ROYAL ASCOT

Richard Onslow

The Crowood Press

ROYAL ASCOT

First published in 1990 by
THE CROWOOD PRESS
Ramsbury, Marlborough
Wiltshire SN8 2HE

Text copyright © 1990 by RICHARD ONSLOW
Design: GRAEME MURDOCH

British Library Cataloguing in Publication Data
Onslow, Richard
Royal Ascot.
1. Berkshire. Ascot. Racecourses: Ascot Racecourse
I. Title
798.4006842298

ISBN 1-85223-215-3

Typeset by NOVATEXT GRAPHIX, Edinburgh.
Printed by BAS PRINTERS, Limited,
Over Wallop, Hampshire.

CONTENTS

ACKNOWLEDGEMENTS

To go back to the origin of this book, I have to thank Jonathan Powell of *The Sunday Express* for suggesting to my publisher Christopher Forster that I should write it. I gladly acknowledge my huge debt to Christopher, for all his help and unobtrusive guidance, most especially with regard to obtaining a balance between writing of Royal Ascot in the various stages of its development, and the meeting during modern times, the horses and personalities of which are well within the memory of so many people, and of correspondingly greater interest. To Graham Hart I am most grateful for his expertly sympathetic editing, and to Graeme Murdoch for the immense amount of trouble he has taken to assemble such a wide variety of interesting, and in many cases original, illustrations. I am very grateful indeed to George Ennor of *The Racing Post* for bringing his great breadth of knowledge of all aspects of The Turf to bear upon the reading of my proofs, thus finding mistakes, that I would blush to mention. To a greater extent than ever I am indebted to Diana Butler and Bronwen Stopford, two greatly valued colleagues of days working on *The European Racehorse*. Diana Butler, now of *Horse and Hound*, compiled the index, and Bronwen Stopford achieved the seemingly impossible task of making fair copy from a perfectly dreadful typescript. Finally, I must thank my wife, Barbara, and our daughter, Harriet, for putting up with me while I wrote this book, which I can only hope will add a little to the knowledge of the long tradition of the most famous race meeting in the world.

Richard Onslow

THE EARLY YEARS

LIKE so many of the brightest threads in the tapestry of English national life, Royal Ascot found its way into the canvas quite haphazardly. In the early part of 1711, Queen Anne was driving through Windsor Forest after a day spent following the Royal Buckhounds in her carriage, when she came across a clearing known as Ascot, originally East Cote, Heath. In common with almost all the other members of the Stuart family, the queen was devoted to hunting, racing and the other sports of the countryside although, like others of that Royal House, she was ill equipped by nature for participation. Her great-grandfather, King James I, had had a near-obsessive love of hawking, hunting and coursing, though cutting a poor figure in the saddle, and had been the first to appreciate the opportunities for indulgence in those pleasures afforded by Newmarket Heath. His grandson and Anne's uncle, King Charles II, was totally dissimilar to him. Tall and lithe, Charles II had been a singularly elegant horseman. He had founded the spring and autumn race meetings at Newmarket, and had ridden winners on the Heath. After girlhood, Anne never had any opportunity to excel as a rider, as she put on ever more weight through a series of miscarriages or pregnancies which gave her children who would die in infancy or a little later. By 1711 she was 46, had been widowed for three years, and was so stout that even walking was a strenuous effort.

Although there was no question of Queen Anne ever riding again, she retained the eye of a horsewoman and readily saw that the large, level expanse of Ascot Heath was ideal terrain over which to gallop horses at full stretch. Accordingly she commanded the Master of the Royal Buck-hounds, the Duke of Somerset, to have it cleared of scrub and gorse, and to have a course laid out so that she could watch racing the next time the Court was at Windsor, six miles away. The cost of constructing the course was not inconsiderable by prevailing values. Nine bills amounting to £558 19s 5d were submitted by William Lowen, who seems to have been the principal contractor, and as such responsible for preparing the ground. William Erlybrown, the carpenter, was paid £15 2s 8d for making and fixing the posts, and Benjamin Culchett £2 15s for painting them, while John Grape received £1 1s 6d for "engrossing the Articles for Her Majesty's Plate run for at Ascot Common".

While the scene was being set the *London Gazette* of 12th July 1711 announced:

> Her Majesty's Plate of 100 guineas will be run for round the new heat [course] on Ascott Common, near Windsor, on Tuesday August 7th next, by any horse, mare or gelding, being no more than six years old the grass before, as must be certified under the hand of the breeder, carrying 12 st, three heats, to be entered the last day of July, at Mr Hancock's, at Fern Hill, near the Starting Post.

Also advertised to be run at Ascot in the same edition of the *Gazette* was:

> A plate of 50 guineas to be run for on Monday August 6th, by any horse, mare or gelding, that had never won the value of £40 in money or plate. Each animal to carry 12 st, in three heats. To be entered on preceding Wednesday, at the Town Hall, New Windsor, or with the Town Clerk or his Deputy, paying 2 guineas, or at the time of starting 6 guineas to the said Clerk or Deputy. The entrance money to go to the second horse in this race.

Despite the races being advertised to be run on the 6th and 7th August, it was not until the end of the week that they were staged, in all likelihood because the course was not ready in time; and on Saturday 11th August 1711, Queen Anne, accom-

Queen Anne – founded the most famous racecourse in the world.

panied by a brilliantly arrayed retinue of courtiers, set off from Windsor Castle to watch the first races ever staged at Ascot. There were seven runners in that £50 plate, the field being composed of:

> The Duke of St Albans' ch h Doctor
> Mr Erwell's gr h Have-at-all
> Mr Smith's gr g Teague
> Mr Smith's bay stone h Dimple
> Mr John Biddolph's b br h Flint
> Mr Charles May's gr g Grey Jack
> Mr Nerrit's iron-grey h Grim

Those seven horses were not the thoroughbreds to be seen at Ascot today, for the thoroughbred was still in the earliest stages of evolution by the mating of Arab stallions, to produce speed, with native English mares, who imparted stoutness. The Darley Arabian, one of three founding sires of the breed, was foaled only 11 years before those first races at Ascot were staged in the presence of Queen Anne; and another, the Godolphin Arabian, would not be born until 13 years afterwards. Those horses that ran at Ascot in 1711, and for many years afterwards, were English hunters, noted for strength and powers of endurance, rather than speed. The two former qualities were quite essential in animals being asked to shoulder 12 st in not just one race, but three heats. The distance was not stipulated in the advertisements in the *London Gazette*, but it was probably four miles, the usual one in those days, which would be two circuits of the Ascot course. Thus the horses were being asked to carry 12 st over 12 miles in the course of the day. Before long they would be subjected to still more ordeals as the system of racing in heats developed, and a horse had to win twice before being the outright winner. That meant that if the first two heats were not won by the same horse, there could be three, four or even five heats before the winner emerged, though runners who clearly had no chance could be withdrawn at any stage. As time went on single heats became increasingly fashionable, distances shorter and weights lower, while the lighter, faster thoroughbreds came into the ascendancy.

Most, if not all, of the horses that ran at Ascot in those early days belonged to courtiers, who followed the Royal Buckhounds, like Doctor's owner the Duke of St Albans (an illegitimate son of King Charles II), while other runners would be the property of officials of the hunt, such as the Yeomen Prickers. Indeed, during the first part of the eighteenth century, hunters necessarily dominated Ascot, where races were confined to "horses that have stag-hunted in Epping or Windsor Forest . . . to be entered at Mr Tempiro's, at Sunninghill Wells" or "Hunters as had been at the death of a Leash of Staggs . . . in Windsor Forest", and bore names like The Yeoman Prickers' Stakes. For close on 200 years, and for long after the thoroughbred had supplanted the hunter, the sovereign continued to delegate the administration of Ascot Racecourse to the Master of the Royal Buckhounds. Coming to the end of the twentieth century, a reminder of the time when racing at Ascot was heavily dependent upon hunting is to be seen in the uniform of the gatemen at the Royal Meeting, whose Forest Green coats with gold facings are adaptations of the livery of the Yeomen Prickers.

We do not know the names of the winners of those races that Queen Anne watched, while surrounded by her courtiers dressed in the very height of fashion, in blues and scarlets, satin and velvet, plumes and lace. For her part, Queen Anne could not know that she had laid the foundations of the most famous race meeting in the world, and given England a cornerstone of its social life. Long after the monarchy of France, which her great general the Duke of Marlborough had defeated at Blenheim, Oudenarde and Malplaquet, had been consigned to history, Royal Ascot would be one of the symbols of the affinity of her successors on the throne of England with their people. Peers of the realm, industrialists, financiers, American millionaires, Eastern potentates, foreign noblemen and Arab sheikhs, to say nothing of small businessmen, farmers, publicans, and thousands of other men and women of far less plentiful resources, would vie with the sovereign for the honour of having a winner at Royal Ascot.

Queen Anne was present at racing at Ascot for the last time in August 1713. On 1st August of the following year she died, and the crown passed to her first cousin once removed George I, the Elector of Hannover, whose mother the Electress Sophia was a granddaughter of King James I. As Ascot is Crown property, the popularity of the racing there is necessarily dependent upon the patronage accorded it by the Sovereign, or close members of the

Royal Family. As neither King George I nor his son and heir King George II took any interest in the turf, the racing at Ascot attracted little interest during the three decades following the death of Queen Anne. In some years, no meeting was held, as there were insufficient funds to provide the minimum prize money stipulated by a recent Act of Parliament, to eliminate a number of smaller meetings, at which some very undesirable practices were rife. Thus Ascot disappeared intermittently, to reappear amidst some strangely incompatible company.

Racing resumed in 1744, and soon afterwards the standard began to rise rapidly as a result of the influence of William Augustus, Duke of Cumberland, the second surviving son of King George II. Cumberland had been a professional soldier, and badly wounded at the Battle of Dettingen at the age of 22 in 1743. Three years later he displayed a ruthless ferocity in the final stages of the suppression of the Jacobite Rebellion, after defeating the army of Prince Charles Edward Stuart, Bonnie Prince Charlie, at Culloden, so that the flower the English named Sweet William after him was known as Stinking Billy in Scotland. He retired from the army following his defeat at Hastenbeck by the French under Marshal d'Estrees in 1757.

The Duke of Cumberland was a compulsive gambler, who won and lost huge sums at cards, and bet heavily on horses. He was Ranger of Windsor Forest, as well as Governor of the state of Virginia in America. Although he never went near the latter territory, he gave its name to Virginia Water, the lovely artificial lake he created a mile or two south of Ascot. It was in Windsor Forest that the Duke established the most successful thoroughbred stud in the country. He took a great deal of pleasure in racing at nearby Ascot, on the southern edge of the Forest, and won many races there with his grey colt Crab and other horses. He was doubtless haughty and, in many respects, far from the most pleasant of men, but as the breeder of Eclipse he made an important contribution to the evolution of the thoroughbred, and was almost entirely responsible for reviving interest in racing at Ascot in fashionable circles.

Like his kinswoman Queen Anne, the Duke of Cumberland became excessively corpulent, probably as a result of vital glands being damaged when

William Augustus, Duke of Cumberland.

he was wounded at Dettingen, and he was only 44 when he died in 1765. Among the stock disposed of at his dispersal sale was a large chestnut colt with a long sock on his off hind and a thin blaze. This was Eclipse, so called because he was foaled in Windsor Forest during the great eclipse of the sun on 1st April 1764. A phenomenon and arguably the greatest racehorse of all time, Eclipse was never beaten, nor even extended, in 18 races, including one at Ascot in May 1769, and at stud became the enduring link in the male line of the Darley Arabian, which is predominant the world over today, and far exceeds in influence the lines of either the Godolphin Arabian or the Byerley Turk.

A still more powerful influence than the Duke of Cumberland in the establishment of Ascot as the most fashionable racecourse in the country, though not on the breeding of the racehorse, was his great nephew George, Prince of Wales, later Prince Regent before ascending the throne as King George IV. For all that his father, King George III, and his tutors tried to inculcate a serious turn of mind into the Prince, and to make him into a man of learning in readiness for the responsibilities of kingship, they never had the slightest chance of weaning him from his pleasures, of which racing was a principal one.

When he commenced owning horses at the age of 21 in 1784, he was an uncommonly good-looking young man, with graceful manners, and enormous charm. His exquisite taste was entirely his own, though he was influenced by the likes of Beau Brummell in the matter of clothes, a consuming interest with him all his life, and in other spheres by different friends. He loved fine buildings, and experimenting with new styles, like the Chinese, in which he created the Royal Pavilion at Brighton. Beautiful women fascinated him, and he entertained his friends, with whom he would revel in his cups long into the night, without any regard to cost. Money, needless to say, or rather the lack of it, presented him with perennial problems.

Determined to be the colossus of the Turf, which he saw as the natural corollary of his position as the undisputed leader of society, he spent huge sums on building up a string of horses, which were trained, at first, by Casborne at Newmarket. In addition he secured the services of the leading jockey of the day, Sam Chifney, to whom he paid the hitherto unheard-of retainer of 200 guineas a year. Although a somewhat foppish, even effeminate, dandy, much given to lovelocks, which protruded from his cap, ruffs and frills, and to bunches of ribbons on the tops of his boots, Chifney was a superb horseman with the lightest of hands. He has the distinction of being the first jockey to employ riding tactics, instead of setting off at a headlong gallop and hoping for the best. Saving up the energy of his mount, he would come with a strong run in the closing stages that became celebrated as "The Chifney Rush". He was certainly a very good jockey . . . whether he was an entirely honest one, Sir Charles Bunbury, the senior steward of the Jockey Club, for one, had his doubts.

Racing on the scale that he did must have cost the Prince of Wales at least £30,000 a year, which meant he had to be a good winner in terms of stake money and betting, as Parliament had voted him an income of only £50,000 a year from the Civil List. Betting provided him with enormous excitement,

Prince of Wales – powerful influence in the development of Ascot.

and he could become exhilarated, almost beyond belief, as he received the congratulations of his friends on the success of one of his horses.

The Prince's first runner at Ascot was a four-year-old bay filly Rosaletta. She finished second to Colonel O'Kelly's Soldier in a two-horse race for a £50 subscription over four miles on 31st May 1785. Later the same day she was successful in a race run in three two-mile heats, winning the first, finishing last of five in the second, and winning the third. She was his only runner at Ascot that year, although he had 17 horses in training. By 1790 he was running no fewer than 40 horses. The most important race that he won at Ascot that year was the £50 Prince's Stakes, in which his filly Louisa beat the Duke of Bedford's Oaks winner Hyppolita and two others.

The glamour of his position, together with his highly personable appearance and graceful manners, combined to make the Prince of Wales enormously popular as a young man. Not since the days when Charles II had indulged his highly developed tastes for pleasure after England was freed from the heavy hand of puritanism by the Restoration of 1660, had any member of the Royal Family commanded the affection of a wide cross-section of the nation to the extent that he did. When it became known that he attended Ascot races every June, people came in their droves from all over the South of England, and in some cases still further afield, to join him in his sport. Lodgings in the area were at a premium during race week, and householders in Bagshot, Wokingham, Sunninghill, Egham, Staines and Windsor could let rooms at the kind of rates that left them eagerly awaiting the following year's meeting.

When the Prince began racing at Ascot, there were still no stands, or any other permanent buildings. Instead, a tightly packed encampment extended almost the length of the straight, surrounded by the wide variety of conveyances by which the visitors had arrived, ranging from the beautifully appointed carriages of the aristocracy to gigs, farm wagons and dog carts. Workmen began pitching the tents a fortnight beforehand. By the time they had finished a canvas village of about 200 booths had appeared, some 30 to 40 of them towering to two stories, with galleries running around them to provide viewing facilities. Amongst all those tents there were a dozen or more gaming tables, whose proprietors provided opportunities of playing for copper, silver or gold, according to the fee paid as a licence to operate, which ranged from 12 guineas to 40 guineas. The income from those tables, at which the odds were nefariously stacked against the players, provided a useful, if tainted, addition to the race fund. A still greater public danger than the manipulators of the gaming tables were the High Tobymen and the Low Tobymen – the mounted highwaymen and the footpads – who infested Bagshot Heath, Chobham Common and the other approaches to Ascot, while the ubiquitous whores plied an equally successful trade.

The racing and the gaming were far from the only forms of amusement to be had at Ascot and its environs during the week of the meeting. There were balls, both private and public, and public breakfasts like that provided by John Marshall of Sunninghill Wells. The theatres at Wokingham, Sunninghill, Windsor and Egham played to full houses all week. In addition there were "mains" of cocks, such as the one between the gentlemen of Berkshire and the gentlemen of Oxfordshire, with 31 birds a side at five guineas a main, while other amusements offered included prize fighting and wrestling.

At first King George III adopted his eldest son's enthusiasm for racing, and for a number of years was present at Ascot, where two large marquees were reserved for the royal party, whose progress through the lanes of tents was one of the principal events of the day. Soon, though, the Prince's debts were mounting at an alarming rate, and it was obvious that the extravagant lines on which he raced were making a substantial contribution to the chaotic state of his finances. It was not only the cost of keeping a large string of horses that caused the King and his advisers to deplore the Prince's involvement in racing. There was also the matter of the company he kept at Ascot, and on other courses, which was hardly conducive to developing his character along the lines envisaged by his father.

Prominent amongst the friends with whom the Prince of Wales raced at Ascot in the early nineties were the three brothers, who were successive Earls of Barrymore, Richard, Henry and Augustus, known in polite society as "Cripplegate", "Newgate" and "Hellgate". The second gentleman owed his soubriquet to his intimate acquaintance with the interior of the penal establishment of that name, and the third to his being a clerk in holy orders. Presumably the eldest suffered from some physical defect. Be that as it may, their sister was always called "Billingsgate" by reason of her vivid turn of phrase.

Richard, Lord Barrymore won a £50 race with his bay colt Ventilator, who was sixth of seven in the first of the nine-furlong heats, and successful in the next two, in 1789, and quite a number of other events during the short time that he raced at Ascot. For a man who could be an amusing conversationalist in the drawing room, and produce amateur theatricals of undoubted merit, he had a sense of humour that was hard to share, and this accounted for Alexander Pope's description of the Duke of Wharton being borrowed to dub him "the scorn and wonder of our age". He once let loose a blind stag for his friends to hunt, and won a bet that he could find a man capable of eating a live cat by producing some depravity from Harpenden, though he always denied the latter achievement. He once walked the length of Newmarket High Street with a town crier's bell shouting "Oyez! Oyez! Who wants to buy a horse that can walk five miles an hour, trot 18, and gallop 20?" When someone was sufficiently gullible to express an interest he replied "I'll let you know when I come across one." One of the favourite pastimes of the Barrymore brothers was the organisation of full-scale shooting parties in the heart of London, to the obvious peril of the citizenry. Richard, Lord Barrymore was only 24 when, in 1793, he killed himself while loading a musket. In the three years since his coming of age he had squandered £300,000.

Other intimates who would be in the Prince's party at Ascot were Charles James Fox, the brilliant Whig statesman, Sir Harry Fetherstonhaugh, who would remain a bachelor until marrying his dairymaid when he was 71, Lord Clermont and George Brummell, whom, for a time, even the Prince acknowledged as the arbiter of taste. Beau Brummell set his face against the bright colours that had long been fashionable among men, and decreed that the ultimate in elegance was achieved by a waisted black coat and white cravat, with pantaloons replacing boots and breeches. The black and grey morning coats worn in the Royal Enclosure today are no more than a modification of the fashion introduced by the Prince's friend 200 years ago.

The closest of all the Prince of Wales' friends was the brother next in age to himself, Frederick Augustus, Duke of York. As well as being Bishop of Osnaburgh, a lucrative though undemanding see to which he was appointed at the age of six months, he was a soldier of a great deal more competence than he is sometimes given credit for. He commanded the British Army in Flanders in the campaigns against revolutionary France from 1793 until 1795. He was appointed Commander-in-Chief in 1798 and held that office until it was discovered that his mistress Mary Anne Clarke was accepting bribes to influence him in the promotion of officers. Like nearly all his brothers, most particularly the Prince of Wales, the Duke was never obsessed by any deep obligation to marriage vows.

The Duke of York was every bit as much of a compulsive gambler as his great-uncle the Duke of Cumberland had been. A good judge of a horse, he might never have got hopelessly into debt had he confined his wagering to the racing he understood, without venturing on to the card table as well.

The most important race at Ascot in the last decade of the eighteenth century was the Oatlands Stakes. This was the first handicap ever run on any course, and took its name from the Duke of York's fine mansion, now a hotel, Oatlands Park, near Weybridge in Surrey. A two-mile event run in a single heat, and for a number of years more valuable than the Derby, the Oatlands Stakes was first run in 1790. The Prince of Wales' five-year-old Escape started hot favourite but was beaten into second place by Seagull, owned by Charles James Fox. The following year the Prince of Wales ran both Baronet, ridden by Sam Chifney, and Escape in the Oatlands. When Baronet beat Express, with Lord Barrymore's Chanticleer third, his owner won more than £17,000 in bets. The Prince's racing career was on the crest of a wave. Nobody could know that he was about to depart the Ascot scene he loved so well.

In October of that year Escape, the horse over which the Prince had lost heavily in the Oatlands of 1790, started at 2/1 on in a field of five for a two-mile race at Newmarket. The following day he was easy to back at 5/1 for a four-mile event, and won from two of the horses that had finished in front of him 24 hours earlier. Rumours of how Chifney had stopped Escape in the first race in order to get long odds to his money in the second were soon rife. The Stewards of the Jockey Club held an enquiry, at the end of which Sir Charles Bunbury let it be known that "If Chifney were suffered to ride the Prince's horses, no gentleman would start against him."

The Prince refused to make a scapegoat of his jockey, and despite the enormous amount of enjoyment he had derived from racing at Ascot, Newmarket and Brighton, sold up all his horses, rather than comply with what he saw as the harsh and unfair ultimatum of Sir Charles Bunbury. Having told Sam Chifney that he was unlikely to own racehorses again, he added:

> But if ever I do, Sam Chifney, you shall train and manage them. You shall have your 200 guineas a year all the same. I cannot give it to you for life. I can only give it to you for

King George III, "Farmer George" – hunting in Windsor Park.

my own. You have been an honest and good servant to me.

The Prince never raced at Newmarket again, though in due course he would return to Ascot.

Had he behaved with the same dignity and loyalty as he did in the Escape affair in other circumstances of his public and private life, the memory of the Prince who became King George IV would be held in infinitely higher respect. For all his many good qualities, and the enormous charm he could exercise, his character was fatally flawed by utter selfishness. Over the years he would betray ministers and mistresses, friends and servants, whenever it suited his convenience, regardless of his obligations to them.

Despite the dullness and utter respectability of his court, and his lacking the charisma of his eldest son, King George III was held in high esteem by the British public, who knew him as "Farmer George" because of his passion for improving methods of agriculture. Never was their affection more apparent than when the Royal Family arrived at Ascot in 1794 while the nation was in almost a frenzy of

patriotic fervour following the defeat of the French fleet off Ushant by Lord Howe a few weeks earlier. All the way up the lane between the tents to the two marquees reserved for the King and his family, their carriages were cheered so loudly that the leading horses of the carriage, in which Princess Elizabeth rode, took fright and bolted. The carriage was overturned, but the Princess and her two companions were brought out, unharmed, by the crowd. Among those present in the brilliantly fine weather of that year were the Duke of Grafton, whose grandfather had been an illegitimate son of King Charles II, the Earl of Jersey, who had been Master of the Buckhounds ten years earlier, the Marquess of Lorne, son and heir to the Duke of Argyll, Earl Grosvenor, and the Prince of Wales' friends the Earls of Clermont and Barrymore.

At about this time the King gave George Slingsby, a Windsor builder, permission to erect the first permanent stand to be seen at Ascot. This stand could accommodate 1650 people, and was to remain in use until 1838.

Although Royal Ascot was beginning to assume

Racing in 1792.

something of the identity by which it would be recognised today, and the wearing of colours had been obligatory since 1783, the racing remained of a very indifferent nature. Races were still run in heats, and private matches abounded. There were only six races in which there were three or more runners in 1794, and each was run in two straight heats. In addition there were three two-horse races, including the £50 sweepstakes for horses that were the property of Huntsmen, Yeomen Prickers and Keepers of Windsor Forest and Great Park, together with seven private matches, and three more for which forfeit was paid.

One of those matches, for £50 over four miles, was won by Lady Lade's Parry, ridden by her owner's husband, from Clifden, the mount of his owner Mr Butler. Lady Lade was among the first of many ladies with a colourful past to be seen at

Royal Ascot. Prior to her marriage to little Sir John Lade, whose money came from a Southwark brewery, she had been Letty Smith, and mistress of the highwayman "Sixteen String Jack", who was hanged at Tyburn. As suggested by the nature of his nuptials, Sir John was far too wild to pay much heed to convention. He bet heavily and rode well, but his main claim to fame lay in being the finest amateur coachman of his day. When particularly low in funds he would accept remuneration to drive his friend the Prince of Wales. He once won a wager that he would drive over two sixpences separated by the distance between his coach wheels. A bet that he seemed a lot less likely to win was with Lord Cholmondeley, a peer of at least twice his own weight, whom he undertook to carry twice round the Steyne at Brighton. News of the wager became public and a large crowd, including many women, assembled to see the settlement of it. Just as a confident Lord Cholmondeley was about to climb onto the others's narrow shoulders, Sir John said sharply "Strip." On being asked what the devil he meant, Sir John explained that he had said he would carry Lord Cholmondeley, not Lord Cholmondeley and his clothes, and had no intention of putting up at least two pounds overweight. Being too modest to strip in mixed company, Lord Cholmondeley paid. Sir John Lade lived on to the beginning of the Victorian era, dying at Egham at the age of 81 in 1838.

The first of the races of the present day to be staged at Ascot was the Gold Cup, inaugurated in 1807, when the three-year-old Master Jackey was the winner in a field of four. Master Jackey may not have been a great horse in the tradition of some of those who would win the race later in the century, and early in the present one, but he must have been more than useful by the standards of that era. He had won at Ascot 24 hours earlier and on his only previous appearance that season had been successful in two two-mile Hedley Stakes at Epsom's Derby meeting, while in his only two subsequent races as a three-year-old he was second to an older horse in a Gold Cup run over four miles at Egham, and a winner at Abingdon.

As single-heat races became ever more popular, handicaps, with their obvious attraction as mediums for betting, rapidly increased in number during the early years of the nineteenth century. Of those still run at the Royal Meeting, the Wokingham Stakes, named after the market town seven miles distant, was the first to be staged. The initial running of that event took place in 1813, two years before the Battle of Waterloo, and the winner was Pointers, a four-year-old belonging to the Duke of York, whose love of racing remained undiminished by the vicissitudes of his public life. The same year Parliament passed an Enclosure Act, which ensured that Ascot Heath, though Crown property, "should be kept and continued as a Race Course for the public use at all times as it has usually been".

Some of the greatest personalities on the European scene attended Ascot on the Friday of the Royal meeting in 1814, and their rapturously enthusiastic reception reflected the festival spirit that pervaded the whole continent following the abdication of Napoleon in April. King Frederick William III of Prussia, and his great general, the 72-year-old Marshal Gebhard von Blücher, were there, and so was Tsar Alexander I, with his general, Platoff, in company with the Prince Regent, the Duke of York and their mother, Queen Charlotte. Among the events seen by those representatives of the victorious allied powers was a match for 30 guineas, in which the Duke of York's unnamed colt by Granicus beat a colt belonging to Mr Ladbroke, the London banker.

In January 1820, King George III died at the age of 81. For the last nine years of his reign he had been incurably deranged, suffering from porphyria, a rare metabolic disorder, and the Prince of Wales had acted as Regent.

Given his love of pageantry, splendid uniforms and liveries, and all forms of elaborate ceremonial, it is hardly surprising that King George IV should have used his influence to ensure that the importance of Royal Ascot, both as a race meeting and as a social event, should be considerably enhanced during his reign. The two enduring features of the meeting that he introduced were the Royal Enclosure and the Royal Procession.

On the instructions of the King, a builder by the name of Perkins constructed a two-storeyed Royal Stand in 1822 to the plans of John Nash, who had already designed Carlton House Terrace for his royal patron. Admission to the lawn surrounding the new stand was strictly confined to those who had received a personal invitation from the King. This was the forerunner of the Royal Enclosure.

Three years later, in 1825, King George IV drove in state to Ascot, instead of arriving in his private carriage. With Lord Maryborough, the Master of the Buckhounds, in attendance on him, King George drove up the course in a coach and four, the Duke of Wellington seated beside him. Four other coaches followed, also drawn by four horses apiece, and a phaeton, with postillions and outriders resplendent in their scarlet liveries. Never had the stamp of royalty been more heavily impressed upon a racecourse than it was when George IV inaugurated one of the most enduring, and popular, constituent parts of England's national pageantry.

George IV had owned horses again for a number of years after the Escape affair, but had no runners at all between 1807 and 1827. In the latter year the Duke of York had died, and the King decided that he would take it upon himself to maintain the tradition of royalty participating in racing. Rather than run horses in his own name, as he had done formerly, however, he had them entered as the property of his racing manager, Delme Radcliffe. They were trained by William Edwards in Newmarket's historic Palace House stable, where King Charles II had stood his carriage horses well over 100 years earlier.

At the time that King George IV resumed ownership, the Ascot Gold Cup was just beginning to be established as one of the principal events in the racing calendar. For a number of years it had been very poorly contested, with only two runners in 1818, 1819, and again in 1824 as well as in 1826, while Banker actually walked over in 1821. In 1827, though, the prestige of the race was greatly enhanced by its being won by Memnon, who had been successful in the St Leger of two years earlier.

King George IV set his heart on winning the Gold Cup. To that end he paid the quite enormous sum of 4000 guineas for the four-year-old The Colonel, greatly to the disgust of Sir William Knighton, Keeper of the Privy Purse, in January 1829. A neat and handy chestnut colt, The Colonel had won the St Leger after running a dead-heat with Cadland in the Derby and being beaten in the decider.

On the opening day of the Royal Meeting of 1829, the four-year-old Zinganee, owned and trained by Bill Chifney, won the Oatlands Stakes. Bill Chifney and his brother Sam, who rode Zinganee, were the sons of the former royal jockey Sam Chifney the elder. Following the Escape scandal of 1791, the older Chifney had never been rehabilitated, and was forced out of racing. He wrote an autobiography, modestly entitled *Genius Genuine*, and invented a bridle with the famous Chifney bit that was calculated to restrain the hardest puller. Neither venture stemmed the rapid deterioration of his financial position. After being obliged to sell the annuity given to him by the Prince of Wales for a lump sum, he soon found himself owing £350 to a saddler called Latchford. The latter had him committed to the Fleet Prison for debt, and there he died at the age of 58 in 1807.

Although the way in which Zinganee won the Oatlands Stakes on that first day of the Royal Meeting suggested that he was the best horse in England, and the probable winner of the Gold Cup on the Thursday, Bill Chifney made it known that he was for sale. Accordingly Lord Chesterfield entered into negotiations to buy the colt, but after mentioning the matter to the King at Windsor Castle that evening, he offered to withdraw his offer of 2500 guineas, lest he be party to preventing his sovereign from winning the Gold Cup with The Colonel.

"My dear Chesterfield," replied the King, "buy the Chifneys' horse by all means. If you don't beat me, Gully will. I don't mind being beaten by you." The son of a Somerset innkeeper, and a remarkably handsome man, John Gully had started life as a butcher, and after a short spell as a prize fighter, became a bookmaker, without earning a particularly enviable reputation. He was soon in a position to run horses, and paid Lord Jersey 4000 guineas for the 1827 Derby winner Mameluke, with whom he was opposing The Colonel and Zinganee in the Gold Cup.

Once again the mount of Sam Chifney, who had all the subtlety of his father and was still the outstanding race rider of the day at 43 years of age, Zinganee, duly won the Gold Cup from Mameluke. Even though denied the Gold Cup, King George did have the pleasure of seeing his favourite mare, a sweet little chestnut called Maria, prevail in a match over two miles for £500 at the last Royal Meeting he ever attended.

A sombre spectacle greeted the crowds when they returned to Ascot for the Royal Meeting of 1830. The Royal Stand was closed, and the rain poured down incessantly. Six miles away the 67-year-old King was dying in Windsor Castle. The once trim figure of "The First Gentleman of Europe" was bloated, and his heart so weak that he could not lie down, so that he had to sleep in an armchair. All the same he retained a keen interest in his horses, which he continually discussed with his factotum Jack Ratford, a former Newmarket stable-boy. In the course of the previous year he had bought Zinganee from Lord Chesterfield, and proposed to run that horse along with The Colonel and a good mare Fleur de Lis in a final attempt to win the Gold

Cup – Sam Chifney having the choice of mounts, as Lord Darlington, who held first claim on him, had no runner in the race. Chifney elected to ride Zinganee, and it was decided not to start Fleur de Lis. The King was desperately anxious to know the result of the race that he had wanted to win above all others, and sent Jack Ratford across Windsor Great Park to the course to bring him news of the outcome, only to learn that Zinganee had completely failed to reproduce his form of 12 months earlier and finished last of four behind Sir Mark Wood's Lucetta, ridden by Jem Robinson, The Colonel being runner-up again. Sixteen days later King George IV died.

Racing always seemed to bring out the best in George IV. Both the loyalty and generosity that he showed to Sam Chifney the elder in the Escape affair, as well as the sportsmanship he displayed at the prospect of being beaten by Lord Chesterfield in the Gold Cup, as well as on other occasions, reflected the most attractive side of a complex character. His principal legacy to Royal Ascot is to be seen every time the Queen drives through the Golden Gates and up the straight to the Royal Enclosure.

As the child of his disastrous marriage to his cousin Caroline of Brunswick, Princess Charlotte of Wales, had died in childbirth shortly after she married Prince Leopold of Saxe-Coburg-Gotha, George IV was succeeded by his eldest surviving brother the Duke of Clarence, who came to the throne as King William IV. While the new king had served with distinction in the Royal Navy, he had not, unlike George IV and the Duke of York, evinced any interest in racing. All the same he followed the example of his father and brother by occupying the Royal Box at Ascot, a maintenance of tradition that came within measurable distance of costing him his life. When he and Queen Adelaide, always more concerned with her needlework than the racing, went to the front of the box to show themselves to the people, a one-legged ex-sailor by the name of Dennis Collins threw two stones at the King, whose hat was dented by one of them, though no blood drawn. Collins, apparently, held the King responsible for his having lost his place as a pensioner at Greenwich the previous year. He was sentenced to death, but reprieved by the

King, and transported to the colonies, where he survived for many years.

Two years after that unpleasant incident, in 1834, the third of the races still run at the Royal Meeting was introduced into the programme. This was the St James's Palace Stakes, which is still staged over the Old Mile and confined to three-year-olds. The race was not an immediate success as the Derby winner Plenipotentiary was allowed to walk over.

As Lord Chesterfield succeeded the Earl of Lichfield as Master of the Buckhounds in 1834, it was appropriate that he should have won six events at the Royal Meeting of that year: in addition to another Gold Cup with Glaucus and the Eclipse Foot with the same horse, the Fern Hill Stakes and a £100 sweepstake with Alexis and another £100 sweepstake with Fortunatus, while his bay colt Mammoth walked over for the Banquet Stakes. The gold-mounted foot of Eclipse, won by Glaucus in 1834, had been presented to the Jockey Club by King William at the pre-Derby luncheon three years earlier to be run for annually by horses belonging to members. It is no longer a trophy for a race, but remains one of the most interesting and valuable treasures of the Jockey Club, and is to be seen in the Rooms at Newmarket.

George Stanhope, 6th Earl of Chesterfield, "Lord Chesterfield the Magnificent" as they dubbed him, was the dominant figure at Ascot during the short reign of King William IV. Born in 1805, he was left an orphan at the age of eight, with the result that a fortune, accumulated during his long minority, awaited him when he came of age. The spending of as much money as he possessed by one man seemed quite impossible. Lord Chesterfield enthusiastically set about proving the task easy of accomplishment. Everything he did was on an almost unbelievably lavish scale. At Chesterfield House in South Audley Street, he gave banquet after banquet, and paid his chef Dolesio, who enjoyed a European reputation, a salary an ambassador would envy. While Master of the Quorn he entertained all and sundry on a princely scale, and took over the whole of The George at Northampton for the hunting season. At a time when men of fashion had such immense pride in their carriages and harness horses, none could match those of the Earl of Chesterfield, who gave his name to the Stanhope, a light gig for two persons.

A tall, handsome man, with chestnut curls beneath a top hat set at a slightly rakish angle, he had, as a young man, been the principal adornment of the retinue that the ageing King George IV had taken to Royal Ascot. In the next reign he had revelled in the office of Master of the Buckhounds, splendidly mounted himself and the hunt servants, and regaled the followers in the same sumptuous manner as he did those of the Quorn. Nothing could cost so much that it prevented Lord Chesterfield from indulging in his tastes.

The first horse of any note that he bought was Zinganee. Shortly afterwards he also acquired Priam, for whom he paid 3000 guineas, another colossal price, from the Chifneys. The winner of the Derby in 1830, Priam would, 60 years later, still be acclaimed by the long-retired Goodwood trainer John Kent as "the best and most perfect racehorse that I ever saw". It was with Priam that Lord Chesterfield won the first running for the Eclipse Foot in 1832. At the end of that season Lord Chesterfield retired the horse to stud at Bretby Park, his home near Burton-on-Trent in Derbyshire. Priam stood at 30 guineas, three times the fee of the Gold Cup winner, Zinganee, who was also at Bretby.

Lord Chesterfield was the most flamboyant of the Masters of the Buckhounds, who tended to be insignificant, if worthy, courtiers, destined to be unknown to posterity. After two seasons he relinquished the appointment, and was succeeded by the 16th Earl of Erroll. During the last two years that William IV was King, the racing at Ascot was hardly noted for its competitive element. Of the 17 events, over and above private matches, that should have been decided in 1835, only two attracted a field of more than four. Pussy, winner of the Oaks the previous year, received forfeit for the Oatlands Stakes, Lord Chesterfield's Eva walked over for the Windsor Forest Stakes, Bran for the Swinley Stakes and Nonsense for a £50 plate, while the St James's Palace Stakes was a two-horse affair won by a colt by the name of Ascot.

Much the strongest field that year was for the Gold Cup, for which there were nine runners. The winner was Lord Jersey's Glencoe, ridden by Jem Robinson. A low-backed golden chestnut colt on whom "Robinson used to look like a man seated in a valley" according to "The Druid" (Henry Dixon, 1822-70), he had won the 2000 Guineas and finished third in the Derby in 1834. Later in 1835 Colonel Jackson, of Alabama, sent an agent to buy the best possible stallion, preferably Priam. As Priam was not on the market, the Colonel's representative settled for Glencoe. In the United States Glencoe proved one of the most influential stallions of that era, largely because his daughters proved the ideal outcross for Lexington. Three of the outstanding horses sired by Lexington – Asteroid, Kentucky and Norfolk – were all out of mares by Glencoe.

Twelve months after the success of Glencoe, the Gold Cup was won the Marquess of Westminster's Touchstone, another high-class colt who was to be influential at stud, proving that the race was established as one of the most prestigious events in the country, even if the overall standard prevailing at the Royal Meeting was at a temporary low ebb. Bred by his owner, Touchstone was a brown colt by Camel out of Banter. The dam of Banter was a thoroughbred hunter by the name of Boadicea, who had once been swapped for a cow. In his early days Touchstone was such an unprepossessing specimen of a thoroughbred that nobody wanted him when Lord Westminster tried to give him away as a foal, but he grew into a fine, robust colt, particularly strong behind, and crowned his three-year-old days by winning the St Leger. He was successful in the Gold Cup again in 1837, thus becoming the second horse to win the race twice, following Lord G. H. Cavendish's Bizarre in 1824 and 1825.

On being retired to his owner's Eaton Stud, Cheshire, where he died at the great age of 31, the dual Gold Cup winner Touchstone sired the Derby winners Cotherstone, Orlando and Surplice. He also got the St Leger winner Newminster, who maintained that branch of the male line of Eclipse, from which Hyperion, Aureole and Vaguely Noble descend.

When Touchstone won the Gold Cup for the first time, he provided the only success in the race enjoyed by John Barham Day, whose great-great-great-grandson Lester Piggott was to win it 11 times. Born at Houghton Down, near Stockbridge,

A close finish in front of the stand in 1843.

in Hampshire, where his father trained in a small way, John Barham Day was one of the most successful jockeys during the second quarter of the nineteenth century, though, like most lightweights, he was unable to ride a strong finish. On the other hand he was an intelligent and reliable rider, who would never become too excited to be able to carry out instructions. As boys he and his brothers travelled around the small meetings in Hampshire, Berkshire and neighbouring counties, with saddlebags slung over the withers of their ponies. It was not until he was 33 in 1826 that John Barham Day came to prominence by bringing off the classic double on Dervise in the 2000 Guineas and Problem in the 1000 Guineas for the Duke of Grafton.

In about 1835 John Barham Day opened a stable at Danebury, near Stockbridge. He was even more skilful as a trainer than he had been as a jockey, as his achievements at Royal Ascot would testify. Like the sons that followed him into the training

profession, Day showed something less than blind loyalty to the interests of the patrons of his stables, and not infrequently ran their horses to suit the family's betting book.

John Day obtained one of his earliest successes at Royal Ascot when he won His Majesty's Plate with his own horse Venison in 1837. Venison was ridden by his son Sam, who died at the age of 19 following a heavy fall while out with Sir John Mills' hounds at Parnell Wood in Hampshire.

On 20th June 1837, a fortnight after Venison won at Ascot, King William IV died and was succeeded by his 18-year-old niece, Queen Victoria. During the 123 years that had separated the reigns of Queen Anne and Queen Victoria, Royal Ascot had emerged as the most fashionable race meeting, owing, for the most part, to the Duke of Cumberland, the foremost breeder of bloodstock of the middle of the eighteenth century, and King George IV, the innovator of the Royal Procession, for whom the first Royal Stand had been built.

VICTORIAN ASCOT

THE crowd that attended Royal Ascot in the first full year of the reign of Queen Victoria was by far the biggest seen there since Zinganee had won the Gold Cup back in 1829. Wearing a lace dress over a pink slip, and a white gauze bonnet trimmed with pink ribbons, the 19-year-old sovereign was loudly cheered as she drove up the course in a procession of seven carriages, escorted by the Yeomen Prickers and other outriders. So far as the crowd was concerned, the presence of the Queen, whom many had never seen before, was more than sufficient compensation for the small fields.

To identify herself with the Royal Meeting, the Queen gave a gold vase valued at £200 to be run for over the mile and a half of the Swinley Course, later to be known as the Gold Cup Vase, and still staged today, with its distance extended to two miles, as the Queen's Vase. The first running was won by Mecca, a chestnut filly owned by Lord Exeter, who completed a notable double that year, as he also won what was to be the final running of the Oatlands Stakes, the race named after the home of Frederick, Duke of York, with Velure. Brownlow Cecil, 2nd Marquess of Exeter, then 43 years of age, was a nobleman to whom any form of false modesty was entirely alien. Not without good reason was it said that "He never forgot by undue familiarity the exalted position to which he was born." Having inherited the title when he was nine years old, he commenced racing as soon as he had come of age in 1816, obtained his first classic success with Augusta in the Oaks of 1821, and was one of the most consistently successful owners over the next 30 years.

There were just three runners for the Gold Cup in that year in which Queen Victoria attended Ascot

for the first time, and the winner was the three-year-old colt Momus, owned by Lord George Bentinck, younger son of the 4th Duke of Portland. Grey Momus, who had also won the 2000 Guineas earlier in the season, was trained at Danebury by John Barham Day, and ridden at 6 st 10 lb by his 15-year-old son Billy.

Lord George Bentinck was then approaching the height of his powers as Dictator of the Turf. A tall, patrician-looking man, more than a little inclined to arrogance, Lord George had introduced some badly needed organisation into racing by reforming the method of starting, giving the starter a flag instead of having him just shout "Go!"; he also insisted the horses carried numbers corresponding to those against their names on the racecards; and he decreed that they should always be paraded in front of the stands after being saddled in the duly appointed place. At the same time he rid racing of many of the pernicious individuals whose activities had brought it into thorough disrepute, such as the welshing bookmakers and the pickpockets who preyed upon the crowds.

As the scourge of wrongdoers, Lord George Bentinck was acutely aware of the smallest mote in anybody else's eye, while happily indifferent to the beam in his own. Although insisting that others should act from the highest possible principles with regard to betting and the running of their horses, Lord George felt himself bound by no such constraints. Had it been generally known that he would go to any lengths to deceive the bookmakers and other owners as to the true ability of his horses, there would have been a public outcry. His cousin Charles Greville, who had been his partner in racing until they quarrelled bitterly, wrote in his diary:

> What a humbug it all is . . . If everybody knew what I
> know of his tricks and artifices, what a rogue he would be

From a Sketch by the Count D'Orsay

LORD GEORGE BENTINCK.

London: Richard Bentley, 1859.

**Lord George Bentinck – scourge of wrongdoers,
he rid racing of many pernicious activities.**

thought, and yet strange to say, I am persuaded he would not commit for anything on earth a clear undoubted act of dishonesty. He has made for himself a peculiar code of morality and honour, and what he has done, he thinks he has a right to do, that the game he plays warrants such deceit and falsehood. . . .

Given the devious means employed by Lord George Bentinck, and the deep-seated belief of the Day family that the Danebury stable should be run entirely for their convenience, rather than the benefit of their patrons, there was never any likelihood of the parties working in harmony. Things came to a head when little Billy Day, who had won the Gold Cup on Grey Momus, wrote to Lord George telling him to back a certain horse, and to a bookmaker advising him to lay the same animal for all that he could take. Unfortunately he posted the letters in the wrong envelopes. In the autumn of 1841 Lord George took his horses away from Danebury to have them trained by John Kent in the Duke of Richmond's private stable at Goodwood.

At the same time that the Gold Vase, and other races that have long been familiar, were being introduced to the Royal Ascot programme, the permanent structures were being greatly improved and increased. By 1838 it was felt that the old betting stand erected about a quarter of a century earlier had outlived its usefulness. Accordingly a grandstand was built on the space between the Royal Stand and what had been the site of the betting stand. The foundation stone was laid by the Master of the Buckhounds, Lord Erroll, on 16th January 1839, and it was ready for the opening of the Royal Meeting on 28th May. Fifty-two feet high and 97½ feet in length, the new stand had a balcony, supported by fluted pillars with Corinthian capitals, projecting 121 feet, which afforded shelter from the rain to part of the lawns. On the ground floor of this stand, which could hold 3000 people, was the betting room, and on the first floor, reached by a staircase at the rear, a drawing room, to which ladies could retire, and various refreshment rooms.

A balcony was constructed for the use of the Master of Buckhounds and his friends, above the weighing room, while the roof behind the balcony was turned into a viewing area for trainers and jockeys. Other improvements effected in 1839 were the building of the first proper box for the judge,

and the demolition of a number of ramshackle, almost derelict, buildings, that had encumbered the far side of the course for longer than anyone could remember. The areas thus cleared provided a parking area alongside the far rails for carriages, from which a first-class view of the running could be obtained.

At that meeting of 1839 the Oatlands Stakes was replaced by the Ascot Stakes, then, as now, run over two and a half miles, and the Windsor Castle Stakes was run for the first time. The Ascot Stakes was won by an unnamed chestnut filly by Merchant belonging to William Forth, a trainer whose enterprise showed little regard for the Rules of Racing. The following season he was to win the Derby with Little Wonder, who was almost certainly a four-year-old.

Whereas the Windsor Castle Stakes is now a five-furlong event for two-year-olds, it was originally run over a mile and confined to three-year-olds, the winner of the Derby, Oaks or 2000 Guineas carrying a 5 lb penalty. The race could hardly have come into being in a more unsatisfactory manner. For one thing there were only two runners, of which The Corsair, a black colt ridden by John Barham Day for Lord Lichfield, beat The Deputy; The Corsair, however, had not carried the extra 5 lb for having won the 2000 Guineas, and was disqualified in favour of the other.

Although the programme was gradually beginning to assume its present form, and was now confined to single heats, while the amenities were being fast improved, the standard of the racing left much to be desired, and the same could be said of the management of the meeting. Not only was the penalty for The Corsair not declared for the Windsor Castle Stakes, but after Lord George Bentinck's filly Sal Volatile won a £30 sweepstakes, the race was found to have started from the wrong post, and had to be run again. In addition to the Windsor Castle Stakes there were six other two-horse races in 1839, as well as a walkover.

The following season the Coronation Stakes was inaugurated to commemorate, somewhat belatedly, the crowning of Queen Victoria two years earlier. As is the case today it was a mile race for three-year-old fillies. The winner of the first running was Lord Albermarle's Spangle ridden by Cotton.

Road to the races – the Long Walk, Windsor, in 1846.

Another of the features of Royal Ascot in 1840 was the five-year-old St Francis becoming the first horse to complete the double in the Vase and the Gold Cup. In the Vase he was ridden by Jem Robinson, while Sam Chifney, son of the Prince Regent's ill-fated jockey, had the mount on him in the Gold Cup. As well as on Zinganee, Sam Chifney had also won the Gold Cup on Memnon in 1827, and quite probably during the years prior to 1823, when the names of the jockeys were not returned.

When winning the Cup on St Francis, Chifney was a veteran of 54 years of age, and still regarded as the outstanding jockey of the day, though not noticeably any more energetic than he had been as a young man. Rather than use his expertise in riding races and trials, he would wander around the Newmarket countryside, a shotgun under his arm, and his lemon-and-white pointer Banker by his side, trying to shoot the odd rabbit. Even though he would only have been required to ride the best horses, he had refused a retainer from Lord Chesterfield in 1838. His incurable idleness thus cost him the Oaks on Industry and the St Leger on Don John. A consummate horseman, he was an even better jockey than his father, and all but perfected the "Chifney Rush". He continued to ride until winning the 1000 Guineas in 1843 on Extempore, his final mount. In 1851 he left Newmarket for Hove, and having paid his last visit to a racecourse to see his nephew Frank Butler win the Derby on West Australian in 1853, died the following year.

Many of the most important races that Sam Chifney won were on horses from the stable of his elder brother Bill, who was the most successful trainer at Newmarket in the 1820s. Bill Chifney was very hard on his horses, of whom only the toughest could survive his methods. He had an implicit faith in sweating horses by giving them gallops of anything up to four miles, wearing heavy rugs and hoods so that they reached maximum fitness by being relieved of every ounce of surplus flesh.

The first man to abandon that primitive, not to say barbaric, method of training was Tom Dawson, a Scot who had been born in Gullane, Haddingtonshire, where his father was a trainer, in 1809. In 1830 Tom Dawson began training in the Brecongill stable at Middleham, and 11 years later sent Mr W. R. Ramsay's six-year-old Lanercost the 250-odd miles south to Ascot to win the Gold Cup of 1841 in the hands of Billy Noble. Lanercost was an extraordinarily versatile horse, who had won the first race for the Cambridgeshire two years earlier, and was not far from the best of that era, though he had been only third to Don John in the St Leger in 1838.

Nat Flatman was the rider in form at Royal Ascot in 1841. As well as the Ascot Stakes on George Payne's Welfare, a filly by Priam, and the Gold Vase on the Marquess of Westminster's Satirist, he won four other races. Elnathan Flatman had been born at Holton St Mary, Suffolk, the son of a small farmer, in 1810, and was apprenticed to William Cooper at Newmarket. Although he would emerge as champion with 81 successes when a tally of winning mounts was published for the first time in 1846, and remained at the top of the list for the next six seasons, he had none of the elegance and subtlety of Sam Chifney – indeed his seat on a horse was rather ugly; nor did he have the flashes of inspiration of Frank Butler. Rightly it was said of him that he was a "good jockey by profession, rather than a brilliant horseman by intuition". He also differed from most of the other fashionable riders of his time in being absolutely honest. In addition he was well spoken, and extremely modest, never accepting a retainer of more than £50 a year from George Payne, his principal employer. Admiral Rous, who abominated jockeys as a species by reason of the conceit and dishonesty of so many of them, actually liked Nat Flatman.

A Northern success in the Gold Cup materialised for the second year running in 1842, when the winner was Beeswing, the nine-year-old mare owned and bred by William Orde, the decidedly eccentric squire of Nunnykirk. This was the mare that had long been hailed as the "Adopted Daughter of Northumberland", and was without doubt one of the very best stayers of her sex ever to have raced at Ascot.

Although no more than 15.2 hands, Beeswing was an impressive individual, with a perfectly delightful head, of great quality, good hips and ribs, and not a trace of white on her rich, dark bay coat. On the debit side, she was light of bone, and had rather upright shoulders. Her lack of bone came from one of the more curious ideas of her breeder, who believed that horses became too gross to train if reared on corn. Consequently she was well into her yearling days before she was fed corn, and the development of her bone was by then already impaired by her insubstantial diet.

Apart from her tendency to pull hard on her way to the start, Beeswing was said to be a lovely ride. In her box she was a lot less amenable. She was likely to lash out on the slightest provocation, and the imprints of her hooves were to be seen five feet high on the wall.

After confining Beeswing to iron rations during her formative years, William Orde had insisted that she should always be kept on the big side while in training. In all likelihood, therefore, she was in need of the race when she came third to St Francis, Sam Chifney's Gold Cup winner of two years earlier, and The Nob in the Gold Vase on the first day of Royal Ascot. At all events the race seems to have brought her on, as she won the Gold Cup by half a length from The Nob, with St Francis third, and Lanercost last of five.

Beeswing, who was probably trained on her breeder's Nunnykirk estate in Northumberland, also won no fewer than 50 other races, including the Doncaster Cup four times. The enormous amount of racing to which she was subjected during eight seasons did nothing to impair her value as a brood mare. To matings with the dual Gold Cup winner Touchstone she bred both Nunnykirk, successful in the 2000 Guineas in 1849, and Newminster, winner of the St Leger in 1851.

The Royal Stand in 1843.

In March 1854, at the age of 21, Beeswing was to be covered by Touchstone yet again, but by that time the walk from Warrington station to the Eaton stud was too much for her. On the evening of her second day at Eaton, she tottered and collapsed. A short while later she struggled to her feet to take a little gruel, and then died. Only her great courage had kept her going. That was to be the quality to predominate in so many of her descendants. In *Bailey's Magazine* of December 1904 G. S. Lowe wrote:

> There was all the leaven of old Beeswing in Apology, and it came out again in Chippendale, the stoutest of his year. This has been the peculiarity of Beeswing. Something of herself has come out almost unexpectedly. A lion-hearted horse like Hampton, a regular glutton to stay like Isinglass, a weight-carrying stayer like Sheen, a determined little runner like Hackler's Pride – the reflections of the old mare through her son Newminster.

Two races destined to be perpetuated, namely the Royal Hunt Cup and the New Stakes, made their first appearance on the Royal Ascot card in 1843. The Royal Hunt Cup was won by three lengths by Lord Chesterfield's chestnut five-year-old Knight of the Whistle, ridden by Nat Flatman, with Garry Owen, Epaulette and Bourra Tomacha running a triple dead-heat for second place. Lord Chesterfield was then 37 years of age, and had long passed that gilded youth during which he had earned the sobriquet "The Magnificent", for the realities of life had caught up with him, especially those having regard to the value of money. Although still extremely rich by the standards of ordinary mortals, he no longer entertained in sumptuous style from what he had fondly regarded as a bottomless purse. To settle the mountain of debts that were the monument to his extravagance, he had sold Chesterfield House, in South Audley Street, to the Duke of

Abercorn, and having resisted the earlier offers, he had finally been obliged to sell Priam to the United States in 1835. The mastership of the Quorn had been relinquished, his private training establishment at Newmarket closed, and his horses sent to the very successful public stable run by John Scott at Malton. Among the relatively few things he retained were his great charm, indolence and good nature, which would never allow him to utter a bad word about anybody. Later he was to have his horses trained by Tom Taylor on his Brocket Park property in Derbyshire, which had been saved from his creditors. In his latter years he would sit for hours on end at Brocket, gazing through a telescope manipulated by his butler. He was only 61 when he died in 1866.

The first running of the New Stakes, which would become the Norfolk Stakes in 1973, was won by Ratan, ridden by foul-mouthed Sam Rogers. The owner and breeder of Ratan was William Crockford. Having started life as a fishmonger, Crockford had become a professional gambler, better known for his courage than any particularly strong addiction to fair play. In 1828 he had opened his own gaming club in the splendid mansion that Benjamin Wyatt had designed for him at the top of St James's Street, where the Duke of Wellington, Lord Sefton, Lord Alvanley, George Payne and almost everybody else prominent in politics, society or the world of sport played the tables. By the early summer of 1844, "Old Crocky" or "The Father of Hell and Hazard" as he was alternatively known, was a very sick man of 69 years of age, and kept alive by little more than the hope of winning the Derby with Ratan, who was again to be ridden by Sam Rogers. Rogers, though, had backed The Ugly Buck, who had won the 2000 Guineas for John Barham Day's Danebury stable. In that most notorious of all Derbies, the first winner of the New Stakes was unplaced to Running Rein, who was subsequently exposed as a four-year-old by the name of Maccabaeus, while Rogers was warned off for stopping Ratan. Two days after the Derby Crockford was dead.

At the same Royal Meeting that saw the founding of the Royal Hunt Cup and the New Stakes, 50-year-old Jem Robinson had ridden his last winner of the Gold Cup, when successful on Lord Albermarle's Ralph. The son of a Newmarket farm labourer, Jem Robinson was one of the most successful jockeys in the first half of the nineteenth century, and the six Derby winners that he rode at Epsom remained a record in the race until surpassed by Lester Piggott on Empery in 1976, more than a century after his death.

Having been responsible for foiling King George IV's final attempt to win the Gold Cup when riding Lucetta to beat The Colonel in 1830, Robinson completed a treble for Lucetta's owner Sir Mark Wood by winning again on Cetus in 1831, and Camarine in 1832. As well as on Glencoe in 1838, he also won the race yet again on Isaac Day's Caravan in 1839. His long career was brought to an end when, at the age of 59, he was thrown from a two-year-old at Newmarket in 1852. Although Robinson earned a great deal of money, he saved very little of it. As soon as the racing season was over, he and his wife would leave Newmarket to take rooms in London, where they indulged themselves in every sort of extravagance throughout the winter. Had it not been for the generosity of the Dukes of Bedford and Rutland, both of whom gave him pensions, this pleasure-loving little man would have spent his last years in greatly reduced circumstances. He died at the age of 72 in 1865.

There was a profusion of royalty at Ascot on the third day of the meeting in 1844, as Queen Victoria and her husband Albert, the Prince Consort, were accompanied by Tsar Nicholas I of Russia and the King of Saxony. A close-run race for the Gold Cup was won by Lord Albermarle's Defence, ridden by Whitehouse, who beat Corranna, the mount of Jem Robinson, by half a length. As a compliment to the Tsar, Lord Albermarle promptly changed the name of the winner to The Emperor. It delighted the ruler of all the Russians to such an extent that he undertook to donate a piece of plate worth £500 annually as a prize for the race, which then became the Emperor's Plate.

The second running of the New Stakes gave rise to a good deal of acrimony after Mr E. Herbert's Bloodstone, ridden by an apprentice called Bell, had beaten John Barham Day's Old England, the mount of his owner's son John Day the younger. John Day claimed the stakes on the grounds that Bloodstone was a three-year-old. Accordingly the Stewards had

John Gully – pugilist turned bookmaker.

the mouth of the colt inspected by two veterinary surgeons, who pronounced him a three-year-old. Whatever the object of this particular piece of villainy may have been, the winning of the New Stakes was, rather surprisingly, no part of it, for the Ascot Stewards concluded their acceptance of the veterinary findings by saying:

> We are further of the opinion that Mr John Newman gave positive orders to the jockey Bell, the rider of Bloodstone, to lose the New Stakes; that Bell having mentioned the orders he received to his master, Planner, before the race, and having afterwards won the race as far as he could, acted in a manner highly creditable to himself.

Even if he had not intended to win the race, Mr Herbert did not like the idea of being deprived of the prize money, and sued John Barham Day for the return of it at Guildford Assizes in August. As the jury brought in a verdict for Day, that was the end of the affair; but it was by no means the last that the Jockey Club was to hear of Old England, whom John Day soon afterwards sold to John Gully, the pugilist turned bookmaker, who had taken another step up in the world by being elected Member of Parliament for Pontefract in 1832. He had acquired considerable coal-mining interests in Pontefract, and represented the borough, albeit inconspicuously, until 1837.

Like Ratan, first winner of the New Stakes, Old England became strongly fancied for the Derby. All the same a number of bookmakers laid heavily against the colt, safe in the knowledge that young Billy Day, who regularly supplied them with information regarding his father's horses, would ensure he was too lame to run. Either the poor animal was to have his foot bruised by a heavy stone, or he was to have a sinew bound by a handkerchief and struck by a stick, in accordance with the plans of William Stebbings, the instigator of the plot. Gully, who had a nose for these things, soon sensed that something was afoot, arrived at Danebury in a towering temper, and extracted a confession from Billy Day. The matter was put in the hands of the Stewards of the Jockey Club, who warned off young Day and his associates, and Old England finished third in the Derby.

Another really splendid mare from the North, in the mould of Beeswing, was seen at Ascot in 1844. This was Alice Hawthorn, trained by Robert Hesseltine at Hambleton in Yorkshire. Without even being out of a canter, Alice Hawthorn beat Robert de Gorham by six lengths in the Gold Vase. A bay by Muley Moloch out of Rebecca by Lottery, she had an action like a hare, so that she seemed to steal along effortlessly over the ground, with her ears pricked. She was bred by John Plummer of New Parks, near Shipton, who was visiting his friend Mr Hawthorn, head of a Newcastle engineering firm, one day when he was so taken by the delightful manners of his host's eight-year-old daughter Alice that he gave her name to his filly, whose descendants would also make their mark at Ascot.

An era came to an end when Lord George Bentinck had his final successes at Ascot in 1845. Slander won the New Stakes for him, Blackcock the Fern Hill Stakes and His Serene Highness the Windsor Plate. A few weeks later he astounded his host and fellow guests at the Duke of Richmond's house party for the Goodwood meeting by offering his entire stud, horses in training, yearlings, foals, stallions and mares to George Payne for just £10,000. With the same energetic thoroughness and singlemindedness that he undertook everything, he had devoted himself to leading the protectionist wing of the Conservative Party in the House of Commons, and was giving up racing completely. After consideration George Payne declined the offer, and it was left to the Hon. Edward Mostyn, later Lord Mostyn, to purchase Lord George Bentinck's bloodstock. Just over two years later, in September 1848, Lord George died of a heart attack, at the age of just 46, while taking a walk on his father's Welbeck Abbey estate.

In 1847 John Barham Day, with whom Lord George Bentinck was never to be reconciled, produced the outstanding stayer at Royal Ascot in The Hero, a chestnut four-year-old by Chesterfield. Partly owned as well as trained by Day, The Hero beat the Duke of Bedford's Bridle by a head in the Gold Vase, and two days later he underlined his excellence over a distance of ground by winning the Emperor's Plate by a length. In both races he was ridden by his trainer's 27-year-old son Alfred Day, a graceful horseman who was a good deal more honest than most of his relations.

Twelve months later, again ridden by Alfred Day,

The Hero won the Emperor's Plate for a second time. John Day owned The Hero in partnership with John Powney, whose family had been settled in Bath since 1628. Powney farmed the land opposite Bath Racecourse at Lansdown, and although it was not until quite late in life that he married Day's niece, he had three sons, John, Hugh and Harry, all of whom trained successfully. Hugh was the father of John Powney, who was private trainer to the late Sir David Robinson until the latter curtailed his racing interests, and later ran a stable in Kent. Thus John Powney, born in 1930, is separated by one generation from the part-owner of the horse that won the Emperor's Plate in 1847 and 1848.

The 13th Earl of Eglinton, John Fobert, who had charge of his private stable at Middleham, and their jockey Charlie Marlow brought off a notable double by winning the Emperor's Plate with Van Tromp in 1849 and The Flying Dutchman the following year. Not only were both horses classic winners, but they were half-brothers. A brown colt by the 1841 Gold Cup winner Lanercost out of Barbelle, Van Tromp had been bred by Colonel Vansittart. He was a five-year-old when he beat the grey Chanticleer by half a length, with the 1847 Derby winner Cossack a length away third in the Emperor's Plate. Van Tromp subsequently went to Russia to become the property of the sponsor of the Emperor's Plate. Nicholas I is said to have become very fond of him.

Not long before Van Tromp had won the St Leger of 1847, Lord Eglinton had formed such a high opinion of the colt that he agreed to pay Colonel Vansittart 1000 guineas for every perfectly formed foal produced by Barbelle. He thus acquired The Flying Dutchman, whom Barbelle bred to a mating with the Derby winner Bay Middleton. The Flying Dutchman won the Derby and St Leger in 1849, and when successful in the Emperor's Plate as a four-year-old cantered home eight lengths clear of Jericho. Before being sold to France for £4000, he had sired the Derby winner Ellighton.

Like Lord Chesterfield, the Earl of Eglinton was a man of great charm, who dispensed hospitality totally regardless of cost. Quite the most spectacular entertainment he ever laid on should have been the Eglinton Tournament of 1839, an elaborate attempt to recreate the pageantry of mediaeval chivalry, for which the novels of Sir Walter Scott had given the Victorians an insatiable taste. Lord Eglinton spent £50,000 on staging this extravaganza, only to see it completely washed out by an incessant deluge of heavy rain. He was not quite 50 when he died of apoplexy at St Andrews in 1861.

In view of the vicious cruelty with which Billy Day had been prepared to nobble Old England, to say nothing of his readiness to betray his father, and rob the colt's backers of a run for their money in that Derby of 1845, it seems strange, by the standards of justice of the present time, that he was no longer a disqualified person seven years later. Not only was he reinstated, but he was training at Woodyates, in Wiltshire, and in 1852 he won the Emperor's Plate with Joe Miller, carrying the colours of Edward Farrance, proprietor of Farrance's Hotel. One of five three-year-olds in a field of nine, Joe Miller won by two lengths, with Voltigeur, winner of the Derby of two years earlier, unplaced.

The Flying Dutchman having been the first Derby winner to crown his career with success in the Gold Cup, or Emperor's Plate as it was still known, in 1850, Teddington became the second to take the Ascot race in 1853. In what was one of the most exciting races seen at Ascot during that decade, Teddington, ridden by Job Marson, won by a head from a better horse than himself in Lord Exeter's Stockwell, winner of the 2000 Guineas and St Leger of the previous season. Teddington must have endured a gruelling ordeal in securing that narrow verdict, as Marson, who rode bolt upright and with rather shorter stirrup leathers than his rivals, was notoriously hard on his mounts, and plied his spurs mercilessly in a close finish.

Teddington was not a success as a sire, many of his stock being soft. Eventually, in 1861, he was sold to the Emperor of Austria, Franz Josef, to stand at the Imperial Stud at Kisber.

On the other hand, Stockwell, the best horse that Lord Exeter ran at Ascot or anywhere else, was an immense success at stud. A really magnificent, masculine chestnut, he was to be acclaimed "the Emperor of Stallions". As well as being champion sire seven times, he got the Derby winners Blair Athol, Lord Lyon and Doncaster.

Lord Palmerston – successful owner and Prime Minister.

Two years after the defeat of Stockwell in the Gold Cup, the second Marquess of Exeter, who had that strong streak of pride of ancestry, was obliged to dispose of his bloodstock to Mr Simpson, a banker of Diss, Norfolk, to pay the price of his shortsightedness. A few years earlier he had haughtily refused to allow the railway company to run a line across a corner of his Burleigh estate. In consequence the businesses of the people of nearby Stamford, most of whom were his tenants, were badly affected. To make good the damage he had done them, he had to find £75,000 to connect Stamford with the main line at Essendon.

Also prominent among the men of fashion to be seen at Royal Ascot in the first half of Queen Victoria's reign was William Temple, 3rd Viscount Palmerston, the Liberal statesman who was Prime Minister from 1855 to 1865 apart from a brief interval from February 1858 to June 1859. He lived at Broadlands, more recently the home of Earl Mountbatten, near Romsey in Hampshire, and had horses in training a comfortable hour or two's ride

away, with John Barham Day at Danebury in the same county. In 1853, when he was vigorously advocating the containment of the aggression of Tsar Nicholas I in the Near East, Lord Palmerston won the Ascot Stakes with the 20/1 chance Buckthorn ridden by Alfred Day.

Apart from Stockwell, the other notable horse to run at Royal Ascot in 1853 was Catherine Hayes, owned by Lord John Scott. On the strength of her having just won the Oaks she started at 5/1 on in a field of three for the Coronation Stakes, but it was only by a head that she beat Mayfair. Catherine Hayes, a tall, rangy brown by Lanercost with no white on her, was trained in Lord John's private stable on his Cawston Lodge property near Rugby by 33-year-old Mat Dawson, who also ran the Yew Tree Cottage establishment at Compton in Berkshire. One of the younger brothers of Lanercost's trainer Tom Dawson, Mat was adamant to the end of his long career that Catherine Hayes, notwithstanding her having only just scraped home at Ascot, was amongst the best horses he ever trained, and certainly the best of many very good fillies.

Almost throughout the 64 years of Queen Victoria's reign, the stocky, immaculately dressed figure of Mat Dawson was a regular sight in the Trainers' Stand at Royal Ascot. Very much the autocrat, rather than the diplomat, even in his relationships with his owners, there was nothing of the rough and ready quality about him that characterised so many of the trainers of that era, such as John Barham Day, who was immensely proud of having been married in a stable jacket. Little Mat Dawson had the most beautiful manners, and spoke in a gently modulated Scottish accent that could render the expletives of vituperations, with which he could express his most extreme displeasure, positively melodious. In time to come the richest peers in the country would be imploring him to have their horses, but he would only have them on his own terms, and on no account would he take any interference in the management of the stable. When the little martinet discovered that Lord Falmouth had given Tom French orders as to how Wheatear should be ridden in the Newmarket Oaks in 1870, he promptly asked the most successful owner-breeder of the day to remove all his horses. The rupture between owner and trainer was healed

**Mat Dawson – autocratic trainer in
second half of the century.**

only through the good offices of Joe Dawson,
another of the brothers to train.

During the early months of 1854 Lord
Palmerston finally persuaded the Prime Minister,
the Marquess of Aberdeen, whose diplomacy he
dismissed as "antiquated imbecility", of the necessity to check the ambitions of Russia. By March
of that year England was at war with Russia, and in
September British troops landed in the Crimea.
Among the Englishmen to survive the dreadful
carnage of that campaign was Colonel Jack Astley
of the Scots Fusilier Guards, later Sir John Astley,
who was wounded at the Battle of the Alma. Soon
after his return to England the charming, utterly
straightforward and perennially impoverished
baronet tried to solve his financial problems by
taking to racing. Although the operation, as was all
but inevitable, failed to achieve its objective, Ascot
was to provide the backcloth to one of its highlights.

With the outbreak of war, further sponsorship of
Royal Ascot's centrepiece by the Autocrat of all the

Russias was neither forthcoming nor wanted, and
the race reverted to being the Gold Cup. In the year
of the resumption of its original identity the race
was won by one of the best of all the horses that
have ever triumphed in it, though it provided him
with the sternest test of his career. This was West
Australian, who had achieved the distinction of
being the first of the 15 horses who have landed the
Triple Crown by winning the 2000 Guineas, the
Derby and the St Leger while racing in the colours
of his breeder John Bowes in 1853. Shortly before
being sent to Ascot, West Australian was bought by
Lord Londesborough for what was then the
enormous price of £5000.

A rather yellowish bay of great scope, standing
15.3½ hands, with a long, thin blaze and a sock on
his off hind, West Australian was trained by John
Scott in the Whitewall Stable at Malton. Despite
obvious brilliance and versatility he posed
considerable problems for Scott as he had very thin
soles to his feet with the result that there were
difficulties in giving him enough fast work to bring
him to peak condition when gallops became firm at
the height of summer. To reduce the possibility of
heat getting into West Australian's feet, John Scott
used to have his box laid with clay. No doubt there
were misgivings as to the wisdom of breeding from
a horse with such a defect, and these impelled John
Bowes to accept the offer made him by Lord
Londesborough.

On the second day of the Royal Meeting of 1854,
West Australian made light work of beating
Vanderdecken by four lengths over two miles, and
24 hours later started at 6/4 on in a field of seven
for the Gold Cup. West Australian, ridden by the
stylish Alfred Day, Kingston, the mount of Job
Marson, and Rataplan, for whom Nat Flatman had
been engaged, kept close company from the start,
each of the jockeys being determined that neither of
the others should be allowed to secure an early
advantage. Turning into the straight Rataplan had
dropped away beaten to the wide, and with West
Australian unable to stride away to settle the issue
with the same authority that he had on other
occasions, Day and Marson settled down to a
prolonged duel as the tension in the stands mounted
with almost every stride. For two and a half furlongs the protagonists were locked together, until

the sympathetic skill of Day paid a slightly better dividend than the desperate spurring of Marson, and it was "The West" by a head.

Six years after West Australian had retired to Kirby Farm at Ulleskelfe, near Tadcaster, Lord Londesborough, who had also acquired Stockwell, died. Both stallions were sold at Tattersalls, where Stockwell was bought for 4500 guineas by Liverpool banker R. C. Naylor, and West Australian for 4000 guineas to go to France as the property of the Duc de Morny, illegitimate son of the Comte de Flahaut and Queen Hortense of Holland. On his death in 1865, the Duc de Morny bequeathed West Australian, first of three Triple Crowned winners to land the Gold Cup at Ascot, to his half-brother Emperor Napoleon III.

As well as the Gold Cup and the other races with West Australian, John Scott also won the Wokingham Stakes with Hobbyhorse, ridden by Nat Flatman, at Royal Ascot in 1854. Hobbyhorse was owned by the 14th Earl of Derby, grandson of the 12th Earl, who gave his name to the race he founded. As a young man the 14th Earl had managed the horses that Bloss trained for his father in Delamere Forest. When he commenced ownership on his own account in 1842 he embarked on a harmonious association with John Scott that would endure for 21 years. A high-spirited and good-natured man, known in the House of Lords as "The Rupert of Debate" from his forceful style of oratory, he was the head of two other Tory governments besides the one which interrupted Lord Palmerston's decade in the premiership. He gave up racing to devote himself to politics in 1863, and died six years later.

Seventeen-year-old George Fordham, who became one of the greatest jockeys of the century – some good judges said he was the greatest – obtained his first success at Royal Ascot on Coroner, for whom he weighed out at 4 st 13 lb, in the Trial Stakes in 1855. The following day he won the Royal Hunt Cup on Lord Clifden's three-year-old filly Chalice.

By no means as elegant a rider as Alfred Day, George Fordham rode with rather short leathers, something in the manner of the modern jockey, and was inclined to slew round in the saddle as he drove his horse out. While he may not have had the style

of such a consummate horseman as Day, he was a great deal more sensitive a rider than Job Marson and the other riders of the primitive school with their blind faith in the power of whip and spur, and was particularly tender in his handling of two-year-olds. He once told Leopold de Rothschild: "When I go down to the post on those two-year-olds, and feel their little hearts beating between my legs, I think why not let them have an easy race, win if they can, but don't frighten them first time out." As well as exerting that wonderfully delicate touch, Fordham rode with great subtlety so that his rivals never knew quite how well his mount was going, or how much he had in hand. Over and over again jockeys would pass him in the final furlong, quite sure that his mount was under heavy pressure and safely beaten, only to find that he came with a late run to beat them close to home.

George Fordham was born into a poor family at Cambridge in September 1837, and was apprenticed to Richard Drewitt, for whom his uncle was travelling head lad, at Middleham. Subsequently Drewitt moved south to Lewes in Sussex, and Fordham went with him. Although he had experienced acute poverty in childhood and adolescence, there was no amount of money that could bribe him. He loathed betting, and would have nothing to do with it. Robert Sly, who had been involved in racing since the early years of the century, once said: "I have seen two great jockeys in my time, Jem Robinson and George Fordham, but George was not only a great, he was an *honest* jockey."

At the end of that season of 1855, in which he had obtained his initial successes at Royal Ascot, George Fordham was leading jockey for the first time. In all he was champion 14 times, finally sharing the title with Charlie Maidment in 1871. Many of the best races he ever rode were at Ascot. As well as on Chalice he won the Royal Hunt Cup on Lord Wilton's See Saw in 1869, and Mr G. Clive's Winslow in 1873, while he rode no fewer than five winners of the Gold Cup.

Tom Parr, owner and trainer of Coroner, the first winner to be ridden by George Fordham at Royal Ascot, was a perfectly extraordinary character who regularly produced horses to beat fancied runners from the fashionable stables, notwithstanding his highly unorthodox methods. Long before com-

George Fordham – leading jockey from 1855 until 1883.

mencing to train at Letcombe Regis, near Wantage, where he often had recourse to hiding in his hay loft to avoid confrontations with his creditors, Tom Parr had been an itinerant tea pedlar between Weymouth and Plymouth. As well as the Trial Stakes with Coroner, he won the Ascot Stakes with Mortimer and Her Majesty's Plate with Saucebox, who went on to win the St Leger of that season, in 1855.

Having spent so much time in almost perpetual motion during his peddling days, he seemed to think it no bad thing if his horses did the same, for he gave them little and infrequent respite from racing. Fisherman was a remarkably hardy individual, who thrived on the heavy demands that Parr made upon his energy. As a three-year-old he won the Gold Vase, with Winkfield, who was to be successful in the Gold Cup two days later, only fourth, and no fewer than 22 other races in 1856. That remains a record number of times that a horse has won during a single season. Following 22 more successes in 1857, Fisherman won another 20 races as a five-year-old, including the Gold Cup. Twelve months later Fisherman won the Gold Cup for a second time. There have been many much better winners of Ascot's most prestigious race, but never a tougher or more genuine one than Fisherman. In all he won 70 of his 121 races. Only Catherina, with 79 races to her credit between 1833 and 1841, has been more successful numerically.

For all the multiplicity of races that he won with the likes of Fisherman, Tom Parr did not prosper in the long run. He had been reduced to poverty again when he died at Letcombe Regis at the age of 70 in 1880.

In 1856, the year that Fisherman won the Gold Vase, the railway line running westward out of London was extended from Staines to Ascot. In consequence the attendance at Ascot was greatly increased. At the same time the congestion on the roads approaching the course was relieved, and those people who continued to drive to Ascot by coach, carriage, trap or cart enjoyed a very much more pleasant journey.

Brilliantly fine weather and the railway ensured that a huge crowd saw Queen Victoria and the Prince Consort drive up the course in 1857. Among those in the royal party was Prince Friedrich Wilhelm of Prussia (later Kaiser Friedrich III), who would become the Queen's son-in-law on his marriage to the Princess Royal the following year. New rails contrived to make the course a great deal smarter than it had been the previous year, and the Queen thoroughly enjoyed the racing, though her pleasure would have been tinged by disapproval if she had been aware of the identity, and activities, of Mr Howard whose black jacket and orange cap were carried successfully by Sedbury in the New Stakes, Arsenal in the Gold Vase and Clydesdale in another event. "Mr Howard" was the *nom de course* of Henry Padwick, a solicitor by qualification, and a moneylender by profession. He derived a handsome income by making loans, at extortionate rates of interest, to young men whose expectations by way of inheritance were greatly in excess of their prudence. A man with a talent for driving hard bargains, and enforcing them rigorously, Padwick was building up an enviable record at Royal Ascot as he had already won the Ascot Stakes with Little Harry in 1854, and the Gold Vase with Oulston in 1855.

Padwick's horses were trained in his private stable at Michel Grove, two miles from Patching in Sussex. In about 1850 John Barham Day assumed control of that establishment, after having handed the Danebury stable over to John Day the younger. The association between Henry Padwick and John Day was not expected to last for long. Nor did it. In 1855 Padwick was convinced that his colt St Hubert would win the 2000 Guineas. So heavily did he back him that St Hubert started 7/4 on, with Lord of the Isles, trained by Billy Day for James Merry, second favourite at 5/2 in a field of nine. What Padwick did not know was that John Barham Day had come to an agreement with his son Billy that St Hubert would give Lord of the Isles a clear run in the 2000 Guineas, in return for the compliment being repaid in the Derby, with the result that Lord of the Isles was able to beat St Hubert by a neck in the Guineas. Beside himself with rage when he came to learn how he had lost his money over St Hubert, Padwick dismissed John Barham Day instantly. The Ascot Stakes of 1854 with Little Harry was thus the last of all the races that John Barham Day won at the Royal Meeting. Telling a friend, some time afterwards, how he had come to the parting of the ways with Padwick, he said self-pityingly, "You will be glad to hear that I have taken care of myself. If I had not, I should like to know who would have done so." He died of softening of the brain in 1860.

For his part, James Merry, who was to figure large at Royal Ascot during the next decade, took his horses away from Billy Day after the 2000 Guineas of 1855. Understandably he felt he would not always necessarily be the beneficiary of his trainer's machinations.

In 1860 when heavy rain made the ground exceptionally testing, the Royal Stand Plate, which had been run over two miles in each of the two previous years, became the Queen's Stand Plate and the distance was reduced to five furlongs. This race, which was to emerge as the most important sprint of the meeting, became the King's Stand Stakes when King Edward VII came to the throne in 1901, but did not revert to its original name on the accession of Queen Elizabeth II in 1952. The first winner of the Queen's Stand Plate was Queen of the Vale, owned by Baron Rothschild and trained in his private stable, Palace House, at Newmarket by Joe Hayhoe. Baron Mayer Amschel Rothschild was the grandson of his namesake, that Mayer Rothschild who had founded the family banking operations from small beginnings in Frankfurt-am-Main towards the end of the previous century. The original Mayer Rothschild had five sons, of whom Nathan took charge of the London branch of the bank, while Carl went to Italy, James to Paris and Salomon to Vienna, with Amschel remaining in Germany. In 1822 the hereditary title of Baron was conferred on all five brothers by Emperor Francis I of Austria as a mark of gratitude for enormous loans received. Baron Mayer Rothschild, the first of many members of the family to race in England, was a younger son of Nathan Rothschild, who had opened the London branch of the family bank. His dark blue jacket and yellow cap were to be seen at Royal Ascot every season for very many years.

The Gold Cup was won by yet another Derby winner in 1861 when James Merry's Thormanby, ridden by Harry Custance, beat Fairwater by two lengths. Thormanby was trained by Mat Dawson at Russley Park, his owner's private stable, a few miles from Lambourn. When Lord John Scott gave up racing in 1857, Mat Dawson had arranged for his

**James Merry – owner of four Gold Cup
winners between 1861 and 1875.**

fellow Scot James Merry, a Glasgow ironmaster, to buy Lord John's bloodstock. At the same time he agreed to go to Russley Park to train them and their new owner's other horses there. In doing so Mat Dawson made the proverbial rod for his own back, for James Merry badly belied his name. As well as being exceedingly mean, and having a highly developed love of money, he was deeply suspicious of his trainers and jockeys, generally quite groundlessly, being convinced that they were in league with the bookmakers to foil his betting.

James Merry displayed the parsimony that was typical of him over the purchase of Thormanby, the first of his Gold Cup winners. A rather rangy chestnut standing near to the ground, by Melbourne or Windhound, out of that wonderful mare Alice Hawthorn, winner of the 1844 Gold Vase as well as 51 other races, Thormanby was originally bought as a yearling on Merry's behalf by Mat Dawson for the surprisingly small sum of £350. The ironmaster, however, took anything but an instant liking to him, and insisted that Mat Dawson should pay for his keep until he finally decided that he would accept the colt. Merry, who died at the age of 72 in 1877, won the 1863 Gold Cup with Buckstone, though only after the four-year-old had endured the ordeal of running off a dead-heat with Tim Whiffler. He then won the race again with The Scottish Chief in 1864, and finally in 1875 with Doncaster.

At the time that Thormanby won the Gold Cup, the stands at Ascot had become a massively impressive conglomeration of buildings. Facing them from the course, one saw the Jockey Club Stand on the right, next to the Royal Stand and opposite the winning post, then the towering structure of the Grandstand, with its huge balcony supported by those iron pillars with Corinthian capitals, and finally a smaller stand of two tiers and capacious roof viewing, but no balcony.

All those stands had been tightly packed when Thormanby won the Gold Cup in 1861, with the exception of the Royal Stand, which was closed as the Queen was in mourning for her mother, the Duchess of Kent, who had died in March. A death of very much more consequence to the nation occurred in the December of that year. On 14th December Albert, the Prince Consort, died of typhoid, probably contracted as a result of the deplorable condition of the drains at Windsor Castle. The Queen was inconsolable, and retired into complete seclusion for close on 40 years, so that she would never again be seen in the Royal Box at Ascot.

Without the panoply of royalty, the sovereign in procession surrounded by her gilded attendants, a necessarily sombre air hung over Ascot in 1862, when the racing went ahead in much the same way as it would have done at any other meeting. The Danebury stable, flourishing to a greater extent than ever before under the management of John Day the younger, brought off a double. The lightly weighted Canary, carrying the colours of his trainer, justified their backing him down to 5/1 favouritism for the Royal Hunt Cup by beating Baron Rothschild's King of Diamonds by half a length, and the Duke of Beaufort's Birdhill was ridden by Alf Day to win a £100 plate for two-year-olds, one of several races at the meeting still without the dignity of a name.

Asteroid, owned by Sir Joseph Hawley of Leyburn Grange near Maidstone in Kent and trained in his private stable at Cannons Heath, Hampshire by George Manning, won the Gold Cup in 1862. The cold, remote figure of Sir Joseph Hawley, with his rather discontented face beneath the exaggeratedly tall top hat, then so much in vogue, was always to be seen in the Jockey Club Stand at Ascot in the first half of Queen Victoria's reign, unless he was abroad indulging his passion for studying literature and science. He was a man whom it was not easy to understand, nor to like, for there was more than an element of hypocrisy about him. Although he bet in very large sums, and took something in the region of £80,000 out of the ring when he won the Derby with Beadsman in 1858, he was constantly inveighing against heavy gambling. In common with his contemporary James Merry, he was intensely secretive and distrustful. His trainer was required to do no more than bring the horses to the peak of condition. Hawley made all his own entries, made the running plans, arranged the trials, and even weighed out the riders, without necessarily telling his trainer what the horses were carrying. Among the virtues of this strange, cultivated man, who never aspired to any part in public life, was considerable generosity. He thought nothing of giving a

The trophies of 1860 – left to right, the Royal Hunt Cup, the Gold Cup and the Gold Vase.

rider £2000, thereby earning the deep disapproval, not to say enmity, of Admiral Rous, who, as mentioned above, loathed all jockeys save Nat Flatman, and deplored their being pampered with lavish rewards.

Admiral Rous was the third of the great Dictators of the Turf, and as such one of the personalities of Royal Ascot where he would watch racing through a telescope, a legacy from service, for some 40 years until his death at the age of 86 in 1877. Unlike Sir Charles Bunbury and Lord George Bentinck, he never made any particular mark as an owner or breeder, and only had the odd horse or two in training in the Newmarket stable of his friend the Duke of Bedford, whose racing interests he managed. By way of contrast to Bentinck, the Admiral was a man of utter integrity, who detested any form of sharp practice. He would write copious

letters to *The Times*, making his views abundantly clear. On occasion, he could be too impulsive, tilting at windmills, and was apt to be left looking faintly ridiculous; but no one ever impugned his motives.

The younger son of the 1st Earl of Stradbroke, the Hon. Henry John Rous served under Sir John Hoste in the Mediterranean during the latter part of the Napoleonic Wars. He subsequently commanded HMS *Rainbow* off India and then in Australian waters. His finest feat of seamanship was to bring the 36-gun frigate *Pique*, badly battered, without a rudder and shipping water, the 1500 miles from Newfoundland to Spithead in 20 days. On retiring from the navy he spent five fallow years as Tory Member of Parliament for Westminster.

Having been elected to the Jockey Club in 1821, Admiral Rous became Steward for the first time in

Admiral Rous – a towering influence whose word was law.

1838. In 1850 he established his position as the supreme arbiter of racing with the publication of *The Laws and Practice of Horse-Racing*, and five years later accepted the post of Public Handicapper, so that he exercised a greater authority and influence over racing than any other man before or since. For the many years during which he was continuously a Steward of the Jockey Club, the Admiral's word was law.

It was in 1862, the year that Sir Joseph Hawley, the Admiral's long-standing adversary within the Jockey Club, won the Gold Cup with Asteroid, that the Royal Ascot Hotel opened its doors. This had been built at the suggestion of John Clark, the judge of the racing, and stood on the left of the Bracknell to Virginia Water road, directly opposite the Paddock bend. As well as providing accommodation for visitors to the meeting, it had 58 boxes that were a welcome addition to the stabling available for runners.

Royalty returned to Ascot in 1863. On 10th March the Prince of Wales, the future King Edward VII, had married Princess Alexandra of Denmark. As it was known that the 21-year-old prince was to take his bride to the meeting, a far larger crowd than usual assembled at Ascot, with the majority of the people trying to catch a first glimpse of the royal couple. Every time the Prince and Princess came to the front of the Royal Box they were greeted by sustained cheering, for the nation was in a mood to make the celebration of the royal wedding last for as long as possible, after the extended public mourning for the Prince Consort.

The day that the Royal Hunt Cup was run was almost oppressively hot without so much as a breath of wind, the big handicap being won by Victor, owned by the bookmaker George Hodgman. It was ironic that diametrically opposite meteorological conditions had been responsible for Hodgman's acquiring the horse. The weather in the late winter of 1861 had been so atrocious that the opening meeting of the season at Lincoln had to be delayed 48 hours. As one expedient to kill time while waiting for racing to begin, Hodgman took a stroll around the city, and on passing the stableyard of "The Saracen's Head", saw a countryman holding a well-ribbed-up brown colt with strong quarters. Taking an instant liking to the horse, Hodgman bought him there and then for £80. This was Victor.

As the spring of 1863 was exceptionally dry, the gallops at Epsom, where Hodgman's horses were trained, became hard. Knowing of a stretch of derelict downland near Winchester that bore a strong resemblance to the straight course at Ascot, the bookmaker expended £100 on having it cleared, and sent Victor to Hampshire to complete his preparation for the Hunt Cup on it. On the strength of his winning a trial with a horse called Libellous soon after arrival, Hodgman and his friends piled money on to Victor with the result that he started hot favourite at 3/1 in a field of 28, and ridden by Morris at 5 st 12 lb, the bargain from the Lincoln stableyard won by four lengths.

As a compliment to the Princess of Wales, the Alexandra Plate, a handicap over the Old Mile, was run for the first time in 1864, and won by Joseph Lowe's Anglo-Saxon by two lengths from James Merry's Crisis. As well as that race, the Princess had

The Marquess of Hastings – high betting and hard drinking adversary of Henry Chaplin.

the Alexandra Stand, a wooden structure to the right of the Grandstand as one faced the course, named in her honour.

Much the most striking of the members of the royal party at Ascot in 1864 was Henry Chaplin, who had become friends with the Prince of Wales while they were up at Oxford together. A tall, thickset young man with a thatch of chestnut hair, he had been born in 1841, the son of the Reverend Henry Chaplin of Ryhall, Rutland, and had inherited the great Blankney estate in Lincolnshire on the death of his father's elder brother in 1859. Rich, without being possessed of positively ducal wealth, the Squire of Blankney was typical of so many men of his background. He was wildly extravagant, demanded the best of everything from boots to horses, and had no doubts as to the privileges to which his position in society entitled him; but, at the same time, he was acutely aware of his obligations to his tenants and to the countryside, in which his roots were deeply implanted. As he chatted easily with the Prince of Wales, nobody could foresee that Henry Chaplin was about to be one of the leading figures in a drama, of which more than one of the minor scenes would be played out at Ascot.

His infatuation with Lady Florence Paget did nothing to set Henry Chaplin apart from his contemporaries, for half the eligible bachelors in London were captivated by that younger daughter of the 2nd Marquess of Anglesey. With her petite, perfectly formed figure, and grey eyes the colour of the plumage of a dove, she was already acclaimed "The Pocket Venus". Her grandfather, the 1st Marquess of Anglesey, had commanded the cavalry at Waterloo and was the famous "One-Leg" whose other limb was taken off by a cannon ball from one of the last shots fired in the battle. Her father, the 2nd Marquess of Anglesey, was an altogether less satisfactory character, a spendthrift who was continually seeking accommodation with his creditors, and hardly qualified to inspire stability in his offspring.

Among the other men aspiring to marriage with Lady Florence Paget was Henry Weysford Charles Plantagenet Rawdon Hastings, 4th Marquess of Hastings. Like her, Harry Hastings had a distinguished soldier for a grandfather, the 1st Marquess

of Hastings having been Commander-in-Chief in India and responsible for securing the loyalty of the Gurkha regiments to the Crown, and a father of little consequence. Harry's father, the 2nd Marquess of Hastings, asked nothing more of life than that he should hunt foxes six days a week. He married the fecklessly delightful Barbara, Lady Grey de Ruthyn in her own right, always know as "The Jolly Fast Marchioness", whose passion for gambling was inherited to such a marked extent by her son Harry.

The 2nd Marquess of Hastings was only 35 when he died in 1844, and when, seven years later, his elder son Paulyn died, the younger son Harry Hastings became Marquess and the owner of vast possessions at the age of eight. With his mother constantly away on visits to continental casinos until her remarriage, Harry Hastings spent an undisciplined boyhood at the family home, Donnington Hall in Leicestershire, with nobody to impose any form of restraint upon him or give any guidance in the formation of his character. He was outrageously spoiled by three elder sisters, and all his life would appeal to the maternal instincts of women, while he had little other company save grooms and gamekeepers, who were in no position to help prepare him for his great responsibilities.

After Eton, where he made no mark at all, Hastings went up to Christ Church, Oxford. He was a handsome young man, with large brown eyes, a strong nose but rather weak mouth, of considerable charm, but little by way of strength of character, and no air of natural authority. At Oxford Lord Hastings fell in with the racing set. He soon discovered the exhilaration to be had from betting, and then revelled in the admiration he aroused by reason of the huge amounts that he would wager on a horse. He may not have been one of the leaders of the social life of the university, like Henry Chaplin, his contemporary at Christ Church and already nicknamed "Magnifico", but he acquired a reputation for being a plunger.

Hastings had at last discovered something that gave him a sense of purpose, and enabled him to prove his virility – as he thought. In addition he had developed a taste for alcohol. While at Oxford he would breakfast on mackerel fried in gin, caviare on toast and a bottle of claret.

On coming down from Oxford, Harry Hastings

Tom Chaloner – strong-riding jockey from Manchester.

runner at the meeting. At that time his principal interest still lay in hunting, as it had been at Christ Church where he had kept his own pack of hounds and was not infrequently observed in the Cathedral with hunting boots visible beneath his surplice.

Ten days after Ascot, on 20th June 1864, the Marquess and Marchioness of Abercorn gave a ball in honour of the Prince and Princess of Wales at Chesterfield House in South Audley Street. At that function Henry Chaplin proposed to Lady Florence Paget, and was accepted. The marriage was to take place in early August.

Engagement to Henry Chaplin did not mean that Lady Florence saw little of Lord Hastings, for the Marquess frequently accepted invitations from her and her fiancé to race meetings and other functions. On Friday 15th July he was in their box to see Adelina Patti in *Faust* at Covent Garden.

The following day Lady Florence announced that she had to buy some items for her trousseau, and was going to Marshall and Snelgrove's in Oxford Street. There she met the Marquess of Hastings, or his emissary, and was driven to St George's Church in Hanover Square, where she married him. Having discovered that she respected, rather than loved, the sophisticated Henry Chaplin, she found herself unable to resist the high betting and hard drinking Harry Hastings, the charming and engaging rake, who could rarely fail to appeal to the maternal instinct in a woman. Society was scandalised.

After a holiday in India, Henry Chaplin returned to England early in 1865 and took up racing in order to have something with which to occupy himself outside the hunting season, rather than on account of any desire to seek opportunities to thwart the betting of Lord Hastings. Conscious that he had behaved quite disgracefully to the man who had once been his friend, though, the Marquess was convinced that Chaplin was seeking revenge by outshining him on the turf. Thus he was perhaps ascribing to the other motives that would have been his own had their roles been reversed. The rivalry between them, therefore, was of the Marquess of Hastings' making, not Henry Chaplin's.

It had been said of Henry Chaplin that "he bought horses as though he were drunk, and backed them as though he were mad". In order to buy into the blood of Queen Mary, whose daughter Blink

determined to break the ring. To that end he began acquiring horses, and sent them to be trained by John Day at Danebury, still the most successful betting stable in the country.

Henry Chaplin had hoped to take Lady Florence Paget to Ascot in 1864, but rather than accompany him to the Royal Box, she allowed herself to be escorted by the Marquess of Hastings, on whose arm she entered the paddock to inspect the filly he had named after her, the equine Lady Florence being a chestnut by Rattle out of Lady Ann by Touchstone, who was about to contest a £100 maiden plate over four furlongs. Little was expected of the filly, who did not figure in the betting, and ridden by Tom Chaloner she finished unplaced to King Charming owned by Count Gustav Batthyany, a Hungarian nobleman resident in England.

On the Wednesday, the Marquess of Hastings won the Fern Hill Stakes with his filly Attraction, who was joint favourite at 4/1, and the following day his chestnut colt Redcap was successful in a £100 maiden plate. Henry Chaplin did not have a

The betting ring in 1866.

Bonny brought off the double in the Derby and Oaks in 1857, he bought the closely related three-year-old colts Breadalbane and Broomielaw from their breeder, the Malton trainer William I'Anson, in whose stable they remained. Breadalbane was by Stockwell out of Blink Bonny and therefore full brother to the Derby winner Blair Athol, while Broomielaw was by Stockwell out of Queen Mary. Both carried the rose-coloured jacket of Henry Chaplin to success at Ascot in 1865, Breadalbane winning the Prince of Wales Stakes by eight lengths and Broomielaw beating Farewell by a length and a half in the Ascot Triennial Stakes; Harry Custance was the successful jockey in each instance. That Ascot meeting of 1865 was a galling one so far as the Marquess of Hastings was concerned, for whereas Henry Chaplin had those two winners, he did not have a fancied horse at the meeting, and each of his three runners was unplaced.

In spite of their pedigrees and their having the ability to win at Ascot, neither Breadalbane nor Broomielaw was much good for racing. Breadalbane was soft and ungenuine, and Broomielaw became so savage that he tried to maul Custance at the start of the Chesterfield Cup at Goodwood. No doubt because of Henry Chaplin's disappointment with these two highly bred colts his association with I'Anson was extremely brief, so that by 1866 he had his horses in Newmarket's Bedford Cottage stable. That establishment was owned and managed by the formidable James Machell, while first the brothers Charles and George Bloss, then Joe Cannon and finally the former steeplechase jockey Jimmy Jewett trained the string for him.

Under Captain Machell, Bedford Cottage was to become an outstandingly successful betting stable, after the manner of Danebury, and rich young men like Henry Chaplin eagerly sent their horses into it so that they could have the assistance of Machell in bringing off coups. In some quarters Machell was blamed for their ruining themselves, but in almost every instance they lost their money through going their own ways or ignoring his advice, rather than by following it.

James Octavius Machell, for whom Ascot was to be such a happy hunting ground, had been born at Beverley, Yorkshire, in 1837, the son of a clergyman. As a young man he was a superb athlete, who excelled as much in jumping as in running, so much so that he could leap onto a mantelpiece from a standstill. While with his regiment at The Curragh, he developed an interest in racing as the owner of a useful sprinter called Grisi, who won him three races there and a couple more at Bellewstown in 1862, and shortly afterwards resigned his commission to set up his stable at Newmarket. As well as being a wonderfully good judge of a horse, he had a thorough knowledge of handicapping, and bet quite fearlessly. A big man with a ramrod-straight back that proclaimed his military background, and a walrus moustache, Captain Machell was apt to be cold and austere, with the result that he was held in awe rather than affection by most of those who knew him.

One of the first horses that Machell bought for Henry Chaplin was the dark chestnut colt by Newminster out of Seclusion by Tadmor for whom he paid 1000 guineas at the sale of the yearlings at the Middle Park Stud in 1865. Given the name of Hermit, this colt never grew to more than 15.2½ hands, but there was no mistaking his class. Although Hermit was beaten in two of his first three races as a two-year-old in the spring of 1866, Captain Machell advised sending him to Ascot, where he justified the decision by beating Dragon by a neck in the Biennial. In addition, Henry Chaplin won the Triennial Stakes with the faint-hearted Breadalbane, who started at 7/2 on to accomplish a very easy task and had things all his own way when beating two opponents by a dozen lengths.

For the Marquess of Hastings Ascot was an utter

Jimmy Jewett – former steeplechase jockey turned trainer.

disaster in 1866. On the strength of his four-year-old The Duke having won four races at Newmarket together with two at Epsom and walked over on the other two of his eight appearances prior to being sent to the Royal Meeting, the Marquess backed him as though defeat were out of the question in the Queen's Stand Plate, so that the bookmakers were asking for 2/1 by the off. With 9 st 12 lb on his back, and giving away as much as 45 lb, The Duke took no part in the finish and was down the field behind Baron Rothschild's two-year-old filly Hippia, who would win the Oaks the following season. In desperation, Lord Hastings brought The Duke out again the following day and backed him down to favouritism for the Gold Vase, but the colt found one too good in Richard Sutton's Elland. For the second year running the Marquess came away from Ascot without a winner.

After his success at Royal Ascot, Henry Chaplin's

Hermit won a couple of races at Stockbridge in June, then Machell put him away for the season. For, like so many of the offspring of Newminster, he was pronouncedly weak as a two-year-old, and needed time in which to develop. All the same his performance at Ascot had shown that he had a sound chance in the Derby of 1867, and the stable as well as the public backed him. For his part the Marquess of Hastings, whose judgement was hardly improved by the losses that he was sustaining any more than by his continual drinking, refused to contemplate his rival winning the Derby, and laid heavily against Hermit. A week before the Derby, Hermit broke a blood vessel, and Henry Chaplin released Custance from his retainer so that he could take another mount, but Hermit recovered from that setback far quicker than expected, though he drifted out to 66/1, and got up close to home in the hands of Johnny Daley to win by a neck. The Marquess of Hastings, nothing if not magnanimous in adversity, was the first man to pat him in the unsaddling enclosure.

His vindictiveness towards Henry Chaplin and insensate prejudice against Hermit had cost the Marquess of Hastings £120,000. By settling day the following Monday he had to find well over a million pounds by present-day values. Rather than have recourse to Henry Padwick, and in the hope of never having to seek assistance from that rapacious individual, he sold the splendid Scottish estate of Loudoun to the Marquess of Bute for £300,000, and settled with the ring in full.

With his top hat worn at the usual jaunty angle, he walked into the betting enclosure, the recently railed-off lawn beside the Jockey Club Stand at Ascot, with all his old assurance, just a fortnight after that fateful Derby, to be greeted by an outburst of cheering from the bookmakers; one after another the layers took up the cry of "The Markis – Gawd bless him!" The most charismatic gambler of the nineteenth century had come to Ascot for his swan song.

The Prince of Wales, who was staying with the Duke of Sutherland at Cliveden, drove up the course in procession, with Lord Colville, the Master of the Buckhounds wearing his silver badge of office, at its head. The weather was unsettled and distinctly chilly, but nothing could dampen the spirits of Lord Hastings whose principal hopes of recovering the huge losses he had incurred over the Derby reposed in Lecturer in the Gold Cup and Lady Elizabeth in the New Stakes, both races being on the Thursday.

Little Lecturer, the gamest horse in the kingdom, had brought off an outsize gamble for the Marquess in the Cesarewitch of the previous season, and was stepping up in class when George Fordham rode him in one of the strongest fields ever assembled for the Gold Cup. A four-year-old bay colt by Costerdale, Lecturer had never grown to 15 hands. When at full gallop he carried his head so low that it almost seemed to be touching the ground, and he had such an exaggeratedly round action that he used to cut his elbows, so that he had to be shod with half-tips.

That season of 1867 remains the only one in which three winners of the Oaks, Regalia, Hippia and Tormentor, have contested the Gold Cup. Henry Chaplin contributed a proven stayer in Rama, winner of the Doncaster Cup and the Goodwood Stakes the previous season, and the irascible Lord Glasgow a typically unnamed colt out of an unnamed mare, while the other four runners included John Davis, who was to make the running for Lecturer. The useful John Davis, who had already won four races that year, set a searching pace which he was able to maintain until they were well into the straight, where his rider, the 21-year-old Tom Cannon, looked round for Fordham on Lecturer. Shrewdly anticipating what would happen next, Tom Heartfield closed on Regalia, and sure enough, Cannon took the tiring John Davis away from the rails to let Lecturer up, but it was Tom Heartfield on Regalia who promptly went through the gap and into the lead. The race was all but over, and the heavily backed Lecturer shut in behind the leaders, as a result of that quick thinking on the part of Heartfield. Great jockey that he was, Fordham kept absolutely calm, and took Lecturer to the outside of the field. Once he had his run, the little colt put his head down to go in pursuit of Regalia, and having got on terms with her inside the distance, fought on to win by a length and a half, and land the Marquess of Hastings a small fortune in bets.

The Marquess, exultant over his change of for-

Parading before the start of the Gold Cup in 1868.

tune, now addressed himself to the serious business of backing the lovely Lady Elizabeth on whom Fordham was to wear his scarlet jacket, with white hoop and cap, again in the New Stakes, the next event on the card. Men of long experience of racing left on record their opinion that there was never a horse that was better as a two-year-old than Lady Elizabeth, not excepting Ormonde. A bay by Trumpeter, of a fraction under 15 hands, she was perfection in head and neck, with magnificent shoulders in true proportion to her wide hips. If she did have a fault it was that she was just a little straight in thighs and hocks.

Lady Elizabeth went to Ascot as the unbeaten winner of five races. Of the 11 that took the field against her, there was not a little confidence behind the French-bred Rabican, and Chelsea from Joe Dawson's Newmarket stable, both unraced, so that the ring offered odds against her in the early exchanges. By the time the Marquess and his commissioners had finished their business Lady Elizabeth was firm favourite at even money with Rabican at 2/1. The result was never anywhere near being in the balance, and Lady Elizabeth won by six lengths from Chelsea.

Henry Chaplin also had his successes at Royal

Ascot that year. Hermit, ridden by Custance, won both the St James's Palace Stakes and the Biennial, and his four-year-old Bertie, on whom his owner's retained lightweight Jeffery had the mount, won the Visitors' Plate. As well as having his colours successfully in those three races, Chaplin cleared £3000 when Baron Rothschild's Jasper won the Royal Hunt Cup, as he had made Jeffery available to the Baron to ride at 6 st 4 lb.

On the final day of the meeting The Marquess brought out Lecturer again, and Chaplin Rama in the Alexandra Plate, which had been extended from a mile to three miles in the second year of its running in 1865. Starting at 11/8 on, Lecturer beat Rama by two lengths. The Marquess of Hastings had very nearly recovered all the money that Hermit had cost him. He left Ascot a happy man.

The remainder of the Hastings story can be simply told, without going into all its ramifications. By the end of the season of 1867 the Marquess was face to face with disaster again, owing the ring some £50,000, and his health deteriorating. All his hopes had to be pinned on his winning the 1868 Derby with Lady Elizabeth, whom he backed through all the credit still available to him. For all that he had plumbed the very depths of folly in the recklessness of his betting, he was still entitled to the loyalty of his trainer. As a patron of Danebury, he was denied even that. Having had a hard season, during which she had won 12 of her 13 races as a two-year-old, Lady Elizabeth lost her form. Rather than inform the owner, John Day exploited the situation by laying against the filly, while Hastings continued to back her. Inevitably she was unplaced in the Derby, and the Marquess, who had already resigned from the Jockey Club as a defaulter, was completely ruined. His health continued to grow worse, and the man who had been a good winner over Lecturer in the Gold Cup the previous year was only 26 when he died on 10th November 1868.

The former Lady Florence Paget never acquired a scintilla of judgement. As her second husband she married Sir George Chetwynd, who was obliged to resign from the Jockey Club for his part in the events that led to his jockey Charlie Wood being warned off for stopping horses. She was 65 when she died in 1907.

Henry Chaplin continued to lead the life of a country gentleman, though the necessity to economise soon led to the reduction in his racing interests. Having married Lady Florence Leveson Gower, daughter of the Duke of Sutherland, in 1876, he became a prominent Conservative Member of Parliament, and a successful President of the Board of Agriculture from 1889 until 1892 with a seat in the Cabinet. He was raised to the peerage as Viscount Chaplin in 1916, and died at the age of 81 in 1923.

Queen Victoria was perfectly appalled by the fate of the Marquess of Hastings. She deeply disapproved of gambling, and was horrified that a peer of her realm, whom she expected to set a good example, should have been ruined by racing. As was usually the case, the Prince of Wales felt the full brunt of her indignation. She wrote to him:

> Dearest Bertie,
> Now that Ascot races are approaching, I wish to repeat to you earnestly and seriously, and with reference to my letters this spring, that I trust you will . . . as my uncle William IV and Aunt, and we ourselves did, confine your visits to the Races, to the two days Tuesday and Thursday, and not go on Wednesday and Friday, to which William IV never went, nor did we . . . Your example can do much for good and can do a great deal of evil. . .

In trying to persuade her heir to limit his patronage of Ascot, which had always been one of his favourite events in the racing and social calendars, she was wasting her time. He replied:

> I fear, dear Mama, that no year goes round without you giving me a jobation on the subject of racing . . . The Tuesday and Thursday at Ascot have always been looked upon as the great days, as there is the procession in your carriages up the course, which pleases the public, and is looked upon by them as a kind of annual pageant. The other days are, of course, of minor importance, but when you have guests staying in your house they naturally like going on those days also, and it would I think look odd and uncivil if I remained at home, and would excite comment if I suddenly deviated from the course which I have hitherto adopted. . . .

Aghast at the tragedy that had befallen the Marquess of Hastings, the Queen failed to prise the Prince of Wales away from Ascot. Out of consideration for his house guests he would continue to attend on all four days.

The outstanding horse seen at Ascot during the Hastings era was the French-bred Gladiateur, who won the Gold Cup in 1866. Gladiateur carried the blue jacket, red sleeves and cap of his breeder Count Fréderic de Lagrange, the son of one of Napoleon's generals, and was trained by Tom Jennings in the Phantom House stables at Newmarket. A bay by Monarque out of Miss Gladiator, who was too unsound to stand training, Gladiateur was left with an unsightly enlargement on his off foreleg after being trodden on as a foal. He grew into a very tall, raking, angular colt with scarcely a vestige of quality about him. Once, after Jennings had shown a party of Frenchmen around the Phantom House yard, they expressed disappointment at not having seen the great Gladiateur. When the trainer took them back to the colt's box, they said "But M. Jennings, you said that was the horse that pulled your cab to the races." Jennings replied, "Yes, though I did not think even you would be such fools as to believe it!" As a three-year-old, Gladiateur dominated the season by winning the Triple Crown, being extravagantly acclaimed by the French press as the "Avenger of Waterloo".

His trainer Tom Jennings, whose father was landlord of The Swan at Bottisham, then a coaching inn on the Cambridge to Newmarket road, was a very reserved man, who kept his own counsel, never answering a question and never asking one. He was a great believer in using the absolutely minimum by way of artificial aids in the training of horses, and very fond of saying "Take off those boots and bandages, and give nature a chance, and you will have far fewer horses break down than is the case now." Although he trained every kind of good horse during his long career, he was particularly adept in the preparation of stayers. He certainly needed to exert all his skills in the handling of Gladiateur, who suffered from navicular disease and was intermittently lame all the time he was training.

For many years afterwards, there was a body of educated opinion that maintained that the performance of Gladiateur in the Gold Cup of 1866 was the finest ever seen at Ascot, though he had just two opponents – the Oaks winner Regalia and the irresolute Breadalbane. The short-sighted Harry Grimshaw, his regular jockey, was instructed to lie up with the other two until the Paddock bend, nurse him down the hill to put the minimum strain on the unsound leg, then kick on along the level ground on the run to Swinley Bottom. These in-

structions Grimshaw elected to interpret in a singularly eccentric manner, so that Breadalbane had set up a lead of 20 lengths from Regalia, who was 10 lengths clear of Gladiateur as they passed the stands. Racing down the hill, Grimshaw rode the big horse so tenderly that he was tailed off, and by the time he reached Swinley Bottom he was actually 300 yards behind the other two. Then, with a little less than a mile to travel, Grimshaw gave Gladiateur his head. Those in the stands could hardly believe the evidence of their eyes, as the big, lanky bay went in hot pursuit of the pair so far ahead of him, in a manner that made a mockery of the old dictum that a good horse can give away weight, but not start. Almost before some people had realised that the uninteresting sight of a straggling procession of three was fast being transformed into a spectacle fraught with tension, Gladiateur had made up a furlong, and then, as he continued to devour the ground with his remorseless stride, the suspect leg totally impervious to the almost bone-hard going, he passed Breadalbane and ranged upsides of Regalia, who had nothing left with which to answer him. Having come from a seemingly impossible position so far behind her, Gladiateur reversed the picture, as it were, so it was she who was tailed off, and he galloped away to win by 40 lengths. Nobody had ever seen a horse win in quite such a magnificent manner. Regalia, a classic winner, had just been galloped into the ground, as she finished totally exhausted, her tongue hanging out like that of a tired dog. As for Breadalbane, he had completely given up the ghost and pulled himself up just after the turn into the straight.

Although Gladiateur was without doubt one of the greatest horses of the last century, he was a failure as a stallion. When his owner sold off most of his stock on the outbreak of the Franco-Prussian war, he was acquired for 5800 guineas by William Blenkiron to stand at the Middle Park Stud at Eltham in Kent and was only 14 when he died of chronic navicular disease in 1876. Gladiateur is one of at least two Gold Cup winners to be commemorated in sculpture. His statue is to be seen at the main gates of Longchamps.

When the Spagnoletti Board, on which the names of the jockeys are shown against the numbers of their mounts, was used on a British racecourse for the first time at Ascot in 1870, the famous Aske spots – red roundels on white – of Lord Zetland were much in evidence. With King Cole, the Yorkshire peer brought off a double in the St James's Palace Stakes and the Ascot Derby, while Brennus, a son of his Derby winner Voltigeur, won the Visitors' Plate and walked over for the Queen's Plate. Both horses were ridden by 26-year-old Jem Snowden, who had been born at Flixton the son of a pedlar. Had he not been so fond of the bottle, Snowden might have been one of the greatest jockeys of the century. He used to say that he would give £5000 to be cured of drinking. Many of the Northern trainers, notably William I'Anson, for whom he won the Derby on Blair Athol in 1864, swore that he was the best jockey in the country whether he was drunk or sober. Others were less tolerant. He once arrived at Chester to ride for the Duke of Westminster, only to find the meeting had taken place the previous week. He never had another mount from the Duke. Jem Snowden had a quaint sense of humour. Arriving in the paddock, more than a little the worse for his tippling, to ride for the Middleham trainer Paddy Drislane, he saw that his mount was wearing blinkers. Pointing to the headgear he said in his broad Yorkshire accent, "Naay, Naay, tak it away, tak it away. A blinnd horse and a blinnd jockey'll nivver deea!" Sadly this natural horseman, and instinctive tactician, was in poverty when he died at the age of 44 at Bentley, near Doncaster, in 1889.

A biting east wind did much to spoil Ascot in 1871, which has gone down in racing history as "The Baron's Year" as Baron de Rothschild won the Derby with Favonius, and the 1000 Guineas, Oaks and St Leger with Hannah, named after his daughter. He also enjoyed his share of success at the Royal Meeting as Corisande, who had won the New Stakes in 1870, returned to land the Coronation Stakes, and Chopette won both the Queen's Stand Plate and the Fern Hill Stakes. Three years later Baron de Rothschild, the first Jew to be elected to the Jockey Club, died at the age of 56. Hannah de Rothschild married the 5th Earl of Rosebery, the future Prime Minister, who would inherit the Mentmore Stud. They were the parents of the late Lord Rosebery, who was to obtain his

final success at Royal Ascot when bringing off a double with Crooner in the Jersey Stakes and Sleeping Partner in the Ribblesdale Stakes in 1969.

There was a far larger attendance than usual in 1873, when the traditional spectacle and glamour of the occasion were not a little enhanced by the attendance of members of the Coaching, Four-in-Hand and Whip Clubs and their equipages. Some 180 coaches lined the far rails, reaching almost to the turn into the straight. Further out towards the centre of the Heath, officers of the Scots Fusiliers, the 7th Hussars, and 12th Lancers entertained their guests in elaborately appointed tents.

That was the year 16-year-old Fred Archer obtained his first success at Ascot, when riding Mr C. S. Hardy's Merodach at just 6 st 10 lb in the Wokingham Stakes. A combination of sheer dedication, horsemanship of the highest order, tactical subtlety, physical strength and intelligence was to make Archer one of the most brilliant jockeys the world has ever seen, though his private life was far from happy. His great friend, and fellow rider, Fred Webb claimed to have found him in tears because he could not be on both horses in a dead-heat. Even if the story was not true, it encapsulated his attitude well. Far taller than the average jockey, hence his later problems with his weight, Fred Archer would go to any lengths to win a race, even if they entailed a little rough riding, or plying his whip with a far greater ferocity than would be tolerated by the Stewards today. Always soberly dressed, with large, solemn, brown eyes, and quiet, dignified, good manners, he seemed more like a bank clerk than a champion jockey when he was not on a horse. He was not without a highly developed appreciation of the value of the rewards that his talent brought him, and they called him "The Tinman", tin having been the Victorian slang for money. The public loved him, as they knew he guaranteed them a run for their money, and many followed his mounts blindly. For 12 brief years, until the consummation of his tragedy, his splendid riding was the feature of Ascot.

Born at Cheltenham in January 1857, Fred Archer was the son of Billie Archer, who won the Grand National on Little Charlie the following year. At the age of 11 Fred Archer was apprenticed to Mat Dawson, who had ended his association with

James Merry in 1866 and opened a public stable in the Heath House yard at Newmarket. Strangely, Archer's first success was on a pony called Maid of Trent in a steeplechase at Bangor, and it was not until September 1870 that he won his first race on the flat on Athol Daisy at the long-defunct Chesterfield meeting. Four years later, in 1874, he was champion jockey at the end of the first of the 13 consecutive seasons that he held the title.

The 5th Earl of Hardwicke, always known as "Glossy Top" in fashionable circles, became Master of the Buckhounds in 1874. Up to this time silk top hats had been made of beaver that was left in its original rough, shaggy state. It was Lord Hardwicke, a fastidious man in all matters sartorial, who had his hat polished so highly that he could see his face in it, and thus introduced headwear still widely seen in the Royal Enclosure today, and favoured by the likes of Sir Piers Bengough, Henry Cecil and Jeremy Tree. A past master in the art of providing light amusement, and as such a close friend of the Prince of Wales, Lord Hardwicke, the descendant of a Lord Chancellor, whose father had been a Dover solicitor, was not without distinction in public life. While still known as Lord Royston prior to succeeding to the earldom on the death of his father in 1873, he had been decorated while serving with the 7th Light Dragoons in the Indian Mutiny, and then for the 10 years from 1863 he was Conservative Member of Parliament for Cambridgeshire.

Thirty-one years after it had been founded, the New Stakes was finally won by a colt destined for Derby honours when in 1874, Prince Batthyany's Galopin beat Vae Victis by a length and a half. Galopin, who had the strange habit of racing with his mouth open as a two-year-old, was trained by John Dawson, younger brother of Tom, Mat and Joe, in the Warren House Stable, Prince Batthyany's private establishment at Newmarket. Before the end of Queen Victoria's reign, three more future Derby winners would have been successful in the New Stakes, namely Donovan in 1888, Isinglass in 1892 and Flying Fox in 1898.

The Sultan of Zanzibar was at Ascot in 1875, when a four-day ticket for the Grandstand could be had for £1. James Merry's Doncaster, trained by Robert Peck, Mat Dawson's successor in the Russley Park Stable, crowned his career with his

Fred Archer – "the Tinman", towards the end of his career.

triumph in the Gold Cup after having won the Derby two years earlier. Ridden by George Fordham in the Gold Cup of 1875, Doncaster went to the front immediately the starter dropped his flag, jumped the tan road that crosses the straight course just before its juncture with the round, and made every yard of the running to come home six lengths clear of his nearest rival. The following day Doncaster came out again to beat Scamp by a length, with a four-year-old filly called Lily Agnes down the field in the Alexandra Plate. As Fordham was claimed by Sir John Astley for Scamp, that powerful welterweight Fred Webb came in for the mount on Doncaster in the Alexandra Plate.

Like Lily Agnes, Doncaster was bred by Sir Tatton Sykes at Yorkshire's famous Sledmere Stud. He was a golden chestnut by Stockwell out of Marigold, and originally rejoiced in the unpropitious name of All Heart And No Peel. Despite the horse's dreadful nomenclature, Robert Peck took an immense liking to him and tried to persuade Merry

Robert Peck – one of the greatest trainers of the last century.

to buy him, but Merry, who was not parting with his money any more freely in illness and old age, refused to go beyond 1000 guineas and insisted on bidding himself, lest his trainer be carried away by his enthusiasm for the colt. Another man had the bid at 900 guineas. Merry countered with 950 guineas, then to Peck's immense relief the hammer fell, and Doncaster was on his way to Russley.

Shortly after he had won the Gold Cup, Doncaster was bought by Robert Peck for 10,000 guineas and a fortnight later sold on for 14,000 guineas to the Duke of Westminster, who retired him to the Eaton Stud. Among the many good horses that he sired was Bend Or, who won the Derby for the Duke in 1880. Mated with Lily Agnes, the mare who had been unplaced to his sire at Ascot, Bend Or got Ormonde, arguably the greatest horse seen at Ascot or anywhere else in the nineteenth century.

Though his career was brief as well as brilliant, Robert Peck rates alongside Mat Dawson and John Porter as being among the greatest trainers of the last century. Born at Malton, where his father ran the Grove Cottage stables, Peck was only 24 when he won the Stewards Cup with Fichu in 1869; he took over the Russley Park Stable the following year. As well as winning the Derby with Doncaster and Bend Or, he won both the Oaks and St Leger with Marie Stuart in 1873. He was still only 36 when he gave up training in 1881. Although plagued with indifferent health he managed both the Park Lodge and Beverley House Stables at Newmarket, while also running his own Howbury Hall Stud in Bedfordshire. As well as being a brilliant judge of a horse, he was quite fearless in his betting, and brought off huge gambles with Hackness in the Cambridgeshire in 1882, and Barcaldine in the Northumberland Plate in 1883. He was 54 when he died at Scarborough in August 1899.

Prince George of Wales, the future King George V, then 12 years of age, and his elder brother Prince Albert Victor were in the royal party at Ascot in 1877 when Tom Cannon obtained his first success in the Gold Cup on the 4th Earl of Lonsdale's Petrarch, trained by his brother Joe Cannon in Captain Machell's stable. The son of a Windsor horse dealer, Tom Cannon had been apprenticed to John Day the younger at Danebury. A particularly graceful rider, with the lightest of hands, he hated to make the running, and whenever possible held his mount up for a late challenge. He married John Day's daughter Kate, and their daughter Margaret married Ernie Piggott, grandfather of Lester Piggott. Cannon was to have easier rides in the Gold Cup than Petrarch, who tried to pull up in order to return to his stable at the Paddock turn, and it took all his rider's persuasive skill to encourage him to continue in the race after he had given away many lengths by his antics. Gradually making up his ground, Petrarch was only six lengths behind the leaders at Swinley Bottom, and going right through with his effort he won by a length from Skylark, the mount of Fred Archer. As he did not ride in the race in 1878, Tom Cannon was successful on five consecutive mounts in the Gold Cup. After winning on Isonomy in both 1879 and 1880, he won again on

Bend Or – a supreme champion trained by Robert Peck.

Robert the Devil in 1881 and Foxhall in 1882. Subsequently he obtained his sixth success in the race on Althorp in 1886. Fred Archer never did ride the winner of the Gold Cup.

A notable absentee from Ascot in 1877 was 82-year-old Admiral Rous. He was taken seriously ill in his Berkeley Square house on the eve of the meeting, and died on 20th June. In his honour Ascot staged the Rous Memorial Stakes, the inaugural running of which was won by Fred Archer on Petrarch in 1878. The champion jockey was at the very top of his form at Ascot that year, riding 11 winners in all. On the second day he won the Royal Hunt Cup by three lengths on Julius Caesar, an elegant, dark brown horse with a filthy temper, trained by his owner Joe Dawson at Newmarket. Joe Dawson lived in what is now the Bedford Lodge Hotel, and built the adjoining Bedford Lodge Stable, which

was generally acclaimed the most modern racing establishment in the country. Julius Caesar was his last notable winner at Ascot. He suffered from diabetes, and died at the age of 55 two years later. His wife Harriet was the niece of the Middleham trainer John Fobert, who had won the Gold Cup with Van Tromp and The Flying Dutchman in the middle of the century.

Forty-eight hours after his success on Julius Caesar in the Hunt Cup, Archer completed the double in the two most important short-distance handicaps of the meeting by winning the Wokingham Stakes on Captain Prime's Trappist, beating George Fordham on Warrior by three parts of a length. Getting the better of Fordham always gave him particular satisfaction, as Fordham, whom a number of good judges rated the better jockey, was the rider for whom he had the greatest respect.

Archer, who was 20 years the younger, never quite knew how much or how little Fordham had in hand. He once said of Fordham:

> He was "cluck-clucking" at his mount the whole way. I thought I had him beaten two or three times in the two miles. But with his infernal "cluck-cluck" he was always coming again. Still 200 yards from home I thought I had him dead settled. I'll "cluck-cluck" you, I thought, but at that moment he swoops and beats me easily.

Among the other races that Fred Archer won at Ascot that year was the Coronation Stakes on Redwing, owned by the 6th Viscount Falmouth, still the principal patron of Mat Dawson's stable. In the Gold Cup he rode Lord Falmouth's Silvio, on whom he had won the Derby the previous year. Silvio was at odds on, but yet again Archer's luck was out in the Cup, and he was beaten six lengths by Count de Lagrange's Verneuil ridden by Jim Goater. Verneuil also won the Gold Vase and the Alexandra Plate that year.

In the March of 1878 Lord Hardwicke, "Glossy Top", sustained serious injury when thrown onto his head as his horse slipped on heavy ploughed land while out with the Royal Buckhounds. In consequence he was unable to carry out his duties at Ascot three months later, and Viscount Colville of Culross, a former Master of the Buckhounds, deputised for him. That year it was decided to sell off the wooden Alexandra Stand by auction at the end of the fourth and final day of the meeting, so that it could be replaced by a larger, more permanent structure alongside the Grandstand. It was also in 1878 that the antiquated sheds in the paddock were at last demolished to make way for a 240-foot range of modern saddling boxes backing on to the main road on the southern side.

Like more than one other member of the aristocracy, that suave and immaculate dandy Lord Hardwicke, whose seat was at Wimpole Hall near Royston in Hertfordshire, all but beggared himself in his endeavours to entertain the easily bored Prince of Wales. Before he died at the comparatively early age of 61 in 1897, he had been living in comparatively reduced circumstances. He had resigned as Master of the Buckhounds in 1879, and that year the Hardwicke Stakes, now a Group Two mile-and-a-half race for older horses, was run in his honour

for the first time. It was always over its present distance, but formerly open to three-year-olds – the first winner, Lord Bradford's Chippendale, ridden by Johnny Osborne, belonging to that age group.

Isonomy, on whom Tom Cannon won the Gold Cup in 1879 and again in 1880, was a bay by Sterling out of a Stockwell mare, trained by John Porter at Kingsclere for Frederick Gretton, a brewer with a taste for heavy betting. A small horse who never grew above 15.2 hands, he first impressed his trainer when Porter saw the spirited manner in which he held his own against much larger yearlings in the paddocks of the Yardley Stud near Birmingham, where he was bred, and thus earned his name, the definition of "isonomy" being "the equal distribution of rights and privileges". Like so many horses foaled as late in the year as May, Isonomy continued to make much more than average improvement when contemporaries had more or less reached their peaks. After he had brought off a huge gamble for his owner in the Cambridgeshire on his only appearance as a three-year-old, rather than having been trained for the classics, Isonomy was clearly top-class as a four-year-old. He beat the Derby winner Silvio by half a length in the Gold Vase at the opening stage of the Royal Meeting of 1879, and then two days later won the Gold Cup by two lengths. To win the Gold Cup for a second time, 12 months later, Isonomy beat Chippendale, winner of the first race for the Hardwicke Stakes, by a length. On retiring to the Bonehill Stud at Tamworth in Staffordshire. Isonomy proved a successful stallion, more than one of whose progeny was to take centre stage at Ascot.

John Porter, the trainer of Isonomy, enjoyed more success at Ascot than the great majority of his profession. He had been born at Rugeley, Staffordshire, in 1838, and apprenticed to John Barham Day at Michel Grove. With the death of George Manning shortly after winning the Gold Cup with Asteroid in 1862, John Porter, intensely conscientious and utterly humourless, took over Sir Joseph Hawley's private establishment at Cannon's Heath in Hampshire in 1863, when still only 25 years old. Four years later he moved Sir Joseph's horses into their owner's newly constructed Kingsclere Stable, and in his first season there won the Gold Cup of 1868 with Blue Gown. When Sir

Joseph Hawley died in 1877, Porter exercised his option to buy Kingsclere, and subsequently spent another £20,000 enlarging it to turn it into one of the biggest and most successful of the public stables.

Exceptionally heavy rain fell at Ascot on the morning of the Wednesday in 1879 and there was grave doubt whether it would be possible to stage that day's card, but fortunately for Captain Machell racing went ahead. With his prodigious knowledge of form, Machell had always enjoyed a tilt at the big handicaps, and the Royal Hunt Cup was to become his favourite. That year he won the race for the first time with his own horse, The Mandarin, ridden by Charlie Wood. Although The Mandarin started at 33/1 in a field of 28, it is unlikely in the extreme that he ran unbacked by his owner. Soon afterwards Captain Machell was responsible for Sweetbread and Elvezir winning the Royal Hunt Cup in the years 1882 and 1883 respectively, as he managed both horses for Mr W. Gerard, later Lord Gerard. A good deal of money would certainly have been won in each instance as Sweetbread, the mount of Jim Woodburn, was joint favourite at 5/1, and Elvezir, ridden, like The Mandarin, by Charlie Wood, was backed down to clear favourite at 5/1. The Bedford Cottage stable was also to win the Hunt Cup on three subsequent occasions while it was under the direction of Captain Machell.

Fred Archer obtained his second success in the Royal Hunt Cup on Sir John Astley's Peter, a brilliant horse whose good humour and co-operation were never to be taken for granted, in 1881. On the first day of the meeting he was ridden by Wood when 3/1 on in a field of three for the Gold Vase. Coming to the racecourse stables by the Paddock bend, this moody individual behaved far worse than Petrarch had done at the same spot in the Gold Cup of 1877, for he simply came to a standstill, and proceeded to buck and kick until Wood had no option but to take him back into the paddock. Despite his having top weight of 9 st 3 lb to carry in the Royal Hunt Cup next day, he started favourite at 100/30. As soon as they jumped off it was clear that Peter was of no mind to race, for he laid back his ears and seemed on the point of pulling up until Archer began to pat him and humour him. With half a mile to go, Peter was hopelessly tailed off, but suddenly he took into that wayward mind of his to respond to Archer's tenderness. On taking hold of his bit, he almost flew as he used his class to overtake horse after horse until he got up by three parts of a length to win from Sword Dance, to whom he was giving 36 lb.

When Peter was brought out for the third time in the course of the meeting to contest the Hardwicke Stakes on the Friday, Sir John Astley was given an insight into the way in which Archer applied his brain to his riding. "I have been thinking over this race, Sir John," said the champion jockey.

> You know the start for the mile and a half we run today is just below the spot where Peter stopped to kick on Tuesday, and it is very likely, if I canter up past it with the other horses, he may take it into his head to repeat his Tuesday's performance. If you will get leave from the Stewards, I will hack him round the reverse way of the course, and will arrive at the starting-post just as the other horses fall in. By doing so, he may jump off and go kindly.

The necessary dispensation having been obtained, Peter arrived at the start in a not altogether characteristically amenable frame of mind, and racing with a will, won by eight lengths from Frederick Gretton's Geologist, the mount of Fordham. The ever impecunious Sir John Astley, having backed him at evens, won a badly needed £1500.

Archer also won both the Prince of Wales' Stakes and the St James's Palace Stakes on Pierre Lorillard's Iroquois, whom he had also ridden when the colt had made history by becoming the first American-bred winner of the Derby a fortnight earlier. On a very different horse, he won the Ascot Biennial on Lord Rosebery's Voluptuary. Three years later Voluptuary, who had been bred by Queen Victoria, won the Grand National without ever having run in a previous steeplechase. This Royal Ascot winner was to finish up on the stage, taking a miniature water jump in the Grand National scene of *The Prodigal Maid* at the Drury Lane Theatre.

Whether the Derby winner Iroquois was necessarily the best American-bred three-year-old running in 1881 is a moot point. Foxhall, trained by William Day for the financier J. R. Keene, was also uncommonly good but could not prove it in the classics, as he was not engaged in them. As a result he had to contest the big handicaps and demonstrated his excellence and versatility by completing the autumn double in the Cambridgeshire and Cesarewitch. He also went across to France to land the Grand Prix de Paris. As a four-year-old Foxhall consolidated his reputation by winning the Gold Cup.

By the time of the success of Foxhall at Ascot, little Billy Day of some 40 years earlier had matured into Mr William Day, the greatly respected trainer. All memories of nobbling horses and sending surreptitious letters to bookmakers, whether or not in the right envelopes, had long been eradicated from his mind. Instead he readily delivered himself of long homilies denouncing sharp practice and every kind of evil that beset the turf. He later had the impertinence to write a book entitled *Turf Celebrities I Have Known*, which was a series of essays that hardly flattered his former owners, most of whom he had treated with scant loyalty. As well as with Foxhall, he won the Gold Cup with Brigantine in 1869. On retiring from training he lost a great deal of money in land speculation and died at the age of 85 in 1908.

A novel event appeared on the card in 1883. This was the £600 Orange Gold Cup, presented by the King of the Netherlands, run over the Old Mile, and confined to horses the property of, ridden and trained by British subjects. The winner was Barcaldine, ridden by Archer, who beat Fordham's mount Faugh-a-Ballagh by three lengths, with Lord March's Alizon a bad last of three. Bob Peck, the winning owner, received the trophy from the Dutch King. Barcaldine, who went through his career unbeaten, was a massive bay with anything but the most pleasant of dispositions, trained by Jim Hopper in his owner's private stable, Beverley House at Newmarket. On his only subsequent appearance Barcaldine brought off the gamble in the Northumberland Plate, and then broke down while being trained for the Cambridgeshire. At stud Barcaldine, who was by West Australian's son Solon, maintained the branch of the male line of the Godolphin Arabian, from which Precipitation and Santa Claus descend.

The horse that everybody went to Ascot to see in 1884 was the Duke of Portland's unbeaten three-year-old St Simon, whom Mat Dawson was to saddle for the Gold Cup. The other four runners were Mr C. J. Lefevre's Tristan, who had won the race for Tom Jennings' stable the previous season, the Duke of Beaufort's Faugh-a-Ballagh, the Duke

of Hamilton's Friday and Iambic, who also belonged to the Duke of Portland. As Archer could not do the weight for St Simon, Charlie Wood came in for the ride. Wood's orders were to win by just two lengths. Although he was probably the strongest middleweight in the weighing-room, Wood never had the remotest chance of carrying out those instructions, for St Simon turned the race into a procession and won by a majestic 20 lengths.

An extraordinarily robust dark bay, with rather a convex profile, St Simon was a very highly strung colt of enormous energy, who took a great deal of knowing and handling. Mat Dawson maintained that he had more "electricity" about him than any horse he had ever known, while his one-eyed lad Charlie Fordham lamented, "Talk about the patience of Job! Job never did no St Simon!" St Simon was bred by Prince Batthyany, an incurably sentimental man as well as a very generous one. On the death of the Prince in the early spring of 1883, the two-year-old St Simon came up for sale along with his other horses and was brought by Mat Dawson for 1600 guineas on behalf of the Duke of Portland. As the rules then stood St Simon's engagements in the classics and the other races that had already closed became void on the death of his nominator. As it happened St Simon had only been entered in the 2000 Guineas, as Prince Batthyany had never been enthusiastic about running his beloved horses in the Derby because of his fear of their breaking down on the undulating Epsom course, and for some reason had not thought it worth putting him in the St Leger. Because of his lack of engagements in the classics and more important juvenile events St Simon had to follow an unorthodox programme in the early part of his career, though was able to crown it with triumphs in the Gold Cup and Goodwood Cup.

St Simon, arguably the greatest of all Gold Cup winners, though comparison with the likes of Gladiateur is impossible, was by Galopin, first winner of the New Stakes to graduate to Derby honours, out of St Angela, by King Tom. At stud he proved one of the most successful stallions in the history of racing, heading the list on no fewer than nine occasions. Moreover he shares with Stockwell the distinction of siring the winners of as many as 17 British classics.

The great Ormonde – winner of two races at Ascot in 1886 and 1887, with trainer John Porter and jockey Fred Archer.

The day after being second to St Simon in the Gold Cup, Tristan won the Hardwicke Stakes for the third year in succession. Ridden by Fred Webb, he beat Waterford by a length, with Harvester, who had dead-heated in the Derby, a bad third. There was no royal procession that year as the Court was in mourning for the Prince of Wales' younger brother Leopold, Duke of Albany, who had died on 28th February.

In 1886 Fred Archer went to Ascot, the course on which some of his finest riding on the likes of Peter had been seen, for the last time. He was still only 29 years of age, but the deep tragedies of his private life, through circumstances that were none of his own making, were clearly reflected in those large, brown eyes that were desperately sad where once they had been solemn. In January 1883 he had

married Helen Rose Dawson, daughter of Galopin's trainer John Dawson, and niece of Mat Dawson. Exactly a year later, in January 1884, she had borne him a son who lived only a matter of hours. In the November of that year he was riding at Liverpool when he received a telegram to inform him that Helen Rose had given birth to a daughter. Dashing home to Newmarket, he found his wife dying in convulsions, though their infant daughter survived. Nothing would ever be able to console him.

To compound his mental misery, Archer was in physical agony as he tried to maintain a racing weight, so that he lived on a near starvation diet, with recourse to drastic purgatives. He was to have ridden his first mount at Ascot in 1886, Toastmaster, owned by Richard Christopher Naylor, the miserly Master of the Pytchley, at 8 st 5 lb, but had to put up 3 lb overweight at 8 st 8 lb. All the same he beat Charlie Wood on Periosteum by a neck in the Trial Stakes, still the opening race of the meeting. In all he rode seven winners in the course of the four days, showing that his talent was quite unimpaired by privation, but his final mount, the Duke of Westminster's Whitefriar, started 2/1 on for the Queen's Stand Plate and finished last of four.

Outstanding among the horses that Archer rode at Ascot in 1886 was the Duke of Westminster's Ormonde on whom he won a three horse race for the St James's Palace Stakes at 100/30 on for John Porter's Kingsclere stable. When Ormonde was brought out again for the Hardwicke Stakes on the Friday, Archer was claimed by Mat Dawson for Melton, winner of the Derby the previous year, and it was George Barrett who rode Ormonde to beat Melton by two lengths.

A massive, rich bay colt, with a neck like a bull, powerful quarters and excellent bone, Ormonde had already won the 2000 Guineas and the Derby, would go on to win the St Leger, and would never be beaten. To many people he was the greatest horse of the last century, but Fred Archer, who rode them both, was firmly of the opinion that St Simon was the better.

Five months after winning on Ormonde and those other six horses at Ascot, Fred Archer, the most successful jockey the world had ever seen, was dead. While recovering from typhoid, he shot himself in a fit of delirium at his Newmarket home on 8th November.

The highlight of Ascot in Golden Jubilee year, 1887, was the seasonal reappearance of Ormonde, who had acquired the status of National Hero, second only in popular affection to the sovereign who had reigned for 50 years. What the vast majority of the people who made Ormonde 4/1 on for the Rous Memorial Stakes on the Thursday did not know was that the great horse had become a roarer. Despite his having become affected in his wind the Duke of Westminster and John Porter decided to keep him in training as a four-year-old, give him extensive treatment with the electric sponge, and rely upon his brilliance to keep his record intact. In the Rous Memorial Stakes, Ormonde, on whom Tom Cannon replaced Fred Archer, toyed with the opposition, beating Captain Machell's

Kilwarlin, who would win the St Leger, by six lengths, Agave being last of three.

The following day Ormonde faced a far, far stiffer task in the Hardwicke Stakes, for which he started at 5/4 on in a field of four. The other runners were Mat Dawson's candidate Minting, who had been favourite to beat Ormonde in the 2000 Guineas and was thought sure to take his revenge, Bendigo, winner of the first race for the Eclipse Stakes the previous season, and the outsider Phil. Minting was ridden by Johnny Osborne, Bendigo by Jack Watts and, ominously, Phil by George Barrett, who had won the 2000 Guineas as well as the previous season's Hardwicke on Ormonde. Never the most stable of characters, Barrett had taken deep offence at Tom Cannon's having been given the ride on Ormonde after the death of Fred Archer, rather than himself, and was determined to do his utmost to engineer the defeat of the colt. As they made the right-hand turn into the straight, Barrett bored hard against Ormonde, and once in line for home continued to ensure that his mount was hanging into the favourite, so that Ormonde was all but carrying Phil, as Minting, racing in the middle of the course, maintained a slight advantage. Eventually the lack of class in Phil told, and he dropped away beaten, but by that time he had done enough harm to ensure that Ormonde was hard put to it to get on terms with Minting as they passed the Grandstand 100 yards from home, and get up to win by a neck.

The crowd went almost mad in their ecstatic delight at seeing their champion triumph at Ascot for a fourth time, and the Duke of Westminster, normally the most reserved of men, led Ormonde round the paddock twice to continuous applause, and then along the course towards the stables. No horse, with the possible exception of Persimmon, would be given such a reception at Ascot until Brown Jack won the Queen Alexandra Stakes for a sixth time nearly 50 years later.

Unfortunately Ormonde was not a success as a stallion. In his second season at stud he was so seriously ill that his fertility was impaired, and fearing that he might transmit his infirmity in the wind, the Duke sold him to the Argentine for £12,000, and in 1894 he was sold again to California for £30,000. His powers of procreation, though, had been

Harry McCalmont – who won the Gold Cup with Timothy in 1888 and Isinglass in 1895.

permanently impaired so that he got very few foals, prior to his being destroyed at the age of 21 in 1904.

A violent thunderstorm, which packed the stands, broke out before Charlie Wood rode Mr Manton's Gay Hermit to beat Pearl Diver by three parts of a length in the Royal Hunt Cup in Golden Jubilee year. The other three races won by "Mr Manton" at Ascot that season were the Prince of Wales' Stakes with Claymore, the Coronation Stakes with Heloise and the Ascot Derby with Timothy.

"Mr Manton" was the *nom de course* of the formidable Agnes, Duchess of Montrose, whose horses were trained by Alec Taylor senior at Manton, there still being a convention that women did not own racehorses, though some, like Mrs Ellen Challoner, widow of the jockey, and Isabella Graham, owner and breeder of Isonomy's sire Sterling, were already running horses in their own names. The ample figure of the imperious Duchess of Montrose, much

given to wearing clothes of a distinctly masculine cut, was readily recognisable in the Royal Enclosure over many years. Not at all easy to please, she would caustically give voice to her vexation. She did not always come off best. One day when she asked the royal trainer Dick Marsh what would win, he mentioned the names of a few fancied runners and she rebuked him, saying, "Marsh, those are newspaper tips." Some time later she touted the trainer again and he replied blandly, "I fear I have not yet read the newspapers today, Your Grace."

The Prince of Wales' Stakes, which the Duchess won with Claymore, was turned into a fiasco. A mounted policeman crossed the course during the race and interfered with a number of runners some 300 yards before the finish. Tom Cannon was thrown from Phil, the horse that had leaned on him in the Hardwicke, and injured his knee, while both Scottish King and Grandison were knocked halfway round. Of more permanent importance, the 118-yard underground passage beneath the lawns behind the Royal Enclosure, leading from the Grandstand to the paddock, was constructed in 1887.

The royal procession was dispensed with again in 1888 as the German Emperor was terminally ill. Kaiser Friedrich, the 100-day Kaiser who had married Victoria, the Princess Royal, was already stricken by cancer of the throat on accession. He died on the final day of the Ascot meeting. In consequence of the Kaiser's illness, his brother-in-law the Prince of Wales only attended the meeting on the Thursday and returned to London the following morning.

The Gold Cup of that year was won by Timothy, carrying the light blue and scarlet quartered jacket of Harry McCalmont, who had followed the example of Henry Chaplin and so many other rich young men by putting his racing interests in the hands of Captain Machell. Having migrated from Scotland to Ulster in the seventeenth century, the McCalmonts laid the foundations of their wealth in the sugar plantations of the West Indies during the Napoleonic Wars. They subsequently entered into banking, building up the most important financial house in the City of London after Baring Brothers, and acquired extensive interests in railways in the United States. At the time that he inherited the entire family fortune from a bachelor great-uncle in 1887, Harry McCalmont was 26 years of age and held a commission in the Royal Warwickshire Regiment.

Gregarious and generous, Harry McCalmont had been an outstanding athlete at Eton. He retained his sporting turn of mind, loved entertaining – giving lavish parties at Cheveley Park, the large estate on the outskirts of Newmarket that he had purchased from the Duke of Rutland, or aboard his yacht – and craved the sort of excitement better afforded by the racecourse than peacetime soldiering. Rather than launch him on to the turf with unknown quantities from the yearling market, Captain Machell bought him the 1887 Ascot Derby winner Timothy, a chestnut colt by Hermit with a quite perfect temperament, from the Duchess of Montrose. First time out in Harry McCalmont's colours, which were those of the Eton football team, Timothy beat Tissaphernes by six lengths in the Gold Cup. For his own part, Captain Machell brought off another coup in the Royal Hunt Cup, when his three-year-old Shilelagh, ridden by George Chaloner at 6 st 3 lb, got home by a neck from Attila, the mount of Seth Chandley.

Dan Dancer, trained by Bob Armstrong on Lord Lonsdale's estate just outside Penrith in Cumbria, won the Ascot Stakes for the North in 1888. A remarkably resilient horse, he had been beaten in a hurdle race in Paris the previous week, arrived back in the yard after a three-day journey on Sunday night, and set off south again the following morning. On arrival at Ascot, Bob Armstrong found no box available, so that Dan Dancer spent the night in a draughty cow byre, with an extra rug. None the worse for the experience, he was as fresh as paint the next day and won by a comfortable three lengths.

An official racecard with leaves replaced the single, cumbersome sheet at Ascot in 1889. With the Queen persisting in her refusal to allow the Prince of Wales to use Windsor Castle during race week, he rented Sunninghill Park, some two miles from the course, and on the opening day of the meeting saw Morglay carry the colours of his close friend Leopold de Rothschild successfully in the Gold Vase. Leopold, nephew of Baron Mayer de Rothschild, combined a passion for racing with

philanthropy, frequently giving prize money, and sometimes multiples of it, to charity, though he could be short-tempered, especially with those critical of his horses. The Prince was frequently a guest on Leopold de Rothschild's shoot at Leighton Buzzard, or at his Newmarket residence, Palace House.

The Coventry Stakes, soon to become Ascot's most prestigious two-year-old race, was inaugurated in 1890, taking its name from George, 9th Earl of Coventry, who had become Master of the Buckhounds in 1886 and continued in office until 1892, serving a second term from 1895 to 1900. Along with the Earl of Chesterfield, Lord Coventry is one of the few Masters to have made an impact well beyond the confines of Ascot. A man of great culture, he was as knowledgeable about pictures and porcelain as he was about horses, and as much in his element at Christie's as at Tattersalls. For many years his steeplechasers were trained on the estate surrounding his Croome Court home in Worcestershire, using the Kinnersley gallops on which the Rimell family have worked such great jumpers as Nicolaus Silver and Comedy of Errors in more recent years. With the full sisters Emblem and Emblematic he won the Grand National in 1863 and 1864 respectively. As an old man he had horses in Willie Waugh's stable at Newmarket, and won the Cambridgeshire of 1923 with Verdict, whose daughter Quashed would be engaged in one of the greatest duels ever seen at Ascot. Lord Coventry had been a member of the Jockey Club for 60 years when he died at the age of 91 in March 1930.

The initial running of the Coventry Stakes was won by The Deemster, from Captain Machell's stable. Just three years later Lord Rosebery's Ladas, who was to land the Derby, became the first future classic winner to be successful in the Coventry Stakes.

Five years after enjoying his initial success as an owner when Fred Archer rode Counterpane at Sandown Park in June 1886, the Prince of Wales had his first winner at Ascot. This was The Imp, on whom the unpredictable George Barrett beat Weldon on John Morgan by three parts of a length in the Ascot High Weight Plate, a handicap over a mile and a quarter in 1891. The royal horses were managed by Lord Marcus Beresford, and, at the

Arrival of the royal party in 1891.

time, trained by John Porter at Kingsclere. The following year the Prince's steadily increasing string was transferred to Richard Marsh, who conducted the palatial Egerton House stable at Newmarket. The official reason for the move was that the horses had to be in a stable more accessible from Sandringham than Kingsclere, but it was widely suspected that relations between the urbane, witty Lord Marcus Beresford and the humourless John Porter were never particularly good. On the other hand Lord Marcus had much in common with Dick Marsh, not least the experience of having ridden in steeplechases, the basis of so many friendships.

A handsome man, with strong features and pleasing manners, Dick Marsh had been born at Smeeth, Kent, in 1851, the son of a farmer. He rode his first winner on Manrico at Dover in 1866, and then went to Newmarket to join Captain Machell's stable, though never formally apprenticed. Not long after winning the New Stakes on Temple at the Royal Meeting of 1869, he became too heavy for the flat, and embarked on a successful career over fences and hurdles. Seven years before riding his last winner on Scots Guard at Kempton Park in 1881, he had begun training in a small way near Epsom, and then in 1876 moved to Lordship Farm, Newmarket, eventually taking over the Egerton House establishment in 1892. Richard Marsh liked to do everything in the grand style, without always taking into account the cost involved. Having installed himself at Egerton House, he found he had to cover overheads of £13,000 a year before he started to make his own living. His second wife, Grace, was the daughter of the Beckhampton trainer Sam Darling. They were the parents of Marcus Marsh, who was to train for the Aga Khan.

As was quite inevitable, the horses of Baron Maurice de Hirsch accompanied those of the Prince of Wales from Kingsclere to Egerton House. The son of the banker to the Bavarian monarchy, Maurice de Hirsch had made a fortune out of financing railways in the Balkans and Turkey, and found the fulfilment of his enormous social ambitions in basking in royal favour – something, to his chagrin, consistently denied him on the Continent. The Prince of Wales had first met Hirsch in Paris in 1890 and accepted the invitation to shoot on his Hungarian estate. The rigidly formal court of Franz Josef, Emperor of Austria-Hungary, was horrified at the prospect of the Prince visiting Hirsch, and the Austrian ambassador vigorously pointed out that the Baron would never be received at the Hofburg in Vienna. The protests made no impression on the Prince of Wales, for whom Hirsch organised the biggest shoot ever known in Europe, with 11,000 partridges killed in five days. Grateful though the Prince of Wales was for the acutely shrewd management of his financial affairs, as well as for the occasional and very considerable loan, he was becoming increasingly irritated by the continual requests for the use of his influence in securing the financier's acceptance at the Viennese court, when Baron de Hirsch died in April 1896. The Baron's only son Lucien had predeceased him.

Although Baron de Hirsch owned horses for less than a decade, he had the good fortune to have his colours carried by one of the best fillies ever seen at Ascot in La Fleche. Bred by Queen Victoria at the Hampton Court Stud, La Fleche was a bay by St Simon out of Quiver by Toxophilite, and cost a record 5500 guineas. At the fall of the hammer Edmund Tattersall enthusiastically called for "Three cheers for Baron de Hirsch, and success to the Royal Stud!" Standing 15.3 hands, La Fleche was a lean, wiry filly with a head brimful of quality, and, when at the peak of her form, pronouncedly ragged. After she had completed the hat-trick in the 1000 Guineas, Oaks and St Leger while with John Porter in 1892, La Fleche was trained by Dick Marsh for her triumph in the Gold Cup as a five-year-old. Ridden by the Egerton House stable jockey Jack Watts, she beat the French-bred Callistrate by three

Baron de Hirsch – owner of La Fleche, winner of 1894 Gold Cup.

lengths. The effort took more out of her than was supposed, and she lost out by half a length to C. D. Rose's Ravensbury in the Hardwicke Stakes the following day.

Not the least part of the fascination of Royal Ascot lies in the sharp contrast in the backgrounds of the owners who enjoy success at the meeting, for the winner's enclosure has never been the exclusive preserve of millionaires. Whereas the Gold Cup winner of 1894 carried the colours of an international financier, who was admitted to the Royal Enclosure, the Royal Hunt Cup winner of that year, Victor Wild, was owned by Tom Worton, who came from the tap room. He was landlord of The Half Moon at Dulwich, and had bought the horse out of a seller at Portsmouth Park as a two-year-old for 330 guineas. Victor Wild, who also won the Kempton Park Jubilee twice, was much the most popular handicapper of his day, especially with Londoners, for there was never any secrecy about whether or not he was fancied. On the evening before he ran, a notice would frequently appear in the saloon of the Half Moon reading, "Don't ask questions over the bar. Victor Wild will win," and he usually did. Jack Horsby, who trained Victor Wild at Wantage, limped badly as a result of having a stiff leg that he swung wide as he walked. He had none of the polished manners of Mat Dawson, Dick Marsh and other leaders of his profession, and was incapable of stringing a sentence together without every other word being an expletive.

Following West Australian and Gladiateur, Isinglass, owned by Harry McCalmont, became the third of the Triple Crown winners to achieve success in the Gold Cup in 1895. With only his own stablemate Kilsallaghan and Baron de Hirsch's Reminder taking the field against him at Ascot, Isinglass started at 11/2 on and beat Reminder by a comfortable three lengths. A fine, big bay of excellent bone, Isinglass was by the dual Gold Cup winner Isonomy out of Deadlock by Wenlock. Captain Machell had bought Deadlock on impulse for 19 guineas while visiting Lord Arlington, but sold her before he was able to appreciate the obvious merit of her first foal. Efforts to locate her proved fruitless, until he saw her drawing a trap driven by a farmer who had come to see him about a nomination to his carthorse stallion Marvellous. Willingly the farmer agreed to swap the mare between the shafts of his trap for a handsome colt by Marvellous. The following year Captain Machell sold Deadlock, with a foal at foot, for £500 to Harry McCalmont.

The skyscape above Ascot was altered dramatically in 1896 by the erection of the clock tower above the Grandstand, which was visible for many miles. Standing upon a balustrade 24 foot square, it rose to a height of 45 feet above the roof.

By the time the clock tower appeared, the men in the Royal Enclosure were dressed in much the same way that they are at the present time, save with regard to neckwear. Wing collars, rather than flat ones, with points turning downwards, were worn, and cravats rather than ties, while frock coats were still as popular as tails. The hirsute look was even more in fashion than it has since become again, with luxuriant moustaches and beards, notably those of the Prince of Wales, very much in evidence; and every man carried a walking cane whether or not infirmity demanded it as an aid to progress. Although the elaborate gowns of the women, which would continue to reach to the ground until after the end of the First World War, varied dramatically

in colour and texture, there was a far greater uniformity of style than there is some 100 years later.

As those to whom the Master of the Buckhounds, Lord Coventry, granted admission to the Royal Enclosure moved in a stately fashion around that most exclusive area, exchanging greetings with elaborate formality, they bore all the outward appearances of the most privileged citizens of the greatest empire the world has ever known, completely united in the enjoyment of their prerogatives. Yet beneath the surface ran deep dissensions, and much ill feeling. Insults were often exchanged as freely as they were in the Silver Ring, albeit more subtly. Old scores were settled, and vendettas wholeheartedly prosecuted. Even the Prince of Wales was not above being slighted.

In a letter written to his private secretary Francis Knollys in 1896, the Prince of Wales said:

> Lord C. B. [Charles Beresford] appeared in the Royal Enclosure, and passed close to me whilst I was talking to someone but totally ignored my existence – as I did his – I afterwards saw that gallant sailor and blackmailer! talking to the ladies and smoking cigarettes so that his statement that I got society to boycott him is as great a lie as most of his statements! He was at the races again today and purposely passed close to me without bowing, but he bowed shortly afterwards to my son and went up to the D and Dss of Devonshire with a "hail fellow well met" kind of manner and said how glad he was to see them again. The Dss came up to me purposely to tell me this, and said they were so taken aback they did not know what to do! His line evidently is . . . to show them that he intends treating me . . . with rudeness.

The origins of the quarrel between Lord Charles Beresford, who had so greatly distinguished himself while commanding the *Condor* before the batteries of Alexandria, and the Prince lay in the infatuation Lord Charles formed for Lady Brooke, the exquisitely beautiful, wife of the heir to the Earl of Warwick. On hearing that Lady Charles Beresford was pregnant, Daisy Brooke wrote to Lord Charles accusing him of infidelity to her, his mistress. As Lord Charles was serving at sea at the time, his wife was empowered to open all his post. On reading Lady Brooke's letter she was horrified, sent it to her solicitor, George Lewis, for safe keeping, and instructed him to threaten Daisy Warwick with prosecution for libel. Fearing the consequences of the publicity arising from such a case, Daisy Brooke, always known as the Babbling Brooke,

Changing skyline at Ascot – the new clock tower erected in 1896.

tried in vain to persuade Lewis to give her back the letter. Daisy then turned for help to the Prince of Wales, another of her more ardent admirers, but even royal intervention would not induce George Lewis to disobey the instructions of his client. Eventually, in response to the blandishments of Daisy Brooke, the Prince let it be known that he wished to be present at no function attended by Lady Charles Beresford, who was, in consequence, ostracised by society. In view of the Prince's treatment of Lady Charles, an entirely innocent party, it is not hard to see why he should have been shunned by her husband in the Royal Enclosure.

That year, 1896, the Ascot Stakes was won in facile fashion by M. Evremond de St Alary's Arlequin, who beat Son O' Mine by 10 lengths. The owner was unable to be present, having fought a duel successfully in France that morning. Less pressing engagements would enable M. de St Alary to witness his horses winning at Ascot in the years to come.

Great Britain celebrated the Diamond Jubilee of Queen Victoria in 1897. The nation was at the very summit of imperial splendour, with the largest empire ever known. From all over the world, royalty, soldiers and statesmen converged upon London to take part in the processions, garden parties and other celebrations that marked the 60th year of the reign of the Queen. In the brilliant sunshine that persisted throughout that memorable summer, Royal Ascot provided an appropriate footnote to the great occasion, when Persimmon, winner of the Derby the previous season, carried the colours of the Prince of Wales to win the Gold Cup. Ridden by Jack Watts, he cantered past the post with his ears pricked, eight lengths clear of Winkfield's Pride, with Love Wisely, winner of the race 12 months earlier, four lengths away third, and the Oaks winner Limasole last of four. The loud cheering that burst out from all over the course continued long after Persimmon had reached the winner's enclosure.

Like Gladiateur, winner of the Gold Cup 31 years earlier, Persimmon has his memory preserved in sculpture. The statue of Persimmon by Adrian Jones, who had qualified as a veterinary surgeon before joining the army, stands outside the administrative offices at Sandringham Stud.

During the 60 years that Queen Victoria had been on the throne, Ascot had been almost transformed. The number of permanent stands had been greatly increased, so that they stretched some two furlongs along the southern side of the course, and the dining rooms and other facilities had multiplied to provide a proper setting for one of the most important social events of the year, while the course itself had been constantly improved to make it worthy of staging the best racing of the season.

A NEW STYLE, A NEW CENTURY AND A NEW REIGN

AS THE 10 runners cantered to the start for the first race at Royal Ascot in 1899, those who had not been racing since the previous year, or had only infrequently attended a meeting, were amused, bewildered, or slightly disgusted by what they saw. The jockey on the favourite, Chinook, could not have looked more out of place on a racecourse if he had been riding side-saddle. Whereas Morny Cannon, Fred Rickaby and the other English riders sat well back, with stirrup leathers the full length of their legs in the traditional style of the hunting field, Tod Sloan, the little American on Chinook, had such a close hold of his mount's head that he was leaning halfway up his neck, while his exaggeratedly short leathers seemed to oblige him to all but kneel on the withers.

The monkey-up-the-stick style had come to Royal Ascot. Although many people laughed at it, as they would at anything unfamiliar, or even worse unfashionable, and purists denounced it as seriously inhibiting the rider's control of a horse, everyone at Ascot, as had been the case elsewhere, soon had to admit that the new method of riding was extraordinarily effective. As well as winning the Coventry Stakes on the chestnut gelding Democrat on the opening day, Tod Sloan won two other races at that Royal Meeting in the colours of Lord William Beresford.

Despite his never having run before, the Prince of Wales' bay colt Diamond Jubilee was made favourite for the Coventry Stakes, largely by reason of his being by St Simon out of Perdita II, and therefore full brother to Persimmon, who had won the Derby, St Leger and Gold Cup for the Prince. Both as a foal at Sandringham, and after he had gone into training with Richard Marsh at Egerton House, Newmarket, Diamond Jubilee had been disgracefully spoilt and cosseted as everybody hoped he would win another classic for the Prince. So much pampering inevitably brought about a deterioration in his character, which did not manifest itself until he was taken to a racecourse for the first time. Just as he was about to saddle Diamond Jubilee for the Coventry Stakes, Richard Marsh remarked to Sir Dighton Probyn, the controller of the Prince's household, that the colt was behaving beautifully. To give the immediate lie to those words, Diamond Jubilee lashed out viciously and kicked a bystander on the hand. Unfortunately the man had his hands in his pockets. Sir Dighton Probyn discreetly retired to the Royal Box as rapidly as he could.

Worse followed at the start, when the royal colt was completely out of the control of the consummate horseman Jack Watts, and made the most deplorable exhibition of himself. First of all he tried to grab the jockey's boot with his teeth. He then reared up continuously, and for a while was walking around on his hind legs. Considering the enormous amount of energy he dissipated while performing these unbecoming antics, Diamond Jubilee did well to finish fourth to Democrat, who beat Vain Duchess by a length. The temperament of Diamond Jubilee never really improved, but, greatly to the credit of Dick Marsh, his ability was successfully developed. Jack Watts, usually the last man in the world to decline a challenge, had to acknowledge that try as he might he would never elicit a sympathetic response from this ill-tempered, all but savage colt, and it was Marsh's hitherto unknown apprentice Herbert Jones, to whose handling he was surprisingly amenable, who rode him to fairy-tale triumphs in the 2000 Guineas, Derby and St Leger in 1900. He was never again seen at Royal Ascot.

Egerton House – successful stable of trainer Richard Marsh.

The Coventry Stakes winner Democrat went on to win the Dewhurst Stakes in the autumn, but became useless for racing as a three-year-old. In due course he passed into the hands of Richard Marsh, who made a present of him to Lord Kitchener, and the Field Marshal used the Coventry Stakes winner as a charger on ceremonial occasions while Commander-in-Chief in India.

But for pure chance, Tod Sloan would never have come to evolve that monkey-up-the-stick style of riding that he introduced to Royal Ascot in 1899. Born near Kokomo, Indiana, in 1874, Tod Sloan was far from a fashionable jockey, nor even a particularly successful one, when his mount bolted with him on the way to the start at the Bay District Track at San Francisco. Desperate to regain control he leaned out of the saddle so that he was crouching over the neck in order to secure a tighter hold of his mount's head. While the other riders jeered at his predicament, Sloan was amazed to find that the horse was striding out even more freely, yet he had it back on the bit. While realising he had discovered

a new dimension to race riding, he demurred from profiting from it in public for fear of bringing more ridicule upon himself. In private, though, he was continually experimenting with different ways of riding horses at top speed, with a view to finding the best possible way in which to balance his mount, while obtaining the maximum control and minimum wind resistance. At the same time he developed an almost uncanny judge of pace. Eventually he gained enough confidence in the efficiency of his new style to begin riding with crouch and short leathers in public. Although inevitably mocked and derided at first, Sloan soon proved that horses went better for him than for jockeys riding in the traditional style. In 1895 he rode 132 winners from 442 mounts, and at the back-end of 1897 arrived in England, where he enjoyed almost sensational success by winning 21 races from just 48 rides in the final month of the season. The following year the little man was again in England in the autumn, and in the season of 1899 rode for Lord William Beresford, whose horses were trained by John Huggins, another American, in the Heath House Stable at Newmarket.

Anything but indifferent to the huge material rewards that his riding brought him, Tod Sloan was able to live in almost unbelievably ostentatious style. He had a large suite of rooms at one of the most luxurious hotels in The Strand, where he indulged in his passion for playing cards for very high stakes, generally at a heavy loss. His exceedingly high opinion of himself as a poker player was never half as well founded as that which he entertained of his jockeyship. He surrounded himself with cronies, who flattered him shamelessly, and it never occurred to him to doubt the sincerity of the compliments that they showered upon him. For his part, he came right up to their expectations by giving them confidential information about the horses he was to ride, from which, for a time, they profited handsomely.

Conceit, rather than egalitarian ideas – such as might have been natural in a citizen of a republic – ensured that Sloan showed no deference to the rich and aristocratic owners who employed him, and did not behave with the modesty of the English jockeys. On the contrary, he would swagger out of the weighing-room with a cigar almost as long as his whip, and continue smoking while receiving his riding orders in the paddock. An almost compulsive gambler, he joined his friends in huge punts on his mounts, though the Jockey Club had amended the Rules of Racing so as to forbid jockeys from betting some dozen years before his arrival in England.

With continual success and an almost uninterrupted diet of flattery convincing him he could do just as he liked, Tod Sloan not infrequently gave considerable offence, and was involved in a number of unpleasant incidents, some of which erupted into minor scandals that found their way into the newspapers. One of the most unpleasant of these occurred at Ascot in 1899, when he was alleged to have hit a waiter over the head with a bottle of champagne. His version of the affair was that he had changed into a white yachting suit – a hardly orthodox sartorial touch – after racing, and was having a drink at a table on the lawn behind the stands when he saw a man, who had been staring at him in a distinctly unfriendly manner, give some money to a waiter. The waiter then approached his table, and seemed about to pour champagne over Sloan's nautical attire in a staged accident when the little American seized the bottle and thrust him away with it. Whatever the truth of the Ascot episode, Tod Sloan did nothing to help his case by agreeing to pay the waiter £5 by way of compensation for injuries supposedly received.

Although Sloan's character left much to be desired, and his choice of friends was really abysmal, there was no denying that he was a genius as a jockey. Freddie Rickaby, who was retained by Lord Derby, went as far as to say that if he were an owner he would never run a horse unless Tod Sloan could ride it.

Lord William Beresford, who brought Sloan to England, was one of the three talented, witty and jauntily carefree younger sons of the 4th Marquess of Waterford, the others being Admiral Lord Charles Beresford, who knocked out the shore batteries of Alexandria when running the *Condor* beneath the trajectory of their fire in 1882, and Lord Marcus Beresford, the Prince of Wales' racing manager. After winning the Victoria Cross by riding back into the path of advancing Zulu tribesmen to rescue a wounded warrant officer at Ulundi in 1879, "Fighting Bill", as *Vanity Fair* dubbed Lord William, became a highly competent Military Secretary to the Viceroy of India. Shortly after his return to England he married the widowed Lily, Duchess of Marlborough, an American by birth. Through her he obtained a knowledge of racing in the United States, and learned of the enormous success of Tod Sloan. Lord William, a familiar figure in the Royal Enclosure in the five years after he came back from India, was a chronic sufferer from recurrence of the dysentery he had contracted there, and only 53 when he died of peritonitis in December 1900.

By far the most important horse to win at Royal Ascot when Tod Sloan rode at the meeting for the first time in 1899 was Cyllene, to whom Northern Dancer, the outstanding stallion of modern times, traces back in tail male line. Ridden by bulbous-eyed Sammy Loates in the colours of Sir Charles Day Rose, the banker who played a large part in the construction of the Canadian Pacific Railway, Cyllene won the Gold Cup in decisive manner, beating Lord Edward II, the mount of Tommy

American Tod Sloan – leading jockey at Ascot in 1900.

Willie, Basil and Jack Jarvis, all of whom figure in the story of Royal Ascot.

Cyllene was one of the Ugly Ducklings of racing in as much as he was not foaled until the end of May, and so puny as a yearling that nobody thought of entering him for the classics. A chestnut with white socks on his near hind and off fore, and a short, narrow blaze on his elegant head, Cyllene nevertheless grew into a remarkably handsome individual, who was sufficiently far forward as a two-year-old to win the National Breeders' Produce Stakes at Sandown Park. The following year he laid claims to being the best of his age by winning the Newmarket Stakes by four lengths, with the subsequent Derby winner Jeddah unplaced.

Like his own paternal grandsire Isonomy, as well as St Simon, Persimmon and many another horse who triumphed in the Gold Cup before stoutness and stamina went out of fashion, Cyllene was an extraordinarily successful stallion. He was champion sire in 1909 and 1910, and got the Derby winners Cicero (1905), Minoru (1909), Lemberg (1910), and Tagalie (1912). It is not, though, from one of the Derby winners that Cyllene sired, but through his son Polymelus, that the great male line of Nearco and Northern Dancer descends. Polymelus's son Phalaris was the sire of Pharos, who got Nearco, the grandsire of Northern Dancer. Unfortunately, at a cost to British bloodstock that we shall never know, the influence of Cyllene, one of the greatest of all Gold Cup winners, was curtailed by his sale to the Argentine for £25,000 in 1908, the year before he was champion sire for the first time.

Whereas American owners of the calibre of Mr Paul Mellon, Mr Charles Engelhard and Mr John Hay Whitney brought nothing but good to the British turf, those who came across the Atlantic in the wake of Tod Sloan at the turn of the century could hardly have had a more baneful effect, until the Jockey Club took vigorous action to suppress the worst of their excesses. As well as having their jockeys stop horses when it suited their betting, they introduced the pernicious practice of doping. An Englishman once said to Colonel Harry Payne Whitney that half the villains of the American racetracks must have come to England. "Half!" exclaimed the Colonel, looking round the paddock.

Loates, by eight lengths; the French horse Gardefeu was three lengths away third.

A colt by Bona Vista out of the Isonomy mare Arcadia, Cyllene was trained at Newmarket by Bill Jarvis, a member of the town's oldest racing family, whose grandfather had sent out Gustavus to be the first grey to win the Derby in 1821. After a brief spell as a jockey, Bill Jarvis trained jumpers, and then gradually built up a string of flat racers in the long-demolished Waterwitch Stable, winning the 2000 Guineas with Cyllene's sire Bona Vista in 1892. He married Norah Godding, whose father had trained the 1863 Derby winner Macaroni. They were the parents of three more successful trainers in

"Why, I guess you've got them all!"

The past master of doping was Enoch Wishard, who brought it to a fine art. He conducted the Red House stable at Newmarket, and trained for James A. Drake, a large and, superficially, genial enough man, and William "Betchamillion" Gates, whose Sobriquet bore eloquent testimony to his subtlety and refinement, with the American brothers Johnny and Lester Reiff, sharing the riding. The speciality of Drake and Gates lay in buying horses with moderate form, backing them heavily for big handicaps on which there was a strong ante-post market, and having Wishard dope them to win. Between 1897 and 1901 this nefarious fraternity extracted a sum in the region of £2,000,000 from the ring, Royal Ascot, being one of the courses at which their activities were best rewarded.

In 1900 Wishard landed a huge coup for the gang with the seven-year-old Royal Flush in the Royal Hunt Cup. While being trained in the North the previous season, the old horse had won minor events at Carlisle, Manchester, Newcastle and Pontefract, achievements that did little to suggest that he would be a factor in as competitive an event as the Hunt Cup; but, given the necessary chemical encouragement by Wishard, he took the big step up in company successfully, when Johnny Reiff rode him to beat Good Luck by a head. In his Eton collar and knickerbockers, fresh-faced Johnny Reiff, "Knickerbocker" Reiff as they called him, looked the picture of youthful innocence. When he first arrived in England, the flightier members of high society made the most ridiculous fuss of him, with fashionably dressed women even kissing him as he made his way to the paddock at Ascot.

Although completely outnumbered by their British rivals, the small band of American riders was able to claim more than half of the winners at that Royal Meeting of 1900, the last in the 64 years of the reign of Queen Victoria. With seven races on each of the four days, as opposed to six a day at the present time, they won 16 of the 28 races.

As well as the Royal Hunt Cup on Royal Flush, Johnny Reiff won a race on Lord William Beresford's Jolly Tar and another on Mr Russell's Rigo. His taller, elder brother Lester, who was already having trouble controlling his weight, did slightly better by obtaining four successes. As well

Lester Reiff – rode four winners at Royal Ascot in 1900.

as the Coventry Stakes on Good Morning owned by Captain Greer, who would become the first Director of the National Stud, Lester Reiff won the St James's Palace Stakes on Bonarosa, the Gold Vase on Solitaire and the Alexandra Plate on Gadfly. Bonarosa, Solitaire and Gadfly were the first winners at the meeting to be owned by the Prince of Wales' financier friend Sir Ernest Cassel, who had been born at Cologne in 1852 and come to England at the age of 16 to work as a clerk for £2 a week in Liverpool. A short, stout, bearded man, with rather cold grey eyes, he was generally seen in the royal party, during the last decade of the nineteenth century and the first two decades of the present one.

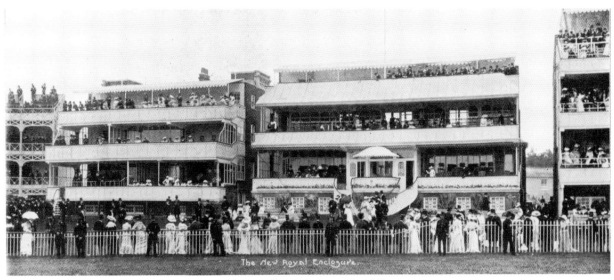

The new Royal Enclosure in 1902.

His grand-daughter Edwina Ashleigh was to marry Lord Mountbatten of Burma.

Leading jockey at Ascot in that last year of the long life of Queen Victoria was Tod Sloan. That talented but excessively opinionated rider reached one of the highlights of his brief and brilliant career by winning six races in the course of the four days. The most important of those races was the Gold Cup in which he rode the Australian-bred Merman in the colours of "Mr Jersey", the *nom de course* of the celebrated beauty Lady de Bathe, who had been known as Lily Langtry in the days when she was mistress to the Prince of Wales. The previous year she had married, as her second husband, Hugo de Bathe, a vapid, ineffectual youth 18 years her junior, who had little to recommend him save his being heir to a baronetcy. The chestnut Merman must have had legs like bars of steel, as he was already an eight-year-old, and still a full horse, when he beat Scintillant by two lengths in the Gold Cup, after having won the Caulfield Cup at home in Australia and a number of other notable events earlier in his career.

The other American jockey to ride winners at Royal Ascot in 1900 was New York-born "Skeets" Martin, who had been champion jockey of the United States two years earlier. As well as the Wokingham Stakes on Mr W. H. Pawson's Bridge, he won two races for Sir Richard Waldie Griffiths.

That was the last Royal Ascot at which Tod Sloan rode. Despite continual warning, the brash little man made no effort to moderate his behaviour, and continued to keep the company of professional gamblers of doubtful integrity, and other undesirable individuals. Matters came to a head when he and his confederates went for a huge win over Codoman, whom he rode in the Cambridge-shire of 1900. After Codoman had been beaten into second place behind Berrill, Sloan treated John Thompson, the successful jockey, to a tirade of vivid and sustained abuse, within the hearing of the Stewards of the Jockey Club and everybody else in the vicinity, as they returned to the unsaddling enclosure. Shortly afterwards Messrs Weatherby informed him that there would be no point in his applying for a licence to ride in 1901. Such was his vanity, that he was actually surprised. Thirty-three years later he died at the age of 59 in the charity ward of a Los Angeles hospital.

Lester Reiff was seen at Royal Ascot for hardly any longer than Tod Sloan. After Reiff had won the Hardwicke Stakes on Colonel Hall Walker's Merry Gal and the King's Stand Stakes together with four other races for Mr William C. Whitney at Ascot in 1901, he rode De Lacy at Manchester's September meeting and was beaten by a head by his brother on Minnie Dee. On the matter being referred to the Stewards of the Jockey Club, Lester Reiff was found to have made no attempt to win the race, and was warned off. Fearful that a similar fate awaited him, Johnny Reiff discreetly retired to France, where standards of probity were somewhat less exacting.

The Royal Meeting that followed the death of Queen Victoria in January 1901 and the accession of King Edward VII was long remembered as Black Ascot, ladies being required to wear dresses, hats and accessories of black, or some other sombre hue, in the Royal Enclosure, where ties and cravats were uniformly black. To give further emphasis to the court being in full mourning for the Queen-Empress, the edges of the racecards were trimmed with black.

The year King Edward came to the throne saw a minor change in the administration at Ascot, though it was of no more than technical significance, as the management of the course remained vested in the nominee of the sovereign. When the Royal Buckhounds were finally disbanded in 1901, the Master, Lord Chesham, was serving in the war against the Boers in South Africa, and his duties at Ascot were being undertaken by Viscount Churchill. Upon the resignation of Lord Chesham from an office that had ceased to exist, later that year, Lord Churchill became the first holder of the post of King's Representative at Ascot, where he was in charge of all aspects of the running of the course, and censoriously allocated the cherished vouchers of admission to the Royal Enclosure. Following the establishment of the Ascot Authority, in place of the old Ascot Grandstand Trust, by Act of Parliament in 1913, the King's Representative assumed the chairmanship of that body, with the clerk of the course as its secretary.

The Royal Enclosure was again ablaze with every imaginable shade of colour after fortunes had been spent in attempts to reach the very height of fashion in 1902. That year, even those people whose ignorance of racing was in direct proportion to their awareness of their social position were eager to see the wonder filly Sceptre, and, if possible, catch a glimpse of her owner. Robert Standish Sievier, who had paid the record sum of 10,000 guineas for Sceptre, always claimed that he had been born in a hansom cab. Whether or not he made such an unorthodox entry into this world – he was always inclined to be economical with the truth – the path

that he followed was never bounded by convention of any sort. A man of considerable charm, and no little wit, both of which were apt to be lost on the frostier members of an establishment he utterly despised, he had already been to South Africa, where he served briefly as a trooper in the Frontier Armed and Mounted Police, and to Australia, where he stood up as a bookmaker, had been married to the sister of a marquess, and had been involved in a great deal of litigation, before becoming the owner of Sceptre. An absolutely fearless gambler, he was not without talent as a writer. He was, in addition, a card-sharp, a blackmailer, and, just possibly, a murderer. At all events he never managed to furnish a credible explanation of how a dead man came to be found underneath his window after an all-night card party in Australia.

The redeeming feature of Sievier's character was his courage. No matter how badly luck ran against him, nor how hard his creditors pressed, nor how many friends deserted him, Bob Sievier always fought back. This, then, was the man that every social butterfly was agog to see at Royal Ascot in 1902.

A hard bay of great range, and all but faultless conformation, Sceptre was by the King's Gold Cup winner Persimmon out of Ornament, a full sister to Ormonde, and had been sold as a yearling following the death of her breeder, the 1st Duke of Westminster. At the time when she won two of her three races at a two-year-old in 1901 she was with Charlie Morton at Wantage, but at the end of that season Morton had become private trainer to Mr Jack Joel. Rather than send a filly with an obvious chance of winning one or more of the classics into another stable, Sievier amazed the racing world by announcing that he would train her himself, and as if to compound his folly engaged Bert Randall to ride her in the 2000 Guineas and 1000 Guineas. Thus arose the apparently ridiculous situation in which Sceptre had an amateur trainer, as well as a jockey who had only recently emerged from that status. The son of Sir Henry Randall, a wealthy Northamptonshire boot manufacturer, Bert Randall had just embarked upon his first season as a professional jockey.

To the amazement of all those hardened racing men who had shaken their heads in horror at the mere idea of Sievier and Randall teaming up to win the classics, they duly brought off the double in the 1000 Guineas and 2000 Guineas with Sceptre. In the Derby, though, Randall's shortcomings were made apparent. After Sceptre had been slow to get away, Randall pushed her up to the leaders far too quickly, thereby expending energy unnecessarily, and she was beaten into fourth place behind Ard Patrick. Despite his jockey being entirely to blame for the defeat of Sceptre in the Derby, Sievier, with a loyalty that was typical of him, allowed Randall to keep the mount on Sceptre in the Oaks, and Randall made partial amends for his performance of two days earlier by bringing her home three lengths clear of Glass Jug.

There was, however, a limit to the loyalty of Bob Sievier, and that limit was reached at Ascot, where Sceptre turned out for the Coronation Stakes on the second day. Always liable to be on her toes, Sceptre was bucking and kicking at the start of that race, in Swinley Bottom, and having deposited Randall in a blackberry bush, got loose. By the time she had been caught she was in no condition to do justice to herself, so that she was unplaced to Sir Ernest Cassel's Doctrine, ridden by Bill Halsey. For some reason, Bob Sievier had not bothered to watch proceedings at the start, and on returning Randall behaved with almost unbelievable stupidity by not telling him the reason for Sceptre being beaten. On eventually discovering that Sceptre had got loose Sievier was furious, and declared that Randall would never ride her again. Accordingly, the apprentice Frank Hardy had the mount on Sceptre when she beat Flying Lemur by a length and a half, without being out of a canter, with the Derby runner-up Rising Glass third in the St James's Palace Stakes the following day.

Despite Sceptre having made him both leading owner and leading trainer, Bob Sievier was again in desperately low water financially at the end of 1902, and soon afterwards had no choice but to sell Sceptre for £25,000 to the brewer William Bass, who sent her to Alec Taylor at Manton. Asked by the solemn, highly professional Taylor how she should be trained, Sievier replied in his usual off-hand way, "Treat her like a selling plater."

Sceptre, the first horse to capture the public's imagination in the twentieth century, made three more appearances at Royal Ascot. In 1903 she earned a long ovation from all enclosures when, again ridden by young Frank Hardy, she carried 9 st 7 lb to give Lord Derby's three-year-old Gay Gordon 2 st and a beating of a very easy five lengths in the Hardwicke Stakes. On being kept in training as a five-year-old in 1904, Sceptre, who had lost her form completely, disappointed the thousands of admirers that she had acquired over the previous two seasons by being beaten in both her races at the Royal Meeting; she came third both in the Gold Cup and when attempting to win the Hardwicke Stakes for the second time.

Among the other winners at that meeting at which Bert Randall had landed in the blackberry bush in 1902 were Ard Patrick and Rock Sand. On the strength of his triumph in the Derby a fortnight earlier, Mr John Gubbins' Ard Patrick was made hot favourite to win the Prince of Wales' Stakes for Sam Darling's Beckhampton stable, only to be beaten three parts of a length by the Duke of Westminster's Cupbearer, ridden by Morny Cannon. Ard Patrick's jockey Skeets Martin promptly lodged an objection for bumping and boring, which was upheld, but the Stewards made it clear that they regarded Cannon in no way to blame as the heavy ground left him no chance of preventing Ard Patrick from rolling.

The Coventry Stakes of that year was won by Rock Sand, a medium-sized brown colt of great quality trained at Newmarket by George Blackwell for Sir James Miller.

Rock Sand may have been some way behind championship class, but he was certainly one of the most successful colts in that era dominated by those wonderful fillies Sceptre and Pretty Polly, and also earned the distinction of winning at Royal Ascot three years in succession. As a three-year-old he completed the Triple Crown in the 2000 Guineas, Derby and St Leger, and at the Royal Meeting won the St James's Palace Stakes at 100/7 on. Then in 1904 he beat Sceptre, to whom he was demonstrably inferior on other form, into third place in the Hardwicke Stakes. Rock Sand was subsequently sold to the United States, where he became the sire of Mahabah, dam of that great horse Man O' War.

Danny Maher, who usually had the mount on Rock Sand, was one of several American riders of

George, Prince of Wales, later George IV, with his good looks
and charm was enormously popular with racegoers.
His love affair with racing endured for well over four decades
until his death in 1830, 16 days after he
failed in a final bid to win the Gold Cup with Zinganee.

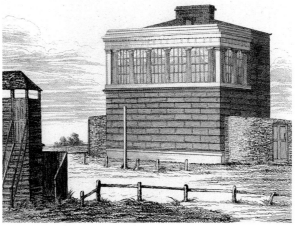

During his reign King George IV considerably enhanced the importance of the Royal Meeting, both as a racing fixture and social event. Apart from introducing the Royal Enclosure and the Royal Procession, which endure to this day, the King commissioned the building of the first Royal Stand in 1822.

Left, racing excitement in 1822, titled "Tom and Bob winning long odds from a knowing one".

Admiral Rous, as the supreme arbiter of racing, introduced the publication
of *The Laws and Practice of Horse Racing* in 1850; and for
some 40 years exercised a great influence and authority over the sport.

GALLERY OF SPORTING CELEBRITIES.—NO. XI.

THE HONOURABLE HENRY JOHN ROUS, CAPTAIN, R.N.

AS a distinguished and zealous member of the Jockey Club, that powerful sporting senate which makes its own laws and enforces them, rather than as a member of St. Stephen's Chapel, Captain Rous finds a niche in our Gallery.

The Hon. Henry John Rous is the brother of the Earl of Stradbroke, one of the oldest families in England, as it has been established, it is said, in Suffolk, since the days of the Saxon Heptarchy. He was born in 1795, and entered the navy in 1818: he served under the late Sir W. Hoste, and has gained as good a reputation in his profession as most men can do in a time of peace. He has just been appointed by Sir Robert Peel one of the Lords of the Admiralty, an office for which a seat in Parliament is not required.

Although a high tory the gallant officer has many of the qualities that win popularity, apart from political opinions. A frank, open, and manly bearing; a bold and ready style of speaking; no hesitation about speaking plain truths in a plain manner; all blended with a spice of humour that smacks too much of the sailor, not to be acceptable to Englishmen of all classes—these were his recommendations to the Electors of Westminster. Some of his speeches in the House were " refreshing " in the midst of the abundance of half-phrased condemnation there to be found. The gallant Captain never hinted faults or hesitated dislikes; he said what he thought, and that was not always very favourable to the Board of Admiralty. He speaks well, however, on other than professional questions; it is said that he has suddenly changed his opinions on the Corn-Laws; this is hardly just as a charge; we believe he supported the Canada Corn Bill, and, on more than one occasion, defended the relaxation of the Protective System. In the House he was much liked; his address and delivery were good, and, on naval questions, his experience was valuable, for he has seen some hard service. To praise his career on the Turf, his bold uprightness on all occasions is quite superfluous.

HINTS ON HORSE DEALERS.

BY HARRY HIE'OVER.

(From the *Sporting Magazine.*)

Having half-persuaded the owner and quite persuaded many others that there is something wrong about the horse—(for the opinion or even insinuation of a third party will in ninety-nine cases out of a hundred go further in persuading people that a horse has some fault than all the owner can say to the contrary)—they now seek a little adjunct in the servant. If he is a fool, they really do satisfy him the horse is worth little

more than they have offered; and then letting him know that a couple of sovereigns will be his if they buy, in no way of course tends to induce him to alter this opinion; so he begins to recommend his master to sell, if possible. Should they, however, find the man has sense enough not to be their dupe, they then try his honesty and bid high; and I fear on this tack they too often succeed. Having paved the way in either case to the assistant offices of the servant, their game is now to appear to have given up all wish for the horse, which one of them, however, keeps a sharp eye on, and also on every one they see even looking at him. Should any one seem disposed to do this, the fellow on the watch accosts him—" Nice nag that, Sir, to look at! I was pretty near putting my foot in it with him."—" Why," says the looker-on, "is anything the matter with him?"—" Oh no, not for some people; but"—and he walks away, imitating a lame horse. This is enough; the looker-on thanks his stars he was not done, and how fortunate he was to have seen that man! The other miscreant, while this is going [on] corner to see if he can start any fresh [...] and repress the owner of the horse as o[...] him up, waiting, hoping, and fully exp[...] appointed) that the owner will come t[...] standing with a longish ground ash i[...] bending about, or has it with his hand [...] very position of the vagabond. Here [...] something like the following very pleas[...] a gentleman on a horse that is not a co[...] voice, " Beg pardon, Sir! what are you [...] a servant be on one that looks in good [...] " Now then, how much for the notom[...] look at you "—this of course loud eno[...] The chance is, that some friend or oth[...] going on, gives the thing a lift, and add[...] (or whatever the fellow's name may [...] Smithfield?" This raises a laugh aga[...] nothing people hate more than to be la[...] so tells the groom to come on one side [...] his escape, he goes. Here both soap a[...] groom would almost sell himself rath[...] sneers of the multitude, it will be no w[...] horse, which he does if the price is left [...] to persuade his master to do so. The [...] that most respectable persons have is o[...] lows work to obtain their ends, either in [...] horses are really sold at half what the o[...] bought, actually to avoid the slang and [...] bonds and their companions.

Now we will suppose, what probab[...] The former gentleman, finding to his [...] the sale of his horse having been purpo[...] made for his horse except by friends of [...] offer him even less than he did, he goe[...] say 10*l.* more than he had offered, and [...] asked: but he now finds the case altere[...] so: it is either that the dealer, having [...] like him at all, or he has bought two o[...] sides, "talking of thirty pounds, Sir; [...] (shewing one belonging to some frien[...] him) for 18*l.*: he is worth two of this h[...] the gentleman, "then you decline him; [...] to that, Sir, I don't mind buying him a[...] —He now tries the civil candid tack; [...] horse; is sure the gentleman would no[...] that!)—dares to say the Gentleman t[...] country gentlemen don't know what su[...] he couldn't sell him as a sound 'un to [...] means: he should sell him for a hom[...] one; he might do a little vork in leathe[...] he could give more; 'twoud be better f[...] could! he has three fivers left; he wou[...] be without him."—It ends in his gettin[...] a-crown openly—(says nothing of the t[...] tells the gentleman " he hopes he'll re[...] a gentleman gives double what the de[...] shillings, half of which goes to the mas[...] horses are sold, and this is often the [...] such places going to fairs to sell their [...] once by such vagabonds as I have des[...] them, and they are legally robbed of th[...] very near it.

A man who may read what I have d[...] so green as to be done in that way. [...] are hundreds who would; and it is still possible, that, had the gentleman not read what I have written on the subject, he might, notwithstanding his confidence in himself, have been done precisely in such a manner. Having had the plot laid bare to him, he thinks it would never have succeeded with him. This cannot be proved; so it only remains a matter

Dominant figures at Ascot during the reigns of King William IV and Queen Victoria included "Lord Chesterfield the Magnificent", (near left) and, Lord George Bentinck, who, as Dictator of the Turf introduced much badly needed organisation into racing. As well as reforming the method of starting, by giving the starter a flag, he had horses allocated numbers.

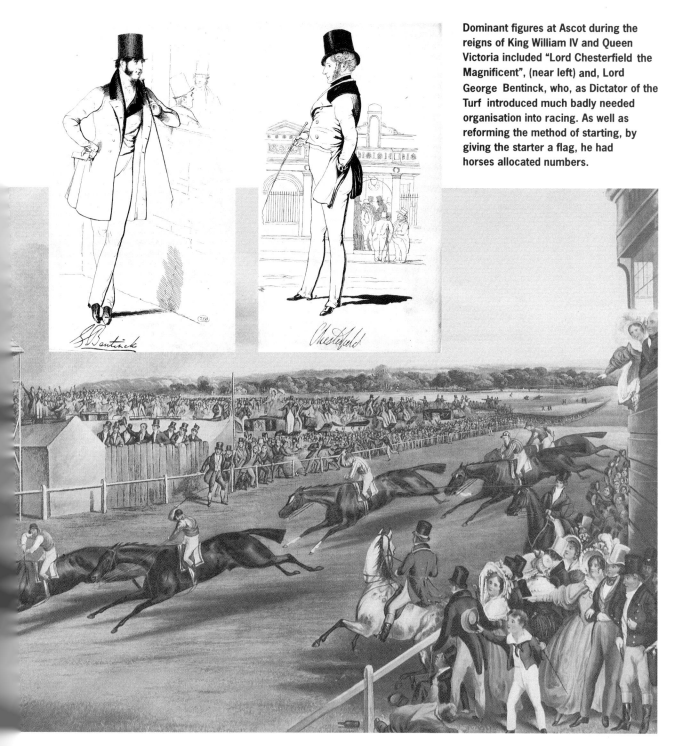

The Royal Meeting in 1837, the last of the reign of King William IV.

In 1839, a number of improvements were effected. A grandstand, with accommodation for 3000 spectators (seen above on Gold Cup day) was built together with a viewing area for trainers and jockeys and a proper box for the judge.

**Beeswing – known as the "Adopted Daughter of Northumberland",
was one of the best stayers of her sex
ever to run at Ascot, where she won the Gold Cup in 1842.**

St Simon, the horse everybody wanted to see in 1884, was
a comfortable 20-length winner of the Gold
Cup from Tristan, the previous season's winner.

ROYAL ASCOT

**The most exclusive enclosure in the world,
ablaze with every imaginable shade of colour.**

ROYAL ASCOT

Pretty Polly, one of the greatest fillies of all time, won the Coronation Stakes
in a canter in 1904, but sustained her only defeat when beaten a length
by Bachelor's Button in the Gold Cup of 1906 on her final appearance (below).

ROYAL ASCOT

After the misery of war, sheer exhilaration was most evident among the fashionable crowds in the enclosures of the early Twenties. High fashion, represented by Mrs Gertrude Shilling, also prevails some five decades later.

FASHIONABLE LONDON GOES TO ASCOT.

A Pretty and Fashionable Racegoer

This picture depicts only one of the many hundreds of delightfully-gowned and fashionable society women who went to this year's Ascot

Some of the Fashions at Ascot

This year's Hunt Cup day was the most brilliant within memory. All London attended, and the display of dresses around the course was almost bewildering

From Kufra to Ascot

Mrs. Rosita Forbes, whose exploits as an explorer are familiar to all "Sphere" readers, with Lieut.-Colonel McGrath on the course

The King and Queen in the Royal Box at Ascot

Amongst those seen here are the King and Queen and Princess Mary. The Duke of York and the Prince of Wales, who were also present, viewed the race from just outside the royal box

More Ascot Fashions

On the Ascot lawns was a real orgy of colour. White predominated, but practically every other colour was also much in evidence

A Beautifully-gowned Racegoer

A Group of Society People on the Course

Miss D'Erlanger and Miss Gellibrand

**Sceptre – after winning the
St James's Palace Stakes in 1902.**

that era to secure a more durable place in British racing than Tod Sloan or the brothers Reiff. A man of pleasing manners and a good deal of intelligence, Maher rode with flair and style, almost invariably had his mount in exactly the right place at every stage of a race, and was never found wanting for strength in a close finish. Lord Rosebery, who owned the Derby winners Ladas, Sir Visto and Cicero, rated him the best jockey of all time. Sadly Maher, the son of an Irish immigrant, had great trouble with his weight, became tubercular, and was only 35 when he died at home in the United States in 1916.

The diamond millionaire Jack Joel had his first winner at Royal Ascot when His Lordship beat Papdale by two lengths in a farcical race for the Wokingham Stakes of 1902. A number of the horses fouled the webbing of the starting gate just as the starter released the lever, and 10 jockeys, including Billy Lane on the favourite Vatel, thinking it a false start, took no part. Having heard the evidence of the starter, Arthur Coventry, formerly an absolutely top-class amateur rider and a grandson of the 8th Earl of Coventry, the Stewards were satisfied that all the horses were behind the barrier when it was released. Leopold de Rothschild, the owner of Vatel, was characteristically incensed at

what he saw as injustice to one of his horses, and vigorously protested that some of the jockeys had broken through the webbing before the start, but the Stewards declined to alter their decision.

Jack Joel and his flamboyant brother Solly, who also embarked upon racing on a large scale at the turn of the century, were the nephews of the famous Barny Barnato. After abandoning a successful career in the London music halls, Barny Barnato tried his luck in the diamond fields around Kimberley, rapidly became a millionaire, and sent for his nephews Jack and Solly, who were soon sharing his financial status. Astute and immensely energetic, Jack Joel would often drive out to his Childwick Bury Stud in Hertfordshire in the early morning, be in his office in the City by 10 a.m., and, if his business commitments permitted, go racing in the afternoon. There were very few days when he was not in his office for some of the time, as he would never delegate the direction of his widespread commercial interests. As well as being permanent chairman of the Johannesburg Consolidated Investment Company, he controlled breweries, collieries and a variety of other businesses.

At first Jack Joel had his horses with Cyllene's trainer William Jarvis at Newmarket, but, as noted above, he persuaded Charlie Morton to turn the Letcombe Regis stable, near Wantage, into his private stable at the end of 1901. In the Wokingham Stakes, the first important race that Morton won for Jack Joel, His Lordship was ridden by Jack Watts the younger, son of the royal jockey.

After continuing to ride for five years after he had first considered retiring, in order to oblige Dick Marsh, Jack Watts the elder began training at Newmarket in 1900, with his health badly impaired by excessive wasting. In July 1902, the month after his son had ridden the Wokingham Stakes winner, he was taken seriously ill at Sandown Park. It was found impossible to move him and he died at Esher at the age of 41 ten days later.

Long before Sceptre had retired, Pretty Polly had burst upon the scene to make the early years of the century memorable as an era dominated by two of the greatest fillies ever seen on the English turf. In sharp contrast to Sceptre, Pretty Polly was able to follow an orthodox career as, unlike Bob Sievier, her owner-breeder Major Eustace Loder would never be obliged to sell her, and all the time she was in training she was in the charge of Peter Purcell Gilpin in the Clarehaven stable at Newmarket. A strong and robust chestnut, of a little under 16 hands, by Gallinule out of Admiration by Saraband, Pretty Polly tended to become excitable, and as she walked round the parade ring, would be preceded by her chestnut companion, Little Missus, a cob with a docked tail, to induce her to settle down.

As Pretty Polly did not make her racecourse debut until late June, she did not run at Royal Ascot as a two-year-old in 1903, but following her successes in the 1000 Guineas and Oaks of the following season, she started at 5/1 on for the Coronation Stakes, which she won by three lengths from Montem. In September she confounded the likes of John Porter, who thought that so fast a filly might just get the mile and a half of the Oaks, but never an inch further, by winning over the mile and three quarters of the St Leger. About a fortnight later Billy Lane, who had ridden her in all her races that year, was so badly injured in a fall at Lingfield that he had to retire. It was Danny Maher, therefore, who rode her when she defended her unbeaten record in her 16th race, the Prix du Conseil Municipal at Longchamps. The outsider Presto II set off to make all the running, and though Pretty Polly made up some ground in the straight, she was unable to produce the terrific burst of acceleration that had mesmerised the crowds at Ascot and elsewhere, so that she was beaten by two-and-a-half lengths into second place. The defeat of Pretty Polly was widely attributed to the effects of an exceptionally rough crossing of the Channel, and the heavy going at Longchamps. Danny Maher knew differently, and was probably alone in his awareness of the real cause of her being beaten. She did not stay. Sheer class had enabled her to win the St Leger, just as it would enable her equally celebrated descendant Brigadier Gerard to win over the mile-and-a-half of the King George VI and Queen Elizabeth Stakes. The knowledge that Danny Maher gained of Pretty Polly at Longchamps was to stand him in good stead at Royal Ascot less than two years later.

Pretty Polly remained in training as a four-year-old with the Gold Cup as her principal objective, but a few days after winning the Coronation Cup,

she slipped while pulling up on Newmarket Heath, and strained muscles in her quarters. As a result of that mishap, she was still on the easy list during Ascot.

Still determined that Pretty Polly should emulate the likes of West Australian, and more recently Isinglass and La Fleche, by bringing her career to a climax with a triumph in the Gold Cup, Major Loder kept Pretty Polly at Clarehaven for a fourth season. Bernard Dillon, who was to become the third husband of the music hall star Marie Lloyd, was riding for the stable that year, and after he had partnered Pretty Polly to win the March Stakes at Newmarket and a second Coronation Cup, he took the mount on her in the Gold Cup.

On arrival at Ascot, Pretty Polly was found to have a wart on her belly, which was lanced without leaving her suffering any ill effects. The weather at the Royal Meeting was exceptionally hot and the going iron hard. Pretty Polly was seen to be sweating freely as she paraded behind her stable-mate Hammerkop, who had become her chaperone on the retirement of Little Missus, but, with the temperature in the eighties, there seemed little significance in her feeling the heat, and such was the public confidence in her that she was backed down to 11/4 on.

The other four runners for the Gold Cup on that gloriously sunny day were Solly Joel's Bachelor's Button, ridden, ominously, by Danny Maher, his pacemaker St Dennis, with George McCall in the saddle, the 1905 Derby winner Cicero, ridden by Herbert Jones, and the French-trained three-year-old Achilles, the mount of the apprentice Arthur Templeman. St Dennis set off at a cracking pace for the benefit of Maher on Bachelor's Button, and managed to maintain it until Achilles went on six furlongs from home, with Pretty Polly, Bachelor's Button and Cicero in close contention, and more or less in line. Once they were well into the straight Pretty Polly began her run and was soon at the girths of Achilles, while Maher waited, confident that he was on the better stayer. At the distance Achilles was a desperately tired horse, and as he hung away from the rails, carried Pretty Polly away towards the centre of the course, and still Maher waited. Back on an even keel again, Pretty Polly went to the front, then at last Maher asked Bach-

The Royal Luncheon Room – built in 1902 but not used by the King until the following year.

elor's Button for his effort and he ran up to within half a length of Pretty Polly.

As the cheering in the stands increased in volume, everyone expected Pretty Polly to sprint clear in the way that she had done in all her other races in England, but this time she had galloped well over two miles at a strong pace, and Bachelor's Button stuck to her, as Maher had been perfectly confident he would do. A hundred yards from home Pretty Polly had nothing left to give, and Bachelor's Button went on to beat her by a length against the background of shocked silence that had suddenly settled upon the stands. Pretty Polly had sustained her first defeat in England. She never ran again.

Peter Purcell Gilpin, the trainer of Pretty Polly, was a tall man of unmistakably military bearing, and a large walrus moustache. He loathed news-papermen, who could expect to be welcomed by a shotgun at Clarehaven, and went to enormous lengths to deceive the touts, even tearing up railings to take his string across a neighbouring trainer's property so as to reach the gallops unobserved. A complete autocrat in the stableyard, he could not abide contradiction, and never, for one moment, did he entertain doubts about the soundness of his own judgement.

Asked how Pretty Polly came to be beaten in the Gold Cup he replied, "In my opinion she lost because the jockey did not obey my instructions. Had he done so I feel sure there would be no defeat for Pretty Polly on an English racecourse to record. I told Dillon this after the race. No doubt he was carried away by excitement." It would never have occurred to him that he might have been quite

wrong in supposing that Pretty Polly had the stamina to stay two and a half miles. For all his high-
handedness, Peter Purcell Gilpin was, as his record
shows, a trainer of outstanding ability.

The day after the Gold Cup, Major Loder, Peter
Purcell Gilpin and Bernard Dillon enjoyed a very
minor measure of compensation when Hammerkop,
who had accompanied Pretty Polly in the paddock,
beat Shilfa by three lengths in the Alexandra Plate.
Hammerkop had also won the Cesarewitch the
previous year, and at stud became the dam of Spion
Kop, whom Gilpin trained to win the Derby in
1920 for Eustace Loder's nephew and heir, Lieutenant-Colonel Giles Loder.

Whereas Solly Joel won the Gold Cup with Bachelor's Button in 1906, his brother Jack Joel won the
Trial Stakes (now the Queen Anne Stakes) with
Dean Swift, arguably the most popular horse of the
day. The public loved this long, lean, ragged-hipped
chestnut gelding, as they could be quite certain that
he would race his heart out, no matter how strong
the opposition. In return Dean Swift, one of the
great equine characters in the story of Royal Ascot,
loved the public, for, as his trainer Charlie Morton
wrote in his reminiscences, "he liked adulation
every bit as much as a popular actor". To show his
appreciation he would often put his fore legs on an
admirer's shoulders, and hug his neck! Dean Swift
was five when he battled on for Bert Randall to get
home by a head from Nero at Ascot in 1906, and
returned to win the same event 12 months later. The
older the Dean grew the better he seemed to be, and
he went on winning until obtaining his final success
in the Chesterfield Cup as a ten-year-old in 1911.

Never has there been a closer race for the Gold
Cup, and rarely a rougher one, than in 1907, when
Colonel Tom Kirkwood's The White Knight, the
even-money favourite ridden by Bill Halsey, and the
French challenger Eider, with George Stern up,
fought a tremendous duel over the last furlong.
Stern was by far and away the most successful
jockey then riding in France, his tactics having
evolved in the permissive atmosphere of his own
country. In the closing stages of that race for the
Gold Cup he not only used his strength to force
Eider to the front, but gave Halsey a very rough
time indeed. After they passed the post locked
together, the judge was unable to separate them and

announced a dead-heat, whereupon a badly aggrie-
ved Halsey lodged an objection. As well as com-
plaining that he had bumped and bored, the English
rider alleged that Stern had gone as far as catching
hold of his leg in an effort to unseat him. Having
heard the evidence, the Stewards, Lords Churchill,
Stanley and Durham, found the charge of deliberate
foul riding unproved, but, to the surprise of absolutely nobody, they disqualified Eider for bumping
and boring, and relegated him to last place.

While all these deliberations were taking place,
some enterprising individual stole the Gold Cup
from the table on which it was exhibited on the
lawn. The identity of the thief was never established, and as the Cup had disappeared for good
and all, Colonel Kirkwood was later presented with
a substitute trophy.

The trainer of The White Knight was 31-year-old
Harry Sadler, whose great-grandfather Isaac Sadler
had owned and trained the 1833 Derby winner
Dangerous. Harry Sadler had a stable at Newmarket, and was only 50 when he died in 1926.

The White Knight, who had already won the
Gold Vase in 1906 and would go on to complete a
notable treble at Royal Ascot with a second Gold
Cup in 1908, was a high-class stayer from a
romantic background. Bred by his owner at Wood-
brook, Co. Rosscommon, The White Knight was a
bay horse by Desmond out of Pella, by Buckshot
out of The Doe. The Colonel had first set eyes on
the grandam of The Doe when she was being taken
to be slaughtered for hound meat, and purchased
her for five shillings (25p), only making the token
payment because he subscribed to the superstition
that it was unlucky to have a horse as a gift.

A new scourge of the bookmakers emerged
during the first years of the century. Captain
Machell, who had masterminded those coups in the
Royal Hunt Cup, had given up the management of
Newmarket's Bedford House stable some time
before his death in 1902, and the more
unscrupulous of the Americans had taken their
leave on cue from the well-deserved fates of Tod
Sloan and Lester Reiff. Now it was the money from
the Druid's Lodge Confederacy the ring feared
most. The confederacy was formed by the clever,
cynical Alan Percy Cunliffe, who owned the lovely
Druid's Lodge establishment, some miles from

Netheravon on Salisbury Plain. The other members were Captain Wilfred Purefoy, who had widespread theatrical and other commercial interests, the hard-riding Captain Frank Forester, for many years Master of the Quorn, J. H. H. Peard, a veterinary surgeon of exceptional skill, and E. A. Wigan. Their horses were successively trained by Jack Fallon and Tom Lewis, neither of whom was any more than a head lad. A. P. Cunliffe provided the principal brains behind the operations, and was responsible for arranging the trials of the horses as well as making the entries, while Wilfred Purefoy used to undertake the delicate task of working the commissions in the ante-post market. The members of the confederacy were generally known as "The Hermits of Salisbury Plain" for no one was allowed within miles of the stable, which was conducted in the utmost secrecy, with the subtle fluctuations in the market providing the only clues to expectations of its inmates.

Years later it emerged that the best horse they ever had at Druid's Lodge was Wilfred Purefoy's Lally. Cunliffe was satisfied that Lally had been tried as a certainty for the Derby of 1906, and they backed him down to 4/1 favourite, but, for once, Cunliffe was wrong. Lally failed to stay and was unplaced. Characteristically, the Confederacy made no attempt to chase their losses immediately, and after he had been beaten in both his subsequent races as a three-year-old, the failed Derby favourite returned to form in unspectacular manner by winning an apprentices' race at Wolverhampton in May 1907, by which time Purefoy had already got down to the serious business of backing him for the Royal Hunt Cup.

Confidence in Lally was duly justified. Ridden by Leslie Hewitt, he held Andover by half a length.

While the Druid's Lodge Confederates were at the height of their success in 1907, two other high-betting men, from very different backgrounds, were beginning to hit the ring. One was Jimmy de Rothschild, the tall, monocled scion of the international banking dynasty, and the other was Henry Seymour Persse, always known as Atty Persse, who came from a family of Galway whisky distillers. Each was a winner at Ascot that year.

Born in Paris in 1878, James Armand de Rothschild was the son of Baron Edmond de Rothschild, whose father James de Rothschild had left the family home in Frankfurt am Main in 1811 to found the French branch of the bank. An individualist who never hesitated to question received wisdom, Jimmy de Rothschild followed his own line in almost all things. Although he could, at times, be high-handed to the point of arrogance, he was guided by a code of ethics that demanded uncompromising integrity. He had exquisite taste in art, which was reflected in his collection of pictures, furniture and ceramics at Whaddesdon Manor, and was an absolutely fearless gambler.

As a man who liked to do things his own way, it was all but inevitable that he would have a private stable, and on commencing racing in 1903, he had his horses trained by Fred Pratt, a nephew of Fred Archer, in the Waltham House yard, now known as Lethornes, at Lambourn. The association between Jimmy de Rothschild and Fred Pratt was to endure for 42 years, and only ended on the retirement of the latter, a singular testimony to loyalty on both sides. The first of several good horses that Pratt trained for Jimmy de Rothschild was Beppo, a brown colt by Marco. Having proved himself of classic calibre by finishing third to Troutbeck in the St Leger, he then won the Hardwicke Stakes at Royal Ascot in 1907. Starting a well-backed favourite, Beppo, ridden by reigning champion jockey Billy Higgs, won by four lengths from Challacombe, ridden by Otto Madden in the colours of the American sewing machine heir Washington Singer.

Atty Persse inherited a taste for steeplechasing from his father and an uncle, Burton Persse, and had it sharpened while at school at Cheltenham. There he heard stories of Billie Archer, who had won the Grand National on Little Charley in 1858, the year after his son Fred was born, and had Tom Pickernell, rider of three Grand Nationals, pointed out to him. On coming down from Oxford, Persse emerged as an amateur jockey, little inferior to the leading professionals. At home in Ireland this tough, autocratic little man, who was as unequivocal in his judgement of men as he was of horses, won the Coningham Cup on Sweet Lavender at Punchestown in 1897, and in England he was successful in the National Hunt Chase of 1902 on Marpessa, while in 1906 he was third in the Grand National on Aunt May.

Tom and Alec Taylor – half-brothers who trained at Manton in Wiltshire.

Long before he had finished riding, Atty Persse had begun training in Ireland, and in about 1905 he opened a stable at Epsom. In those days most of the leading trainers ran betting stables, without, for the most part, planning their operations with quite the foresight and meticulous precision of the Druid's Lodge Confederacy. Although he had not served any apprenticeship in his profession in the way that the likes of Alec Taylor, Charlie Morton and Sam Darling had done, Persse soon showed that he was a match for any of them. To land his first major gamble he sent an unraced two-year-old called Sir Archibald to Newmarket, of all places, and brought off a starting-price coup. The bookmakers having unsuspectingly lumped the colt with the rest of the

20/1 outsiders in a field of 29, Sir Archibald proceeded to win by a length from the hot favourite Mocassin, owned by the high-betting Barney Barnato. A month later Persse obtained his first success at Royal Ascot when Sir Archibald, again ridden by the American Lucian Lyne, beat Sir Ernest Cassel's Araminta by a length and a half in the New Stakes.

The way in which Persse had backed the unraced Sir Archibald to beat fancied horses from the most powerful stables in the country was absolutely typical of him. He had a confidence in his own judgement that has rarely been matched by any other trainer before or since. There was no nonsense about the man. He knew his job, and he made sure that his horses knew theirs. Many years later he was to write:

> I have known trainers so to coddle their charges, that they would even weigh them every week to see just how they were doing, just as a proud nurse weighs a Royal baby. This may be an excellent way of reassuring oneself if one has doubts; but to my mind if a trainer cannot tell how his charge is getting along by giving him the once-over, he is not born to the job.

Atty Persse was born to the job.

In 1908, the year after he had won the New Stakes with Sir Archibald, Atty Persse bought the Chattis Hill Stables, near Stockbridge in Hampshire. Before long he had established himself as a past master of the art of training precocious two-year-olds, many of whom, and one in particular, were to lay the foundation of their reputation at Royal Ascot.

Alec Taylor came to the forefront of the Ascot scene for the first time in 1908, at the age of 45. He was the grandson of Tom Taylor, who had been private trainer to Lord Chesterfield at Bretby Park in the first half of the previous century, and the son of Alec Taylor the elder, who had run the Fyfield stable until building the lovely Manton yard on the Wiltshire Downs in 1870. On the death of Alec Taylor the elder in 1894, Manton came under the joint management of his sons, the half-brothers Tom and Alec. For reasons that have long been lost in the mists of Manton history, fraternal harmony was not forthcoming, and the great days of the stable began to return only after Alec had taken complete charge in 1902. Amongst the owners with horses in the stable was Mr Alfred W. Cox, who never saw fit to explain why he chose to race as "Mr Fairie". After he had disappointed his family by failing the army entrance examination, his father, a Liverpool jute merchant, packed young Cox off to Australia with £100 in about 1875. In a game of poker, at which he was already adept, on the voyage out, A. W. Cox won a sheep station. On inspecting it he found it so derelict as to be beyond repair, but noticed the sun reflected by something in the dusty soil. It was silver. From what became the famous Broken Hill Mine, A. W. Cox made a fortune that enabled him to return to England to lead a life of leisure in the West End of London, and indulge his passion for Havana cigars, old brandy and racing.

It was for A. W. Cox that Alec Taylor saddled Bayardo for the New Stakes at that Royal Ascot meeting of 1908.

Although always immaculately dressed, and never anything but courteous, Alec Taylor was a long way from being in his element as he mingled with the cream of Edwardian society in the Ascot paddock. Leading a life that approached the monastic in more ways than one, he never married, and never took one of those exotic foreign holidays that were becoming increasingly popular with other successful trainers. Indeed he never left Manton, where the regime was frugal in the extreme, except to attend a race meeting or a sale.

Nor was A. W. Cox better calculated than his trainer to delight in the company of the famous and fashionable. Brusque and abrupt to well beyond the point of actual rudeness, A. W. Cox never cared whom he offended. He had not taken up racing with any intention of making friends, and was totally indifferent to unpopularity.

On the Monday of the week before Ascot Alec Taylor staged a full-scale trial of his New Stakes candidate Bayardo, with jockeys brought down to Manton to ride each of the eight participants, though Cox was unable to witness it by reason of a minor indisposition, probably a surfeit of his favourite brandy. Former champion jockey Otto Madden had the mount of the horse that mattered, Herbert Toon rode the three-year-old Seedcake, who was meeting Bayardo at level weights, and the rest were two-year-olds. After Bayardo had beaten the older horse by an easy six lengths, success at Royal Ascot looked assured.

Just before breakfast on the first day of the meeting Alec Taylor met Otto Madden in their hotel, where Taylor asked the other if he knew what he would be riding for Manton over the next four days. When Madden replied that he was not quite sure they began going through the entries together, and on coming to the New Stakes Alec Taylor pointed to a name, and said, in a matter-of-fact way "There's the horse you have to ride."

"Which horse?" asked a puzzled Madden.

"Why, Bayardo" exclaimed the trainer.

"But," protested Madden, "I don't ride Bayardo."

"Yes, you do. That's the one."

Only then did it occur to Otto Madden that he

had made an incredibly silly mistake. Because his mount had won that trial at Manton with such ridiculous ease he had assumed that it was the older horse, and having calculated the two-year-olds in the stable were no more than moderate, had engaged himself to ride a Cyllene filly called Doro. Bernard Dillon, therefore, came in for the mount on Bayardo, who beat Lord Rosebery's Perdiccas by a length and a half without being out of a canter, with Doro unplaced.

Without doubt Bayardo was one of the outstanding horses to win at Royal Ascot during the reign of King Edward VII. A bay to brown colt with lop ears, he was by Bay Ronald out of the Galopin mare Galicia, who had won for his owner at the Royal Meeting as a two-year-old. A long, low-slung individual of 15.3 hands with nothing flashy about him, he did not take the eye immediately, but, in fact, was perfectly proportioned.

While there was no doubting his ability, as was made clear in that trial as well as when he made his racecourse debut at Royal Ascot, he was exceptionally hard to train because of his fleshy, shelly feet, especially those in front, and Alec Taylor had great difficulty in keeping him sound. The hard winter was all against Bayardo in the spring of 1909, and contrary to the advice of Taylor, his strong-minded owner insisted on sending him to the post for the 2000 Guineas, in which he was fourth to Minoru; then in the Derby, also won by Minoru, he was badly hampered by the fall of Sir Martin and came only fifth.

By the time Royal Ascot came round again in 1909, Bayardo was back to his brilliant best, and Danny Maher rode him to give the Duke of Portland's Cattaro 6 lb and a beating of three parts of a length in the Prince of Wales' Stakes, in which Otto Madden, who had lost the mount on him for good, was unplaced on King Charming. In the autumn Bayardo achieved the classic honours he so richly deserved by winning the St Leger. Kept in training as a four-year-old in 1910, he was seen at Royal Ascot for the third season in succession, and he easily took the measure of the unattractively named French horse Sea Sick II by four lengths in the Gold Cup.

Bayardo had the strange habit of banging his manger with his chin. This could be heard all over the yard at Manton, where the lads called it "Bayardo's Drum". Whereas Bayardo's career on the racecourse had been hampered by his shelly feet, his career at stud was curtailed by death following a thrombosis at the early age of 11 in 1917. He was, however, highly successful as a stallion and had two outstanding sons in Gay Crusader and Gainsborough, winner of wartime Triple Crowns in 1917 and 1918 respectively. Gainsborough was to prove instrumental in founding the male line of Bayardo, which, through Hyperion, has been maintained by High Line, Empery, Mummy's Pet and Mummy's Game.

A. W. Cox was not the only owner with an element of the "Wild Colonial Boy" about him to have his colours carried successfully at Royal Ascot in 1908. There was in addition Richard Croker, for whom the Irish-trained Rhodora was a winner. A brown filly by St Frusquin out of Rhoda B, she was half-sister to Orby, who had won the Derby for Croker the previous season.

Born in Ireland in 1841, Richard Croker was taken to the United States as a small child when his father emigrated. By early manhood he displayed all the qualities that equipped a man to make his mark in American politics in that era, being extremely tough, vain and not even on nodding terms with any code of ethics. In due course he became undisputed boss of New York's Tammany Hall, where he exerted enormous power, and, being totally corrupt, quickly accumulated a large fortune. Although the citizenry in New York never judged their municipal leaders by particularly exacting standards, opposition to the way things were run at Tammany Hall eventually became so strong that Boss Croker very sensibly retired to his native Ireland, where he lived with a Cherokee wife 50 years his junior.

As a three-year-old Rhodora trained on to win the 1000 Guineas for Boss Croker. He then retired her to stud, and taking in-breeding to its ultimate extent, implemented his disgusting plan of mating her with her half-brother Orby. The resultant foal had be cut away from her in pieces, and Rhodora died in the course of the ordeal.

By contrast to poor Rhodora, Americus Girl, who won the five-furlong Fern Hill Stakes at Royal Ascot in 1908, had a wonderfully successful career at stud. She was a three-year-old chestnut by

Americus, who had raced in the United States as Rey del Carreras before being brought to England by Boss Croker, out of Palotta by Gallinule. An enormously important influence for the transmission of pure speed, Americus Girl founded a flourishing female dynasty, from which brilliant Royal Ascot winners of many years in the future, such as Tudor Minstrel, were to descend.

By 1909 King Edward VII was growing old, – he would be 68 in November – but nobody thought that he was attending Ascot for the last time. His popularity was greater then ever, especially amongst the racing community, from Stewards of the Jockey Club to stable lads, with whose interests he had identified himself so closely for more than 30 years. Towards the end of the previous month Minoru had become the first horse to carry the colours of a reigning sovereign successfully in the Derby, and received an ovation of unprecedented length and enthusiasm after the judge had awarded him a short-head verdict over Louviers. Reappearing in the St James's Palace Stakes, Minoru faced a far easier task, and, again ridden by Bertie Jones, beat The Story, owned by Jack Joel, by two lengths.

The King also won with Princesse de Galles, who obtained a somewhat overdue success in the Coronation Stakes, at his last Ascot. Princesse de Galles had been second to Electra in the 1000 Guineas, and had been unluckily beaten in the Oaks as she had come heavily into season shortly before being runner-up to Perola. At Ascot the royal filly had her revenge on Electra, whom she beat by a neck.

Having made a consummate fool of himself by declining the mount on Bayardo in 1908, Otto Madden was soon to find himself with greater reason to look back with regret upon the Royal Meeting of 1909. In the Ascot Stakes he rode Mr Douglas Jardine's Sir Harry, who started a well-backed favourite at 3/1, for Dobson Peacock's Middleham stable. Sir Harry was unplaced to Rush Cutter, who won by three lengths from Laughing Mirror, with Wedding Ring third. That might have been that, had not Sir Harry reappeared in the Northumberland Plate at Newcastle just eight days later. Again ridden by Madden, Sir Harry managed to turn the Ascot form upside-down by beating Laughing Mirror by six lengths, with Wedding Ring third. Incensed by such a blatant reversal of the

Ascot running, the Stewards of the Jockey Club asked Madden to explain his riding of Sir Harry in the Ascot race. Madden, no stranger to such enquiries, blithely declared that he had been tied down by orders to wait at Ascot, but would have won had he been able to ride the way he had done at Newcastle. Asked to corroborate that evidence, that bluff old Yorkshireman Dobson Peacock, who was never slow to speak his mind, was absolutely furious. He maintained that he had certainly not given Madden orders to hold up Sir Harry at Ascot, and, for good measure, added that he and Douglas Jardine were deeply dissatisfied with the way the horse had been ridden there. In their findings the Stewards attached no blame to either owner or trainer, and Madden escaped by the skin of his teeth by receiving a reprimand, and being strongly cautioned as to his future conduct.

Otto Madden and his works had never much commended themselves to the Stewards of the Jockey Club. While reigning champion jockey in 1902 he had been refused a licence to ride for "associating with persons of bad character", and he was widely suspected of pulling Wool Winder when that colt was second to Orby in the Derby in 1907. Be that as it may, he was replaced by Bill Halsey when Wool Winder justified favouritism in the St Leger.

Born in Hungary in 1872, Otto Madden was the son of a Manchester man who rode that great Hungarian mare Kincsem in most of her races. The young Madden spent most of his apprenticeship with the royal trainer Dick Marsh, for whom he won the Derby on the 100/1 chance Jeddah in 1898. The following year he became champion jockey. He headed the list again in 1901, and after reinstatement in 1903 and 1904. He retired to train in 1909, but with the dearth of jockeys created by the First World War, resumed riding in middle age, and won a substitute Oaks on Sunny Jane in 1917. He was a highly esteemed churchwarden at Newmarket at the time of his death in 1942.

Also successful at Ascot in 1909 were Lemberg and Charles O'Malley. A. W. Cox's Lemberg, a rather tall bay colt by Cyllene, emulated his half-brother Bayardo by winning the New Stakes first time out, and Charles O'Malley landed the Windsor Castle Stakes for the Druid's Lodge Stable. A little less than a year later Lemberg won the Derby, with Charles O'Malley third, then both returned to Ascot, Lemberg being successful in the St James's Palace Stakes and Charles O'Malley in the Gold Vase.

That Royal Meeting of 1910 was another "Black Ascot". King Edward VII had died on 6th May, expressing with his last words delight at the news that his lovely little filly Witch of the Air had just won at Kempton Park. Without any ordinance from the Ascot Office at St James's Palace, racegoers in all enclosures wore mourning and the brilliant hues of the silks and taffetas, usually essential ingredients of the scene, were replaced by uniform black in tribute to the sovereign who had always derived so much unconcealed enjoyment from the meeting, and did so much to enhance its social importance.

Ironically, or appropriately, two of the winners carried the black jacket of Lord Derby. Decision beat Admiral Hawke by a length in the Ascot Derby, and Swynford was successful in the Hardwicke Stakes.

Swynford was a horse with very large feet, and in the spring he was causing his trainer George Lambton considerable concern by the way he used to clip his off hind joint. Lambton mentioned this to the celebrated painter of horses Lynwood Palmer, who, rather surprisingly, declared that he thought he could cure the trouble, though there would be an element of risk involved. On Lambton agreeing to take the chance, the painter took a sharp knife to Swynford's near hind hoof, and pared it to exactly the right extent to prevent the colt catching his joint. Subsequently Palmer was constantly consulted with regard to the conditions of the hooves of Lambton's horses. Asked how he had come to be an expert in this extraordinarily specialist field, Lynwood Palmer explained that as a young man he had charge of the horses of one of the largest hackney cab proprietors in New York. As his income depended upon the amount of work his charges did, it had been in his interests to acquire some superficial veterinary knowledge, and he learned that the cause of lameness in horses was usually to be found in the hoof.

In his last gallop before Ascot Swynford had gone so well that George Lambton became very sweet on his chances of beating the Derby winner

The Hon. George Lambton – who trained for the Earl of Derby.

Lemberg in the St James's Palace Stakes. It was not to be. Starting at 8/1 on, Lemberg won by three lengths at the end of the mile with Swynford third of six. Pulled out again the following day, Swynford showed his appreciation of the extra half-mile of the Hardwicke Stakes by beating Marajax by three parts of a length. In the autumn he fulfilled the promise of that performance by winning the St Leger. The following year he was successful in the Hardwicke for a second time.

The Hon. George Lambton, who was responsible for the successes of Swynford and so many of the other great horses owned by the 17th Earl of Derby, had been born in 1860, the fifth son of the 2nd Earl of Durham. A remarkably handsome man, with large, generous eyes and finely chiselled features, never anything but elegantly dressed, he went through life with a carefree charm. Originally intended for a military career, he developed a fascination for racing, abandoned all thoughts of the army, and as a young man devoted himself to riding as an amateur. Being perennially short of money, and sometimes heavily in debt, he was largely dependent upon successful betting, and the odd bit of horse coping, for funds in those days. After riding his first winner on Pompeia at Nottingham in 1880, he made the acquaintanceship, and in many cases the friendship, of Fred Archer, Mat Dawson, Captain Machell and almost everybody else of consequence in racing, while developing into an increasingly successful race rider under both codes.

George Lambton's riding career came to an end as a result of a heavy fall on Hollington in a steeplechase at Sandown Park in February 1892. The legacy of the severe injuries to his spine sustained in that crash would be with him for the remainder of his life, and for several years afterwards he was virtually a cripple. All the same he started a minor social revolution by opening a small stable at Newmarket later in 1892. Up to that time it was considered inconceivable for the son of a peer, an officer, or anyone else aspiring to be a gentleman to train racehorses, and if, like the Hampshire squire Arthur Yates, they did, they maintained the fiction that the head lad was the trainer. George Lambton changed attitudes to training completely, and made it a profession recognised as suitable for gentlemen. Hitherto, only the Church, the army and the navy had been so regarded.

The year after he had opened his stable George Lambton accepted the offer to become private trainer to the 16th Earl of Derby, who was reviving the family's racing interests, in Newmarket's Bedford Lodge yard. In 1903 he moved the string into the palatial Stanley House establishment, and on the death of Lord Derby in 1908, continued to run the stable for the latter's son, the 17th Earl.

Winkipop, successful in the Coronation Stakes at that "Black Ascot" of 1910, had a strange background for the winner of such a race. While up at Oxford, her owner Waldorf Astor, later the 2nd Viscount Astor, bought a mare called Conjure, by the sprinter Juggler, for £100 with a view to her breeding him a horse on which he could win the Grand National. Having exhibited her in a show ring, where she was highly commended, Waldorf

Astor had intended sending her to King's Premium stallions to produce the required steeplechasers. Changing his mind, however, he mated her with horses of the quality of William the Third, to whom she bred Winkipop, and John O'Gaunt. In due course Winkipop became the dam of five winners, and one of the foundation mares of Waldorf Astor's Cliveden Stud near Maidenhead.

In those last few seasons before the outbreak of the First World War, Hornet's Beauty, the first horse owned by the dapper little Yorkshire baronet Sir William Cooke, commanded a huge public following at Ascot. A bay gelding by Tredennis, he was bred in Ireland by Michael Collins, who could not sell him for £100 early on in his two-year-old days in 1910; but after he had gone on to win each of his three races at that age, Sir William gave £2000 for him on the advice of Steve Donoghue. The model of consistency, Hornet's Beauty was wonderfully versatile, and effective at all distances from five furlongs to a mile and a half, but probably most in his element as a sprinter. As a three-year-old in 1911 he carried all before him at home by winning each of his 15 races, but was down the field in the Grand Prix d'Ostende. At Ascot he won the seven-furlong Trial Stakes on the opening day, the five-furlong Fern Hill Stakes on the Wednesday, and after being hampered when Hallaton swerved across him at the start of the King's Stand Stakes on the final day, he recovered to beat Jack Joel's Sunningdale by half a length.

As Hornet's Beauty was off the course for most of 1912 he was not seen at Ascot, but the following season he returned. Having landed the odds of 9/1 laid on him in the All-aged Stakes on the Thursday, he won the King's Stand Stakes for the second time by carrying the jump weight of 10 st 7 lb to beat Jarnac II by half a length. Finally, in 1914, the old horse maintained his unbeaten record at Ascot; he obtained his sixth success there by winning the All-aged Stakes again. In all, Hornet's Beaty won 31 races.

An enthusiastic man to hounds, Sir William Cooke was Master or Joint Master of several packs, including the Sinnington and the Derwent, at various times. He was also a keen polo player. When he had to give up polo on medical advice, he took to coaching, and was often to be seen driving the then famous "Venture", in which he had a share, between Harrogate and Scarborough. After becoming ever more involved in racing he left his native county, and in 1913 founded the Wyld Court Stud at Hampstead Norris, near Newbury in Berkshire. He obtained his only classic success with Happy Knight, ridden by Tommy Weston for Henri Jellis's stable, in the 2000 Guineas in 1946, and lived to be a very old man, dying at the age of 91 in June 1964. Despite his enthusiasm for such a wide variety of equine sports gaining him the acquaintanceship of so many people, there was an essential shyness about Sir William, which was accentuated by increasing deafness as he grew older.

In the year that Hornet's Beauty won at Ascot for the first time, 1911, the long-distance races were dominated by Willonyx, the outstanding stayer of the era. After winning the Ascot Stakes by four lengths on the first day, he defeated the classic horse Charles O'Malley by a neck in the Gold Cup. A powerful brown colt by William the Third with two small socks behind, Willonyx had failed to make his reserve at Doncaster as a yearling, and was bought privately for £700 by the Beckhampton trainer Sam Darling, who promptly found an owner for him in C. E. Howard, a successful building contractor, who lived at Coombe Park, near Whitchurch in Oxfordshire. Blessed with a really beautiful temperament, Willonyx was too backward to be of any account as a two-year-old in 1909, improved as he developed strength compatible with his frame throughout his second season, and came to his peak as a four-year-old. In addition to the Gold Cup and the Ascot Stakes, he won the Chester Cup, the Jockey Club Cup and the Cesarewitch under the record weight of 9 st 5 lb. In all those races he was ridden by the Beckhampton stable jockey Billy Higgs. Having enjoyed very little success while an apprentice at Lambourn, Higgs made his name in Ireland, and returned to England to become champion jockey with 149 winners in 1906. Although Mr Howard refused an offer of £5000 for Willonyx, the horse made no significant mark as a stallion until reaching the famous Chapadmalal Stud, owned by Senor Martinez de Hoz, in Argentina.

Sam Darling, the trainer of Willonyx, was the grandson of the jockey of the same name who had won the St Leger of 1833 on Rockingham. He had been born in 1852 at Bourton-on-the-Hill, where he was apprenticed to Edwin Weever. After riding successfully he began training at Kinnersley, and in 1880 purchased the Beckhampton stable. After handing over that establishment to his son Fred on his retirement in 1913, he died in 1921. Sam Darling was an extremely methodical man, who was almost obsessed with neatness. In his will he ordained that the village streets of Beckhampton should be freshly swept and sanded on the day of his funeral and specified the colours in which the farm carts that carried his coffin should be painted.

By comparison with his son and successor, Sam Darling was easy-going. Fred Darling was the ultimate martinet, totally intolerant of weakness in men and horses. When he was in charge of the Home Guard during the Second World War, he found Templeton, his head lad of many years and a brilliant stableman, absent from his post. Templeton was not only dismissed from the Home Guard, but lost his job at Beckhampton. Fred Darling was totally dedicated to the success of Beckhampton. He made no friends at all, not even among the rich and influential men whose horses he trained, and only with great reluctance did he permit them to visit the stable. This abrupt, autocratic little man, with sharp features, actively discouraged the lads from making friends with each other, obliged them to do all their betting through him, and insisted they rode out in breeches and highly polished leggings. Everything in the stable ran like clockwork, and the horses were dressed over with such thoroughness that the "Beckhampton Bloom" became their trade mark. Fred Darling's German-born wife returned to her own country at the outbreak of war in 1914. He never saw her again. He never spoke of her, but her picture was never taken down from the wall at Beckhampton. He would make his mark on Ascot to a still greater extent than his father had done.

A new era had opened at Ascot in 1911 when Lieutenant-Colonel Sir Gordon Carter was appointed Clerk of the Course. Gordon Carter had had a remarkable military career as he had been commissioned from the ranks of the Life Guards, an unprecedented achievement in those days, except in the case of riding masters and bandmasters. He had taken part in the relief of

Sam Darling – trainer of Willonyx, the outstanding stayer of 1911.

Kimberley, and became second-in-command of the regiment. Running Ascot with the same military precision which he brought to every aspect of his own life, he was a disciplinarian, who would instantly dismiss any man found smoking at work; yet he was absolutely fair, and his word could never be doubted. He was quite devoted to Ascot, and over a period of 30 years he was constantly trying to devise means of improving every aspect of the Royal Meeting. Always a cavalryman, Sir Gordon, as he became, went everywhere on horseback, and would cover miles every day as he rode around the course supervising the work of groundsmen, painters and others, giving instructions and encouragement, and where necessary delivering the occasional rebuke. This tall, soldierly man knew everybody's job, and was singleminded in his determination to ensure that it was done to the highest possible standard. For close on a third of a century Ascot was his life.

There was an unusual outcome to the St James's

Palace Stakes in 1912 when an American-bred maiden, Mr Augustus Belmont's Tracery, beat the 2000 Guineas winner Sweeper II by four lengths. As racing in the state of New York had been suspended because of the anti-betting laws, Augustus Belmont sent Tracery to be trained by John Watson in the Rothschild family's private stable, Palace House, at Newmarket, there being a close commercial affinity between the Belmonts and the Rothschilds, as the former had long been the representative of the Rothschilds' bank in the United States.

As a two-year-old Tracery was beset by spavin trouble and a variety of other ailments, so that he could not run at all at that age. The following season the big brown colt, who was never particularly impressive in his work, was slow to come to hand, but by early June was ready to make an extremely unorthodox debut in the Derby. Inevitably he was one of the rank outsiders at 66/1, but to everybody's surprise finished third to Tagalie. His running at Ascot suggested that he was training on to be the best of his generation, and in the autumn he furnished proof of his having reached that status by winning the St Leger by five lengths with Tagalie unplaced.

When Tracery reappeared at Royal Ascot as a four-year-old he lined up against Prince Palatine for what was widely expected to be an exciting race for the Gold Cup. After Jackdaw had made the running for a mile and a half "Snowy" Whalley sent Tracery to the front. With four furlongs to run, Tracery still held a commanding lead, Prince Palatine being still some 20 lengths in arrears, though going very comfortably in the hands of Billy Saxby. At this point a man whose name was subsequently ascertained to be Hewitt rushed on to the course waving a little suffragette flag and a loaded revolver. There was not the remotest possibility that a horse galloping at racing pace could avoid him, and Tracery was brought down, though happily he came out of the incident unharmed and "Snowy" Whalley was no more than badly shaken. Hewitt, on the other hand, was severely injured without having promoted the cause of votes for women one iota. With Tracery so dramatically removed from contention, Jackdaw resumed the lead, closely pressed by the French challenger Gorgorito. As soon as they had made the turn into the straight Prince Palatine threw down his challenge to Jackdaw, and quickly securing the upper hand, went away to win in a canter, beating Lord Derby's Stedfast by a length and a half with Jackdaw fifth. The previous season Jackdaw had won the Queen Alexandra Stakes. He was to sire a horse who would do a lot more than win that race just once.

Four weeks later Tracery and "Snowy" Whalley were reunited in the Eclipse Stakes at Sandown Park, where they beat the 2000 Guineas winner Louvois by four lengths. In the middle of the October of that year Tracery brought his career to a close by winning the Champion Stakes, and was retired to the Southcourt Stud at Leighton Buzzard in Bedfordshire. He got a number of good winners, including The Panther, successful in the 2000 Guineas, before being sold to Argentina for 53,000 guineas. After his son Papyrus had won the Derby of 1923 he was bought back by a syndicate of English breeders, only to die of a rupture of the diaphragm and a hernia of the stomach at the Cobham Stud in August 1924.

The horse that everybody was agog to see at Ascot in 1913 was The Tetrarch, a two-year-old belonging to Major Dermot McCalmont, and trained by his cousin Atty Persse at Chattis Hill. They said he was a phenomenon, a freak, the greatest horse the world had ever seen. Ever since he had spreadeagled a huge field at Newmarket two months earlier he had been the talk of the racing world. Nobody had ever seen a racehorse quite like The Tetrarch, who was by Roi Herode out of Vahren. He was remarkable for his size, and even more so for his appearance. Iron-grey in colour, he had splashes of white all over his coat, some as large as a goose's egg and others as small as a marble, so he looked as though someone had daubed him with lime. Seeing him as a yearling in his paddock at Straffan Station, a well-known Irish racing personality asked his breeder Mr Edward Kennedy what he was going to do with the colt with those strange markings.

"Send him to Doncaster Sales, of course," replied Kennedy.

"If he were mine," said the visitor, "I should have him cut, and put him away as a steeplechaser."

When he arrived at the sales paddocks at Doncaster, the Vahren colt was dubbed "The Rocking Horse", and rated too big and coarse to make a racehorse by most of those who inspected him. One of the exceptions was Atty Persse, who outbid Sir William Cooke at 1300 guineas and passed him on to Dermot McCalmont, who had inherited the fortune of his cousin Colonel Harry McCalmont, the owner of Isinglass.

The Tetrarch proved uncannily easy to break. As soon as the tack was put on him, he seemed to know exactly what to do. He had nothing at all to learn. Persse's stable jockey Steve Donoghue, who was to ride him in all his races, always swore that The Tetrarch had done it all before, and that it was "his second time on earth".

One morning early in April 1913 Atty Persse was about to gallop four small, sharp two-year-olds, who would be ready to run soon, when he decided to throw in The Tetrarch to see how he shaped, telling the lad on the big grey to drop him out if the others began to leave him. Persse could not believe his eyes. Instead of toiling behind, The Tetrarch was well clear of the others after two furlongs, and still going away. Two days later The Tetrarch was formally tried with two older horses, and another two-year-old that had just won at Newbury. Within a few strides of jumping off, The Tetrarch had the other three off their feet, and streaking away won the trial by many lengths. He almost pulled Steve Donoghue's arms out of their sockets.

The Ascot racegoers eagerly awaited a performance way out of the ordinary from The Tetrarch in the Coventry on the opening day; they were not to be disappointed. Making all the running, he won by 10 lengths from Courageous, and was still cantering. Men who had been coming to Ascot since the middle of Queen Victoria's reign vainly searched their memories for another two-year-old who had won with quite so much authority. Never before had they seen quite such a horse as The Tetrarch. It was not only the colouring of his coat that set him apart from other horses.

Staying on course as quite invincible, The Tetrarch went on to win the National Breeders Produce Stakes at Sandown Park, the Rous Memorial Stakes at Goodwood, the rather pretentiously named Champion Breeders Foal Stakes at Derby and the Champagne Stakes at Doncaster. In October he was to have gone for the Imperial Produce

The Tetrarch – the "Spotted Wonder", invincible in 1913, ridden by Steve Donoghue.

Stakes at Kempton Park, but had to miss that event after rapping his off fore in a gallop. In consequence he was retired for the season.

As the idea of The Tetrarch ever being beaten was patently absurd, he was winter favourite for both the 2000 Guineas and the Derby. Though the odds were very cramped indeed, the public piled money on to him, to identify with the wonder horse and savour vicariously a share in his success.

By the early spring of 1914 The Tetrarch was nowhere near as far forward as he had been at the corresponding time in his two-year-old days, and Major McCalmont and Atty Persse decided not to run him in the 2000 Guineas. As the weather grew warmer The Tetrarch came to himself, and any doubts there may have been about his being too fast to be able to stay the mile and a half were dispelled for good and all after he had worked brilliantly over the distance a fortnight before the Derby.

Then came disaster. Three days after the gallop he struck his off fore again in the course of half-speed work. The leg filled, and The Tetrarch became so lame that there was no alternative to scratching him from the Derby. He never ran again, and retired to the Ballyinch Stud, Co. Kilkenny at a fee of 300 guineas, later increased to 500 guineas. His stock, and one filly in particular, would ensure that his association with the Royal Meeting had not ended when he was led out of the winner's enclosure after the Coventry Stakes. Incontrovertibly, "The Spotted Wonder" was one of the most exciting horses ever seen at Ascot.

Steve Donoghue, who rode The Tetrarch in all his races, had the most lovely hands, which enabled him to establish an instant rapport with any horse that he rode, and to handle the hardest puller as though it were a child's first pony. In addition he was a wonderful judge of pace, a quite instinctive tactician, and fearless without ever being reckless. Thus he was both a polished horseman, and also an accomplished race rider, which is far from the same thing.

There was about him an irresponsibility, almost amounting to fecklessness, redeemed by his charm, a legacy of his father's Irish ancestors. While never averse to accepting enormous sums for first claim upon his services, he had only the haziest idea of the obligations which he had undertaken, and was constantly engaging himself for a fancied mount when his retaining stable had a runner. At various times Lord Derby, Fred Darling and other leading owners and trainers held claims upon him only to become utterly exasperated. In the end they had to recognise that Steve Donoghue was a law unto himself, and though only too pleased to have him ride when available, they made no further efforts to enter into formal arrangements with him.

Steve Donoghue had been born in Warrington, Lancashire, in 1884, the son of a steel worker. His early attempts to become a jockey were badly frustrated, and although attached to three different stables, he was never formally apprenticed in England. He began with John Porter at Kingsclere, but ran away after being thrashed because his mount had got loose and upset the Derby winner Flying Fox. Subsequently he spent short spells with Dobson Peacock at Middleham and Alfred Sadler at Newmarket.

On seeing an advertisement for a job with the American trainer Edward Johnson in France, he was successful in his application for it, and eventually rode his first winner on Hanoi at the small course at Hyères in 1905. He used to say that experience of riding the sharp little provincial tracks in France enabled him to master the intricacies of Epsom, where he won the Derby on Humorist, Captain Cuttle, Papyrus and Manna.

He was champion jockey for each of the ten years up to and including 1923, and after The Tetrarch was to ride two other of the famous horses in the story of the Royal Meeting – lovely little Diadem, and the seemingly immortal Brown Jack. The public loved this friendly, modest little man. For close on three decades the cry of "Come on, Steve!" was taken up on every racecourse in England, and nowhere louder than at Ascot.

For the most part the weather during the summer of 1914 was almost unbelievably beautiful. There was hardly a cloud in the sky, metaphorical or otherwise, and no sense of impending doom or dire threats to the established order of things. True, Kaiser Wilhelm II, a grandson of Queen Victoria, was much given to attitudinising, preferably in a gorgeous uniform, and not averse to a little sabre-rattling, but there was no harm in him, as the

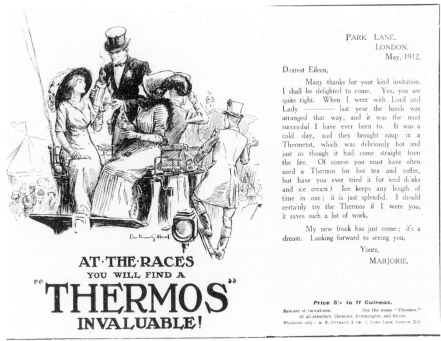

An advertisement of the day – extolling the creature comforts of the Thermos in 1912.

Agadir incident had shown. In 1911 the German Emperor had sent the gunboat *Panther* to the Moroccan port of Agadir to protect what he saw as his country's interests in North Africa. On the British Government making it clear that another naval presence could not be tolerated so close to Gibraltar, the *Panther* was withdrawn.

The Pax Britannica had been preserved. England was at the very apogee of empire. Her statesmen exercised unprecedented authority worldwide, and the leaders of her society lived in a style scarcely imaginable in more egalitarian times. Their opulence was never more in evidence than at Royal Ascot, which was, for so many of them, the high point of the London season. All week they entertained on a lavish scale. Rather than stay in their London houses, though, those whose country seats were many miles distant had a substantial house in East Berkshire or across the nearby county border in North Surrey solely for use during the Royal Meeting. The Earl of Derby, for instance, whose principal landholdings were in Lancashire, took up residence at Cowarth Park in Sunninghill, some three miles from the course. There he dispensed hospitality to a house party whose members had arrived accompanied by coachmen, valets and ladies' maids.

On his magnificent Maiden Erlegh estate, on the outskirts of Reading, Solly Joel set the tenor of a week in which expense was totally immaterial. In the huge marquees erected on the lawn he entertained 300 people to lunch. As well as prominent members of the Jockey Club and other owners, along with trainers and jockeys, his guests included prominent statesmen, and the leaders of the literary and artistic worlds. Lord Dewar, the whisky magnate, King Edward's yachting friend Sir Thomas Lipton, the most successful grocer the world had known, the thriller writer Edgar Wallace, and the Labour Party luminary J. H. "Jim" Thomas, who behaved like a licensed jester, were all amongst the wide variety of people who had memories of Solly Joel's pre-Ascot parties.

Lord Derby and Solly Joel both enjoyed success at the Royal Meeting of 1914. With Glorivanna the Earl won the Gold Vase, and two days later Solly Joel landed the Rous Memorial Stakes with Maiden Erlegh, the horse that he had named after his Berkshire estate. To wind up the proceedings Adular, bred in Hungary, won the King's Stand Stakes. Nine days later shots rang out at Sarajevo.

BETWEEN THE WORLD WARS

SHEER exhilaration was the predominant emotion in the crowds that flocked back to the enclosures in June 1919. Four years of almost indescribable horror had come to an end the previous November. The fighting was over, and everybody was bent upon picking up the threads of peacetime pleasures. Yet however wholehearted that feeling of national relief may have been, there was an ineradicable sorrow, only thinly veiled by the gaiety. So many people who should have been at Ascot that year would never be seen on the course again. Like those in every other part of the population, racing families had suffered heavy losses in the war. The veteran statesman Lord Rosebery had lost a much-loved younger son; Freddy Rickaby, who had seemed set fair to become an even better jockey than his father, had been killed in the final phases of the conflict; Major Charlie Beatty had left Newmarket's Bedford Lodge stable to die on the Western front in 1917; Charlie Morbey, one of the leading jockeys of the eighties, was left inconsolable in old age by the death in action of his only son. The list was seemingly endless.

But life had to go on, and Royal Ascot returned to the forefront of the social life in England. There were new faces, and new money coming into racing, in addition to owners of a very different type to those who had traditionally supported it. As well as those men whose businesses had thrived during the war, there were the financiers, who made fortunes from their dealings in the City. Foremost amongst these was Mr James White, on whose horse Irish Elegance rested the hopes of thousands upon thousands of small punters in the Royal Hunt Cup.

Originally a bricklayer in Rochdale, Lancashire, Jimmy White had a wonderful flair for finance, and for a while made huge sums of money by the manipulation of the stock market, buying at the right time and selling at the right time with what seemed a quite uncanny knack, without ever being involved in the creation of any sound commercial venture. In due course he began racing, perfectly convinced that he could break the bookmakers as easily as he had overcome rivals in the City, with his fellow Lancastrian, the champion jockey Steve Donoghue, as his mentor. From the theatrical impresario Frank Curzon he bought the Foxhill Stable, situated on the Wiltshire Downs a few miles from Swindon, and engaged Harry Cottrill, yet another Lancastrian, as his trainer. Brash and bombastic, he loved to make a splash by laying £1000 just before a race was off; and with the generosity which was much his most attractive characteristic he lavishly rewarded all concerned when he won.

Irish Elegance was a really magnificent animal, though half-bred, by Sir Archibald, with whom Atty Persse had landed the New Stakes in 1908, out of a mare called Sweet Clorane, and therefore half-brother to Cloringo, who had been successful in the National Hunt 'chase over four miles at Cheltenham. After he had won a couple of races at Newmarket in the colours of Mr R. B. Thorburn as a three-year-old in the summer of 1918, Irish Elegance was bought for 2000 guineas by Harry Cottrill, who passed him on to Jimmy White. With his powerful physique, the big chestnut looked as though he would have no difficulty in carrying a big man for a whole day in the hunting field, so it was not altogether surprising that he was to prove quite indifferent to weight and earn the reputation of being one of the greatest handicappers of all time.

First time out in 1919, Irish Elegance delighted Jimmy White by carrying 9 st 9 lb to win the Salford Borough Handicap on the financier's home course at Manchester, where he was ridden by Steve Donoghue. For that success he earned a 10-lb penalty for the Royal Hunt Cup which brought his weight up to 9 st 11 lb. With Donoghue claimed to ride Jutland for King George V, Fred Templeman came in for the ride on Irish Elegance. Notwithstanding his huge burden, which would have been considered prohibitive in the case of any other horse, the big chestnut was heavily backed by his owner and the public alike so that he started joint favourite at 7/1 with Jutland, to whom he was giving no less than 34 lb. The outcome was never in any real doubt, and Irish Elegance won by a length and a half from Lord Jersey's Arion, winner of the Kempton Park Jubilee earlier in the season and in receipt of 26 lb. In his own felicitous phrase, Jimmy White had "won a bundle", and the champagne flowed.

Had he known the eagerness with which his bets were accepted by the bookmakers, White would have been insulted to the point of incredulity. The tribal memory of bookmakers is very long indeed, and the lore of their trade is full of once recklessly confident men who plunged too often for too long in the certainty that they would break the ring, like the Marquess of Hastings who had destroyed himself and dissipated a huge fortune by the age of 26. The ring bided its time, as well it knew it could afford to do. White took £80,000 from them when he won the Cesarewitch with Bracket later in 1919, but before long the luck began to run against him. At the same time the financial empire of this cold, grasping egoist, whose ruthlessness was masked by an earthy geniality, began to crumble while having no firm foundations on which it could be sustained. In one last desperate bid to stave off ruin Jimmy White tried to corner the shares in the British Controlled Oilfields Company in the early summer of 1927. When settling day came on 29th June he needed another £750,000 in cash to complete the operation, and nobody wanted to lend to the man who had displayed such overweening arrogance during the days that he was in clover. Jimmy White had never given any quarter, and he would not beg for it. That afternoon he went to his fine mansion, King Edward's Place, near Foxhill, and sending the staff into Swindon for the evening, he retired to his bedroom with a bottle of prussic acid and some

Lord Glanely – "Old Guts and Gaiters".

chloroform. The following morning they found the body of the man who owned Irish Elegance, the finest weight-carrier the English turf has ever seen.

While Irish Elegance created the sensation of that first post-war Royal Ascot in 1919, much the most successful owner was Lord Glanely, whose horses were trained by Frank Barling in a private stable at Newmarket. As well as landing the St James's Palace Stakes with his Derby winner Grand Parade, and the Prince of Wales' Stakes with Dominion, Lord Glanely (pronounced "Glan-eely") won the Wokingham Stakes with Scatwell, the Windsor Castle Stakes with Bright Folly, and the Granville Stakes with Lady Juliet, while Sky-Rocket ran a dead-heat for the Visitors Handicap, and He, a bay colt by the 1901 Gold Cup winner Santoi, walked over for the Churchill Stakes, giving the shipping magnate seven successes in all.

With his luxuriant moustache, Lord Glanely was an unmistakably flamboyant figure, with a powerful personality in which energy and shrewdness were combined to a remarkably high degree. Born in Appledore in Devon as William Tatem in 1868, he spent a short time at sea before joining the staff of a mercantile office in Cardiff, already determined to own his own shipping line, and in 1909 realised his ambition by founding Tatem S. N. Co. Ltd. In 1918 he received a baronetcy, followed by a peerage. Lord Glanely, generally known as "Old Guts and Gaiters", gave many of his horses names like Rose of England, Chulmleigh, Glorious Devon and Westward Ho, which reflected his patriotism and deep pride in his native county.

By riding five of those winners owned by Lord Glanely, Arthur Smith, who was still indentured to Frank Barling, set a record for success obtained by an apprentice at a Royal Meeting. In the Derby, Smith had chosen to ride Dominion, who was unplaced, rather than Grand Parade, another chance mount for Irish Elegance's Hunt Cup rider Fred Templeman. At Ascot Arthur Smith rode both Grand Parade and Dominion, as well as Bright Folly, Sky-Rocket and He. Smith never fulfilled that early promise, although he won the St Leger on Caligula in 1920. He gradually dropped out of racing after about 1936, and died of a heart attack at his home in Cheltenham at the age of 71 in 1969.

Those seven winners at Royal Ascot following the winning of the Derby represented instant success for Frank Barling, who had taken charge of Lord Glanely's stable at the outset of the season. Barling had practised as a veterinary surgeon in Monmouthshire until he began to train steeplechasers. A serious illness in 1924 brought an end to his brief and successful association with Lord Glanely. On recovery he opened a public stable at Primrose Cottage, Newmarket. Frank Barling died at the age of 66 in 1935.

While Irish Elegance was the hero of the meeting in 1919, Lord d'Abernon's lovely little chestnut mare Diadem, who had taken classic honours in the 1000 Guineas two years earlier, was the heroine, and, in the eyes of the professionals, every bit as much a star. Following The Tetrarch, she was the second of the famous horses with whom Steve Donoghue was to be associated at the royal fixture. On the Thursday they shared success in the Rous Memorial Stakes, then 24 hours later beat the Duke of Portland's Best Born Boy by a decisive two lengths in the King's Stand Stakes. A beautifully moulded little chestnut, though perhaps a trifle light of bone, by Orby out of Donnetta, by Donovan, Diadem was bereft of white save for a shield-shaped star on her intelligent head. Her trainer George Lambton wrote of her that she was "the sweetest and most gallant little mare that was ever seen on the racecourse".

Diadem reappeared at Royal Ascot in 1920 to win the King's Stand Stakes for a second time after beating her solitary rival, Tetrameter, by six lengths in the All-aged Stakes, and being given a walk-over in the Rous Memorial Stakes. By the end of her career she had won 24 of her 39 races, finished second eight times, third three times and been unplaced on just four occasions. She is commemorated at Ascot today by the Diadem Stakes, a Group Three race run over six furlongs at the September meeting.

As well as winning those two races on Diadem at Royal Ascot in 1919, Steve Donoghue had, for a licensed jockey, the unique distinction of having bred the winner of the Gold Cup, and the mortification of finishing second to it himself. Ridden by George Hulme in the colours of Mr W. T. de Pledge, the five-year-old By Jingo beat Donoghue's mount Air Raid by three parts of a length. The champion jockey had bred By Jingo from the mating of Aquascutum with the Velasquez mare Minnesota, and sold the colt for £100 as a yearling. Being perennially short of money, the easy-going Donoghue was not best pleased when he heard that By Jingo had been passed on to Mr de Pledge for £2000.

Although King George V relished the social side of racing a great deal less than the gregarious Edward VII had done, he was a better judge of a horse than his father, and always derived a great deal of pleasure from winning a race at his own meeting at Ascot. The King obtained his first postwar success there when Viceroy, ridden by his father's old jockey Bertie Jones, beat Lord Derby's Danegelt four lengths, with Lord Glanely's Starshot third, in the Waterford Stakes in 1919.

The old-fashioned Triennial Stakes were at last discontinued after the end of the First World War. Those were the races run in a three-year cycle, with the entries eligible to meet over the five furlongs as two-year-olds, over the extended seven furlongs as three-year-olds, and finally over two miles as four-year-olds in the third season. The two-mile race became the Churchill Stakes, named after the King's representative, for which He had walked-over in 1919; the seven-furlong middle leg of the Triennial became the Jersey Stakes, commemorating the 4th Earl of Jersey, who had been Master of the Buckhounds in 1782 and 1783, and won by A. E. Barton's Knight of the Air ridden by Fred Templeman; and the two-year-old race was continued as the Chesham Stakes. The first running of the Chesham Stakes, named after the 3rd Lord Chesham, last of the Masters of the Buckhounds, was won by Mr Lionel Robinson's unnamed chestnut colt by Prince Palatine, with Australian Brownie Carslake up.

The other event inaugurated in that first season following the end of the Great War was the Ribblesdale Stakes, which takes its name from the 4th Lord Ribblesdale, Master of the Buckhounds from 1892 to 1895. Today the Ribblesdale is a Group Two race for three-year-old fillies over a mile and a half, but in its original form it was run over a mile and open to three-year-olds and four-year-olds of either sex. The initial running was won by Milton, ridden by the 15-year-old apprentice George Scott Colling, son of the Newmarket trainer Bob Colling. In all, George Colling rode 72 winners that year, but was far too tall to have prospects of anything but a brief spell on the flat. Severe trouble with his weight soon obliged him to give up riding, and after being assistant to his brother, he embarked on his career as a trainer which culminated in his winning the Derby with Nimbus in 1949. He married Frank Barling's daughter Kathleen.

The feature of Royal Ascot in 1920 was the success of offspring of The Tetrarch, who had inherited his colouring. Of his colts, Caligula, who was destined to give Arthur Smith his classic success in the St Leger, won the Ascot Derby, Syrian Prince won the Chesham Stakes and Tetratema, who would be back to land the King's Stand Stakes next year, the Fern Hill Stakes; then his daughter Tete-a-Tete won the Jersey Stakes. Thus in the first two seasons that he was represented at Royal Ascot, The Tetrarch was responsible for six winners, as, besides Viceroy winning the Waterford Stakes, another of

his sons, Sarchedon, had won the Coventry Stakes in 1919.

Jack Jarvis, third and youngest son of Cyllene's trainer Bill Jarvis, obtained the first of many successes at Royal Ascot when Sir William Cooke's Golden Orb was ridden by Fred Slade to win the Wokingham Stakes in 1920. Then just 32 years old, Jarvis had ridden his first winner in 1902 and won the Cambridgeshire for the Druid's Lodge Confederacy on Hackler's Pride in 1903. By the time that increased weight obliged him to ride over hurdles for a short while he had 121 winners to his credit. After serving as a signals N.C.O. attached to the Tank Corps during the war he moved into Newmarket's spacious Park Lodge Stable, once the property of the notorious gambler William Crockford, with only three horses in 1919. One of those horses was the filly Winfrith, whom he had bought from a farmer for £30. After Winfrith had finished third in a selling race at Birmingham in April 1919, Jarvis wanted to exercise his right of first claim, to which the rules then entitled him, on the runner-up Wrecker, trained for Captain G. C. H. Davy by Vandy Beatty. As Captain Davy was anxious to keep Wrecker, he persuaded Sir William Cooke, who was a friend of Jarvis's father, to negotiate the withdrawal of the claim. Eventually Jarvis agreed to forego his rights in the matter, and shortly afterwards Sir William Cooke sent him Golden Orb and other horses. Winfrith may not have been very good, but she played a big part in giving Jack Jarvis that first success at Royal Ascot so early in his career.

Always inclined to be irascible, Jack Jarvis had a frightening temper until he began to mellow with age; but at heart he was a kind and considerate man, and intensely loyal to anyone associated with himself or his family. It was typical of him that he gave 50-year-old Billy Warne the winning ride on Starflower II at York in 1919. Warne had served his apprenticeship with Jarvis's uncle Jimmy Ryan, and badly needed to establish himself after being interned in Germany during the war.

Another member of the Jarvis family occupied the limelight in 1921 when Basil Jarvis, the second son of Cyllene's trainer, sent out Periosteum to win the Gold Cup for Mr Ben Irish, a farmer in a big way at Sawtry in Huntingdonshire. Ben Irish was a particularly lucky owner, who had paid only 260 guineas for Periosteum as a yearling. Two years later he won the Derby, with Papyrus, whom he had bought for 3500 guineas.

Rather taller than his somewhat mercurial younger brother, Basil Jarvis was of a very much more relaxed disposition. Entering into the social life of Newmarket to the full, he was a keen cricketer and hunted regularly. His genial nature ensured that he had a widespread circle of friends, amongst whom he was invariably the life and soul of any party.

The mount on Periosteum in the Gold Cup was taken by the 36-year-old Australian Frank Bullock, whose riding was the feature of the meeting. In addition he won the St James's Palace Stakes on Lord Astor's Craig an Eran for Alec Taylor's Manton stable, which had first claim on his services, the Gold Vase on Copywright, and six other races, giving him a total of nine successes in the course of the four days. Frank Bullock was widely regarded as the most likeable of the riders who had come to England from Australia. He was a sound all-round jockey, whose subtlety and judgement of pace made him particularly effective in matches, events that were a great deal more common when there were so many fewer horses in training than there are today. By the time he retired in 1925 he had ridden 589 winners in Britain. He subsequently trained in France and India, as well as England, and was only 61 when he died in 1946.

Felix Leach performed one of the most notable feats of his long and distinguished career when he brought off the double in the Ascot Stakes and Queen Alexandra Stakes with Sir Hugo Cunliffe-Owen's Spearwort, a four-year-old colt by the Derby winner Spearmint, in 1921. Born at Wigan, Lancashire in 1868 and long one of the most popular personalities in Newmarket, Felix Leach all his life retained a style and elegance redolent of the Edwardian era, in which he had been a young man. He had come into racing as a member of Mat Dawson's staff at Heath House, Newmarket, though never formally apprenticed, as his parents wished him to keep his career options open, and was later head lad to Richard Marsh at the time that Persimmon was in the Egerton House Stable. Among his many other notable achievements was

the winning of the Wokingham Stakes of 1927 with Sir J. B. Jardine's Nothing Venture, who was ridden by his son Jack. Like his brothers Felix Leach junior and Henry Beresford Leach, always known as "Chubb" Leach, Jack Leach was apprenticed to his father. All three brothers inherited their father's debonair charm, which accounted for their being among the best-liked men on the racecourse during that era between the wars, though to the sadness of their many friends Felix died during the course of an operation for appendicitis in 1930. Felix Leach senior combined training with the management of his Meddler Stud at Kentford, near Newmarket, while his several hobbies included the breeding of game fowl and wire-haired fox terriers.

That Royal Meeting of 1921 saw the inaugural running of the Queen Mary Stakes, a five-furlong race for two-year-old fillies, named in honour of the consort of King George V. The runner-up was destined for a far more important place in history than the winner, as Mr W. E. Whineray's Wild Mint, ridden by Joe Shatwell, beat Lord Derby's Selene, the mount of Steve Donoghue, by half a length. Selene was to be the mother of Hyperion, who was to become one of the most influential sires of the present century after mixed fortunes at Ascot.

The green and brown hoops of the Aga Khan, who was to make such a strong impression of the top echelons of British racing for close on 40 years, were seen at Ascot for the first time in 1922, when he won the Queen Mary Stakes with Cos and the Windsor Castle Stakes with Tricky Aunt, a bay filly by that great stayer Son-in-Law. Aga Sultan Sir Mohamed Shah, the spiritual leader of the Ismaili sect of the Shia Muslims, was the grandson of the first Aga Khan, a Persian nobleman who had fled to Bombay with a retinue of 1000 relations and servants during a time of civil war. The family was subsequently accorded princely status by the British Raj.

The Aga Khan, born in 1877, raced horses in western India as a young man, when his interest was whetted by his friendship with Lord William Beresford, who, as already mentioned, had gone to the sub-continent as Military Secretary to the Viceroy. Coming to Europe towards the end of the century, the Aga Khan saw his first Derby in 1898, and following a visit to Lord Wavertree's Tully Stud in Ireland, set about an intensive study of the theory of bloodstock breeding, with a view to racing in England in partnership with his cousin Aga Shamsuddin. The death of the latter in 1910, increased political responsibilities, and then the First World War, caused implementation of these plans to be postponed until 1921, when he commissioned George Lambton to purchase a number of yearlings. Lambton's position as private trainer to Lord Derby precluded his training them, so the Aga Khan accepted his recommendation that they should be sent to the Irishman Dick Dawson, who had the Whatcombe stable on the Berkshire Downs.

Although endowed with a fortune befitting his rank, the Aga Khan had a highly developed sense of the value of money. On occasions he could give very serious consideration to the question of whether to tip his caddie half-a-crown or two shillings. The acquisition of wealth came as naturally as the conservation of it to this highly intelligent and cultivated man, with his cosmopolitan background. He was a natural trader for whom everything had its price, and he was to do little to endear himself to England's racing establishment by selling the Derby winners Blenheim, Bahram and Mahmoud to the United States.

Cos, the Aga Khan's first winner at Royal Ascot, returned to land the Fern Hill Stakes the following season before becoming one of the foundation mares of his stud. The most notable of her offspring was Rustom Pasha. Having run a dead-heat for the Chesham Stakes at Royal Ascot in 1929, he was successful in both the Eclipse Stakes and the Champion Stakes.

Jack Jarvis consolidated his reputation by landing the stayers' double of the Gold Vase and the Gold Cup with Sir George Bullough's Golden Myth in 1922. The four-year-old was ridden in both races by Jarvis's 17-year-old apprentice Charlie Elliott, whose father was travelling head lad in Lord George Dundas's Newmarket stable. A natural rider of superb style, Elliott was blessed with unlimited self-confidence. The previous year Golden Myth had provided him with the second leg of the double he had brought off at Nottingham on his first two mounts in public. When Jack Jarvis congratulated him he replied, "Thank you, Sir; the other kid rode well too." The "other kid" was Freddie Fox, who

Charlie Elliott – one of the greatest of all English jockeys.

had ridden his first classic winner ten years earlier.

Charlie Elliott shared the jockeys' championship with Steve Donoghue in 1923, and was still an apprentice when he won the title outright with 106 winners in 1924. He was, without doubt, one of the greatest of English jockeys. Unfortunately his incorrigible betting, which incurred the displeasure of the Jockey Club, his extravagance, and his indulgence in high living, prevented him from exploiting his natural talents to the full.

Like so many of the horses that are links in the most famous male lines, Pharos made his mark at Royal Ascot. By Cyllene's grandson Phalaris, he was ridden by Teddy Gardner to win the Chesham Stakes by six lengths in 1921. He became the sire of that great Italian horse Nearco, whose dominant line has been maintained through stallions of the calibre of Northern Dancer and Nasrullah.

The meeting of 1922 ended on a somewhat unusual note as the King's Stand Stakes was won by King Sol, ridden by Steve Donoghue in Mr J. C.

Galstaun's colours, which were not often to be seen in the rarefied atmosphere of Royal Ascot. A little Armenian of faintly comical appearance, Galstaun had arrived from India, and had horses with Captain Ossie Bell at Lambourn. His speciality was laying long odds on horses that he liked to run way below their class in selling plates, sometimes having as much as £12,000 on to win £2000. The diminutive Armenian used to scamper along the rails, while the bookmakers shouted, "Take 9/4 Corporal [or whatever the Galstaun horse was] – and not much of it!" One of his biggest coups was with King Sol, the horse destined for the sprinters' crown at Royal Ascot. He entered the horse to be sold for £100, thus obtaining a 7-lb allowance, in the Milton Selling Plate at Doncaster's St Leger meeting in 1921, and after being backed down to 7/2 on by his intrepid owner, King Sol won by four lengths. He had his inevitable reverses, but by and large the bookmakers did not enjoy the "Galstaun Era".

Racegoers at Royal Ascot in 1923 saw another of those horses that are so brilliant as to be outstanding even by the standards that invariably prevail at the meeting, for it was evident that the Aga Khan's Mumtaz Mahal had inherited the almost unbelievable speed of her sire, The Tetrarch, as well as his grey coat. On the strength of her having won at Newmarket in May on her only previous appearance "The Flying Mumty", as she was soon to be dubbed, started at 4/1 on for the Queen Mary Stakes, which she won by 10 lengths without so much as being out of a canter. Like Cos and Tricky Aunt the previous year, Mumtaz Mahal was ridden by George Hulme, a 24-year-old native of Leeds, who had served his apprenticeship with Dick Dawson. Two years later he was superseded by Charlie Smirke as the Aga Khan's jockey, and in 1929 went to Hungary to ride for his father-in-law Herbert Reeves. He remained there till his death, some fifty years later.

As many people suspected, Mumtaz Mahal was far too fast to have any chance of staying the mile of the 1000 Guineas. After being six lengths clear two furlongs out, she compounded quickly to be beaten into second place behind Plack. She was given one more chance over a mile in the Coronation Stakes at the Royal Meeting but was unplaced. On reverting to sprinting she won the King George

Mumtaz Mahal – the brilliantly fast foundation mare of the Aga Khan's breeding empire.

Stakes at Goodwood and the Nunthorpe Stakes (now the William Hill Sprint Championship) at York.

Mumtaz Mahal, who had the characteristic Tetrarch spots, played a still more important part in the development of the Aga Khan's breeding empire than Cos. Her daughter Mah Mahal was the mother of the Derby winner Mahmoud as well as Star of Iran, who bred Petite Etoile, winner of the 1000 Guineas and the Oaks for the Aly Khan, elder son of the Aga Khan. Mumtaz Begum, another of the daughters of Mumtaz Mahal, was the dam of the Champion Stakes winner Nasrullah, and of Dodoma, who bred Diabletta, winner of the Queen Mary Stakes in 1949.

King George V won both the Coventry Stakes with Knight of the Garter and the Royal Hunt Cup with Weathervane in 1923. The veteran royal jockey Bertie Jones had the mount on Knight of the Garter, but the up-and-coming lightweight Staff

Ingham rode Weathervane at 6 st 12 lb. Ingham was apprenticed to the Epsom trainer Stanley Wootton, who was responsible for coaching many of the outstanding young riders of that year including Charlie Smirke and Jackie Sirrett, and, later, Ken Gethin. Before very long, Staff Ingham grew too heavy for the flat, and after proving an outstanding rider over hurdles, began training at Epsom in 1939.

Knight of the Garter and Weathervane were the last winners at Royal Ascot to be trained by Richard Marsh. He retired at the age of 73 at the end of 1924, and lived in retirement at the Shelfords, near Newmarket, until his death in 1933.

The successor to Richard Marsh as royal trainer was Willie Jarvis, elder brother of Basil and Jack Jarvis. A man of complete integrity, Willie Jarvis was taller and more reserved than his brothers, but beneath his reticence was the same generosity and capacity for friendship. The first race at Royal Ascot that he won for the King was, appropriately, the Queen Mary Stakes with Aloysia, a bay filly by Lemberg, ridden by Joe Childs in 1925.

Joe Childs, who was intensely proud of being the King's jockey, was a great deal taller than his colleagues in the weighing-room. With dark, bushy eyebrows that gave him a somewhat gloomy appearance, he was strong-minded, apt to be argumentative to the point of being cantankerous, and convinced that the only way to win a race was to come from behind. After making all the running to win the Derby on Coronach, in accordance with the orders given him by Fred Darling, in 1926, he was so furious that he threw his saddle on the weighing-room floor in disgust.

His grandfather had been head lad to Peter Price at Newmarket, and his father had ridden with some success in France, where Joe Childs himself was born in 1884. After being apprenticed to Tom Jennings junior at Phantom House, Newmarket, he spent much of the early part of his career on the Continent. He enjoyed an excellent relationship with Willie Jarvis, whose professionalism he respected profoundly, and continued to ride for the royal stable until he retired in 1935. He died in 1958.

The 17-year-old apprentice Charlie Smirke obtained his first successes at Royal Ascot when com-

Joe Childs – proud of being the King's jockey.

pleting a double on George Hardy's Scullion in the Ascot Stakes and C. F. Kenyon's Audlem in the Gold Vase on the opening day of the meeting in 1924. The following day he rode Haine to beat Steve Donoghue on Norseman by a short head in the Bessborough Stakes. Before long Smirke would become one of the finest riders in that golden age of British jockeyship between the wars.

A cockney from Lambeth, where his father sold fruit and vegetables, Charles James William Smirke was ebulliently, often aggressively, self-confident. He never knew what it was to be nervous, and was as cool and imperturbable on Derby Day as he was at a mid-week meeting at Brighton. With his highly developed judgement of pace, his courage and his formidable strength in a finish, together with the elegant style that was the hallmark of the Wootton academy, he had all the attributes of a really great jockey. Unfortunately his abrasive manner not only made him enemies in the weighing-room, but frequently alienated owners accustomed to deference from the riders who wore their colours. Moreover his propensity for betting was soon to become common knowledge amongst the professional element on the racecourse, and to incur the displeasure of the Stewards of the Jockey Club. Four years after riding those three winners at Ascot his licence was withdrawn and he was warned off as a result of allegations that he had made no effort to start on an odds-on favourite at Gatwick. Only after five years, during which his resilience in adversity commanded respect on all sides, was his licence restored to him, in the autumn of 1933.

The sprinting star at Ascot in 1925 was Diomedes, and the staying star Santorb. Ridden by Jack Leach for Harvey Leader's Newmarket stable, Diomedes completed the double in the Granville Stakes on the Thursday, and the King's Stand Stakes on the Friday. Twelve months later he would return to obtain a third success at the Royal Meeting in the Cork and Orrery Stakes. Diomedes had been a present to 25-year-old Sidney Beer from his mother. A dapper, slightly saturnine young man, Sidney Beer belonged to a family of wealthy cotton spinners, and began owning horses when he was still in his teens. He bet very heavily indeed, and as Diomedes started hot favourite for both those races in 1925, would have been a good winner over the meeting.

Jack Leach – Diomedes' jockey in strict training.

As well as on his horses, Sidney Beer bet on his coursing greyhounds, which included the 1920 Waterloo Cup winner Fighting Force, and he loved to gamble in the casinos. Despite his youth, he was extremely shrewd, and never averse to taking the advice of his trainer. In consequence he made his betting pay.

Following a winning run in the casinos at Cannes, Sidney Beer indulged himself in another of his passions by undertaking an extensive study of classical music in London, Vienna and Salzburg. He subsequently founded the National Symphony

Orchestra, with which he toured in England and on the Continent.

Not for the first time, nor the last, St Leger form was reversed in the Gold Cup when Steve Donoghue rode Santorb to beat the Aga Khan's Salmon Trout by a length. In the previous year's St Leger Salmon Trout had beaten Santorb into second place by two lengths. Santorb was owned by Barclay Walker, a member of the Lancashire brewing family, and trained by Jim Rhodes at Lambourn. Jim Rhodes had ridden against Fred Archer and lived until 1966. He was born at Pocklington, Yorkshire, the son of a butcher, and the nephew of Jem and Luke Snowden. Apprenticed to Paddy Drislane at Middleham, Rhodes was only 20 when he went south to join Garrett Moore's stable at Lambourn. Santorb was the second winner of the Gold Cup that he trained, as he was also responsible for the success of By Jingo in 1919.

In retrospect the Trial Stakes, won by Lord Glanely's Sunderland in 1925, could be seen to be a race of some significance, as it was the one in which Gordon Richards, then 21 years of age, enjoyed his initial success at Royal Ascot. He had ridden his first winner of all at Leicester in 1921, and at the end of that season of 1925, would be champion jockey for the first of 26 times. Short and stocky, with a thick thatch of black hair that gave him his nickname "Moppy", he had been born the son of a miner at Oakengates in Shropshire in 1904, and was apprenticed to Martin Hartigan, then private trainer to Jimmy White in the Foxhill Stable. When Hartigan left to take over the Ogbourne Maizey yard, Gordon Richards went with the trainer, although White had offered £3000 for his indentures.

In the years to come Gordon Richards would set an example to younger riders by his complete integrity and utter reliability, rather than his style which was anything but orthodox. As he slewed his body round in the saddle in a finish, his weight was unevenly distributed, yet his mounts never became unbalanced and ran as straight as a die under his powerful driving. Gordon Richards would never give in until he had passed the post, and with his immense strength, which often seemed out of proportion to his size, he would wring the last vestige of energy from a horse to secure a verdict in a close

finish. Unlike Tom Cannon and other riders of the old school and his own contemporary Joe Childs, he had no special predilection for coming with a long run from the back of the field, and if he had a fault, albeit one seldom in evidence, it was impatience, as he always seemed eager to be up with the leaders. That, though, is to be hypercritical, for as the late Lord Rosebery said so succinctly, the greatness of Gordon Richards lay not in the number of races that he won, but by the few that he lost when he should have won.

One of the greatest stayers to have won the Gold Cup is Sir John Rutherford's Solario, who was successful in 1926. A really magnificent brown colt by Gainsborough, he was trained at Newmarket by Reg Day, and had won both the Ascot Derby and the St Leger in 1925. In the Gold Cup he was, as usual, ridden by Joe Childs, who could hardly have enjoyed the experience, as he had to force the pace to make full use of Solario's stamina when he found that the riders of none of the other five runners wanted to set the pace. Coming out of Swinley Bottom, Solario, the 6/4 on favourite, was still in front, with the fancied French challenger Priori II going well in second place, followed by Warminster, Zambo and Plack, winner of the 1000 Guineas for Lord Rosebery two years earlier, and finally Pons Asinorum. Almost as soon as they had turned into the straight Priori II threw down his challenge, and to the horror of thousands in the stands, headed Solario, but Childs, with the combination of caution and cunning that characterised his riding, had something in hand. With a little under a furlong and a half to cover he asked Solario to settle the issue. In a few strides the big brown colt took the measure of Priori II and, ridden out by Childs, drew away to win by three lengths, with Pons Asinorum, on whom Harry Wragg wore the pink and green stripes of Sol Joel, four lengths away third.

As a yearling Solario had been bought for 3500 guineas by Sir John Rutherford, a bachelor brewer from Blackburn, Lancashire, who outbid George Lambton, acting for the Aga Khan. In the early months of 1926 Jack Joel offered Sir John £75,000, which was politely declined. Then the Aga Khan began to have regrets that his man had been outbid for the horse, who was so obviously a stayer a great deal out of the ordinary, and asked Sir John if he would accept £100,000, an absolutely enormous sum for those days, but that too was refused. Six years later, though, Solario did have to be sold. Sir John Rutherford died at the age of 78 in February 1932, and his executors sent the 10-year-old Solario to the Newmarket July Sales. A syndicate headed by Lord Glanely was prepared to go to 40,000 guineas, only to find itself forced to go to 47,000 guineas in face of determined opposition from the United States. That 47,000 guineas paid for the Ascot Gold Cup winner was a record price for a horse sold at public auction in England, which reflects the high value placed on stoutness and stamina in that era.

Solario proved well worth the money paid for him. He was champion sire in 1937, when his son Mid-Day Sun won the Derby, and was in the the first four in the list of winning stallions on five other occasions. He got a second Derby winner in Straight Deal, successful in a wartime substitute race in 1943, and a number of other good horses including Orpen and Dastur. Among the fillies he sired were Exhibitionnist, winner of the 1000 Guineas and Oaks, Solar Flower, the mother of Solar Slipper, and Sun Princess, whose son Royal Charger was to be an influential stallion on both sides of the Atlantic.

Reg Day, the trainer of Solario, was a firm believer in giving his horses plenty of strong work in the old-fashioned way of doing things. An animal doing a good half-speed at Newmarket used to be said to be having "one of Reg Day's canters". His methods were certainly drastic by comparison with those employed today, yet they produced some impressive results from sound, tough and genuine horses, and earned him an enviable reputation as a trainer of high-class stayers. The other really outstanding horse that he had in Newmarket's Terrace House stable was Son-in-Law. As he ran during the First World War, Son-in-Law could not contest the Gold Cup, but he won the Goodwood Cup of 1914 as a three-year-old, the Jockey Club Cup twice and the Cesarewitch.

No relation to the Days of Danebury, Reg Day was the son of Fred Day, "Bushranger" Day as they called him, who had practised as a veterinary surgeon in his home town of Cheltenham before training in Australia and then returning to resume the latter profession at Newmarket. Reg Day rode at the last steeplechase meeting held at Newmarket in 1907, the same year in which he began training. Thirty-five years after he had won the St Leger with Solario, he obtained his only other classic successes when Sweet Solera brought off the double in the 1000 Guineas and the Oaks in 1961. He finally retired in 1968, and died at the age of 89 in 1972.

On the day before the triumph of Solario in the Gold Cup of 1926, the mile and a half race for three-year-olds known as the Ascot Derby since its foundation in 1834 was run as the King Edward VII Stakes for the first time, to perpetuate the memory of the sovereign who had made such a contribution to enhancing the prestige of the Royal Meeting. The winner of the first running under the new nomenclature was M. Evremond de St Alary's French-bred bay colt Finglass ridden by George Archibald and trained at Newmarket by Peter Purcell Gilpin, then a veteran of 68. Finglass, whose temperament was by no means his most endearing attribute, became a specialist at the Royal Meeting. In 1927 he brought off the double in the Churchill Stakes and the Queen Alexandra Stakes, and after being beaten a length by Ivershin in the Gold Cup 12 months later, won the Queen Alexandra again. Five months after Finglass had won at Royal Ascot for a fourth time, Peter Purcell Gilpin died at his Dollanstown home in Co. Kildare in November 1928. He had never recovered from a seizure in the spring of that year so that Finglass and the other horses in the Clarehaven stable in 1928 were trained by his son Victor.

M. de St Alary had obtained his first success in England back in 1896, when his three-year-old Arlequin had beaten Lord Durham's Son O' Mine by ten lengths in the Ascot Stakes, as already mentioned. He owned the Haras Saint-Pair du Mont near Lisieux, and was a permanent member of the committee that advised the French Ministry of Agriculture on the country's Stud Book. The best horse that he owned was Finglass's sire Bruleur, who won the Grand Prix de Paris in 1913. For a period of more than 30 years M. de St Alary had horses with the Gilpins, father and son. He was elected an honorary member of the Jockey Club in 1932, and died nine years later.

Much the most impressive winner in 1926 was

Fashionable ladies on parade.

Lord Woolavington's Coronach, on whom a highly indignant Joe Childs had been obliged to make all the running in the Derby two weeks earlier. Reverting to a mile in the St James's Palace Stakes, the huge chestnut, with his long blaze and flaxen mane and tail, beat Lex by 20 lengths.

Unlike the majority of the winners of the Queen Mary Stakes, whose precociousness was exemplified in the extreme by Mumtaz Mahal, Lord Astor's Book Law, successful in the race in 1926, trained on to stay. She obtained her second success at Ascot in the Coronation Stakes the following year, and went on to win the St Leger and the Jockey Club Stakes both over a mile and six furlongs. Book Law was the first of the three classic winners who have won the Queen Mary Stakes at the time of writing. The

other are Masaka (1947), who won the Oaks, and Waterloo (1971), who won the 1000 Guineas.

Book Law was trained by Alec Taylor, who won the Prince of Wales' Stakes with Mr Washington Singer's Chantrey and the Ribblesdale Stakes with Mr Somerville Tattersall's Foliation in 1927. Foliation was a daughter of Tracery, who had been brought down by that fanatic in the Gold Cup in 1913. Book Law, Chantrey and Foliation were the last winners at Royal Ascot trained by Alec Taylor. At the end of 1927 he handed the Manton Stable over to his former assistant Joe Lawson. In retirement Alec Taylor lived at Thorpe, near Chertsey, a few miles over the Surrey border from Ascot, until his death at the age of 80 in 1943.

The Coventry Stakes of 1927 was won by Lord

Captain Cecil Boyd-Rochfort – trained the first of a long succession of winners in 1928.

Derby's Fairway, one of the best horses to have been successful in that race. A full brother to Pharos, Fairway, a somewhat highly strung colt, started favourite for the Derby but sweated away his chance after being mobbed by his enthusiastic supporters. He did not run at Ascot as a three-year-old, and in the autumn won the St Leger, then in 1929 this great horse was back at Ascot to win the Rous Memorial Stakes by a length and a half from Winton.

Captain Cecil Boyd-Rochfort had the first of a long succession of winners at the meeting in 1928, when Captain G. P. Gough's Royal Minstrel was ridden by Joe Childs to beat Solly Joel's Porthole by three lengths in the St James's Palace Stakes. Over the next 40 years, Captain Boyd-Rochfort would achieve some of the greatest of all his feats of

training at Royal Ascot, though not without meeting more than one dramatic reversal too. For close on half a century he was to be one of the outstanding personalities there.

Tall and handsome, with an unmistakably military demeanour and perfect manners, he could have been just as successful as a diplomat or a courtier as he was at training racehorses. At the same time he had an exceptionally strong character that commanded the respect of his owners no less than it did that of his staff. He liked to do things his own way, and would not tolerate owners interfering with the minor aspects of the management of their horses. Almost without exception his owners came from the wealthiest ranks of the British aristocracy, or were American millionaires, while in the second half of his career he was also to train the royal horses. Always careful to choose his friends from men with an impeccable social background, like those for whom he trained, he kept himself aloof from the more raffish elements of Newmarket society, and was never to be seen in the racing clubs along the High Street. He remained a bachelor until he was 57.

Cecil Charles Boyd-Rochfort was born in 1887, a younger son of Major Hamilton Boyd-Rochfort of Middleton Park, Co Meath. From earliest childhood he had an affinity with bloodstock, as several members of the family owned horses, rode as amateurs or had married into racing families. After leaving Eton he became assistant to his fellow Irishman Atty Persse in 1906. Two years later he joined Captain R. H. Dewhurst at Bedford Lodge, Newmarket, and in 1912 was appointed racing manager to Sir Ernest Cassell. Serving with the Scots Guards during the First World War, he was wounded on the Somme, and, after the armistice, resumed his duties as Sir Ernest Cassell's manager, while acting in the same capacity for the American millionaire Marshall Field. He commenced training in 1923, having borrowed the £6000 with which he bought Newmarket's Freemason Lodge stable from his mother and Marshall Field.

Priory Park, the most popular handicapper of his day, was ridden by the Australian Brownie Carslake in the colours of Jack Joel, to win the Royal Hunt Cup in 1928. Earlier in the season Priory Park had been successful in the City and Suburban, while the previous year he had completed a notable double in the Lincolnshire and the Stewards Cup. The last of the 24 races Jack Joel won at Royal Ascot was the King's Stand Stakes with the grey gelding Tag End, the mount of Harry Wragg, in 1929. Both Priory Park and Tag End were saddled by Charlie Peck. Following the retirement of Charlie Morton at the end of the season of 1924, Peck had succeeded him as private trainer to Jack Joel, and the string moved to the Foxhill Stables, on its purchase from the executors of Jimmy White.

As suggested by the lack of winners at Royal Ascot, Jack Joel was considerably less successful in the second part of his racing career than he had been in the first. Rather than use stallions of the calibre of Polymelus, as he had when amongst the foremost breeders, he sent his mares to moderate

sires like Spanish Prince, in whom his faith proved badly misplaced. In consequence the stock of the Childwick Bury Stud, which he had acquired in 1907, declined.

Even the most discerning racegoers could not recognise the opening of an epoch at Royal Ascot, when a four-year-old gelding beat a colt of the same age in the Ascot Stakes in 1928. The name of the winner was Brown Jack. He was to make a more enduring impression on Ascot than any other gelding has ever done, and earn the affection of racegoers to a quite unprecedented degree. By Jackdaw, winner of the Queen Alexandra Stakes in 1912, out of Querquidella, by Kroonstad, he was owned by Major Harold Wernher (later Major-General Sir Harold Wernher), and trained by Aubrey Hastings at Wroughton in Wiltshire. His remarkable story had begun in Ireland, where he was bred by George Webb. As a yearling he was put into the Birr Show, where his breeder was perfectly confident that he would be awarded first prize, especially as there were only three other animals in his class. To his intense disappointment, Brown Jack was placed last of four, and, still worse, failed to elicit so much as a bid when submitted to the Dublin sales. Thus it was in a private deal that Brown Jack was sold for £110 to Marcus Thompson, of Kilmore House, Cashel, Co. Tipperary, shortly after leaving the ring.

Some time later the well-known trainer Charlie Rogers ran out of petrol in the vicinity of Cashel while driving to the race meeting at Limerick Junction, where he had a runner in the first race. Accordingly he called on Marcus Thompson, who obligingly agreed to run him to the course. As they were going down the drive Rogers had his eye taken by a gelding grazing in the company of a donkey. On learning the horse was by Jackdaw, to whose stock he was greatly partial, Rogers liked him still better, and forgetting all about his runner, stopped to make a thorough inspection, but eventually found the price asked by Marcus Thompson too high. Once more Brown Jack was unsold. Charlie Rogers, though, had second thoughts, and was not long in ringing his friend with a view to making a deal, with the result that Brown Jack changed hands for £275.

Rather than train Brown Jack as a two-year-old Charlie Rogers turned him out, and by way of company for him bought another gelding of much the same sort, by Achtoi, later to be known as Arctic Star. Whereas Brown Jack had been intractable and unruly as a yearling, he had become so amenable since being cut that he was positively lethargic. When in his box, he would lean against his hay net, fat, contented and dozing fitfully.

In February 1928, Charlie Rogers wrote to the Epsom trainer Vic Tabor to say that he had a couple of nice staying two-year-olds for sale, in which the other might be interested. Tabor made the journey to Co. Meath – and bought Arctic Star. Yet again Brown Jack was rejected.

Left with the three-year-old on his hands, Rogers began to train him. Towards the end of May Brown Jack had his first outing when down the field at Proudstown Park, Navan. A month later he reappeared at Phoenix Park. Although unplaced again, he left his trainer with the distinct impression that with only a bit more work he would begin to make a racehorse. Moreover Charlie Rogers noticed how the racecourse transformed him. Gone was the lackadaisical attitude he displayed at home. With his ears pricked, he was continually looking around him with an insatiable curiosity. And once out on the course, instead of slopping along as he did on the gallops, he took hold of his bit with a vengeance. The lamb had become a lion.

Scenting an imminent profit, Charlie Rogers put Brown Jack on the market by apprising Aubrey Hastings of his having something that could make a jumper for sale. As it happened, Hastings was looking for a potential top-class hurdler for Major Wernher, who lived at Thorpe Lubenham Hall, near Market Harborough in Leicestershire. The Joint Master of the Fernie, Major Wernher raced hunters and steeplechasers enthusiastically, and particularly cherished hopes of winning the newly instituted Champion Hurdle, first run the previous year, 1927.

Even though Brown Jack was still a long way from being fully furnished, Aubrey Hastings, a fine judge of a horse, recognised an element of quality in him, and was greatly attracted by his intelligent head and bold eye. The outcome of negotiations was that Brown Jack was sold to Major Wernher for £750, with a contingency of another £50 to be paid if he won a race.

The Hon. Aubrey Hastings, then 50 years old,

was the third son of the 13th Earl of Huntingdon, and one of the foremost jumping men of his generation. He rode and trained Ascetic's Silver to win the Grand National in 1906, and subsequently trained three other winners of the race, namely Ally Sloper in 1915, Ballymacad in 1917 and Master Robert in 1924.

Major Wernher, whose green and yellow vertically halved colours were to be carried by Brown Jack throughout his long career in England, was the son of Sir Julius Wernher. After being educated at Eton and Sandhurst he was commissioned into the 12th Lancers, and served throughout the First World War, being mentioned in dispatches. He retired from the army shortly after the end of the war, to become an industrialist of distinction and imagination as chairman of Electrolux Ltd and other companies.

Brown Jack made an inauspicious beginning to his life at Wroughton. Soon after his arrival he became very ill with a high fever and a temperature of 105°. All the same, he ate up with his customary relish, with hot beer, eggs and whisky supplementing his diet. As part of his treatment the top door of his box was left open 24 hours a day, and never shut again, summer or winter.

After being third on the now long defunct Bournemouth course first time out over hurdles, Brown Jack won six of his eight races before Bilby Rees rode him to beat Peace River by a length and a half in the Champion Hurdle. Steve Donoghue was at Cheltenham that day, and Aubrey Hastings asked him to watch the running of Brown Jack closely so as to be able to give an opinion whether he would be good enough for the flat. Not only did the former champion declare that Brown Jack could certainly win on the flat, but enthusiastically offered to ride him. In this way began one of the greatest partnerships in the history of English racing.

Following the totally unexpected death of Aubrey Hastings after he had played in a polo match at Cirencester in late May 1929, the Wroughton stable was taken over by Ivor Anthony, one of three sons of a Carmarthenshire farmer, who rode with conspicuous success over fences before turning to training. It was Ivor Anthony, therefore, who saddled Brown Jack when he reappeared at the Royal Meeting to try to repeat his success of 12 months

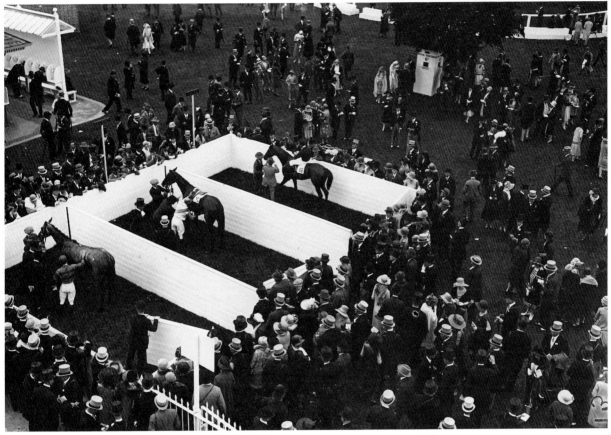

The 1st, 2nd and 3rd in the Coronation Stakes in 1926.

earlier in the Ascot Stakes. With top weight of 9 st he was undertaking no mean task. Tradescant made the running, and coming out of Swinley Bottom led from the French horse Zopyre, but once they had made the turn into the straight the race turned into a duel between Steve Donoghue on Brown Jack and Freddie Lane on Old Orkney, as the pair drew away from the rest of the field. At the lower number board Old Orkney held a slight advantage and seemed to be going rather the better of the two. But Brown Jack would never give in, and rallied all the time for Steve Donoghue. Coming to the last 100 yards Brown Jack was all but upsides, and still closing. Old Orkney, in receipt of 10 lb, was no quitter either, and in a desperately close finish Old Orkney was home by a short head.

Brown Jack came out of the race well. Ivor Anthony told the owner, now Colonel Wernher, that he was sure to win the Alexandra Stakes three days later, and the horse duly justified confidence by coming home four lengths clear with his ears pricked. The runner-up was none other than Arctic Star, who had been his fieldmate at Charlie Rogers' place back in Ireland. It was after he had won the Alexandra Stakes for the first time that Bob Lyle, racing correspondent of *The Times*, noticed that Brown Jack broke his gait as he walked back to the unsaddling enclosure, and did a sort of shuffle as though he were trying to do a jig, or dance with joy, in the knowledge that he had won.

To those who knew Brown Jack well, his having taken no harm from his ordeal in the Ascot Stakes was no surprise at all. On the contrary, they were aware he was almost certainly all the better for it. He was still every bit as indolent as he had been in Ireland, and probably even more so, as he grew older and more knowing. His intelligence told him that exerting himself on the gallops at Wroughton,

Brown Jack – six times winner of the Queen Alexandra Stakes from 1929-1934.

when he was so obviously not racing, was a waste of energy. In any case he was bored to distraction by routine in familiar surroundings. That being Brown Jack's frame of mind, Ivor Anthony had great difficulty in inducing him to put his back into his work, to bring him to racing fitness. To stimulate his interest, which was essential if he were to extend himself, Anthony consequently had to resort to boxing him up, and sending him to the working grounds at Lambourn, Manton, Beckhampton or Ogbourne Maisey.

The prospect of a new experience could always be relied upon to kindle the horse's enthusiasm.

Nothing, though, so far as Brown Jack was concerned, matched Royal Ascot. He could sense the importance of the occasion, and revelled in the glamour of it, especially when he knew that he was the star.

As had been the case in 1929, Brown Jack turned out for both the Ascot Stakes and the Queen Alexandra Stakes as a six-year-old in 1930. In the Stakes his chance was ruined in the running. After being badly placed at Swinley Bottom, he was boxed in as he tried to improve his position in the straight, with the result that he was unplaced to Bonny Boy II, whom he had beaten into second place in the race two years earlier. Three days later he met his old rivals Old Orkney and Arctic Star, now owned by Lady Curzon of Keddleston, in a field of six for the Alexandra Stakes, and avenged his defeat of 12 months earlier at the hands of Old Orkney by beating him by a length and a half, with Arctic Star a head away third.

A few months later Mailed Fist arrived at Wroughton. As a three-year-old in 1928, he had won at Sandown Park and Newcastle, while trained by Captain Boyd-Rochfort for Colonel Wernher's wife, Lady Zia Wernher. Subsequently he proved a bitter disappointment. On the gallops he showed form that guaranteed he would win a race, but would never reproduce it on the course, and Lady Zia decided to send him to Ivor Anthony to see if he were any good for hurdling. When Anthony discovered that, if nothing else, Mailed Fist could go a blistering pace for a mile and a half at home, he knew that he had the ideal horse to lead work for Brown Jack on the gallops, and make the pace for him in public. Lady Zia agreed to his being given both roles. The arrangement was ideal. As Ivor Anthony said, "One was good before breakfast and bad in the afternoon, and the other was bad before breakfast, and good in the afternoon."

Top weight of 9 st 7 lb put paid to Brown Jack's chance in the Ascot Stakes in 1931, but his third success in the Queen Alexandra Stakes, as the race was now styled, came when Mailed Fist, ridden by Steve Donoghue's son Pat, appeared at Ascot in his capacity as pacemaker for the first time. In an exact replay of the 1929 running of the race, Brown Jack came home four lengths clear of the luckless Arctic Star.

The friendship that developed between Brown Jack and Mailed Fist did nothing at all to dissipate the lethargy of the former on the working grounds. By way of refinement in idleness, Brown Jack had taken to sitting in his manger, squatting in it on his haunches as though it were an armchair. Always eager to indulge the stable favourite, Ivor Anthony covered the bare iron manger with felt to make the repose of Brown Jack more comfortable. Such fripperies were not appreciated. Next morning the felt was found in the yard, having been thrown out of the box through the ever open top door. Thinking that it was his own amateur attempt that

was inadequate, Anthony sent for a saddler, and had him lace a leather covering on to the manger. Brown Jack was not having that, either. Next morning the leather was also found in the yard. As the saddler had done his job thoroughly, Brown Jack must have taken all night to rip off the covering.

In 1932 Brown Jack was favourite to win the Gold Vase under the jumping weight of 10 st 4 lb, but was unplaced to Silvermere, to whom he was giving 34 lb. He then won the Queen Alexandra Stakes for the fourth time. Taking the lead rather earlier than usual, as he was in front before the bell rang to mark the field's entry into the straight, he ran on in great style to beat Brulette, winner of the previous year's Oaks, and more recently the Prix du Cadran, by two lengths.

Brown Jack was nine years old when he turned out for the Queen Alexandra Stakes for a fifth time in 1933. He had always been inclined to ease up when he thought he had a race in safe keeping, and the trait was becoming more accentuated. This time it very nearly cost him dear. As he eased into a common canter at the distance, Joe Childs, riding Corn Belt for Captain Boyd-Rochfort's stable, realised there was a chance of catching the 5/1 on favourite. In seconds the cheering in the stands faded into a horrified silence, as Childs, a powerful welterweight riding for all he was worth, drove Corn Belt to the quarters of Brown Jack. By the time Steve Donoghue came to appreciate the seriousness of the situation, it seemed too late, but Brown Jack was equal to the occasion. A flick of Donoghue's heel had him back to top gear, and he went away to win by a length and a half from a horse that had been foaled in the year he had won the Alexandra for the first time.

The season of 1934 promised to be rich in excitement. Lord Glanely's Colombo had been unbeaten in seven races as a two-year-old, and there seemed no knowing what he might achieve. The 2000 Guineas seemed at his mercy. Whether he would stay the mile and a half of the Derby, though, was a subject of endless discussions over the winter. Yet for many people, especially those with no more than a casual interest in racing, the classics paled into insignificance compared with the prospect of Brown Jack winning the Queen Alexandra Stakes for a sixth time at 10 years of age. Colombo was not a national hero. Brown Jack was. The public adored the old horse who had never run a bad race.

The weather was changeable and stormy on the first three days of the Royal Meeting of 1934, then, as though nature was determined to provide a perfect setting for the great occasion, the sun shone brightly from an almost cloudless sky when Brown Jack and Mailed Fist arrived at the course at 11.30 on the morning of the Friday. In large red letters the *Evening Standard* proclaimed BROWN JACK TODAY. The excitement was intense. Brown Jack was already the only horse to have won at Royal Ascot six years in succession. Now he faced a truly fearsome task for a horse of his age. Arctic Star, Old Orkney and other rivals of his youth had long departed the scene, and he was being asked to beat equally well proven opposition from a much younger generation.

Apart from Mailed Fist, seven rivals took the field against Brown Jack on that long-remembered day. As well as the good mare Nitischin, winner of the Cesarewitch, Harinero, winner of the Irish Derby, Joe Child's mount Our Hope, successful at Gatwick last time out, the useful Solatium, Benskin and Dark Dew, the French horse, there was the strongly fancied local hope Loosestrife, winner of the Newbury Autumn Cup, trained by Miss Norah Wilmot at Binfield a few miles from the course, and ridden by Gordon Richards.

A dense crowd was packed around the parade ring to watch Brown Jack being led round by his lad, Alfie Garratt. Eventually the jockeys came in. Steve Donoghue touched his cap to Sir Harold and Lady Zia Wernher, and then produced a pair of spurs.

"Shall I put these on?" he asked.

"Put on everything today," replied Sir Harold, though they both knew that Brown Jack's flanks would never feel the rowels.

Cantering down to the start Brown Jack looked as fresh as a horse of half his 10 years. All along the stands cheers, and thousands of wishes of good luck, greeted him. Alone, beneath the shade of the trees in the paddock, sat Ivor Anthony. He could not bear to watch the race.

At 4.34 the cry of "They're off!" rang out from the stands. Mailed Fist went into an immediate lead, but could not hold it for long. Passing the stands, Benskin, the mount of the champion's brother Cliff Richards had the edge on Mailed Fist. They were followed by Loosestrife and Solatium, while Brown Jack raced in company with Nitischin some lengths further away. They made the right-hand turn round the Paddock bend, then soon after they had entered the back straight, Gordon Richards sent Loosestrife to the front from Solatium. For a moment or two it looked as though the issue was already settled and that Loosestrife was poised to draw right away, but he was already under pressure shortly after coming out of Swinley Bottom, and Brown Jack went to the front, pressed by Solatium on the rails. The pair of them swept into the straight well clear of the others. While Solatium showed no signs of weakening, Brown Jack gradually, inch by inch, began to gain the upper hand, then as cheers rose, and reverberated, from the stands he established a clear lead, which he had extended to two lengths as he passed the post to win his last race.

Pandemonium broke out all over the enclosures. Hats flew in the air, staid peeresses gathered up their skirts, and men well advanced in years joined younger racegoers in the hectic rush to get a view of Brown Jack returning to be unsaddled. As he walked through the huge crowds along his path from the course to the winner's enclosure, Brown Jack looked from one side to the other, ears pricked, enjoying his ovation to the full, and totally indifferent to the souvenir hunters plucking hairs from his tail. At the gate to the enclosure, he stood stock still, oblivious to Donoghue's gentle urgings to relish the cheers a little longer, before languidly walking in to be greeted by Sir Harold, Lady Zia and the greatly relieved Ivor Anthony.

Better horses, greater horses, have won at Royal Ascot, but never one as popular as Brown Jack. Seven times he had triumphed at the meeting, and it is unlikely that his record will ever be broken. In company with his old friend Mailed Fist, he retired to the paddocks surrounding Thorpe Lubenham Hall. There he died at the age of 24 in September 1948. The memory of him is kept alive by the Brown Jack Stakes at Ascot's July meeting. During the running of both that event and his own race, the Queen Alexandra Stakes, a bronze of Brown Jack stands on a plinth at the top of the steps from the paddock to the Royal Enclosure.

In 1929, the year in which Brown Jack won the Queen Alexandra Stakes for the first time, the Aga Khan's runners dominated the two-year-old races. Blenheim, who would win the Derby the following year, beat Press Gang in the New Stakes; Tea Cup won the Windsor Castle Stakes; Qurrat-al-Ain the Queen Mary Stakes, and Rustom Pasha, a son of the first Queen Mary Stakes winner Cos, ran a dead-heat for the Chesham Stakes.

When Qurrat-al-Ain reappeared to win the Coronation Stakes in 1930, the airless atmosphere was all but stifling in its closeness, and the funereal black of the sky guaranteed a thunderstorm. Shortly before the running of the Royal Hunt Cup, the second race on the card, came the lightning, then the thunder, followed by the rain that teemed down in stair-rods, so that it seemed that The McNab came through a curtain of water to win the Cup by a length from Grand Idol. All but the police, who stood their ground steadfastly, ran for cover. Even the gatemen in their forest green coats deserted their posts in the face of such a terrifying natural phenomenon. A bookmaker sheltering beneath an umbrella in Tattersalls was struck by lightning, and killed instantly. Another flash of lightning struck the ground just in front of Somerville Tattersall as he walked down a glass-covered passage near the weighing-room, so that The McNab's trainer Fred Darling and Lord Ellesmere, who were standing nearby, believed him dead.

Very soon the paddock was awash. The track was covered with water at the junction of the round course and the straight, as well as at the Paddock bend to the left of the stands. Even the Thames Valley had never seen a storm of such ferocity. The Stewards had no option but to abandon the rest of the card and order the remaining five races to be divided between the last two days of the meeting as the bedraggled crowd dispersed.

Inevitably the Gold Cup, and the other nine races on the extended Thursday card, were run on very heavy going indeed. Lord Derby had kept Fairway in training as a five-year-old to enable him to prove his stamina in the Gold Cup, but the horse injured a tendon of a fore leg in May, and was retired immediately. This left Bosworth, a four-year-old by Son-in-Law, to represent the Stanley House stable in the

Using chairs as stepping stones after the thunderstorm in 1930.

Gold Cup, and, ridden by Tommy Weston, he gave Lord Derby his only success in the race by beating Hotweed by a length.

Two days earlier the meeting had opened with the running of the first Queen Anne Stakes, as the Trial Stakes had been renamed in honour of the founding sovereign. The winner was The Recorder, on whom Cliff Richards wore the colours of the whisky millionaire J. A. Dewar, and beat his brother Gordon on Lord Glanely's Grand Prince by a length.

The Whatcombe trainer Dick Dawson, who had been responsible for the Aga Khan obtaining instant success at Royal Ascot with Cos and Tricky Aunt in 1922, saddled his last winners at the meeting for that owner when Pomme d'Api beat Amfortas in the Gold Vase and Taj Kasra dead-heated in the Windsor Castle Stakes in 1931. Always inclined to be autocratic, Dawson was greatly given to making entries and riding engagements, as well as taking other matters into his own hands, with scant regard

Frank Butters (right) – the Aga Khan's trainer from 1932 until 1949.

for the wishes of his owners. This manner of doing things was far from being to the liking of the Aga Khan, who had a number of ideas of his own with regard to the management of his horses. Matters came to a head when there was an all but public row between owner and trainer at Newbury in the autumn of 1931, following which the Aga Khan removed his horses from Whatcombe and sent them to Frank Butters at Fitzroy House, Newmarket. This was the beginning of an almost spectacularly successful association lasting 18 years, during which many of its highlights were to come at Royal Ascot.

Like Dawson, Frank Butters completed a double at Royal Ascot for the Aga Khan in the first season that he was training for him, as Udaipur followed up her success in the Oaks by beating Lord Astor's Pennycross in the Coronation Stakes, and Dastur, who had been runner-up in the Derby, won the Kind Edward VII Stakes in 1932. Born near Vienna in 1877, while his father, Joe, was training there, Frank Butters was educated in England, and then

returned to Austria to train successfully. After undergoing nominal internment during the First World War he resumed his career in Italy. He did not train in England until he was very nearly 50, when he took over the Stanley House stable from George Lambton, who became Lord Derby's racing manager in 1927. While at Stanley House he was responsible for the successes of Fairway, that of Bosworth in the Gold Cup, and the winning of many other races, being leading trainer in both 1927 and 1928. At the end of his four-year contract, Lord Derby decided that the circumstances of the worldwide recession left him unable to afford both a trainer and a manager, and George Lambton combined both capacities again. Consequently Frank Butters moved to the Fitzroy House yard without the promise of a single horse, to conduct a public stable for the first time in his life at the age of 54 in 1931.

Frank Butters had no interest in betting, and disliked intensely having to give an assessment of a horse's chances. By way of contrast to Dick Dawson, he was deeply conscious of his obligation to the owners whose horses were in his charge. Along with Reg Day and so many other trainers rooted in the traditions of the nineteenth century, Butters believed in giving his horses plenty of strong work, despite the contingent risks of their breaking down. The Aga Khan thoroughly approved of his methods. In his memoirs, published in 1954, the Aga Khan was to write:

> In general, trainers nowadays spare their horses a great deal more than did . . . the man whom I consider the greatest trainer of all, Frank Butters. There is far too much coddling at present, far too much cotton wool.

At the end of the first season that the Aga Khan's horses were at Fitzroy House, Frank Butters was leading trainer. He also finished at the top of the list in two of the next three years, 1934 and 1935.

Although he could not match the double that his former trainer brought off for the Aga Khan at Royal Ascot in 1932, Lord Derby was not without his success at the meeting, as his bonny little chestnut colt Hyperion beat Nun's Veil, the hot favourite, by three lengths in the New Stakes. In his early days Hyperion was so puny and unprepossessing that the prospect of his ever making a racehorse

Order Out of Chaos

The central control of the totalisator at Royal Ascot which has risen on the site of the demolished luncheon rooms bordering the grandstand lawn.

Extensive rebuilding in 1931 – a new Tote building, the largest on a British racecourse.

Hyperion – Lord Derby's bonny little chestnut colt.

seemed negligible. When George Lambton took Tommy Weston to see Lord Derby's foals in 1930, he pointed to the little chestnut and said to the stable jockey, "I'm afraid I shall have to put that one down, Tommy. He'll never be any use."

As it happened, Hyperion, who was by the wartime Triple Crown winner Gainsborough out of Selene by Chaucer, did furnish up a bit, though he never grew to more than 15.2½ hands, and was sent into training. On the working grounds he did nothing to justify the decision to persevere with him, but merely seemed to confirm the first impressions of his being useless, so that George Lambton did not even bother to go to see him run when he made his racecourse debut at Doncaster in late May.

To the utter amazement of Tommy Weston, the racecourse transformed the little colt, just as it used to transform Brown Jack. Instead of ambling along in the way he did at home, Hyperion strutted round the paddock as if he owned it, and though he did not win, gave Tommy Weston a completely different feel to that which he had given on the gallops, and

ran with enormous promise behind the Aga Khan's Aidetta.

A few days later Lord Derby, Lambton and Weston were going round stables. When they came to Hyperion's box Weston said, "He'll win the New Stakes at Ascot." Lord Derby smiled indulgently at his jockey's optimism, while Lambton retorted, "Do you know what you're talking about? Have you seen what we're up against? There's Fred Darling's Nun's Veil, for one, and she hasn't been beaten yet."

"Don't worry guv'nor," replied Weston. "You ought to have been at Doncaster, and seen him run. He's a different horse as soon as he gets on a racecourse."

At Royal Ascot Hyperion showed the world that he was a racehorse. The following year he won the Derby, and then reappeared at Royal Ascot to win the Prince of Wales' Stakes before beating the Aga Khan's Felicitation in the Leger.

If the rupture between the Aga Khan and Dick Dawson the year after they had won the Derby with Blenheim was a sensation, the parting of the ways between Lord Derby and George Lambton at the end of the season in which Hyperion had won the Derby was a nine-day wonder. Lambton was then 73, and had been seriously ill for six weeks during the early summer, so that he had not been at Epsom when Hyperion won the Derby. In the circumstances Lord Derby felt he was unable to carry the responsibility of running a large stable. Lambton did not agree. He promptly bought Newmarket's Kremlin House establishment, and opened a public stable.

Lambton had trained for Lord Derby, and his father before him, for a period of 40 years. The ending of the association ensured that Hyperion's racing career ended in disaster. In place of George Lambton as trainer at Stanley House, Lord Derby appointed Colledge Leader, one of the four sons of old Tom Leader, trainer of the 1874 Derby winner George Frederick, to have stables at Newmarket, the others being Diomedes' trainer Harvey Leader, Tom Leader the younger, who concentrated on jumpers, and Fred Leader. Their sister Ethel married Jack Jarvis.

Now Coll Leader did not understand Hyperion, who was kept in training as a four-year-old in 1934 with the Gold Cup as his principal objective. He did not know that the little horse was so lazy that he needed a great deal more work than far bigger animals to bring him to racing fitness. In consequence he worked him in the conventional manner, with the result that he was a long way from being completely straight in condition when he went to Ascot for the Gold Cup. Felicitation, ridden by Gordon Richards, went into an immediate lead, lost it briefly passing the stands, and led again rounding the Paddock bend. Running into Swinley Bottom Felicitation was 10 lengths clear. With seven furlongs to run, Weston made a forward move, and shortly after entering the straight asked Hyperion for a burst of speed with which to cut down Felicitation. Hyperion responded briefly, but could not go through with his effort, and the French colt Thor II, ridden by Charlie Elliott, ran him out of second place behind Felicitation. Hyperion was also beaten in his only subsequent race, but proved an outstanding success at stud. Six times he was champion sire, and his offspring included the likes of that brilliant filly Sun Chariot, the Derby winner Owen

Tudor, Godiva, who completed the double in the 1000 Guineas and the Oaks, and the Queen's high-class colt Aureole.

Tragedy struck the Leader family during the Royal Meeting of 1933. On the opening day Fred Leader, named George Frederick after his father's Derby winner, had won the Gold Vase with H. J. Simms' Gainslaw, ridden by Tommy Weston. Returning to Newmarket he and his wife were driven by their nephew Geoff Leader, the veterinary surgeon. Between Knebworth and Stevenage the car ran into a stationary lorry. The body of the car was ripped off the chassis, and Fred Leader and his wife were killed instantly. He was only 52.

Probably the fastest filly seen at Royal Ascot in the decade before the outbreak of the Second World War was the grey Myrobella. By The Tetrarch's son Tetratema out of Dolabella, by White Eagle, she was bred by the National Stud, leased to the Earl of Lonsdale for her racing career, and trained by Fred Darling. Having failed to stay the mile when third to Brown Betty in the 1000 Guineas in 1933, Myrobella went to Ascot for the five-furlong Fern Hill Stakes and put up a splendid performance by beating Stairway by five lengths. In due course she became the dam of that brilliant miler Big Game, who won the wartime 2000 Guineas before becoming a successful stallion. Myrobella also bred Snowberry (by Cameronian), whose son Chamossaire won a substitute St Leger at York in 1945.

The Earl of Lonsdale, whose colours were carried by Myrobella, was absolutely in his element amidst the splendour and glamour of Royal Ascot. He loved anything of a theatrical nature and, in particular, enjoyed dramatising himself. Known as The Yellow Earl, on account of the colour of his carriages, the livery of his servants and the inevitable carnation in his buttonhole, he had been born in 1857. He lived in great state in Lowther Castle, near Penrith, and derived his huge income from the coal mines beneath the sea off the nearby Cumbrian Coast.

This flamboyant peer always made a point of crossing the course a few minutes before the start of the Derby, smoking a large cigar, thereby raising a huge cheer from the crowds. He was very proud of his friendship with Kaiser Wilhelm II, once a frequent guest at Lowther. As well as being a member

Directing the fashionable arrivals to the course on the first day in 1936.

of the Jockey Club, he was for many years Master of the Cottesmore and an enthusiastic patron of the prize ring. When not engaged in sport, few things gave him greater pleasure than regaling his companions with stories of his adventures in the Wild West as a young man, or how he had beaten the American bare-knuckle champion John L. Sullivan. Edward VII used to call him "the biggest liar in my kingdom". Perhaps somebody else was nearer the mark when they described Lord Lonsdale as "almost an emperor, and not quite a gentleman".

Frank Butters had his horses in all but unbeatable form at Royal Ascot in 1934, when he saddled no fewer than nine winners. For the Aga Khan he won the Churchill Stakes as well as the Gold Cup with Felicitation; the Rous Memorial Stakes with Alishah; the Waterford Stakes with Badruddin; the Coventry Stakes with Hairan; the Chesham Stakes with Shahali, and the Windsor Castle Stakes with Theft. In addition Butters won the Queen Anne Stakes with Spend a Penny owned by the theatrical magnate Sir Alfred Butt, and the Prince of Wales' Stakes with Achetan, who carried the colours of Mr Tommy Lant.

It was also in 1934 that Lord Hamilton of

Dalzell succeeded Viscount Churchill as the King's Representative at Ascot. A close personal friend of King George V, Lord Hamilton was a man of considerable vision. He was among the first to appreciate the desirability of the betting industry making a contribution to the sport on which it thrived, and was largely instrumental in the introduction of the Tote in 1928. Although a member of the Jockey Club for 44 years, and Senior Steward for three of them, he only had the occasional horse in training with Matt Peacock at Middleham, the best that he owned being Quothquan, who won the Free Handicap in 1930.

The best of those three-year-olds to win for the Aga Khan at Royal Ascot in 1934, Hairan, Shahali and Theft, was Theft, who was running for the first time. On his next appearance he was much fancied for the National Breeders Produce Stakes at Sandown Park, in which the Aga Khan was also represented by the newcomer Bahram, a 20/1 chance. To the disgust of the many backers of Theft, he was beaten by the unconsidered Bahram.

Bahram, a good-looking and powerful bay colt by Blandford, was yet another horse cast in the mental mould of Hyperion and Brown Jack, whom it was quite impossible to judge by his performance on the gallops. When he ran at Sandown Park nobody had any idea of his merit, let alone his potential, as he never did anything more than was necessary at home. Whereas Brown Jack would sit on his manger to save himself the trouble of standing, Bahram used to lean against a wall, with his fore legs crossed, revelling in admiration.

Without doubt, Bahram was one of the outstanding horses to be seen at Royal Ascot, or anywhere else, between the wars. After winning the 2000 Guineas and the Derby, Bahram provided the focal point of the Royal Meeting of 1935, and duly justified confidence by beating Portfolio by a length, on reverting to a mile in the St James's Palace Stakes. He then went on to be the 14th winner of the Triple Crown by taking the St Leger. He was never beaten, nor even extended in nine races, and they certainly never got to the bottom of him at home. Talking of the horses that he trained many years later, Frank Butters said: "Bahram was certainly the best . . . . As he was very lazy all the time, not even I knew how good he was."

On the same day that Bahram beat Portfolio in the St James's Palace Stakes, a local boy who made good was 17-year-old Douglas Smith; he obtained his first important success by riding Sir Abe Bailey's grey mare Doreen Jane to win the Ascot Stakes. She was trained at Lambourn by Harry Cottrill, who had bought her out of a selling race at Sandown Park for 360 guineas six weeks earlier. Doug Smith and his elder brother Eph had been brought up on their father's farm at Shottesbrook, just a few miles from Ascot, and had learned the rudiments of horsemanship following the Garth as well as the Berks and Bucks Staghounds. Both the Smith brothers were apprenticed to Major Fred Sneyd at Sparsholt, near Wantage. Sneyd was a harsh, humourless man, who readily commanded respect without ever inspiring affection; but he was a wonderfully good tutor of aspiring race riders, not least because of his insistence on perfection in all things. He did not believe in wasting money on pampering his apprentices. The first quarters occupied by Doug Smith at his establishment consisted of a former coal shed, shared with two other lads.

Eph Smith, two and a half years older than Doug, brought off a double at the Royal Meeting of

1935. On C. W. Gordon's Sea Bequest he won the Waterford Stakes, and on Theio, owned by Sir Laurence Philipps, later Lord Milford, the Wokingham Stakes. Both were trained by Jack Jarvis, who had had first claim on him since 1933.

As far as most people were concerned the safest bet at Royal Ascot in 1936 was Omaha in the Gold Cup. A magnificent chestnut four-year-old of 16.2½ hands, with strands of grey in his tail, belonging to the New York banker William Woodward, he was reputed to be the best horse ever to come to Europe from the United States. In 1935 he had emerged as the champion of his generation by completing the American Triple Crown: he won the Kentucky Derby on Churchill Downs, the Preakness Stakes at Pimlico near Baltimore, and the Belmont Stakes at New York's Belmont Park. Following those successes he went lame, so that he had to be retired for the season. He had arrived at Captain Boyd-Rochfort's stable in early February, and any doubts as to whether he was completely sound again were resolved when he beat Montrose by a length and a half over a mile and a half at Kempton Park in early May. Three weeks later, again ridden by Captain Boyd-Rochfort's stable jockey Rufus Beasley, he had done well to give Lord Derby's useful horse Bobsleigh 7 lb and a beating of a neck at the end of two miles on the same course.

The principal dangers to Omaha were Quashed and Valerius. Quashed was a wiry bay filly, very much on a leg, leased by Lord Derby's son Lord Stanley from her breeder Lady Barbara Smith. She had won the Oaks for the Stanley House stable in 1935. Sir Abe Bailey's five-year-old Valerius had beaten Enfield by a short head in the two-mile Yorkshire Cup the previous month. As he was by Son-in-Law he was expected to be still more effective over another half-mile. Also in the field of nine were Baron Edouard de Rothschild's French-trained Bokbul, the mount of Charlie Elliott, for whom Chaudiere was to make the pace, Robin Goodfellow, another of Sir Abe Bailey's horses, who had been second to Bahram in the Derby, Lord Glanely's Buckleigh, Evremond de St Alary's Samos II and Jimmy de Rothschild's rank outsider Patriot King.

Chaudiere made the early running, but soon gave way to Buckleigh. Approaching the straight, Buckleigh still showed the way, with Quashed close up, along with Bokbul and Chaudiere, and Omaha going ominously well in between them. Coming round the bend Bokbul ran out towards the centre of the course, carrying the improving Omaha wide. Once in line for home Quashed went to the front from Buckleigh, while Omaha, on whom Rufus Beasley was still sitting as quiet as a mouse, continued to close on them. With a furlong to go Omaha was upsides of Quashed and going rather the better of the two, so that it looked as though he would be able to come away. But not for nothing was Quashed a daughter of Verdict, who had vanquished Epinard, the pride of France, in the Cambridgeshire of 1923. With all the courage that her dam had shown on that never-to-be-forgotten occasion, Quashed fought back against the giant American colt, as they became locked in the most desperate duel seen at Ascot for many a year, while sustained and vociferous partisan encouragement came from the feverishly excited crowds in the stands. The graceful Irish rider, Rufus Beasley, made full use of his legs to keep the fast-tiring Omaha balanced, as he drove him out with his whip. On Quashed, the little Londoner, Dick Perryman, worked frantically to hold the filly together, to make the most of the last vestiges of her energy that she was giving so generously. A hundred yards out they came very close together. Inadvertently Dick Perryman knocked Rufus Beasley's whip out of his hand, but, though all too close to total exhaustion, the enormous American horse fought on in response to hands and heels, and Verdict's daughter went with him. At the post it was Quashed by a short head.

As King George V had died on 20th January 1936, the Court was still in mourning during Ascot week. Consequently the royal horses ran in the name of Lord Derby, and it was the black jacket and white cap that Dick Perryman wore when he rode Fairey to win the Waterford Stakes for Willie Jarvis's stable, beating the Aga Khan's Derby runner-up Taj Akbar by three lengths.

Captain Boyd-Rochfort soon obtained compensation for the defeat of Omaha in the Gold Cup. Twelve months later, in 1937, he sent out Lady Zia Wernher's splendid stayer Precipitation to beat Sir Abe Bailey's Cecil by two lengths. Precipitation was a chestnut by Hurry On out of Lady Zia's Cambridgeshire winner Double Life, who was by Bachelor's Double. At stud Precipitation made an important contribution to maintaining the minority line of the Godolphin Arabian, whose tail male descendants are overwhelmingly outnumbered by those of the Darley Arabian through Eclipse. As well as Airborne, winner of the Derby and the St Leger, and the St Leger winner Premonition, Precipitation got a substitute St Leger winner in Chamossaire, sire of the Derby winner Santa Claus, and the Gold Cup winner Sheshoon, who got the Prix de l'Arc de Triomphe winner Sassafras.

Fearless Fox, trained for Allan Gordon Smith by Jack Jarvis, won the Gold Vase in 1937, but was unplaced to Precipitation in the Gold Cup, and came back from the race with his offside flank covered with paint from the rails. He had certainly had a very rough passage indeed. Jack Jarvis, never a man to accept such a situation with anything remotely like patient resignation, was convinced that Tommy Burns on Raeburn had deliberately ridden to spoil the chance of Fearless Fox. Entering the jockeys' room, as trainers were allowed to do in those days, livid with rage, he secured confirmation of this impression both from his own jockey Eph Smith and from Bill Rickaby, who declared he had pulled Suzerain out from behind Fearless Fox, as he feared the latter was about to be brought down. The awful wrath of Jack Jarvis then fell upon Tommy Burns, who was designated, among a good many other things, an "Irish bastard". As Burns had been born in wedlock in Scotland, he took deep offence. Not only did he report the affair to the Stewards, who fined Jack Jarvis £25, but he brought an action for slander. Burns was represented by no less an advocate than Sir Patrick Hastings, K.C., and Jack Jarvis by another quite his match in Mr Norman Birkett, K.C., but the case was eventually settled out of court.

If Jack Jarvis looked back upon the meeting with regret, Sir Abe Bailey, most of whose string was trained by Joe Lawson at Manton, could remember it with nothing but satisfaction. As well as the Prince of Wales' Stakes with Cold Scent, Sir Abe won the Ascot Stakes with Valerian and the Rous Memorial Stakes with Dan Bulger, while in the New Stakes he ran Caerloptic, winner of the Woodcote

Stakes at Epsom, and the hitherto unraced Ram Tapa. Tommy Weston, then his retained jockey, opted for the ride on Caerloptic, and was beaten by a short head by Jack Brennan on Ram Tapa.

Sir Abe Bailey, whose black and gold hoops were so prominent at Ascot during the first 30 years of this century, was one of the greatest personalities in the heyday of the British Empire. He took part in the infamous Jameson Raid on the then Boer republic of Transvaal, and was sentenced to two years' imprisonment, subsequently commuted to a fine. A large man, with a leonine shock of grey hair in old age, Sir Abe was born in 1864, the son of the Hon. Thomas Bailey of Queenstown, Cape Colony. He played a large part in the public life of South Africa, whose parliament he entered in 1915, and was an extremely progressive farmer. At home in South Africa he ran a large stable while still a young man, and was so successful with his betting that the bookmakers were obliged to form a market without his runners. In 1895 he had his first success in England, where he bet every bit as fearlessly as he had done in his own country. A man of keen acumen and remarkable energy, he had played both cricket and football in his younger days, and was more than competent as a boxer. Even after both his legs had to be amputated when he was over 70, he would allow his activities to be circumscribed by that misfortune only to the minimum extent, and maintained his many interests. He was 75 when he died in 1940.

Captain Boyd-Rochfort, whose patience made him such a past master of the art of training stayers, won the Gold Cup for the second successive year in 1938 when Flares, carrying the Omaha colours of William Woodward, beat Buckleigh by a neck. On the first day of the meeting, by way of contrast, he had produced an outstandingly fast horse in Mrs James Corrigan's Panorama, who beat Wheatland by three lengths in the Coventry Stakes. Panorama, a fine, robust chestnut who already looked like a three-year-old became an outstandingly successful sire of fast horses. Among them was Whistler, who would emulate him by winning the Coventry.

In all, Captain Boyd-Rochfort won five races at the Royal Meeting of 1938. He was also responsible for the Duke of Marlborough's River Prince being successful in the New Stakes, J. E. Widener's Un-

Miss Dorothy Paget – heavy betting owner.

breakable in the Waterford Stakes, and Marshall Field's Foray in the King's Stand Stakes.

In common with Captain Boyd-Rochfort, and many other trainers of an earlier generation, Geoffrey Barling particularly enjoyed training stayers. In 1932, at the age of 30, he had taken over the Primrose Cottage stable at Newmarket from his father, the trainer of Lord Glanely's Derby winner Grand Parade, and appropriately gained his first notable success with James Westoll's Frawn in the two and a half mile Ascot Stakes in 1938. The following year Frawn, with Eph Smith in the saddle again, won the race for a second time.

The gaiety and pleasure-loving atmosphere at Royal Ascot in 1914 had enabled it to prolong the carefree Edwardian era four years after the death of the eponymous sovereign. The First World War had come as suddenly as a summer's storm. The Second would not. The atmosphere at Royal Ascot in 1939, therefore, was very different to that in the summer of 25 years earlier, and was fraught with tension and apprehension. The increasingly aggressive policies of Nazi Germany were making another

The course and stands in 1931.

European war look all but inevitable. Since violating the Treaty of Versailles by reoccupying the Rhineland in 1936, Hitler had seized Austria in 1938, and only as recently as March had annexed the Czechoslovakian provinces of Bohemia and Moravia. Only the politically naive could look forward with any degree of confidence to Royal Ascot taking place in 1940. All the same, everybody was determined to enjoy themselves, while the professionals got on with the business of winning races.

Basil Jarvis, who had charge of Lord Glanely's stable, while also having the horses of his older owners in the yard, provided the shipping magnate with his final successes at the meeting he had dominated in that first year of peace back in 1919. With the unnamed bay colt by the Guineas winner Colombo out of the Oaks winner Rose of England, Jarvis won him the Chesham Stakes, and with Olein, also by Colombo, the Coronation Stakes. Both mounts were taken by the stable jockey Tommy Lowrey, a sound and singularly stylish rider, who had served his apprenticeship with Fred Leader. Snowberry, daughter of that very fast mare Myrobella, and also leased to Lord Lonsdale by the National Stud, won the Queen Mary Stakes, and Sir Abe Bailey's Caerloptic made amends for being beaten by his less fancied stablemate at the meeting two years earlier by winning the Royal Hunt Cup.

The millionairess Miss Dorothy Paget had a huge bet, even by her standards, on her four-year-old Colonel Payne in the Cork and Orrery Stakes. A knee injury had prevented him from running as a three-year-old, but the brilliant speed he had shown in a gallop at Beckhampton in the late spring had convinced Fred Darling he would win at Ascot. Accordingly Darling told Miss Paget that she should have her maximum on him. Her first bet was £10,000, and by the time she had finished Colonel Payne was 11/10 on. After Colonel Payne had completely failed to reproduce his home form and finished unplaced, the owner stormed up to Gordon Richards as he was unsaddling, and demanded to know where Fred Darling was.

"I wouldn't be quite sure, Miss Paget," replied Gordon, taking the heat out of the situation, "but I've a pretty shrewd idea he's on top of the stand cutting his throat."

A large woman, with a round face and short straight hair, usually dressed in a grey overcoat that nearly touched her ankles, and a blue felt hat, Miss Paget was an unmistakable, and unapproachable, figure, usually surrounded by a large retinue of female secretaries. She rarely spoke to a man. The second daughter of Lord Queenborough, by his marriage to Pauline, daughter of the American politician William C. Whitney, she was as much out of place at a social function like Royal Ascot as Lord Lonsdale, for his part, found himself in a setting that might have been designed for him. She lived almost as a recluse in her house at Chalfont St Giles, turning night into day, satisfying her voracious appetite with colossal meals in the small hours of the morning, and then holding long conferences with her sorely tried trainers on the telephone. All arrangements with regard to her horses, very heavy betting, and almost everything else, had to be done on the telephone, or through one of those numerous secretaries. Only very occasionally would she visit a yard to see her horses. Fortunately, perhaps, for the trainers concerned, they were generally spared the ordeal of having to cope with Miss Paget for any protracted length of time, as she was constantly moving her horses from one stable to another.

Despite all the money she spent on bloodstock, she had very few good horses on the flat. With her steeplechasers she was a great deal more fortunate, as she owned the brilliant Golden Miller, winner of the Grand National and five Cheltenham Gold Cups, two other Gold Cup winners in Mont Tremblant and Roman Hackle, and other top-class performers. On the other hand she paid the top price of 6600 guineas at Doncaster sales in 1931 for an animal called Tuppence, whose homely name so caught the imagination of the nation's housewives that they backed him from 100/1 to 10/1 for Hyperion's Derby, in which he was naturally unplaced. His only meagre taste of success came when he dead-heated at Hamilton Park, thereby earning £56. The best horse that she had before the war was Wyndham, who was trained by her cousin Donald Snow and ridden by Steve Donoghue when he won the New Stakes at Royal Ascot in 1935.

The Cork and Orrery Stakes of 1939 was calamity for Miss Paget in particular, and the final race of the meeting, the King's Stand Stakes, a disaster for backers in general. Portobello, who had whipped round at the start when hot favourite for the Granville Stakes the previous day, was made favourite again. In the Granville Stakes the mount on him had been taken by Rufus Beasley, who did not seem to be riding at his best while he anticipated his wedding to the lovely, teenaged Lady Alexandra Egerton, for he had missed the break on a number of occasions recently. With Gordon Richards replacing Rufus Beasley, Portobello started at 5/2 for the King's Stand Stakes, but could only finish third to the 20/1 chance Mickey the Greek, who had been unplaced in the Cork and Orrery along with Colonel Payne.

The last winner at Royal Ascot before the outbreak of war was trained by Chubb Leach, and ridden by his brother-in-law Harry Wragg. Within a very short while Chubb Leach would be serving with the Royal Air Force Police. While being interviewed for suitability, he was asked if he could keep a secret.

"I've held a licence to train at Newmarket for 10 years. What's your next question?" replied Chubb Leach with that urbanity which characterised his family.

Thus the curtain came down on Royal Ascot for seven years, and one of the most brilliant of those lights all over Europe went out.

THE POST-WAR ERA

A S ENGLAND emerged from the horror, squalor and sheer, soul-destroying misery of the Second World War, the Royal Ascot Meeting of 1946 was one of the slightly more colourful milestones on the long, drab road back to peacetime conditions. In that era of reconstruction, dire austerity and horrendous shortages of almost everything under the sun, there could be no question of the meeting being held amidst the splendour and glamour brought by high fashion that used to make it the most important social event of the year. The King and Queen arrived in procession only on Gold Cup day, with postillions wearing blue and gold liveries instead of the traditional scarlet. Ladies wore day dresses with hats, and their escorts lounge suits or service uniform. Haute couture and morning coats would have to wait for kinder times.

For close on six years King George VI had epitomised the unity of the nation while he steadfastly refused to quit his capital at the height of the blitz, or when invasion was most imminent. Now with that solitary drive in state from the Golden Gates to the Royal Enclosure the sovereign symbolised the gradual regeneration of the country. Within the severe limits imposed by clothing coupons dressmakers had done their best to bring back a modest touch of chic to the lawns and stands, and everybody could be glad that Royal Ascot had been revived at long last, albeit in a utility edition.

The arrival of the jockeys at the weighing-room was like the reassembly of the cast of a much-loved play. There was the stocky figure of Gordon Richards, already champion 18 times, and at the age of 42 at the very height of his powers. Charlie Smirke, the irrepressible cockney with nerves of steel, was back in the saddle after going through

heavy bombardment while with the army in Italy and the Middle East. Tommy Weston, too, had known the rigours of war as a petty officer in the Royal Navy, having spent 72 hours adrift in the Atlantic after the sinking of the *Empress of Canada* in December 1943. Bill Rickaby had taken part in the North African campaign as a major in the Royal Artillery, and was picking up the threads of a career that had been shaping up well when war broke out.

Harry Wragg, the subtlest tactician of them all, had served in an anti-aircraft regiment in East Anglia, and was coming to the end of his career. Bobby Jones, as strong a man in a finish as you could wish to see, had also reached veteran status. Then there was the Irishman Michael Beary, a superb horseman with exquisite hands, Jackie Sirrett, who could still weigh out at 7 st 4 lb at the age of 40, and Billy Nevett, the "Cock o' the North", more than able to hold his own with the riders from Newmarket and Epsom. Charlie Elliott, the supreme stylist, was over from France to ride for the powerful stable of M. Marcel Boussac, while the Smith brothers Eph and Doug, who had emerged from the thirties as the leading lightweights, were very much on home ground when they came to Ascot. Of the riders who had appeared during the war, much promise was being shown by Frankie Durr, Tommy Gosling and Joe Sime, each of whom was still claiming the allowance.

When the number board was filled, the names of several riders who had been so familiar to the racegoers of the thirties were seen to be missing. Dick Perryman and Rufus Beasley, who had fought that historic duel on Quashed and Omaha in the Gold Cup in 1936, had both retired to train, Perryman at Newmarket and Beasley at Malton. And no board proclaimed the mount of S. Donoghue. The rider of the immortal Brown Jack, lovely little Diadem, and

Harry Wragg – the subtlest tactician of them all.

Stud and his bloodstock to his son Jim, whose love of racing was already well known, while the death of the 74-year-old Lord Glanely in an air raid in June 1942 had been followed by the dispersal sale of his horses. Viscount d'Abernon, for whom George Lambton trained Diadem, was 83 when he died in 1942, and St Simon's owner, the 6th Duke of Portland, whose enthusiasm for the turf had waned in later years, was 85 at the time of his death in 1943. Memories of the great coup landed over Lally in the Royal Hunt Cup in 1907 had been evoked by the deaths of three of the leading members of the Druid's Lodge Confederacy, A. P. Cunliffe, Captain Frank Forester and E. A. Wigan, in 1942.

The new era had opened, and in the hard struggle back to peacetime conditions everybody wanted a champion to help inspire their faith in the future. That champion was duly furnished by the mighty Beckhampton stable, still run by peppery little Fred Darling with his first claim on Gordon Richards. In the two-year-old Tudor Minstrel, Darling trained a colt of unmistakable class. According to the most extravagant rumours that flew around the racecourse he really was that mythical beast "The Horse of the Century", and would never be beaten over any distance, on any ground.

Owned by the whisky distiller J. A. Dewar, Tudor Minstrel was a bay colt by the wartime Derby winner Owen Tudor out of Sansonnet by the 1924 Derby winner Sansovino. A strong and robust individual of great quality, he was particularly deep through the middle, had massive quarters, and a good sloping shoulder. Making his debut at Bath on 25th April, he had beaten Wild Revel, already a winner, by five lengths with consummate ease. Just over a month later he had enjoyed another routine canter at Salisbury.

As Tudor Minstrel walked round the parade ring at Ascot prior to the Coventry Stakes, still run over five furlongs, even the most censorious racegoer found it impossible to fault the horse. Meanwhile, in the ring, those that could afford to do so, or did not care that they were unable to do so, backed him as though they were buying money, eventually laying 13/2 to the bookmakers.

Tudor Minstrel never for a moment looked like letting them down. Royal Barge, ridden by Cliff

that phenomenon of speed The Tetrarch, had died at the early age of 60 in March 1945. Another rider of the other days, never to be at Ascot again, was Freddie Fox, who had ridden Bomba, the last three-year-old to win the Gold Cup, back in 1909. He had been killed in a car crash in December 1945.

There were other absentees too. The immaculately trim figure of George Lambton was not to be seen, nor were the more substantial ones of Jack Joel and Lord Glanely. George Lambton, who remained the embodiment of Edwardian elegance long after the era had receded into history, had died at the age of 85 on 23rd July 1945, just two days after he had finally retired and handed over the Kremlin House stable to his son Teddy. Jack Joel had died in 1940, bequeathing the Childwick Bury

Fred Darling – trainer of six winners the last time he saddled runners at the Royal Meeting in 1947.

Richards, led until halfway, then Tudor Minstrel went to the front with no more effort than he had gone down to the start and drew right away to win from Patrol and Firemaster without being out of a canter. The judge gave the winning distance as four lengths. Phil Bull said it was nearer six lengths, and photographs of the race definitely support that estimate. Royal Ascot had thrown up another champion in the mould of The Tetrarch and Mumtaz Mahal, ominously – as it would prove – half-sister to Tudor Minstrel's second dam Lady Juror.

While the English racing fraternity could take patriotic pride in the emergence of a horse of the calibre of Tudor Minstrel, other events at that Royal Meeting of 1946 gave no grounds at all for satisfaction. The fact of the matter was that the French-trained horses had obtained absolute domination of the stayers' races, and were making a heavy impact in other divisions too. Wearing the orange jacket and grey cap of the textile magnate Marcel Boussac, Charlie Elliott won the Gold Cup on the hot favourite Caracalla II with the places going to two of the other French runners Chanteur II and Basileus. The following day the superiority of the French stayers was consolidated when Elliott won the Queen Alexandra Stakes on Marsyas II, another of M. Boussac's horses, with Urgay second,

and Rising Light, on whom Doug Smith wore the King's colours, third. On the same card Elliott also won the Hardwicke Stakes on M. Boussac's Pan II, while a fourth French success had been obtained by Mme J. Lieux's Sayani, the mount of Roger Poincelet, in the seven-furlong Jersey Stakes. By the end of the meeting the outlook for the English stayers and middle-distance horses was bleak.

As the riders went into the paddock before the Queen Mary Stakes, the race that followed upon the Coventry, only the professional element recognised the jockey in the light terracotta jacket with crimson chevrons, or knew the owner of the colours. They belonged to the Maharajah of Baroda, and were being worn by the 33-year-old Australian Edgar Britt, who had made his name in his own country and then in India.

The first the English knew of Yuvaraj Shimant Pritapsinha, Gaekwar of Baroda, was when he gave £50,000 to purchase a squadron of Spitfires, and undertook to replace every one that was shot down at his own expense. The ruler of a state with 3,000,000 inhabitants, he had an income of £2,000,000 and was determined to enjoy it to the utmost. Smoking huge cigars, he was a gregarious man, who loved giving parties, played a good game of golf, and was extremely generous, frequently giving half the prize money to his jockey.

After buying 10 horses from the Aga Khan for £20,000 in 1941, when he was still only 32, the Maharajah of Baroda raced extensively in India. One of those horses that he bought from the Aga Khan had the Mohammedan name of Bisharin, which Baroda, a Hindu, promptly changed to Golden Fawn. With Golden Fawn Baroda achieved the first of his racing ambitions by winning the Eclipse Stakes of India in both 1942 and 1943, Edgar Britt, whom he retained, being the successful jockey on each occasion.

Having won the Eclipse Stakes at home in India, the young Maharajah set his heart on winning the Derby, and establishing a stud in England to rival that of the Aga Khan. To that end he commissioned the Middleham, Yorkshire, trainer Sam Armstrong to buy him yearlings in 1945. At the Newmarket September Sales of that year Armstrong caused a sensation by giving 28,000 guineas, a new record price for a yearling, for the handsome brown colt by Nearco out of Rosy Legend. This colt, whose brother Dante had won the Derby earlier in the year, was named Sayajirao after one of Baroda's sons. In all 92,000 guineas was paid on his behalf for yearlings that autumn.

As well as horses, the Maharajah acquired property. For £52,000 he bought the Warren Place stable at Newmarket from Sam Darling. He paid £40,000 for a London house, and £25,000 for Hedley Grove, a country property near Epsom, where he played golf with members of the racing community. At the end of 1945, he persuaded Sam Armstrong to leave Middleham and take charge of Warren Place stable.

Frederick Lakin Armstrong, always known as Sam and then aged 41, was a son of Bob Armstrong, who had won the Ascot Stakes with Dan Dancer all those years ago in 1888, and was still training in a small way in the Tupgill Park stable at Middleham. After being apprenticed to his father, Sam Armstrong had a brief and successful career as a jumping jockey, riding his first winner at his home meeting at Carlisle in 1921. When a bad fall obliged him to give up riding in 1924, he already had 50 successes to his credit. After a spell of training in Ireland, Sam Armstrong took over the Ashgill stable at Middleham in 1926, and obtained his first success

at Royal Ascot with Bold Ben in the Wokingham Stakes in 1938.

A remarkably astute trainer, with a good head for business, as well as a horseman, Sam Armstrong would certainly have made money had he turned to commerce. He was one of the first members of his profession to realise that stables could no longer rely on the patronage of the landed aristocracy and gentry, in the way that they had traditionally done, by reason of the sea-change in the social structure of Britain, and the redistribution of wealth accelerated by the policy of the socialist government that was in office from 1945 until 1951. In consequence he relied, to a large extent, on owners from overseas to fill his yard, and would travel extensively during the close season, visiting sales and studs, and convincing wealthy men and women of the attractions of British racing.

Sam Armstrong was also a skilful coach of young riders, whose careers he promoted assiduously, thus earning a reputation comparable to that enjoyed by Stanley Wootton between the wars. Many jockeys who served their apprenticeship with him were to ride winners at Royal Ascot. As well as the champion jockey Willie Carson, they included Willie Snaith, "the pocket Hercules", Charlie Gaston, David East and the late Michael Hayes.

The Maharajah of Baroda, the new Croesus of the turf, had his first runner at the royal meeting when dapper little Edgar Britt rode Lalita in the Queen Mary Stakes. As Lalita struck the front just below the distance it looked as though the Maharajah would fulfil one of the most cherished dreams of any owner by obtaining instant success at England's most prestigious fixture; but Gordon Richards, with characteristic strength and tenacity, rallied the early leader Apparition to such good effect that she got up to beat Lalita by a neck. Apparition was owned by Mrs Reginald Macdonald-Buchanan, and, like Tudor Minstrel, trained by Fred Darling.

Another of the races won by Darling at the meeting that year was the Bessborough Stakes with Esquimault, owned by Lord Porchester, now the Earl of Carnarvon and the Queen's racing manager. Esquimault was the first of the winners that Lord Carnarvon has had at Royal Ascot over a period of more than 40 years.

In the very first race after the fixture had been

restored to The Calendar, backers nearly suffered one of those reverses that cause those who talk most vehemently through their pockets to dub Royal Ascot "The Graveyard of Good Things". Royal Charger was made hot favourite for the Queen Anne Stakes, but to the consternation of those who had laid the odds on him he lost a lot of ground by swerving when the tapes of the starting gate rose – stalls still being 21 years in the future. Fortunately Eph Smith soon had him on an even keel, was on terms with the field soon after halfway, and won by a length from Langton Abbot. Contesting the last race of the meeting as well as the first, Royal Charger was third to Vilmorin and Golden Cloud in the King's Stand Stakes. Like Reynard Volant, winner of the Ascot Stakes that year, Royal Charger was trained by Jack Jarvis for Sir John Jarvis, owner and trainer being unrelated.

The Irish took something in the order of £50,000 out of the ring when The Bug, who was still only a three-year-old, beat the older horses in the Wokingham Stakes at 7/1. Trained by the Hon. Gerald Wellesley for Mr Norman Wachman and ridden by Charlie Smirke, The Bug beat Commissar by three lengths in a canter.

As had always been the case before the war, the colours of the Aga Khan were very much in evidence, and Michael Beary was wearing them when winning the Princess Elizabeth Stakes, a five-furlong race for two-year-old fillies, on Neocracy. The first foal of Neocracy was a little colt called Tulyar, who won the Derby for the Aga in 1952.

The year prior to that first post-war Royal Ascot Meeting, Bernard Marmaduke Fitzalan-Howard, 16th Duke of Norfolk, had succeeded Lord Hamilton of Dalzell as His Majesty's Representative at Ascot. The Duke was a man whose achievements came from the conscientious determination with which he applied his mind to problems, rather than flashes of inspiration. Another of his assets was the ability to think in the long term as a result of the foresight he had developed while holding a number of public offices. He was determined to enable Ascot to maintain its position as one of the greatest racecourses in the world, with regard to both the standards of the racing and the amenities afforded to racegoers, in the face of the ever increasing competition from France, the United States and else-

where around the globe. To an extent that must have been far beyond his expectations, the Duke realised these objectives, and by the time that he relinquished office the racing at Ascot was more competitive than it had ever been, while the course itself, and the viewing and ancillary facilities, had changed out of all recognition.

Early in 1946 Sir John Crocker Bulteel became Clerk of the Course at Ascot. The son of Mr J. G. Bulteel, who had won the Grand National with that great horse Manifesto in 1899, Sir John had been a handicapper between 1926 and 1937, and subsequently obtained wide experience as Clerk of the Course by officiating at Newbury, Hurst Park and elsewhere. Sir John was unquestionably the outstanding administrative official in racing during that era, and the first to realise that as a result of social changes brought about by the redistribution of wealth, racing had to appeal to the general public as well as to owners if it were to survive.

When Tudor Minstrel reappeared at Royal Ascot to contest the St James's Palace Stakes in 1947, he was looked upon in rather a different light than he had been 12 months earlier. On the one hand he had enhanced his enormous reputation by winning the 2000 Guineas by no less than eight lengths. On the other, the limitations of his stamina were exposed when he failed to stay the mile and a half of the Derby, in which he was only fourth to Pearl Diver. Thus it was abundantly clear that he was not a horse apart from other horses; yet there remained every reason to suppose that he was one of the greatest milers ever seen. In the circumstances it is hardly surprising that he started at the old-fashioned price of 100/6 on to beat his only two rivals in the St James's Palace, Tite Street and Welsh Honey, nor that he had to do no more than canter to dispose of them, coming home five lengths clear of Tite Street, with Gordon Richards sitting right up against him. Following that second triumph at Royal Ascot Tudor Minstrel had just two more races. Unfortunately too much was asked of his stamina again when he was second to Migoli in the mile-and-a-quarter Eclipse Stakes. Then he wound up his career by returning to Ascot to win over the mile of the Knights Royal Stakes in the autumn.

Before being exported to America in 1959 Tudor

Minstrel managed to found a sprinting branch of the Hyperion male line by getting Sing Sing, the sire of Mummy's Pet. Mummy's Pet and his son Mummy's Game are among the most successful sires of fast horses at the present time. Tudor Minstrel also got Tudor Melody, the sire of the 2000 Guineas winner Kashmir II.

That Royal Ascot of 1947 was the most melodious part of the swan song of 63-year-old Fred Darling, who was to retire at the end of the season on account of his deteriorating health. As well as the St James's Palace Stakes he won the Queen Anne Stakes with Woodruffe, the Rous Memorial Stakes with Combat and the King's Stand Stakes with Greek Justice for Mr J. A. Dewar. In addition he won the Coventry Stakes with The Cobbler, who traced back to Pretty Polly in the tail female line, for Colonel Giles Loder, and the Jersey Stakes with Nebuchadnezzar, owned by the diplomat Sir Percy Loraine.

Whereas today it is fashionable to bring out the most highly regarded two-year-olds towards the end of the season, and there are now more widespread opportunities for horses of all ages than there used to be, Fred Darling and his contemporaries always set their stalls out to win at Royal Ascot. It is, of course, impossible to say which was the best of the horses with which he won there. Tudor Minstrel was certainly one of them, but Myrobella, successful in the 1933 Fern Hill Stakes, was wonderfully fast, and Coronach, who came home 20 lengths clear in the St James's Palace Stakes in 1926, was a Derby winner out of the ordinary. Fred Darling died in 1953, a few days after Pinza, whom he had bred, won the Derby.

By contrast to the St James's Palace Stakes of 1947, the Coventry Stakes was the most exciting race of the meeting, with the Maharajah of Baroda's Lerins, the mount of Edgar Britt, running a dead-heat with Mr J. Coltman's Delirium, ridden by Charlie Smirke for Jack Leach's stable. Lerins drew clear from the distance, but under the forceful driving of Smirke, Delirium finished so fast that he caught the other colt on the post.

The Maharajah of Baroda was so impressed that a jockey could enable a horse to achieve a dead-heat with Lerins, the apple of his eye, that he gave Smirke a large retainer to ride for him in each of the next two seasons. It was Smirke, therefore, who rode My Babu, as Lerins was to be renamed, to win the 2000 Guineas in 1948.

The French domination of the stayers' races continued, with Souverain winning the Gold Cup from his compatriot Chanteur II, while Monsieur l'Amiral, ridden by Smirke, beat Reynard Volant, who had won the Ascot Stakes for a second time three days earlier, in the Queen Alexandra Stakes. As Monsieur l'Amiral had been only fifth in the Churchill Stakes on the Wednesday the Stewards enquired into the apparent discrepancy in running, and, not being satisfied with the reasons offered, referred the matter to the Stewards of the Jockey Club. The latter accepted Smirke's explanation that he did not know Monsieur l'Amiral when riding him in the Churchill, never having been on his back before, and dismissed the case, after cautioning all concerned. Two other French successes were obtained at that meeting of 1947 as Charlie Elliott brought off a double for M. Boussac on Djerid in the Chesham Stakes and Nirgal in the Hardwicke Stakes.

As well as winning on Monsieur l'Amiral and achieving a dead-heat on Delirium, Smirke won two other races at the meeting. On The Bug, who had been transferred from Ireland to Marcus Marsh's Newmarket stable during the previous year, he won the Cork and Orrery Stakes, and on Masaka the Queen Mary Stakes. Masaka became the first winner of the Queen Mary to graduate to a classic triumph in the Oaks.

While Royal Ascot was necessarily dominated by the large stables of the likes of Fred Darling, Captain Boyd-Rochfort, Frank Butters and Jack Jarvis, Herbert Blagrave had an enviable record with the few runners he sent out from his small private yard. In 1947 he brought off a notable double with Master Vote, ridden by the apprentice Tommy Sidebotham, in the Royal Hunt Cup, and Saucy Sal, with Rae Johnstone up, in the Coronation Stakes. A member of a family of Berkshire squires, who owned a good deal of land in Reading and elsewhere in the county, Herbert Blagrave trained about 15 horses belonging to himself and his wife Gwen in a beautiful thatched stable at Beckhampton, just up the Bath Road from Fred Darling's establishment. He was a great friend of

The King and Queen, accompanied by Princess Elizabeth, arrive at the course for the first day in 1947.

the Paris theatrical impresario Leon Volterra, a firm believer in breeding from an admixture of the best of French and English blood, and imported several horses from France including Atout Maitre, with whom he won the Gold Vase in 1939. His other important success at the meeting before the war had been with Couvert, ridden by Cliff Richards, in the Royal Hunt Cup in 1938. For many years Colin Richards, younger brother of Gordon and Cliff, was on his staff.

As the bookmakers knew to their cost, Herbert Blagrave's winners rarely ran unbacked. A genial and kindly man, who had played cricket for Gloucestershire, Herbert Blagrave died at the age of 82 in July 1981.

Another of the winners at Royal Ascot in 1947

was Major W. N. Hillas's Oros, who gave the 37-year-old Thirsk trainer Noel Murless his first success at the meeting when Gordon Richards rode him to beat Buckthorn in the Britannia Handicap. Having taken the lead at the halfway stage of the extended seven furlongs, Oros won by five lengths without being challenged.

The son of a Cheshire farmer, Noel Murless had been a professional steeplechase jockey before beginning to train at Thirsk in 1935. After the war had interrupted his career at a vital stage in its development he quickly made his impact, being leading Northern trainer by winning 34 races in 1946 and 33, including the Stewards Cup at Goodwood as well as that race at the Royal Meeting, in 1947. Nobody had been more impressed by

Murless's attitude to his professional responsibilities than Gordon Richards. The champion jockey was struck by his absolute dedication to his horses, and tireless attention to every detail that affected their welfare. On the recommendation of Gordon Richards Murless was invited by the patrons of the Beckhampton stable to succeed Fred Darling at the end of 1947, and the offer was accepted.

When the Royal Meeting opened on 15th June 1948 racing's professionals were quite confident that the traditional success of Beckhampton would be maintained by Noel Murless, even though he was temporarily without the services of Gordon Richards, who had broken a couple of ribs in a crashing fall at Brighton shortly after the Derby. Murless had very quickly shown his aptitude for handling horses of the highest class, and had almost brought off a double with his first classic runners. Two days after The Cobbler had been beaten by a head in the 2000 Guineas, Queenpot had won the 1000 Guineas.

Readily meeting all expectations, Noel Murless produced a new star in Lt-Colonel Reginald Macdonald-Buchanan's grey two-year-old Abernant, whom Charlie Smirke rode to beat El Barq by an effortless five lengths at the end of the five furlongs of the Chesham Stakes. Bred by his owner's wife, Abernant was a colt by Tudor Minstrel's sire Owen Tudor out of Rustom Mahal, an unraced mare bred by the Aga Khan, who was by Rustom Pasha out of the flying Mumtaz Mahal. Abernant would go on to prove that he had all the absolutely brilliant speed of his grandam, and is widely regarded as the fastest horse seen in England since the end of the Second World War. He was also a great character, with a wonderfully docile temperament and an insatiable curiosity. Once when Gordon Richards had him down at the start at York he noticed some boys playing marbles, wandered over to see what it was all about, and put out a fore foot as though he wanted to play too.

As well as the Chesham, Noel Murless won the Coventry Stakes with Colonel Macdonald-Buchanan's Royal Forest, who beat the future Derby winner Nimbus, and the Rous Memorial Stakes with Oros, one of the horses he had brought with him from Thirsk to Beckhampton. Like Abernant, Oros was ridden by Charlie Smirke,

while Cliff Richards deputised for his brother on Royal Forest. The engagement of Smirke for those Beckhampton runners renewed an old association, as he had ridden the first winner Noel Murless ever trained – Rubin Wood – on the now defunct Lanark course back in 1935.

Once again the French dominated the Gold Cup, which Arbar, ridden by Charlie Elliott, won in a canter from one of his compatriots, Bayeux II. The other French stayer to win at the meeting was Estoc, who beat Vulgan by three parts of a length in the Gold Vase. Solina got the invaders off to a good start when providing Jacko Doyasbere with a successful ride in the Queen Anne Stakes, and Coronation V ran out the narrow winner of the Queen Mary Stakes.

Nirgal started hot favourite to win the Hardwicke Stakes for France for the second year in succession, but was foiled by the Maharajah of Baroda's record-priced colt Sayajirao. Making all the running in the hands of Smirke, Sayajirao beat Nirgal by two lengths, with the previous year's Derby winner Pearl Diver five lengths further away last of three. The Maharajah also won the New Stakes with Makarpura, on whom Smirke beat Edgar Britt on Golden Triumph.

The Hardwicke Stakes was the last race that Sayajirao won. He was a strong and robust colt of considerable quality, who had already justified his price by taking classic honours in the St Leger. At stud he gained a reputation as a sire of stayers by getting the likes of Indiana, who also won the St Leger, and that splendid mare Gladness, who won the Gold Cup.

Master Vote made history by becoming the first, and, at the time of writing, the only horse to have won the Royal Hunt Cup twice. With the bookmakers offering 100/8 in a field of 27, he was ridden by Rae Johnstone to come home four lengths clear of Prince Peto, for whom the 18-year-old apprentice Manny Mercer had weighed out at 6 st 10 lb. The following day Herbert Blagrave won the King Edward VII Stakes with one of his French importations, Vic Day, also ridden by Johnstone. Third to Vic Day was a long-striding low-slung liver chestnut colt belonging to Lord Derby and called Alycidon. The way he ran at the finish made it evident to the most amateur race reader that he would appreciate a very much longer distance in due course. Subsequently Alycidon finished second to Black Tarquin over the mile and three quarters of the St Leger, thereby confirming impressions that he would train on to be an absolutely top-class stayer as a four-year-old.

Seven years after inheriting the bloodstock interests of his father, Mr Jim Joel had his first winner at Royal Ascot when Joe Sime rode Lake Placid to win the King George V Stakes of 1948. Rather curiously, Lake Placid was saddled by Jack Watts, who had ridden Jack Joel's first Royal Ascot winner – His Lordship in the Wokingham Stakes in 1902. Jack Watts, who had trained for Marcel Boussac in France for a spell after winning the 1927 Derby with Call Boy, had been appointed Mr Jim Joel's private trainer in 1942. He held that post for the ten years until his retirement in 1952, dying at the age of 72 in 1959.

Mr Jim Joel is a kind and modest man of great charm, from whose generosity many a charity has benefited. Although a member of the Jockey Club, he has never taken part in the administration of racing, but has always been most approachable, and is at his happiest when talking about horses, of which he has acquired a profound knowledge during his long life. Born in September 1894, he has never lost that love of racing acquired from watching his father's horses in boyhood, and at the age of 90 braved the rainstorm that swept Ascot on the final day of the Royal Meeting in 1985 to watch Protection carry his black jacket and scarlet cap to win the Britannia Handicap.

On becoming the owner of the Childwick Bury Stud Mr Joel was faced with the problem of how to revive the fortunes of that establishment. Not only had his father bred no winner of a race at Royal Ascot in the last dozen years of his life, but he had bred no winner of any race of consequence anywhere else during that period. After much careful thought, Mr Joel decided to place his faith in mares that traced to his father's great foundation mare Absurdity, whose son Black Jester had won at Royal Ascot in 1914, as it was the only line that had consistently served the stud well, and to cull the mares from the other lines. Events were to prove he had found the right formula, and he had his first winner from the Absurdity family when King's Evidence,

who had the mare for his fourth dam, beat Poona in the Windsor Castle Stakes in 1953.

One of the highlights of the Royal Ascot of 1949 was the second meeting of Black Tarquin and Alycidon in the Gold Cup. Like Omaha, Black Tarquin was trained by Captain Boyd-Rochfort for William Woodward. Edgar Britt, who had ridden Black Tarquin in the St Leger because the Captain's stable jockey Harry Carr was out of the saddle as a result of a fall earlier in 1948, had kept the mount on him. Alycidon was to be ridden by Lord Derby's retained jockey Doug Smith, who excelled in long-distance races by reason of his superb judgement of pace. Along with the rest of the horses in the Stanley House stable Alycidon was in the temporary care of Fred Archer's nephew Willie Pratt, as his trainer Walter Earl was suffering from the tumour on the brain that was to prove fatal.

Black Tarquin had shown sufficient pace to win the Gimcrack Stakes at York as a two-year-old, and Britt had used his great acceleration to head Alycidon inside the final furlong after being towards the rear of the field of 14 for most of the way in the St Leger. Freemason Lodge was relying on the finishing speed of Black Tarquin, maximised by superb fitness. Captain Boyd-Rochfort was a past master at bringing a horse to the very peak of condition, and set about preparing Black Tarquin for the Gold Cup with characteristic thoroughness. As well as working him on the Heath in the morning, the Captain had Black Tarquin led out for a strong walk before evening stables, so that the sight of the St Leger winner striding along Bury Road in late afternoon became familiar to the people of Newmarket in May and early June 1949.

At Stanley House they had a plan that was quite simple, and utterly ruthless. Black Tarquin was to be galloped into the ground so that his speed was of absolutely no avail at all. To this end Alycidon was to have not one, but two pacemakers, with Tommy Lowrey on Benny Lynch and Percy Evans on Stockbridge.

Partisanship amongst the public was as intense as the rivalry between the two stables. Although King George VI, whose homebred horses had been at Freemason Lodge since 1943, was already a sick man he went down to the paddock to inspect Black Tarquin as excitement mounted all over the course.

So evenly was opinion divided that Black Tarquin was favourite at 11/10, with Alycidon at no more than 5/4. For the first time in four years everyone agreed that the French were out of the reckoning so that their candidate Turmoil II was a forlorn third favourite at 100/6, with Vic Day, who had been only fourth in the Leger, 20/1, the Irish horse Heron Bridge 25/1 and Alycidon's pacemakers Benny Lynch and Stockbridge at 100/1.

Stockbridge jumped off in front at such a rare gallop that he was already finished after a mile, at which point Benny Lynch went on. After another seven furlongs Benny Lynch, too, could do no more, and Doug Smith, who was just behind him as Benny Lynch began to weaken rapidly, glanced over his shoulder to see Black Tarquin still unaffected by the terrific tempo of the gallop, with Edgar Britt poised to unleash that burst of speed that had won the St Leger. Desperately Doug Smith shouted to Tommy Burns on Heron Bridge to beg him to go on, but whether or not the Scotsman on the Irish horse wanted to accede to that request, he could not, as the pacemakers had done for Heron Bridge as surely as they had done for themselves.

Realising that even the slightest slackening of the pace would play right into the hands of Black Tarquin, Doug Smith did the only thing that would ensure it was maintained by sending Alycidon to the front as Benny Lynch dropped out. Black Tarquin turned for home, ominously just behind Alycidon, then once into the straight Britt brought Black Tarquin into contention. As they raced stride for stride, Stanley House must have thought they had seriously underrated the stamina of the American horse, until Edgar Britt went for his whip at the distance. The pace had told at last. Black Tarquin cracked. This time it was Alycidon who found the speed, as he strode away over the final furlong to win the Gold Cup by five lengths.

Alycidon was undoubtedly the finest stayer to be seen in England during the 25 years that followed the end of the Second World War, and in retrospect we may see him as the best of the second half of the century, with the possible exception of Sagaro. After winning the Gold Cup Alycidon went on to complete the stayers' Triple Crown with triumphs in the Goodwood Cup and Doncaster Cup. He retired to Lord Derby's Woodland Stud at Newmarket, and

sired a number of top-class horses, to whom he transmitted his stamina, such as the St Leger winner Alcide, but after five years at stud his fertility became low, and by 1962 it was no more than 30%. The following year he was painlessly destroyed.

The last of the great horses bred by the 17th Earl of Derby, Alycidon was by Donatello II out of the Hyperion mare Aurora. Lord Derby died at the age of 82 in February 1948, when Alycidon, still a maiden three-year-old, was inherited by his grandson, the present earl. Lord Derby was much the most successful of the breeders of the thoroughbred of his era. Three of the most influential stallions of the first half of the twentieth century came from his studs – the brothers Pharos and Fairway, and gallant, indolent little Hyperion. Each, as has been seen, enhanced his reputation at Royal Ascot. Pharos won the Chesham Stakes; Fairway won the Coventry Stakes and the Rous Memorial Stakes; and Hyperion triumphed in the New Stakes and the Prince of Wales' Stakes.

Portly and rubicund, with a well-trimmed walrus moustache, Lord Derby was a genial, popular man, who smiled in public a great deal more often than most men of wealth and influence, at a time when Victorian conventions still demanded that they rigidly suppress all expressions of emotion outside the circle of their intimates. Known as "The King of Lancashire" because of his huge estates in that county palatine, he was Lord Mayor of Liverpool in 1912, four years after he had inherited the title from his father, who had engaged George Lambton to train the family's horses. Lord Derby also played a large part in public life far beyond the borders of Lancashire. After being Private Secretary to Field Marshal Lord Roberts during the Boer War he became Postmaster-General with a seat in the Cabinet in 1903. At the height of the First World War he was Secretary of State for War, then from 1918 until 1922 Ambassador to France. His eldest son, Lord Stanley, whose colours were carried to win that great race for the Gold Cup of 1936, died at the age of 44 in 1938.

The third day of the Royal Meeting of 1949 was one to remember for the 31-year-old 18th Earl of Derby. As well as the Gold Cup with Alycidon, he won the King Edward VII Stakes with Swallow Tail, who had been beaten by a head and the same into

Frank Butters' Fitzroy House yard at Newmarket.

third place in the first photo finish to the Derby earlier in the month.

Captain Boyd-Rochfort was by no means without compensation for the defeat of Black Tarquin in the principal race of the meeting. For the King he won the Coronation Stakes with Avila, ridden by Michael Beary, Harry Carr having elected to ride the heavily backed second favourite Three Weeks. On the opening day the Captain won the Gold Vase with Lone Eagle, another of William Woodward's horses, and on the final one the Hardwicke Stakes with Lady Zia Wernher's Helioscope. As the luckless Carr had no hope of making the 7 st 12 lb carried by the former, let alone the 7 st 6 lb of the latter, Lone Eagle was ridden by Britt and Helioscope by Joe Sime.

The splendidly consistent riding of Gordon Richards was, not for the first time, the feature of the four days, and by the end of the last of them the champion had seven more winners to his credit. On Abernant he made all the running in the King's

Stand Stakes to beat Cul-de-Sac by four lengths without ever having been challenged. The other two races that he won for Noel Murless were the Wokingham Stakes on The Cobbler, who defied top weight in a field of 35, giving away 41 lb in one instance, and the St James's Palace Stakes on J. A. Dewar's Faux Tirage.

For the Aga Khan and Frank Butters, Gordon Richards won the Coventry Stakes on the grey Palestine, and the Windsor Castle Stakes on Tabriz, making all the running in each instance. Gordon Richards' other two successes came on Pambidian, whom he rode for Epsom trainer Walter Nightingall in the Queen Anne Stakes, and the Irish-trained Solonaway in the Cork and Orrery Stakes.

As well as the Coventry Stakes, in which he was obtaining his sixth success, and the Windsor Castle Stakes, Frank Butters won the Queen Mary Stakes for the Aga Khan. For that event he saddled Diableretta, a granddaughter of Mumtaz Mahal, and with Rae Johnstone in the saddle she came home a very easy three lengths clear of Quarterdeck, ridden by Gordon Richards for the Beckhampton stable.

No one was to know that this was the last Royal Ascot at which Frank Butters would saddle a winner, or even attend. Although it was four years since the armistice, he continued to go everywhere on the bicycle he had used during the war in order to economise on petrol. One evening in late 1949 he was leaving Fitzroy House in the dark for a meeting of the management committee of the Rous Memorial Hospital, when he was knocked down by a lorry, sustaining serious brain injury. Despite receiving the very best surgical and neurological treatment at the expense of the Aga Khan, he never recovered the full use of his faculties, and was obliged to retire.

Frank Butters was one of the best examples of the old school of Newmarket trainers. He was a firm believer in giving his horses plenty of strong work to make them as hard and fit as possible, though the more delicate of them inevitably broke down. He was completely devoted to the interests of the patrons of his stable, and concerned only with obtaining the best possible from their horses. He never bet, and had a profound dislike of giving an opinion on the chances of his runners. He survived that terrible accident for eight years, living quietly in Newmarket until his death in 1957.

With the retirement of Frank Butters, Marcus Marsh, son of Persimmon's trainer Dick Marsh, accepted the offer to take over the Aga Khan's horses and those of the other owners at Fitzroy House, Newmarket. While training at Lambourn as a young man he had won the Derby with Windsor Lad in 1934, and having enlisted in the R.A.F. on the outbreak of war, had been shot down over Amsterdam in 1941 and taken prisoner. Resuming his career after liberation he moved into his father's old quarters at Egerton House, Newmarket.

Rufus Beasley, who had been beaten on Omaha in the Gold Cup in 1936 and won it on Precipitation 12 months later, had his first success at Ascot as a trainer in 1949. With Mr J. B. Townley's Sterope, ridden by Joe Caldwell, he won the Royal Hunt Cup.

If ever there was a year in which Royal Ascot deserved its reputation with backers as "The Graveyard of Good Things", that year was 1950.

For a long time the meeting was ruefully remembered for two horses that were beaten, rather than for any that won. In the King Edward VII Stakes Prince Simon finished second, which was beginning to become a habit on his part, and in the King's Stand Stakes Abernant was runner-up, a decidedly unusual position for him.

Had the bookmakers of 40 years erected a statue of a horse as a mark of gratitude, that horse would assuredly have been Prince Simon. He started favourite for each of the five races that he ever contested, and was second in the three that really mattered, the 2000 Guineas, the Derby and finally the King Edward VII Stakes, for which he was 8/1 on.

Another of the horses that Captain Boyd-Rochfort trained for William Woodward, Prince Simon, an American-bred bay colt by Princequillo out of Dancing Dora by Sir Galahad III, was a really magnificent specimen of the thoroughbred, with quality in proportion to his size. As the firm ground persisted throughout that dry summer of 1949, and on into an almost rainless autumn, Captain Boyd-Rochfort did not bring him out as a two-year-old for fear of prejudicing his future by running him on ground to which he was totally unsuited. The Captain, though, was looking forward to Derby Day 1950 more than he had any other, and almost everybody else in Newmarket had high expectations of the fine big colt seen out with the Freemason Lodge string every morning.

Prince Simon seemed sure to fulfil the high hopes of him when he won the Wood Ditton Stakes in a common canter first time out, but the artistry with which Smirke used the speed of the 1949 Coventry Stakes winner Palestine brought about the short-head defeat of Prince Simon in the 2000 Guineas. Prince Simon rehabilitated himself by winning the Newmarket Stakes effortlessly, then in the Derby Harry Carr had to send him to the front earlier than he had wanted, was caught by Galcador, and came again only to be beaten by a head.

On Derby form winning the King Edward VII Stakes was a formality for Prince Simon, as he had only three to beat. That trio consisted of Lord Derby's Exodus, winner from horses far below classic standard at Newmarket last time out, the Maharajah of Baroda's Babu's Pet, whose recent success had been in a maiden event at Kempton

Park, and Cagire II, who had not been out again since being fourth at the Guineas meeting.

Babu's Pet, the 20/1 outsider of the four, jumped off in front and Harry Carr, whom the Captain had instructed to ride a waiting race, held Prince Simon up some way off the very strong pace in close company with Exodus, on whom Doug Smith was executing similar orders. Never before in his life, either on the gallops or on the course, had Prince Simon been restrained, and the big colt showed how much he resented it by fighting Harry Carr all the way. Having dissipated so much energy trying to get his head Prince Simon had nothing left when at last asked to make up a considerable amount of leeway on the leader. In the short Ascot straight Prince Simon gained ground rapidly, but could not quite go through with his effort so that he failed by a head to catch Babu's Pet, and became the hottest favourite to be beaten at Royal Ascot for years.

A filling of the near fore necessitated Prince Simon being scratched from the St Leger, and he never ran again after Ascot. He returned to America to stand at stud, where he was also a failure. Eventually he was given away as a hack. So ended the sorry story of one of the most handsome horses ever to grace the paddock at Royal Ascot.

Babu's Pet, much the worst of the three horses to beat Prince Simon, was trained at Epsom by George Duller, who had been the outstanding jockey over hurdles in the years between the wars. Early in 1949 the Maharajah of Baroda, with rather characteristic capriciousness, had decided that he wanted his horses trained at Epsom so that they were nearer his Surrey home. Sam Armstrong, who had already moved from Middleham to Newmarket at his behest, had no wish to change stable again. The Baroda horses, therefore, went to Tommy Carey's Epsom yard and, as the arrangement was not a success, they passed on to George Duller.

Shortly after the sensational success of Babu's Pet at the expense of Prince Simon at Royal Ascot, the Maharajah of Baroda became deeply involved in political problems at home in India, which culminated in his deposition in 1951. In consequence it was not long before the colours of the brightest flash in the pan of post-war racing disappeared from the scene altogether. The Maharajah was only 59 when he died in 1968.

Eighteen other favourites, besides Prince Simon, had been beaten as Abernant, heavily backed at 11/4 on, and the three-year-olds Tangle and Skylarking II, ridden by Eph and Doug Smith respectively, cantered down to the post for the King's Stand Stakes, the last race of the last day. Gordon Richards had Abernant in front at halfway, and at the distance Eph Smith produced Tangle, to whom the favourite was giving a massive 23 lb. The concession of so much weight to a horse as fast as Tangle, a winner at Alexandra Park and Salisbury on his two previous appearances of the season, was too much even for Abernant, who failed to hold his challenge by half a length. Tangle was trained for Lady Baron by Bill Payne, who had been champion steeplechase jockey in 1911, in Lambourn's Seven Barrows stable, now the quarters of Peter Walwyn.

The big public gamble of the meeting had been on Gold Mist, whom Noel Murless, a strictly non-betting trainer, saddled for the Wokingham Stakes. After early backers had had 100/7 to their money Gordon Richards' mount was returned clear favourite at 6/1. A very long way from home it was clear that the money was staying in the book-makers' satchels, and at the post Gold Mist was only tenth of 24 behind Blue Book, ridden by Edgar Britt for Marcus Marsh's stable.

Some people, though, were left with happy memories of the Royal Ascot meeting of 1950. Palestine followed up his success in the 2000 Guineas by beating Rising Flame by five lengths in the St James's Palace Stakes. The Aga Khan, Marcus Marsh and Charlie Smirke also shared the success of Tambara in the Coronation Stakes.

Fulke Walwyn, who had been champion jumping trainer in each of the three seasons that followed the war as he was to be in subsequent ones, had one of his few runners at Royal Ascot when he sent Miss Dorothy Paget's Aldborough to the post for the Queen Alexandra Stakes with Gordon Richards in the saddle. Taking the lead two furlongs from home, Aldborough won by an extremely comfortable two lengths from the French-trained favourite Val Drake. The French were not to be denied success altogether, and produced another stayer of the requisite class in Baron Guy de Waldner's Fastlad, on whom Freddie Palmer beat Edgar Britt's mount Rainfall by a neck in the Gold Vase.

Another of the more positive features was a first success at the Royal Meeting for the Australian jockey Scobie Breasley, who had come to England at the outset of the season to ride for Noel Cannon, private trainer to the flour millionaire J. V. Rank in the Druid's Lodge stable. On Mr Rank's Hyperbole Breasley won the Royal Hunt Cup from Gordon Richards on the Beckhampton-trained favourite Wat Tyler, who had been shut in two furlongs out.

Another Australian newcomer, 28-year-old Neville Sellwood, was seen to still greater advantage at Royal Ascot in 1951, the year that the Festival of Britain was celebrated. He was riding for the Lambourn stable of the veteran trainer Atty Persse, who was responsible for three of his winners. Wearing the light blue and scarlet quartered colours of Major Dermont McCalmont, which had been carried by The Tetrarch before the First World War, Neville Sellwood won the Royal Hunt Cup on Val d'Assa, while on Lord Sefton's Bob Cherry he was successful in the Cork and Orrery Stakes and on Jack Olding's Stephen Paul the King's Stand Stakes. Among the foals of Val d'Assa was Verbena, who would breed the colts Vervain and Linden Tree to matings with Crepello. Vervain won the King Edward VII Stakes at the Royal Meeting in 1969 and Linden Tree was runner-up to Mill Reef in the Derby. The other race that Neville Sellwood won at the 1951 meeting was the Bessborough Stakes on Major Stanley Bates' Proud Scot, trained by Major Peter Nelson, whose stable was also at Lambourn.

Neville Sellwood, who was born in Queensland, rode very short, even by the standards of the Australians, had beautiful hands and was a fine judge of pace. Despite their success he never really had a happy working relationship with Persse, who was then 82 years of age, and went back to Australia at the end of that season. In 1961 he returned to Europe to ride for the Aga Khan in France, but was killed when the filly Lucky Seven fell with him in a race at Maisons-Lafitte in 1962.

The pink jacket with chocolate sleeves of Sir Winston Churchill, who was re-elected Prime Minister later in the year, was carried by his splendidly game grey horse Colonist II, ridden by Tommy Gosling, in the Gold Cup. On a really sweltering hot day Colonist II made most of the running, and

Major Dermot McCalmont's Val d'Assa, Royal Hunt Cup winner in 1951.

as he led into the straight aroused expectations of one of the most popular successes ever witnessed in the history of the Royal Meeting. Alizier, one of the four French challengers, came through to wrest the lead off him, as Roger Poincelet improved on another of the Frenchmen, Pan II. Colonist II fought back with all the courage of his owner and had the lead back from Alizier just as Pan II threw down his challenge at the distance. Finding the better turn of foot Pan II went away to beat Colonist II by three lengths with Alizier third.

In the King Edward VII Stakes Mrs T. Lilley's Supreme Court beat the Derby runner-up Sybil's Nephew by a length, with Fraise du Bois II, who was to win the Irish Derby, half a length away third. Supreme Court was one of many horses who began lives as ugly ducklings to find themselves swans at Royal Ascot. He was so unprepossessing as a yearling that he was not entered for the classics, and after he had failed to make a modest reserve as a yearling his breeder gave him to his wife, who sent him to Marcus Marsh. Before long Marsh returned him in order to make room for the Aga Khan's yearlings, and Mrs Lilley then sent the colt to

Flowers in the Royal Enclosure in 1952.

Kingsclere to be trained by Evan Williams, who had won the Grand National on Royal Mail in 1937. A month after his success in the King Edward VII Stakes, Supreme Court, again ridden by Charlie Elliott, returned to Ascot to win the King George VI and the Queen Elizabeth Festival of Britain Stakes, the race of the year.

Having won the Ascot Stakes with Honourable II the previous year Herbert Blagrave obtained another success at the meeting with his wife's filly Chinese Cracker, ridden by Scobie Breasley, in the Ribblesdale Stakes. Chinese Cracker, who had been second in the Oaks, was probably the best horse of either sex to be trained by Herbert Blagrave. Classic form also worked out well in the Coronation Stakes that year as Belle of All, with Gordon Richards up, became the first filly to follow up her success in the 1000 Guineas by winning that event since the end of the war. She was owned by the Hon. H. S. Tufton, and trained by Fred Darling's former travelling head lad Norman Bertie in the Bedford House Stable,

which was owned and managed by Major Jack Clayton, at Newmarket.

There was drama at the finish of the Ascot Stakes. Bill Rickaby's mount, Robin McAlpine's Royaliste IV, was sent to the front on the outside of the field a furlong and a half from home. Hardly had he gone ahead when he swerved violently to his right, interfering with Mr Maurice Kingsley's Guerrier, ridden by the apprentice Tommy Mahon for his master Willie Stephenson. The inevitable objection to Royaliste IV followed, and the race was awarded to the 20/1 chance Guerrier. While no one could quarrel with the verdict of the Stewards there is no doubt that Royaliste IV was the better horse, and would have won had he kept to a straight line. When they met again on the same terms in the Brown Jack Stakes at the July meeting Royaliste IV beat Guerrier by four lengths. Royaliste IV was one of those horses that seem to have a jinx on them. By the end of the season he was dead.

King George VI had been too ill to attend Royal

Ascot in 1951, being confined to Windsor Castle with pneumonitis. By the time the Royal Meeting of 1952 took place he had died, on 6th February, worn out by duties for which he had no training, but which he carried out with such conscientious dedication.

The most significant event at Ascot in the opening year of the reign of Queen Elizabeth II, in retrospect at any rate, occurred when 16-year-old Lester Piggott, the boy wonder of the day and champion apprentice of the two previous seasons, won his first race at the Royal Meeting when riding Mr H. E. Elvin's Malka's Boy in the Wokingham Stakes for Walter Nightingall's stable. Two furlongs out Malka's Boy took the lead and then drew away to win by three lengths from Mr Phil Bull's Orgoglio, ridden by Edgar Britt. This was the prelude to more than 100 other triumphs by Piggott at England's most prestigious fixture, and, on the darker side of the picture, to the bitter controversy of which he would be the central figure two years hence.

Although Gordon Richards was still riding with consistent brilliance as he approached his 50th birthday, Doug Smith was top jockey at that Royal Meeting of 1952 with five winners. On the opening day he landed the Ascot Stakes for Epsom trainer Johnny Dines when bringing Mrs F. B. Jackson's Flighty Frances a length and a half clear of that remarkable horse Crudwell, on whom Piggott had the mount; Crudwell was, perhaps, the most versatile performer ever to have been seen at the fixture. By the end of his career he had won no fewer than 50 races – four on the flat and seven over hurdles together with 39 steeplechases – for Frank Cundell's stable. On the final day of the meeting Doug Smith won the Queen Alexandra Stakes on Mr P Bartholomew's Medway for the stable of his father-in-law Fred Winter senior, and he also won the Bessborough Stakes on Hoar-Frost, the New Stakes on Blue Lamp and the King Edward VII Stakes on Castleton.

Although the Maharajah of Baroda had departed to cope with the problems that beset him in India, the Maharanee, who was never averse to having a good bet, continued racing. She kept one or two horses with her husband's original trainer Sam Armstrong and a few more with Major Nelson.

Each provided her with a winner at the Royal Meeting of 1952. For the Gold Cup Sam Armstrong saddled her French importation Aquino II, who had been bought from the Marquis de Nicolay after he had won two races very easily and finished fourth in the Prix Morny as a two-year-old in 1950. Gordon Richards sent Aquino II to the front just before they came to the turn into the straight and though strongly challenged by Bill Rickaby on Eastern Emperor throughout the final furlong, held on to win by three parts of a length.

On the strength of his having won at Wolverhampton, Kempton Park and Epsom on his three previous appearances, Whistler, trained for the Maharanee by Peter Nelson, started at 5/2 on for the Coventry Stakes, and, ridden by Edgar Britt, came home an easy four lengths clear of Mr W. Humble's Nearula, a newcomer from Captain Charlie Elsey's Malton stable in Yorkshire. Nearula improved out of all recognition after that first effort at Royal Ascot and won the 2000 Guineas in 1953. On retiring to stud, Whistler, a cleverly named son of Panorama and Farthing Damages, readily transmitted his speed and sired a lot of fast horses like Sound Track, Tin Whistle and Sammy Davis; he died in 1975.

The big gamble of the 1952 meeting was on Fleeting Moment in the Royal Hunt Cup. After opening offers of 10/1 had been eagerly accepted he was backed down to 6/1 to win for Tommy Bartlam's stable, but Charlie Elliott could never get him into the race, and he was unplaced to Queen of Sheba, ridden by Frankie Barlow. Like Val d'Assa, who had won the race the previous year, Queen of Sheba was a filly trained by octogenarian Atty Persse for her breeder Major McCalmont.

The Rous Memorial Stakes, the first event of the final day, was won by Wilwyn, ridden by Manny Mercer and trained by George Colling for the Kent fruit farmer Robert Boucher. The skill with which Colling placed Wilwyn was one of the features of that season, during which the four-year-old won 10 consecutive races, and then crossed the Atlantic to win the first running of the Washington D.C. International at Laurel Park. Racing was acquiring an increasingly international character as methods of transport continually improved, but standards at Royal Ascot were unimpaired.

THE NEW ELIZABETHAN AGE

ALL EYES were on the Queen, 27 years old and at the height of her beauty, practically throughout the Coronation Year of 1953, and, apart from the day on which she was actually crowned, never more so than at Royal Ascot. Second only to the Queen in the awareness of the racing community was Sir Gordon Richards, who had become the first jockey to receive a knighthood when the Coronation Honours were published in early summer. Everybody knew that the honour bestowed upon Sir Gordon was not simply a reward for professional achievement, in having ridden almost 5000 winners in 32 years, but a token of recognition of his complete integrity, and the splendid example he set younger riders. A few days after the announcement of his knighthood Sir Gordon achieved his ambition to win the Derby by riding Pinza to beat Aureole, owned by the sovereign who had so recently conferred the accolade upon him.

It was at Royal Ascot, a fortnight later, that the defeat of Aureole was avenged to some extent when the Queen's four-year-old Choir Boy won the Royal Hunt Cup from Brunetto, ridden by Sir Gordon Richards. As Captain Boyd-Rochfort's jockey Harry Carr was again unable to do the weight, Doug Smith had come in for the mount on Choir Boy.

Hats were raised by men in every enclosure as the stands exploded in an emotional volcano of delight when Choir Boy passed the winning post. As the newly crowned sovereign made her way from the Royal Box to the winner's enclosure to greet her horse and thank Captain Boyd-Rochfort, she passed through a crescendo of cheering that could be compared only with that which had acclaimed her on Coronation Day itself.

Everybody was looking forward to the first jockey ever to be knighted riding a winner for his Queen at her own meeting in the year of her Coronation. As well as her homebred horses with Captain Boyd-Rochfort, the Queen had the horses she leased from the National Stud for their racing career with Noel Murless, who had moved from Beckhampton to Newmarket's Warren Place stable towards the end of the previous season, while retaining first claim on Gordon Richards. Unfortunately the only runner that Murless saddled for the Queen at Royal Ascot in 1953 was the two-year-old Landau, a black colt by Dante out of the brilliant but temperamental triple classic winner Sun Chariot, on whom Sir Gordon was unplaced in the Windsor Castle Stakes.

By his own high standards Sir Gordon Richards obtained disappointing results at the Royal Meeting of 1953. In contrast to the mounts he had had in each of the 24 races, which yielded seven winners, on his way to setting a seasonal record with 269 successes in 1947, he had only 16 mounts at the fixture in 1953 and rode just two winners. The first was Major E. Kay's Rhinehart, trained by Major Derrick Candy, in the Jersey Stakes, and the second, which was for Noel Murless's stable, on Colonel Loder's Blood Test in the Cork and Orrery Stakes.

By far the most successful trainer in Coronation Year was Jack Jarvis. On the first day he won the Britannia Stakes with Lord Milford's Stormy Hour, a well-backed favourite at 6/1, and on the second brought off a treble with Sybil's Niece, also owned by Lord Milford, in the Queen Mary Stakes, Mr H. D. H. Wills' Happy Laughter in the Coronation Stakes and Lord Rosebery's Skye in the Ribblesdale Stakes.

If the multiple success enjoyed by Jack Jarvis at the meeting caused Eph Smith a pang of regret for ending his association with the Park Lodge trainer

Lester Piggott, with trainer Harry Wragg, won the first of over 100 races at Royal Ascot in 1952.

at the end of 1948, it was no more than natural. Eph Smith was almost stone deaf, and Jack Jarvis could be something more than forceful in his criticism of jockeys. The Gospel According to Newmarket High Street, by no means the most reliable of the testaments, had it that Eph Smith, never a man to spend his money recklessly, eventually invested in a hearing aid in 1948, found out what Jack Jarvis had been calling him for 15 years, and promptly accepted a retainer to ride for Mr Joel's stable at Sefton Lodge. Jack Watts had been succeeded by the former champion steeplechase jockey Ted Leader, who had won the Grand National on Sprig in 1927, as Mr Joel's private trainer on retirement in 1952.

Although Ted Leader did not enjoy success on the same scale as Jack Jarvis, his uncle by marriage, at the Royal Meeting 1953, he did enable Eph Smith to ride two winners for Mr Jim Joel. The two-year-old High Treason, who was one of the fastest horses of his generation, made all the running to justify favouritism by beating Ozbeg by two lengths in the Chesham Stakes, and King's Evidence won the Windsor Castle Stakes.

That year the French mounted a massive onslaught on the Gold Cup by fielding Talma II, winner of the St Leger of two years earlier, Feu de Diable, Aram, and Le Bourgeois as well as Le Flamand, and they were all beaten by Souepi. He got home by a short head from Aram, who was supposed to be making the pace for Talma II. Souepi was trained by George Digby at Exning, on the outskirts of Newmarket, owned by him in partnership with Mohammed Bey Sultan, and ridden by Charlie Elliott. Jack Jarvis always used to say it was the greatest race he ever saw Elliott ride. "A stride before the post Elliott was beaten, a stride after the post he was beaten, but on the post he won," he used to say.

The Royal Ascot Meeting of 1954 will always be remembered as the one at which 18-year-old Lester Piggott was involved in his first major confrontation with authority. Having caused a minor sensation by winning the Derby on Mr R. S. Clark's 33/1 chance Never Say Die for Joe Lawson's Newmarket stable he rode the colt again in the King Edward VII Stakes, which turned out to be one of the roughest races ever seen on Ascot Heath. Blue

Prince II, ridden by Harry Carr, led into the straight from the Derby runner-up Arabian Night (Tommy Gosling). Behind them, more or less in line abreast came Dragon Fly (Doug Smith) on the rails, Garter (Bill Rickaby) in the middle, and, on the outside, Rashleigh (Gordon Richards), with Never Say Die tucked in just behind them. As they came round the bend first Rashleigh, and then Garter, hung away from the rails towards the centre of the course so that the gap opened up between Dragon Fly, on whom Doug Smith continued to hug the rails, and Garter veering towards the middle of the course. Piggott sent Never Say Die through the gap.

About a furlong and a half from home Arabian Night passed the pacemaking Blue Prince II to take the lead without undue difficulty. Shortly afterwards the hind legs of Arabian Night seemed to lose their footing as though he had struck a patch of false ground, and he struck sharply right, crossing Blue Prince II and colliding with the rails. To prevent Blue Prince II galloping into the quarters of Arabian Night, Harry Carr took his mount away from the rails, thereby carrying the improving Tarjoman to the left. Meanwhile on the outside of the field Gordon Richards had got a run out of Rashleigh, who was hardly any better balanced than he had been when going wide on the turn. All the time that he was improving Rashleigh was hanging towards the rails so that when he passed Tarjoman, contact was made. At the post Rashleigh was a length clear of Tarjoman, with Blue Prince II half-a-length away third and Never Say Die fourth.

The Stewards, the Duke of Norfolk, Lord Allendale and Lord Derby, did three things. They lodged their own objection to Rashleigh for crossing. They withdrew their own objection to Rashleigh for crossing. They held an enquiry into the incident that had occurred during running. Now, three incidents had taken place. The first was when Lester Piggott brought Never Say Die through on the inside of Garter and Rashleigh. The second came about through Arabian Night losing his footing, cutting across Blue Prince II, who, in turn, carried Tarjoman left. The third arose when Rashleigh made contact with Tarjoman, while coming through to win the race. The Stewards, rather surprisingly, seemed to find that the last two incidents were of no relevance, and that Piggott was responsible for all subsequent trouble by going on the inside of Garter and Rashleigh on the final bend when there was insufficient space to permit such a manoeuvre.

The Ascot Stewards suspended Lester Piggott for the remainder of the Royal Meeting, and reported him to the Stewards of the Jockey Club. These were Major-General Sir Randle Feilden, Lord Willoughby de Broke and Sir Humphrey de Trafford (acting for the Duke of Norfolk), and they met for just 20 minutes the following day and informed Piggott that they had "taken notice of his dangerous and erratic riding, both this season and in previous seasons, and that, in spite of continuous warnings, he continued to show complete disregard for the Rules of Racing, and the safety of other jockeys". They withdrew his licence to ride indefinitely, and let him know that no consideration would be given to an application for its renewal until he had served at least six months in the stable of a trainer other than his father.

So Ascot, where so many of his greatest triumphs were to be obtained, provided the backdrop against which Lester Piggott received punishment of almost unprecedented severity. More than all the success that he was to enjoy at Ascot during the coming third of a century, the bitterness aroused in him by the treatment that he received from the Stewards of the Jockey Club there seemed to colour his attitude to life in general, and to authority in particular. Because of his nine previous suspensions, it appeared to many people that he had been made a scapegoat for all that had happened in a very rough race. There had been a gap between Dragon Fly and Garter on the turn into the straight. It had not only been his right, but his duty, to go through it.

Born at Wantage, then in Berkshire but now in Oxfordshire, on 5th November 1935, Lester Piggott comes from a family whose members have been prominent in the story of Royal Ascot for more than 150 years, as has already been noted intermittently. Ninety-nine years before his birth, his great-great-great-grandfather John Barham Day had won the Gold Cup on Touchstone. Of the several sons of John Barham Day, John, William and Alfred all obtained their successes training and riding successes at Ascot. John Day the younger's daughter Kate married Tom Cannon, who won the Gold Cup

on those five consecutive mounts in the race between 1877 and 1882. Tom Cannon was the father of the champion jockey Mornington Cannon, Lester Piggott's great-uncle, who won the Royal Hunt Cup on Laureate II in 1891 and Clorane in 1895 together with many other races at Ascot; Tom's daughter Margaret married Ernie Piggott. The son of a Cheshire farmer, who became landlord of The Crown at Nantwich after his stock had been wiped out by foot-and-mouth disease in the early years of the century, Ernie Piggott made his name, not at Ascot, but as a steeplechase jockey, winning the Grand National on Jerry M and Poethlyn. Ernie Piggott's son Keith was also a leading jump jockey, and married Iris Rickaby, whose father Fred won the Gold Cup on Santoi, owned by the theatrical impresario George Edwardes, in 1901. Keith and Iris Piggott became the parents of Lester Piggott.

The Royal Ascot Meeting of 1954 was the last at which Sir Gordon Richards rode. Appropriately the champion obtained his final success there when wearing the colours of the Queen on Landau in the Rous Memorial Stakes. In addition to that event and the highly controversial King Edward VII Stakes on Rashleigh, Sir Gordon won the Cork and Orrery Stakes on Key, also trained by Noel Murless, and the New Stakes on Lord Porchester's Tamerlane for Norman Bertie's stable. Three weeks later he was thrown when leaving the paddock at Sandown Park, sustained multiple injuries, including a broken pelvis, and was obliged to retire from riding immediately, rather than at the end of the season as he had planned to do.

The second winner that the Queen had at the 1954 meeting was her classic colt Aureole, whom Eph Smith rode to beat the French-trained Janitor by a short head in the Hardwicke Stakes. Like so many of the other offspring of Hyperion the bright chestnut Aureole was very highly strung, and anything but an easy ride. Eph Smith had first had the mount on him when he won the Cumberland Lodge Stakes at Ascot the previous autumn. Captain Charles Moore, the Queen's racing manager, formed the impression that the colt went better for Smith than he did for Carr, and suggested that Smith should keep the ride on him. Very reluctantly Captain Boyd-Rochfort, who was intensely loyal to his stable jockey, agreed.

A notable two-year-old double was completed for Major L. B. Holliday by Noble Chieftain in the Coventry Stakes, and Bride Elect in the Queen Mary Stakes. Both were ridden by Frank Barlow, and trained by Humphrey Cottrill in their owner's private stable at Newmarket. Bride Elect traced back in tail female line to the Major's foundation mare Lost Soul, and became the dam of his St Leger winner Hethersett.

Major Holliday, the governing director of L. B. Holliday & Co., manufacturers of aniline dyes at Huddersfield, was the most successful breeder of racehorses in Britain during the immediate post-war era. Having begun his breeding operations at the Cleaboy Stud in Co. Westmeath in 1914, he acquired a profound knowledge of bloodstock and became a good judge of horses, but was far from being a sympathetic personality. He had far too much confidence in his own opinions to give serious consideration to the views of other people. In consequence he rarely worked in harmony with his trainers and jockeys, whose association with him was not infrequently brief. For many years his horses were trained by his fellow Yorkshireman Bob Colling, an equally forceful character. Then in 1947 he purchased Newmarket's Lagrange Stable. There a succession of trainers – Major Geoffrey Brooke, Humphrey Cottrill, Major Dick Hern, Captain Jimmy James and finally Walter Wharton – had charge of the 50-odd horses for varying periods of time. Major Holliday had no doubt that training his horses was inevitably a stepping-stone to a successful career, and once remarked, "My trainers come to me on bicycles, and leave in Bentleys."

Jockeys found it equally hard to give satisfaction. Stan Clayton, who was his favourite rider, reckoned he had been sacked 11 times.

If the withdrawal of Piggott's licence was the most sensational feature of the meeting, the success of twin brother apprentices in two of the big handicaps was the most remarkable. On the first day John Forte won the Ascot Stakes on Major C. E. Raphael's Corydalis, and on the second Dominic Forte was successful in the Royal Hunt Cup on Baron P. Hatvany's Chivalry. John Forte was apprenticed to Bob Read, and Dominic, like Lester Piggott, to Keith Piggott. As the top-weight King of the Tudors led into the final furlong of the Royal

Hunt Cup, Mr F. W. Dennis's high-class horse looked assured of success, but young Dominic Forte forced Chivalry up in the very last stride to win by a short head for Tom Rimell's Lambourn stable. Next time out, King of the Tudors won the Eclipse Stakes.

The Royal Hunt Cup so narrowly won by Chivalry was the last run over its old distance of seven furlongs and 155 yards. Up to that time the start of races over that distance took place in front of the Golden Gates, which left the early running out of sight of the public, hidden by the stands. At the end of the 1954 Meeting the Duke of Norfolk gave news of the Queen having given her approval to the construction of a new course by extending the final stretch of the round course in an easterly direction sufficiently to obtain an absolutely straight mile, all of which could be seen from the stands. The realignment of the course to improve the racing as a spectacle had first been considered when Lord Ribblesdale had been Master of the Buckhounds in 1895, but he came to the end of his term of office shortly afterwards, and the matter was not pursued by his successors. The idea of a straight mile was revived by Lord Hamilton of Dalzell when he was the King's Representative at Ascot in the 1930s, only to be necessarily shelved with the outbreak of war. Finally the laying out of a straight course was begun under the supervision of the Duke of Norfolk, 60 years after it had first been mooted, and was completed in time for the Royal Meeting of 1955.

As it happened there was more time in which the work could have been carried out than was supposed. In this day and age, when the majority of racegoers come to Ascot along the motorway and trunk roads, and the runners are transported in horseboxes, it may seem strange that as recently as 1955 the success of a major meeting was dependent upon the railways. Consequently when there was a railway strike during the early part of 1955, the Royal Meeting had to be postponed for a month.

Eventually the fixture opened on 12th July, when the Queen Anne Stakes, the first race to be run over the straight mile, was won by Mr P. Bartholomew's Golden Planet, ridden by Doug Smith and trained by Fred Winter senior. Following the retirement of Sir Gordon Richards the previous summer, Doug

The TV camera position on one of the stands – on extreme right of the top tier in 1952. Under the canopy on the very top are commentators and race readers.

Smith had wound up the season at the top of the list with 129 winners to his credit. The second winner that Doug Smith rode at Royal Ascot as reigning champion jockey was the Queen's Jardiniere, trained by Noel Murless, in the King George V Stakes. Fourth to Jardiniere was Peter Pan, on whom Barry Hills, one of the outstandingly successful trainers of the present time, claimed the 7-lb apprentices' allowance.

Later on the first day Lord Porchester's Tamerlane supplemented his success in the New Stakes by winning the St James's Palace Stakes, and Miss Dorothy Paget's high-class, but ill-fated colt Nucleus was ridden by a reinstated Lester Piggott to win the King Edward VII Stakes. Nucleus was subsequently second in the St Leger, but a fortnight after he won the Winston Churchill Stakes on the old Hurst Park course in the May of his four-year-old days a tumour on his brain was diagnosed and he had to be put down in early June 1956.

The Coventry Stakes was run over six furlongs for the first time at that postponed meeting in 1955, instead of five furlongs as hitherto, and won by Sir Malcolm McAlpine's Ratification, ridden by Harry Carr for the Epsom trainer, former top jockey Vic Smyth, who had won the Gold Cup on Happy Man back in 1923. Ratification was to achieve a certain amount of success at stud, especially as a sire of brood mares. Of his daughters, Volley was the dam of the St Leger winner Commanche Run, and Ruta of Sassafras who was successful in the Prix de l'Arc de Triomphe in 1970.

The English stayers were once more vanquished in the Gold Cup, but this time by a challenger from Italy, not France. The winner was Botticelli, a bay colt by the 1939 Derby winner Blue Peter, trained by his owner the Marchese Incisa della Rochetta and ridden by Enrico Camici. Taking the lead two furlongs out, Botticelli ran on in really great style to win by three lengths from Blue Prince II, the colt that had been runner-up to Rashleigh in that highly contentious race for the King Edward VII Stakes at the meeting the previous year. Earlier in his career Botticelli had won the Derby Italiano.

The first Royal Hunt Cup run on the straight mile proved a triumph for the handicapper and a disaster for backers. The winner was the 50/1 shot Nicholas Nickleby, on whom Willie Snaith, the

"pocket Hercules", beat Doug Smith's mount Coronation Year by a short head, with Comic Turn another short head away third. Nicholas Nickleby was trained by Sam Armstrong for the South African steel manufacturer Mr Jack Gerber.

On the third day Gratitude, ridden by Doug Smith in the colours of Major Holliday, justified favouritism in the New Stakes, then after Mr Jabez Barker's Prince Barle had been ridden by Manny Mercer for Joe Lawson's stable to win the Gold Vase, Ascot Heath was struck by one of the most highly charged thunderstorms ever known in the Thames Valley. A streak of lightning shot the length of the straight. One woman was killed, and many people were knocked to the ground; a number of them had to be taken to hospital.

The Ribblesdale Stakes was delayed 40 minutes while the storm abated, and when at last the race could be run Oaks form was upheld, with Mr R. D. Hollingsworth's Ark Royal winning by four lengths from Reel In; the pair of them had been second and third respectively to Meld in the Epsom classic. Following that success on the part of Ark Royal, proceedings for the day were concluded. Of the two races that it had not been possible to run the Bessborough Stakes was run on the Friday and the Rous Memorial Stakes on the Saturday, which is not part of the Royal Meeting.

The Aga Khan had his first success at the meeting since concentrating his horses in training in France at the end of the season of 1952 when Palariva, whom he had with Alec Head, won the Chesham Stakes. Making all the running, she won by an impressive three lengths from Gilles de Retz, who would be successful in the 2000 Guineas the following year.

Palariva was yet another Royal Ascot winner for the Aga Khan to descend from Mumtaz Mahal in tail female line. She was by Palestine, who had completed the double in the Coventry Stakes and the St James's Palace Stakes, out of Rivaz, winner of the Queen Mary Stakes at a one-day meeting in 1945. Rivaz was by Nearco out of Mumtaz Begum, who was by Blenheim out of Mumtaz Mahal.

Lady Zia Wernher's Meld, possibly the best filly to be seen at Ascot during the decade, reverted from the mile and a half of the Oaks to a mile in the Coronation Stakes. With odds of 9/4 laid on her she

The Queen's Alexander, ridden by Harry Carr, winning the Royal Hunt Cup from Jaspe and Blue Robe in 1956.

beat Gloria Nicky by five lengths without even being challenged, and then went on to win the St Leger from Nucleus. At stud she became the dam of the Derby winner Charlottown.

Having lost heavily over the Royal Hunt Cup, backers were dealt another blow in the Wokingham Stakes when there was a wholesale gamble on Lord Rosebery's three-year-old grey filly Aberlady, who had been runner-up to Meld in the 1000 Guineas. Having opened up at 8/1 she was backed down to start clear favourite at 4/1, but after showing speed for four and a half furlongs, dropped back to be unplaced to Lord Ashcombe's 25/1 chance The Plumber's Mate, on whom Duncan Keith claimed the 7-lb allowance.

As the Australian rider Rae Johnstone brought Adare back to the unsaddling enclosure after a comfortable success in the Jersey Stakes in 1956, his trainer looked rather out of place to English eyes. The previous year he had won the Grand National for the third season in succession, and he had also

saddled four winners of the Cheltenham Gold Cup and brought off a hat-trick in the Champion Hurdle. Now Vincent O'Brien was enjoying his first success at Royal Ascot, where he was to become so familiar with the winner's enclosure over more than three decades.

Later the same afternoon the Queen won the Royal Hunt Cup for the second time. Ridden by Harry Carr for Captain Boyd-Rochfort's stable, Alexander justified favouritism by beating Jasper, the mount of Rae Johnstone, by half a length. Captain Boyd-Rochfort and Harry Carr had also shared the success of Mr T. J. S. Gray's Zarathustra in the Ascot Stakes the previous day.

Harry Carr, who was successful on Meld, Zarathustra and so many other high-class horses at Ascot, rode for Captain Boyd-Rochfort for the 18 years until he retired from the saddle in 1964. Throughout that period he performed his duties as stable jockey in exemplary manner, sparing no pains to get to know every horse in the Freemason Lodge yard, and riding out with the string almost every morning, not just on galloping days. Moreover it would never have occurred to him to beg off one of the Captain's runners if he were offered the mount on a more fancied horse.

When Harry Carr was born in November 1916, his father Bobby Carr was travelling head lad to Bob Armstrong, who was still training on Lord Lonsdale's estate near Penrith. On Armstrong's moving into the Tupgill stable at Middleham in 1923, Bobby Carr and his family went with him, and it was there that Harry Carr served his apprenticeship with Armstrong, riding his first winner on Knight's Folly at Ayr in 1931. At the end of his apprenticeship he became one of the leading jockeys in India during the seasons preceding the outbreak of war. Returning to England in 1946, he was given very little riding and was seriously considering returning to India, but despite limited opportunities impressed a number of good judges in the North, notably Lieutenant-Colonel A. P. Curzon-Herrick, the stipendiary steward, by his quiet competence, good manners and natural dignity. It was on the recommendation of Curzon-Herrick that this little-known rider, as much to his own astonishment as that of almost everybody else, was appointed to succeed Doug Smith as first jockey to Captain Boyd-Rochfort for the outset of the season of 1947. As the man who wore the royal colours more often than any other jockey, Harry Carr was to be one of the central figures at Ascot for close on two decades.

In retirement he ran the Genesis Green Stud, which he had founded in 1958, at Wickhambrook near Newmarket. He died suddenly in October 1985. His daughter Anne married Joe Mercer.

The French horses dominated the Gold Cup to a greater extent than ever before in 1956 by filling five of the first six places. Charlie Elliott, who had retired from the saddle at the end of 1953 to train for M. Boussac in France, provided the winner in Macip, ridden by Serge Boullenger. Making every yard of the running, Macip won by a length and a half from Bewitched III, the mount of Jean Massard, with Freddie Palmer third on Clichy.

It was not only in the tests of stamina that the French horses triumphed. Palariva returned to win the King's Stand Stakes and Alec Head also won the Coronation Stakes with M. Pierre Wertheimer's Midget II, a fine, big grey who belied her name. Palariva became the grandam of the French 2000 Guineas winner Kalamoun and Habat, while Midget II was the dam of Mige, winner of the Cheveley Park Stakes in 1968.

The Irish obtained their second success of the meeting when Mr F. Blackall's Skindles Hotel, trained by Paddy Prendergast, beat the hot favourite Ennis by a comfortable three lengths in the New Stakes. Skindles Hotel was ridden by Brian Swift, the son of the successful bookmaker Jack Swift. Brian Swift, who married Scobie Breasley's daughter Loretta, subsequently trained a lot of winners, notably fast two-year-olds like Skindles Hotel, at Epsom, but, sadly, died when only 48 in 1985.

The Royal Meeting of 1957 opened in an atmosphere of apprehension brought about by tension in the international situation, and uncertainty on the political front at home. The previous November the nation had been embroiled in the Suez crisis, which had culminated in the unsuccessful attempt by the Anglo-French forces to occupy the Canal Zone. The same month Russian tanks had rolled into Budapest to suppress the popular rising in Hungary. In January the Prime Minister, Sir Anthony Eden, then a sick man, had resigned. His successor, Harold Macmillan, was an experienced politician of proven ability. All the same it seemed far from certain that he would be able to save a government which had pursued such a disastrous policy with regard to the Suez crisis.

The effect of those events was to undermine confidence in the economy at home, the repercussions of which were quickly felt by the racing industry. With everybody playing safe, there was no money for investment in horses. When The Plumber's Mate, winner of the Wokingham Stakes in 1955, came up at Messrs Botterill's Ascot Sales, the Devonshire trainer Gerald Cottrell, who had not yet turned to the flat, was amazed to secure a fine big chestnut gelding, with form, for his opening bid of 100 guineas.

There was nothing uncertain about the way in which Lord Howard de Walden's chestnut colt Amerigo won the Coventry Stakes on the first of the four days in 1957. Ridden by Eph Smith, he beat Major Holliday's Trimmer by eight lengths in a

The Queen, with the Duke of Norfolk, and the Royal party in 1956.

canter in one minute 15.22 seconds, a new record for Ascot's six furlongs.

Amerigo was trained in the Heath House stable by Jack Waugh, a member of the well-known racing family. His grandfather Jimmy Waugh had left Scotland in the middle of the nineteenth century to succeed his friend Mat Dawson at Russley Park. Subsequently he ran the most successful stable in Austria-Hungary before settling at Newmarket. Jimmy Waugh began the family's long association with Ascot by bringing off the double in the Ascot Stakes and the Alexandra Stakes with Eurasian in 1887, and in 1899 was responsible for Refractor winning the Royal Hunt Cup.

After the one brilliant performance, Amerigo never won another race in England. Instead he did a great deal to strengthen the prejudice against the chestnut offspring of Nearco, as he became increasingly foul-tempered, hard to handle and disinclined to exert himself. Next time out in the National Breeders Produce Stakes at Sandown Park he was beaten by a short head and three lengths into third place behind Promulgation and Trimmer, whom he had slammed so comprehensively at Ascot; and when favourite for the Dewhurst Stakes at Newmarket in the autumn he was only sixth of seven. He was also beaten in each of his three races as a three-year-old, but after being sent to the United States he was often to be found in a more amenable frame of mind, and won the San Capistrano Handicap and other prestigious events. Before dying at the early age of ten Amerigo, a winner of the Coventry Stakes in the manner of The Tetrarch and Tudor Minstrel, sired a number of good horses including Fort Marcy, twice winner of the Washington D.C. International.

As the weather had been hot and sultry throughout the week preceding the opening of the 1957 meeting, Clerk of the Course Major-General David Dawnay had refrained from using the watering apparatus in the belief that thunderstorms, so often produced by such conditions, would ease the ground. The weather, though, never showed any signs of breaking. As a result the ground was unacceptably firm to a large number of trainers, and many horses arrived only to be taken away again without their having had a race. The fields, therefore, were a great deal smaller than would normally be the case, there being only eight runners for the Wokingham Stakes, for example, as opposed to 28 the previous year.

Northern stables made a splendid start to that Royal Meeting of 1957, and carried on in winning vein almost throughout, although all six winners on the third day came from Newmarket. The Queen Anne Stakes was won by Hugh Leggat's Baron's Folly, ridden by Edgar Britt for Rufus Beasley's Malton stable, and Britt promptly completed a Malton double by winning the Gold Vase on Lord Allendale's Tenterhooks, who was trained by Captain Charles Elsey. The third race on the card, the Ascot Stakes, also produced a success for the North as the 25/1 winner was Mr J. E. Wood's Bonhomie, ridden by the diminutive apprentice Michael Hayes at 6 st 8 lb for Eric Cousins' Cheshire stable.

The first race of the following day, the Jersey Stakes, was won by Quorum, who had been second in the 2000 Guineas, for Colonel Wilfred Lyde's stable. Quorum was ridden by Alec Russell, who was in the midst of an exceptionally successful season and rode all six winners on the card at the now defunct course at Bogside the following month. In due course Quorum became the sire of Red Rum, the only horse to have won the Grand National three times.

There were three more winners from the North on the last day of the meeting. Mrs J. C. B. Cookson's Meldon, ridden by Edward Hide for Rufus Beasley, was successful in the Rous Memorial Stakes, Edgar Britt rode Phil Bull's Dionisio to win the Wokingham Stakes for Captain Elsey, and finally Lester Piggott won the King's Stand Stakes on Right Boy, trained by Bill Dutton for G. A. Gilbert.

Captain Charles Elsey was the most successful trainer at Malton during the 15 years that followed the end of the Second World War, and though Bill Dutton, who had the Grove Cottage stable in the same quarter, never enjoyed any success in the classics, he won many good races at Royal Ascot as well as elsewhere. The son of William Edward Elsey, who had turned from farming in Lincolnshire to training, Captain Elsey opened a stable at Middleham when he was 30 in 1911. After winning the Military Cross in the First World War, he followed the guidance of an uncle, who advised him not to resume training in the post-war economic

Zarathustra and Lester Piggott in 1957.

conditions, and took a lease on a farm in Lincolnshire. Following the sale of the farm in 1921 he trained at Ayr until buying the historic Highfield stable at Malton in 1926. Three years later he won the Wokingham Stakes with H. F. Clayton's Six Wheeler, ridden by Tommy Weston.

An extremely hard-working trainer, Captain Elsey always had a large string, and could elicit the best from any sort of horse, from a very high-class miler like the 2000 Guineas winner Nearula to that grand old handicapper Crusader's Horn, who was 11 years old when he won the last of his 18 races for the Highfield stable. At the end of the season of 1960 he handed the string over to his son Bill, who acquired the distinction of winning with his first runner at Royal Ascot when Mr Jim Joel's Black King beat Polyktor in the Queen's Vase in 1961. The award of the C.B.E. to Captain Elsey for his services to racing that year was extremely popular, especially in the North. Captain Elsey was 84 when he died in 1966.

Originally intended for a career in the legal profession, Bill Dutton, the son of a Cheshire farmer, was still articled to a solicitor when he won the Grand National on Tipperary Tim in 1928. He never practised law. Instead he trained at Hednesford, Staffordshire, until 1939, and after moving to Malton at the end of the war earned a reputation for his shrewdness in buying good horses cheaply for small owners. With Mrs E. Goldson's Pappa Fourway, who had cost just 150 guineas, for instance, he won the King's Stand Stakes, as well as the July Cup and Diadem Stakes, in 1955. Bill Dutton obtained his final successes at Royal Ascot with Sandiacre in the Ascot Stakes and Right Boy, who had been bought for just 575 guineas, in the Cork and Orrery Stakes in 1958; he died at the age of 57 in the December of that year.

Midget II reappeared under 9 st 2 lb in the Royal Hunt Cup and started a well-backed favourite at 5/1, but it was another case of weight-for-age form not quite working out as expected in a handicap. Rae Johnstone came through with a strong run on her in the final furlong only to fail by a length to overhaul Lady Zia Wernher's Retrial, ridden by Peter Robinson for Captain Boyd-Rochfort. Alec Head was not long in obtaining compensation for the defeat of Midget II as he won the next race, the Coronation Stakes, with the Aga Khan's Toro. That was the last of all the many winners that the old Aga Khan had at Royal Ascot. He died in Geneva at the age of 79 the following month.

With the reverses met by Prince Simon and Black Tarquin, and still further back in time Omaha, no more than memories, Captain Boyd-Rochfort was now at the very peak of his brilliant career. As well as the Royal Hunt Cup he won three other races at the Royal Meeting in 1957. For the Queen he won the Ribblesdale Stakes with Almeria as well as the New Stakes with Pall Mall, who was successful in the 2000 Guineas the following year. In the Gold Cup the Captain ran both the Queen's Altas, ridden by Harry Carr, and Zarathustra, for whom Lester Piggott had been engaged, but neither was generally expected to be able to cope with another strong challenge from abroad. The Italian colt Tissot, who had won his previous five races with the greatest of ease, was favourite to emulate Botticelli, and the French-trained Cambremer, winner of the St Leger the previous season, second in the market. For once England had a horse with the requisite class and stamina: Zarathustra went to the front two furlongs out, and held the renewed efforts of Cambremer by

Zarathustra, with Lester Piggott up, beat a strong challenge from abroad to win the 1957 Gold Cup.

a length-and-a-half, with Tissot half-a-length away third and Altas fifth.

To those who saw Zarathustra in the paddock, his success can have come as no surprise. By the time he was a six-year-old he had developed into a magnificent black horse of great strength and depth, and as he was by Persian Gulf, with whom the Captain had won the Gold Cup in 1937, his stamina could be taken for granted.

The going was firm on all four days that year, and Mr Stanhope Joel's Matador set a new record for six furlongs when winning the Cork and Orrery in one minute 14.35 seconds, the previous best time having been one minute 15.22 seconds. Taking the lead a furlong and a half out, he beat Wasps Fifteen by a very easy four lengths. Like Amerigo, he was ridden by Eph Smith for Jack Waugh's stable.

Sir Gordon Richards had his first success at Royal Ascot as a trainer when The Tuscar, with Scobie Breasley up in the colours of John Lewis, won the Bessborough Stakes. Riding a waiting race that was typical of him, Breasley did not put The Tuscar into contention until half a furlong out and

got up close to home to win by a head from Casmiri, the mount of fellow Australian Eddie Cracknel.

On the first day Sir Gordon had been widely expected to win the St James's Palace Stakes with his classic colt Pipe of Peace, who had been third in both the 2000 Guineas and the Derby. As they came to the final furlong Pipe of Peace disputed the lead with the Irish colt Chevastrid, but could not go through with his effort and finished third to Chevastrid, who held the challenge of the fast-finishing Tempest by a head. The winner was ridden by Jimmy Eddery, father of the future champion jockey Pat Eddery, and of another excellent rider of the present day, Paul Eddery.

By the last day the ground was so firm that three of the five runners in the Queen Alexandra Stakes, the previous year's winner Borghetto, Cabalist and Souverlone were badly stumped up and returned lame. The race was won by the French-trained Flying Flag II, who held a strong late challenge from Strait-Jacket by half a length after making all the running. The rider of the runner-up, better known at Cheltenham than Ascot, was Aubrey Brabazon, who had won three Gold Cups for Vincent O'Brien.

Having given notice that he would henceforward be a power at the Royal Meeting by winning the Jersey with Adare two years earlier, Vincent O'Brien made his first major impact on the fixture by bringing off the long-distance double with Even Money in the Gold Vase and Gladness in the Gold Cup in 1958. Although still a newcomer to the more rarefied reaches of flat racing, O'Brien was already operating internationally, and the previous month Gladness had run the French horse Scot II to a length in the Prix du Cadran at Longchamps, where she had been ridden by T. P. Burns.

As Burns had met with an accident in the early summer Lester Piggott, still only 22 years old, rode Gladness, a powerful, slightly common, five-year-old mare, with a dark brown coat. She was made joint favourite with Scot II, whom she met on 7 lb better terms than she had done in France. High hopes were entertained of the Queen's Doutelle, whom Carr rode for Captain Boyd-Rochfort, as the royal colt had beaten the previous year's St Leger winner Ballymoss in the Ormonde Stakes at Chester five weeks earlier. There was also confidence behind Court Harwell and Hornbeam, as they represented classic form, having been runners-up in the St Leger in 1957 and 1956 respectively. The Queen and her party went down to inspect Doutelle in the paddock, where Gladness was seen to be sweating up.

As Flying Flag II had led from pillar to post in the Queen Alexandra Stakes 12 months earlier, Jean Massard tried to make forcing tactics pay off again. Turning into the straight, Flying Flag II was still in front of the other seven runners, but when Piggott brought Gladness through to challenge on his inside two furlongs from home, the leader could find nothing extra and rapidly dropped back. Staying on strongly, Gladness held the challenge of Hornbeam, ridden by Joe Mercer, by a length; Doutelle, who clearly failed to get the trip, was five lengths away in third place.

Gladness carried the colours of the American building contractor Mr John McShain, the son of an Irish immigrant, whose firm built the Pentagon and undertook extensive repairs to the White House. He had flown across the Atlantic to see the

race the previous day. On being mated with her owner's St Leger winner Ballymoss, Gladness became the dam of Merry Mate, who was successful in the Irish Guinness Oaks in 1966.

The meeting had opened under dull, sombre clouds, and the weather showed no signs of brightening up throughout the four days, though the rain held off, apart from a brief downpour on the first day. Among fashionably dressed women the somewhat unedifying "Sack" line was surprisingly popular. Running straight from neckline to hem, and generally wider at the former than the latter, it nullified many elegant waists.

Apart from Gladness becoming the first mare to win the Gold Cup since Quashed 22 years earlier, the other feature of the meeting was Captain Boyd-Rochfort's remarkable achievement in winning the King Edward VII Stakes with the Queen's Restoration, a neat, strong bay colt by Persian Gulf out of the 1000 Guineas winner Hypericum. Restoration had been very weak in the early part of his two-year-old days, and when at last ready to run met with a setback. Then, at the outset of his three-year-old career, he succumbed to an inexplicable bout of lameness, so that he had still not seen a racecourse when the Captain sent him to Ascot to take on the French-trained favourite Capitaine Corcoran and eight other experienced colts. Ridden by Harry Carr, Restoration took up the running approaching the final furlong, and won by a comfortable two lengths from Capitaine Corcoran, with All Serene, owned by the Queen's aunt, the Princess Royal, three lengths away third. Curiously enough Restoration never won another race, though kept in training as a four-year-old.

A notable Northern success came about when Tudor Melody, trained by Dick Peacock at Middleham, won the Chesham Stakes. Tudor Melody became one of the most important stallions to have been trained in the North in that period, as the sire of the 2000 Guineas winner Kashmir II, the Queen Elizabeth II Stakes winner Welsh Pageant, the July Cup winner Tudor Music and other good horses. Among the high-class performers produced by his daughters was the champion sprinter Marwell.

Major Dick Hern, in his first season as private trainer to Major L. B. Holliday, gave one of several hints that he was destined to reach the top of his profession by winning the Ribblesdale Stakes with None Nicer. Born in 1921, Major Hern was brought up among horses on his father's farm in Somerset, hunting with both the West Somerset and the Quantock Staghounds from early boyhood. After service with the Northern Irish Horse throughout the North African and Italian campaigns, he took a riding instructor's course at Porlock, after which he stayed on at that establishment to become chief instructor, and coach to the British Equestrian Team that won a Gold Medal at the Olympic Games in 1952. The same year he became assistant to his old friend and former brother officer, Major Michael Pope, who was training at Streatley, in Berkshire. During the five years in which he learned every aspect of training in Major Pope's stable, he rode as an amateur under National Hunt Rules, winning steeplechases on Sir John IV. Then in 1957 he answered Major Holliday's advertisement for a private trainer to succeed Humphrey Cottrill in Newmarket's Lagrange stable.

A horsemaster of the old school, Major Hern proved to have immense patience, and always looked at an animal's career in the long term, specialising in turning out middle-distance horses of the highest class, rather than precocious two-year-olds. With his unmistakably military bearing, Major Hern has never sought the limelight but is far too straight-forward and fair-minded a man to be unapproachable. He has been exceptionally successful at Royal Ascot.

Having gone a long way towards making his name as a trainer by winning the Cork and Orrery Stakes of 1936 and other races with that fast horse Bellicose while training at Newmarket, Jack Colling turned out a number of notable stayers, many of them belonging to the Astor family, following his move to the West Ilsley stable, near Newbury in Berkshire, shortly after the end of the war. In 1958 he obtained a substantial measure of compensation for Lord Astor's Hornbeam being beaten into second place by Gladness in the Gold Cup by winning the Queen Alexandra Stakes for his brother, Mr J. J. (later Sir John) Astor, with the six-year-old gelding Rally, also ridden by his stable jockey Joe Mercer, the popular younger brother of Manny. Making every yard of the running over the extended two and three quarter miles, Rally won by a length

and a half from the former Derby hope Induna, with the French horse Magic North third of four. That was the only winner that Joe Mercer rode at Royal Ascot that year, while Manny obtained his solitary success of the meeting by winning the Bessborough Stakes on Sir Foster Robinson's four-year-old Huguenot for George Colling, to whom he had been apprenticed. One of the features of the racing during that era was the rivalry between two brothers riding for two brothers – Joe Mercer for Jack Colling and Manny for George Colling.

Huguenot, on whom Manny won the Bessborough, was a rather angular chestnut gelding with a mind of his own and decided ideas of what he would, and what he would not, do while out at exercise, but went on racing until he was a 15-year-old in 1969. He became the last of the offspring of Hyperion to be returned a winner when he was awarded a race at Bath as an 11-year-old.

Jack and George Colling, the latter being four years the younger, were the sons of Bob Colling, who was apprenticed to Bob Armstrong at Penrith, subsequently training at Middleham, then for Major Holliday and other owners at Newmarket. Although both the Colling brothers were tall for jockeys, each had a successful, albeit necessarily brief, career in the saddle. Jack Colling rode for Major Waldorf Astor, later the 2nd Lord Astor, on whose Blink he was second in a wartime substitute Derby in 1918. A handsome man, who was never anything but immaculately dressed, Jack Colling opened a stable at Newmarket shortly after the end of the First World War.

At the age of 15 George Colling finished fifth to Steve Donoghue in the list of winning jockeys in 1919. Among the 72 races that he won that year was the Northumberland Plate on Lord Derby's Trestle. While retained by Lord Derby the following year, George Colling won the Park Hill Stakes for him on Redhead, but by the age of 18, in 1922, was already too heavy to continue riding. After being assistant to his elder brother, George Colling commenced to train at Newmarket in 1935. Although never the most robust of men George Colling enlisted in the Royal Artillery a few days before the outbreak of war, only to be demobilised in 1942 on account of ill health. In 1949 he won the 2000 Guineas and the Derby with Nimbus, ridden by

Charlie Elliott, though too ill to get to Epsom to see the Derby. Ten years later he died, when only 55 years of age.

The Mercer brothers, two of the outstanding jockeys of their generation, were born in Bradford, Manny in 1930 and Joe in 1934. After beginning his apprenticeship with Jim Russell at Mablethorpe, and coming to prominence by winning the Lincolnshire on the 100/1 chance Jockey Treble in 1947, Manny Mercer had his indentures transferred to George Colling. Modelling himself upon Charlie Elliott, then Colling's stable jockey, Manny Mercer became a superb stylist. As well as for George Colling, Manny Mercer rode regularly for Jack Jarvis and Harry Wragg, whose daughter Susan he married.

Having followed Eph and Doug Smith into the spartan regime of the stable that Major F. B. Sneyd ran at Sparsholt near Wantage, Joe Mercer rode his first winner on Eldoret at Bath when he was 15 in September 1950. Two years later he was champion apprentice, and still an apprentice when he became first jockey to Jack Colling in 1953, the year that he won the Oaks for the West Ilsley stable on Lord Astor's Ambiguity. Like Manny, he became a fine stylist in the tradition of Charlie Elliott.

Huguenot was the last winner Manny Mercer ever rode at Royal Ascot, as he was beaten on each of his 16 mounts at the meeting in 1959. On 26th September that year he was taking Sir Foster Robinson's Priddy Fair to the post for the start of the Red Deer Stakes at Ascot, and as she turned to go down to Swinley Bottom the filly reared and slipped, unseating her rider. While struggling to her feet, Priddy Fair twice kicked Manny in the face, and he was killed instantly at only 29 years of age. Manny Mercer was a natural jockey, who did the right thing by instinct, rather than in accordance with carefully devised tactics. Jack Jarvis used to say, "I don't understand that boy. I give him his orders, then he goes and does the exact opposite, and still wins!"

Manny Mercer left behind him the memory of an extremely kind little man, especially among the Newmarket lads, who knew that he was always good for a generous present when he rode a winner on horses they looked after. Once, on hearing that a particularly parsimonious owner had economised on his overheads by declining to give a lad a present, Manny made good the deficiency from his own pocket. Although offered large sums for first claim on his services by Jack Jarvis, he could never be tempted to desert George Colling.

The weather was quite beautiful at Royal Ascot in 1959, though too hot for the men who had, perforce, to swelter in morning coats in the Royal Enclosure, particularly on the second day, when the temperature soared to close on 80°F. The Queen was present only on the Tuesday and Wednesday, as she left the country for a tour of Canada on Gold Cup day, but Queen Elizabeth the Queen Mother and Princess Margaret came on all four days.

For Queen Elizabeth, well known for her enthusiasm for National Hunt racing, it was a memorable meeting, as she won the Queen Alexandra Stakes with Bali Ha'i III, a six-year-old bred in New Zealand. While she had been on a visit to that dominion in the February of 1958, Queen Elizabeth had watched Bali Ha'i III win the St James's Cup at Trentham, and presented the trophy to his owner Sir Ernest Davis, who asked her to accept the horse as a present. Unfortunately almost as soon as he arrived in Captain Boyd-Rochfort's yard Bali Ha'i III split a pastern, and was unable to run at all in 1958.

He was the only English-trained runner in the Queen Alexandra Stakes, as his three rivals consisted of Magic North from France, together with the Irish pair Smiley, the last horse Charlie Smirke rode at the Royal Meeting, and the well-known hurdler Havasnack. After Havasnack had made most of the running Smiley went on two furlongs from home, only to be challenged by Harry Carr on Bali Ha'i III after another half-furlong.

Riding with a strength and vigour rarely seen in a man of 52, Charlie Smirke conjured every last ounce from the brave but stricken Smiley, but at the post the royal horse had prevailed by half a length. As they pulled up, poor Smiley could be seen to have broken down, and Charlie Smirke, one of the greatest of all the riders in that golden age of British jockeyship before the war, dismounted to lead the horse as he entered the unsaddling enclosure at the Royal Meeting for the last time.

Towards the end of that season Bali Ha'i III finished third in the Cesarewitch on ground that was far too firm for him, and broke down. In consequence he was off the course again throughout 1960. Reappearing as an eight-year-old at Kempton Park in May 1961 he pleased by finishing third to Vienna, but after one more race he broke down again. With his racing days finally over, Queen Elizabeth sent Bali Ha'i III home to New Zealand, where he spent his retirement in Sir Ernest Davis's paddocks.

Captain Boyd-Rochfort, who had won the Derby with Parthia a fortnight earlier, sent an impressively strong team to the Royal Meeting that year, and came away from it having experienced decidedly mixed fortunes. On the credit side the Captain won the St James's Palace Stakes with the Queen's Above Suspicion and the Jersey Stakes with Mrs J. W. Hanes' Welsh Guard, as well as the Queen Alexandra, but on the debit the classic winners Alcide and Pall Mall who spearheaded the Freemason Lodge party met with reverses, while Restoration and Hieroglyph, another of Mrs Hanes' horses, were also beaten into second place.

As Sir Humphrey de Trafford's Alcide, a son of Alycidon, had beaten that good filly None Nicer by eight lengths in the St Leger of the previous year, and was fresh from successes at Kempton Park and Hurst Park, he was confidently expected to make his stamina tell in the Gold Cup. Having started favourite at 11/10 in a field of six, Alcide took the lead a furlong and a half out, and all seemed plain sailing until Freddie Palmer obtained a great run from the French colt Wallaby II. Responding splendidly to the pressure from Harry Carr, Alcide clung tenaciously to his advantage, but Palmer was not giving up either, and in the very last stride forced Wallaby II to snatch the verdict by a short head. The winner was owned by Baron Guy de Waldener, whose Pearl Diver had been successful in the Derby 12 years earlier, and was trained by Percy Carter.

Pall Mall, winner of the 2000 Guineas of 1958 for the Queen, stepped down in company by taking on the handicappers in the Royal Hunt Cup, after being successful in the Lockinge Stakes at Newbury on his previous appearance. Although he inevitably had top weight, which was still 9 st 7 lb in those days, and was giving as much as 39 lb to the likes of Doctor Tadgh and Tantrum, backers were happy to rely on the class of the royal colt who started favourite at 5/2 after opening at 7/2, with Faultless Speech, trained by his owner Harold Wallington at Epsom, next in the betting at 3/1. Having wrested the lead from Small Slam when approaching the final furlong, Pall Mall was unable to withstand the challenge that Geoff Lewis unleashed from Faultless Speech. At the post Faultless Speech had drawn a length and a half clear of him, with Small Slam the same distance away third.

A physical defect rather than lack of the requisite ability probably brought about the defeat of Hieroglyph in the King Edward VII Stakes. Unfortunately he was so short-sighted in his near eye as to be almost blind, and when Harry Carr produced him to challenge Lester Piggott on Pindari, he hung to the side of his good eye, in behind Pindari. By the time that Carr had carried out the necessary corrective procedure the race was as good as over, and although Hieroglyph finished the faster, Pindari held on to win by half a length.

A brown colt by Pinza out of Sun Chariot, Pindari was one of those horses that the Queen leased from the National Stud. His dam Sun Chariot was one of the greatest fillies of the first half of the century, but never had the chance to demonstrate her brilliance at Royal Ascot, as it was in wartime conditions that she completed the fillies' Triple Crown in substitute races for the 1000 Guineas, Oaks and St Leger.

Queen Elizabeth was not the only personality prominent in the jumping world to win a race at Royal Ascot in 1959. Monamolin, winner of the Windsor Castle Stakes, was trained at Lambourn by Fulke Walwyn for his wife, a daughter of the owner of the luckless Alcide.

Like Captain Boyd-Rochfort, Noel Murless trained three winners at the meeting. As well as the King Edward VII Stakes with Pindari, he landed the Britannia Handicap with Macquario and the Rous Memorial Stakes with Mr Steuart's Pinicola. Macquario carred the colours of the third and last Earl of Feversham, a sporting Yorkshire peer of great charm, who dearly loved a good bet. There was another side to Lord Feversham's character. Despite his widespread business commitments, he devoted much time to work in connection with his deep and abiding interest in the welfare of those whom the world had treated less kindly than himself. In many respects a long way ahead of his

Royal Ascot

Aerial view of the course and enclosures in 1921.

Officials view the racing from their vantage point, and, below,
the successful team of Willie Carson and Major
Dick Hern with the 1979 Queen's Vase winner Buttress
watched by the Royal party.

Lester Piggott had his first success at the age of 16 on Malka's Boy in the Wokingham Stakes in 1952. Among the many races he was to win later, were the 1975 Gold Cup on Sagaro (bottom left) and the Jersey Stakes in 1975 on Fandango from Joe Mercer on Joking Apart (main picture). On turning to training, he won the Coventry Stakes of 1986 with Cutting Blade, his first runner at the Meeting.

ROYAL ASCOT

The Royal Procession has held the huge crowds in thrall for generations.

**Captain the Hon. Nicholas Beaumont, clerk of
the course at Ascot since 1969.**

time in his thinking on social issues, he was patron of the Probation Officers' Association and president of the Mental Health Association. Few men practised in their private lives what they advocated in their public ones quite so conscientiously and unobtrusively as he did. Sadly, he died at the early age of 56 in 1963.

Lord Faversham's only child, Lady Clarissa, married Major "Nico" Collin, the successful bloodstock agent and a former amateur rider, whose Sir Giles became the first horse to win a jumping race at Ascot in 1965. Lady Clarissa Collin owned Clip Joint, whom Sam Hall trained to win the King George V Stakes at Royal Ascot in 1970.

On the first day of the 1959 meeting, R. N. Webster's good colt Martial, ridden by Walter Swinburn senior for Paddy Prendergast's stable, justified hot favouritism in the Coventry Stakes. At the time of writing Martial is the last winner of the Coventry Stakes to go on to success in the 2000 Guineas, though three subsequent Coventry Stakes winners – Silly Season (1964), Mill Reef (1970) and Chief Singer (1984) – were all runners-up in the Guineas.

Following the success of Martial, Paddy Prendergast completed an important two-year-old double by winning the Queen Mary Stakes with Mrs J. R. Mullion's Paddy's Sister (by Ballyogan), whose half-brother Paddy's Point (by Mieuxce) had been second to Hard Ridden in the Derby the previous year. On being retired to the Ardenode Stud, which Mrs Mullion ran in partnership with her husband, Paddy's Sister became a successful brood mare. Mated with the home stallion Ragusa in 1968, she became the dam of Ballymore, winner of the Irish 2000 Guineas.

Pat Rohan, who had taken over the Grove Cottage stable at Malton on the death of his father-in-law Bill Dutton, earned the credit for Right Boy winning at Royal Ascot for the third consecutive year, following successes in the King's Stand Stakes in 1957 and the Cork and Orrery Stakes in 1958. As in the previous two years, Right Boy was ridden by Lester Piggott, and won the Cork and Orrery for the second time by beating Capuchon by three parts of a length with quite a bit in hand.

Billy Nevett, so long the champion jockey of the North, obtained much the most important success

Noel Murless, trained three winners at the 1959 meeting.

as a trainer when his old rival Joe Sime rode Chris to beat Sir Winston Churchill's Welsh Abbot in the King's Stand Stakes. Chris carried the colours of his breeder Mr Hugh Hartley, a wool manufacturer from Harrogate, and was a grey colt by Vilmorin out of the Ballyogan mare Tie Silk, on whom Nevett had won the Gosforth Park Cup for Mr Hartley at Newcastle. Billy Nevett had begun training with just 11 horses in the Newby Park stables a few miles from Ripon in 1958, but despite the highlights provided by Chris, the venture never really prospered and he relinquished his licence after five seasons.

In May 1960 racing people throughout the world were shocked to learn of the death of Prince Aly Khan. The elder son of the late Aga Khan, and for many years a partner in his studs, had been killed at the age of 48 in a car crash in a suburb of Paris. Aly Khan was a charismatic personality who captured the imagination of almost all the thousands of people that he knew, as well as the millions who only read about him. Slim and elegant, he used his wealth to enjoy life to the full, was immensely energetic, and brought terrific enthusiasm to everything he undertook, not least his innumerable courtships, one of which resulted in marriage to the film star Rita Hayworth for a while. In addition he was a fine judge of a horse, who had been more than proficient as an amateur rider, and was never afraid to bet. A few days before he was killed, his colt Sheshoon stumbled close to home and was beaten by a short head in the Prix du Cadran. Looking at a print of the finish Aly Khan turned to a friend and said, "I'm afraid my luck is running out."

While Aly Khan's estate was being wound up, his horses, who were trained by Noel Murless in England and Alec Head in France, ran in the name of his executors. At Ascot, Head brought off a double with his late owner's horses when Sheshoon outstayed Exar by a length and a half in the Gold Cup, and Venture VII, who lost out by a head in the 2000 Guineas, landed the prohibitive odds of 33/1 on by beating his only rival in the St James's Palace Stakes.

In view of the apprehension and misgiving that had permeated the nation in the wake of the Suez crisis, Russian intervention in Hungary and then the Eden resignation, it seemed little short of miraculous that three years later, the Royal Meeting of 1960 should take place in an atmosphere of resurgent national self-assurance. Against all odds, Eden's successor as Prime Minister, Harold Macmillan, had mended the fortunes of the Conservative Party to such good effect that he had led it to success for the third consecutive time in a General Election in October 1959, and was already being dubbed "Supermac". He loved it. With his carefully cultivated air of languor, which suggested he had never quite left the carefree Edwardian era of his youth, this handsome man with a military moustache steadfastly refused to let himself become excited by any crisis, brushing one aside as a "little local difficulty", and radiated an almost contagious confidence. They said he was unflappable. And he loved that, too.

The weather was not particularly pleasant on the Tuesday, and it was in a torrential rainstorm that the appropriately named Typhoon became a second consecutive winner of the Coventry Stakes for Paddy Prendergast's stable. Ridden by the Australian Ron Hutchinson in the colours of N. S. McCarthy, Typhoon beat Blue Sail by a length, as the huge crowd huddled in the stands to keep dry.

The remaining three days of the meeting, though, were warm and sunny.

The four-year-old Shatter furnished evidence of the shrewdness of his trainer Tom Masson by defying his penalty in the Ascot Stakes, then worth £2788. At the December Sales of the previous year Masson had bought Shatter out of Jack Colling's stable for 900 guineas. Three months after his success at Ascot he was sold for 7300 guineas to dissolve the partnership in him. In the Stakes Shatter was ridden by Masson's 19-year-old apprentice Bobby Elliott, who landed another big handicap the following day when he was successful in the Royal Hunt Cup on Mr Philip King's Small Slam, trained by Geoffrey Barling at Newmarket.

Pat Rohan, responsible for the final success of Right Boy at the Royal Meeting, produced another fast horse in B. W. Grainger's Tin Whistle. The three-year-old was ridden by Lester Piggott in the Cork and Orrery Stakes, and made all the running to win by a very comfortable four lengths from Sovereign Path, the mount of future champion jump jockey Josh Gifford.

Mr Jim Joel's Predominate, arguably the most popular horse of the day, won the Queen Alexandra Stakes with ridiculous ease when Eph Smith brought him home six lengths clear of Fabius. The eight-year-old had already won the Goodwood Stakes in each of the last two seasons, and the following month would add to his laurels when winning that race for the third time, then in 1961 he won the Goodwood Cup.

Newmarket stables had a distinctly thin time in 1960, winning only six races, and even Captain Boyd-Rochfort's Derby winner of the previous year, Parthia, met with a reverse. He tried to make all the running in the Hardwicke Stakes, but Aggressor, ridden by Jimmy Lindley, took the lead off him approaching the final furlong and won by a length and a half for Towser Gosden's stable.

Despite the eclipse of Parthia, who started at 15/8 on, the bookmakers did not have a good meeting. Silver King, from Sam Hall's Middleham stable, brought off a wholesale gamble in the Wokingham Stakes after being backed from 10/1 to 15/2 favourite. Joe Sime took him to the front with 150 yards left to cover, and though Lester Piggott came through with a late run on the top-weight

Work in progress on the new Queen Elizabeth II Stand in 1960.

Sovereign Path, he never looked like catching Silver King, who won by three lengths. In addition to the unbackable Venture VII, nine other favourites and a joint favourite were also successful.

There was a minor change of nomenclature that year as the Gold Vase became the Queen's Vase, and was won by Prolific, ridden by Duncan Keith for Walter Nightingall. The three-year-old stormed home five lengths clear of the older horse Farrney Fox, leaving connections of St Leger aspirants heartily thankful that he was not engaged at Doncaster.

When the crowd flocked back to the Royal Meeting of 1961 evidence of very much more substantial changes was to be seen. The old buildings in Tattersalls had disappeared, and in their place stood the imposing Queen Elizabeth II Stand. With a frontage of 570 feet, it provided accommodation for 13,000 racegoers. There were 280 boxes, and reserved seating for 1600 people.

Once again in 1961 the unpleasant controversy as to whether or not the course should be watered reared its head. As a dry spell had persisted through late May into June the decision to water had been taken, then on the Monday before the meeting opened there were 12 hours of heavy rainfall. Consequently the going was artificially soft on the first day, and although the ground dried out over the following three, horses drawn on the far side of the straight course had their chances all but ruined. The only horse to overcome that huge disadvantage was Mrs Dermot McCalmont's Xerxes, who made all the running to win the Coventry Stakes very easily.

Prince Aly Khan, sadly killed in a car crash in 1960, bred the wonderful grey mare, Petite Etoile, winner of the 1959 Rous Cup.

Noel Murless and Lester Piggott shared five successes, two of which were with classic winners, and another with a future classic winner. That wonderful grey mare Petite Etoile, who had brought off the double in the 1000 Guineas and Oaks in 1959, was kept in training by Noel Murless as a five-year-old to carry the colours of H. H. Aga Khan, elder son and heir of her breeder Aly Khan. She started at 2/15 to beat her four rivals over the mile of the Rous Stakes. After Right of Way had led on sufferance until 150 yards from the post, she cruised to the front and won by a length without being out of a canter.

For the Hardwicke Stakes, Noel Murless provided St Paddy, Sir Victor Sassoon's Derby winner of the previous year, with a pacemaker in Sunny Way. St Paddy also started at odds on, as his only other rivals were the Irish colt Die Hard, and Sir Winston Churchill's Vienna, who had been second and third to him in the St Leger. Sunny Way brought them along at a fair gallop for a mile, then St Paddy went into the lead. Although Vienna ran on under pressure from Tommy Gosling, Sir Winston's horse never looked like getting on terms with St Paddy, who won by a comfortable length. Both St Paddy and Vienna were by the Queen's horse Aureole, himself winner of the Hardwicke seven years earlier, and both became successful stallions. St Paddy sired Connaught, winner of the Eclipse Stakes and runner-up in the Derby, Welsh Saint and Jupiter Island, while the outstanding son of Vienna was the Prix de l'Arc de Triomphe winner Vaguely Noble, who, in turn, was sire of that brilliant filly Dahlia and the Derby winner Empery.

With the evil-tempered Aurelius, another son of Aureole, Noel Murless and Lester Piggott won the

King Edward VII Stakes for Mrs Vera Lilley. Three months later Aurelius franked the form with success in the St Leger. At stud Aurelius was an utter disaster. He had to be gelded, and was sent to Ken Cundell for jumping. Seven years after he had won at the Royal Meeting, this classic winner returned to Ascot to win a steeplechase in which he was ridden by Stan Mellor. Noel Murless and Lester Piggott were also responsible for Aiming High, yet another of the horses that the Queen leased from the National Stud, winning the Coronation Stakes, and Favorita the Jersey Stakes in 1961.

Lester Piggott won two other races at Royal Ascot that year. On Abermaid he won the New Stakes and on Pandofell the Gold Cup. Abermaid, who ran as the property of the executors of Sir Percy Loraine, was trained by Harry Wragg, and is one of the relatively few classic winners to have won at Royal Ascot as a two-year-old during the last 30 years. Carrying the colours of Mr Roderick More O'Ferrall she won the 1000 Guineas in 1962.

Pandofell has to rate amongst the greatest bargains secured since the end of the Second World War. After he had been unplaced in both his races as a two-year-old in 1959 his breeder, Mr Jim Joel, sent him to the Newmarket December Sales, where Lambourn trainer Freddie Maxwell was able to buy him for just 600 guineas on behalf of H. Warwick Daw, a 72-year-old surveyor from London. As a three-year-old he was still so little regarded that he was given only 7 st 3 lb in the Cesarewitch. During his third season, he improved almost out of recognition. In May he won the Yorkshire Cup, then at Ascot he struck the front two furlongs from home in the Gold Cup and went right away to beat Jet Stream by five lengths without being challenged. Prolific was just a neck away third, Shatter fourth, and Puissant Chief, who had been made odds on to win for France, only seventh of ten.

A few weeks later Pandofell was the centre of a major sensation. He was to have returned to Ascot to run in the Sunninghill Park Stakes, but when Freddie Maxwell entered his box on the morning of the race, he was horrified to find Pandofell in a terrible state. Dazed and only half conscious with his eyes badly cut, he was propping himself up against the wall with great difficulty. Laboratory tests established that a large dose of phenobarbitone had

been administered to the Gold Cup winner. Despite intensive investigation by the police the identity of those who nobbled Pandofell was never discovered.

For a week Pandofell was a very sick horse, and for three weeks he was unable to do any work at all. He had to miss the Goodwood Cup, then recovered in time to obtain a well-deserved success in the Doncaster Cup.

The Irish trainer "Brud" Fetherstonhaugh performed the extraordinary feat of running three horses belonging to Mr Stanhope Joel at the meeting and winning with all of them. On the Thursday he landed the Cork and Orrery Stakes with Bun Penny, and the following day he brought off a double by winning the Windsor Castle Stakes with Prince Tor and the King's Stand Stakes with that horse's older half-brother Silver Tor.

As became a man who had spent the formative part of his career with Atty Persse, trainer of The Tetrarch, and arguably the greatest handler of two-year-olds of all time, Geoffrey Brooke, who had the Clarehaven stable at Newmarket, excelled in producing fast first-season horses. After winning the Coventry Stakes with Xerxes on the first day of the 1961 meeting he completed an important juvenile double with Mr David Robinson's My Dream in the Queen Mary Stakes 24 hours later. The following year Brooke landed the same double, when Crocket, owned by the American Danny van Clief, won the Coventry Stakes unchallenged, and Lt-Col D. S. Cripps' Shot Silk was successful in the Queen Mary Stakes. In addition Major Brooke and his stable jockey Doug Smith won the Jersey Stakes with R. F. Dennis's Catchpole in 1962.

Whereas Brooke excelled in the handling of precocious two-year-olds, the Manton trainer George Todd, whose patience had long been legendary, was a past master of the art of preparing long-distance horses. At the Royal Meeting of 1962 he won the Ascot Stakes on the first day and the Queen Alexandra Stakes on the last with Mrs Leonard Carver's six-year-old brown gelding Trelawny, who was ridden by Scobie Breasley in both races. Trelawny, who had so much more stamina than his sire Black Tarquin, was bred by the Astor Stud, and originally trained by Jack Colling at West Ilsley for Sir John Astor. After winning two minor races at Birmingham and another at Catterick Bridge as a three-year-old he was sold for 2500 guineas at the December Sales, and sent to Syd Mercer, who proceeded to win the Chester Cup of 1960 with him for Mrs Carver. As a five-year-old he was back with Jack Colling, who sent him to Ascot to win the Brown Jack Stakes, and continued his peregrinations by going to George Todd.

In 1963 Trelawny became the only horse who has ever completed the double in the Ascot Stakes and the Queen Alexandra Stakes twice. For a while, however, there was the dreadful possibility that he would lose the first leg in the Stewards' Room. In the Ascot Stakes he had to carry the jumping weight of 10 st, and Scobie Breasley, understandably anxious to conserve his energy for his second engagement of the meeting, eased him as soon as he had taken the lead from his stablemate Sea Leopard, to whom he was giving no less than 49 lb, a furlong and a half from home. As Breasley tightened his rein, Trelawny momentarily veered from a straight course, slightly hampering Lost Property, who bumped the Queen's Golden Oriole, ridden by that good lightweight Derek Morris. Almost instantly, Breasley had Trelawny back on an even keel, and he ran on to beat Sea Leopard by three parts of a length, with Lost Property a length and a half away third, and Golden Oriole fourth. The Stewards objected to the first three, and then withdrew their objection.

The reception accorded Trelawny after his success in the Queen Alexandra Stakes was likened by veteran racegoers to that given Brown Jack after he had won the race for the sixth time 29 years earlier. The cheering began as he took the lead from Sannazaro four furlongs from home, and steadily grew in volume until it reached a crescendo as he passed the post three lengths clear of Grey of Falloden, with Sannazaro 20 lengths away third. The staid decorum of the Royal Enclosure suddenly dissolved as men threw top hats into the air, and there was a headlong rush from all parts of the course to see the fine old horse unsaddled.

Trelawny bid for his hat-trick in the Ascot Stakes as an eight-year-old in 1964. As he began to improve rapidly four furlongs from home, hopes of his winning yet again rose high, only to be dashed when age at last took its toll, as he could not go through with his effort in the final furlong, so that

he failed by two lengths to give 40 lb to Mary Lady Delamere's Delmere, trained by Willie Stephenson at Royston. The abnormal weather in the second part of Ascot week that year robbed him of the formality of the compensation that would have come to him on the Friday. Had the meeting not been abandoned after the second day by reason of the course being waterlogged, Trelawny would have walked over for the Queen Alexandra Stakes.

It was a shame that the story of Trelawny at Royal Ascot had to end on a note of anti-climax. By the time he turned out for the Queen Alexandra Stakes as a nine-year-old in 1965 he had lost his form, and finished last of six to his old rival Grey of Falloden.

George Todd, the third of Trelawny's trainers, had been born into a farming family in Lincolnshire in 1894, and apprenticed to Bert Lines at Newmarket. Being too tall to have any chance of ever being a jockey, he devoted himself to the study of all aspects of stablecraft. After five years with Lines he spent two at Hednesford with Tom Coulthwaite, who had already trained two Grand National winners. Commencing to train in a small way at Royston, Todd obtained his first success with Social Event in a selling race at Nottingham in 1928. Twenty years later he brought off an enormous gamble with Dramatic in the Stewards Cup, taking £57,000 out of the ring, as he confided to Geoffrey Hamlyn, formerly chief starting price reporter of the *Sporting Life*. With his winnings he proposed to buy the palatial Manton establishment, which Tattersalls were to sell by auction at their Knightsbridge premises. Unfortunately his taxi got stuck in the London traffic, and he arrived too late to bid. As it happened, though, Manton had not made its reserve, and he was able to buy the stable.

George Todd was the complete perfectionist in the conduct of his stable, and a meticulous planner who thought in terms of years, not months, when laying out a horse, particularly a stayer, for a race. He lavished the same sort of affection on his horses that other men do on their children, and had a marvellous way with bad-legged animals. Other good races that he won at Royal Ascot included the St James's Palace Stakes with Roan Rocket in 1964, the Ribblesdale Stakes with Parthian Glance in 1966 and the Ascot Stakes with Shira in 1967.

After being severely wounded on the Western front in the First World War, George Todd promised himself that should he survive he would never again set foot outside England. True to that vow, he never saw Sodium give him the biggest success of his career in the Irish Sweeps Derby in 1966. He died in 1974.

Lester Piggott was a notable absentee from the weighing-room in 1962, as the result of an incident at Lincoln in late May. Riding Ione for Bob Ward, he had been beaten two lengths by that horse's stablemate Polly Macaw, the mount of Peter Robinson. Being dissatisfied with the manner in which the race had been run the Lincoln Stewards reported the matter to the Stewards of the Jockey Club, who held an enquiry and then issued a statement saying they considered "L. Piggott, the rider of Ione, had made no effort to win the race", and withdrew his licence until July 28th inclusive. It was Scobie Breasley, therefore, who was successful in the Hardwicke Stakes on Aurelius, Noel Murless's only winner of the meeting.

Having won the Grand Prix de Paris, over its old distance of a mile and seven furlongs, the previous season, the French horse Balto justified favouritism in the Gold Cup by beating Captain Boyd-Rochfort's Yorkshire Cup winner Sagacity by an exceedingly comfortable three parts of a length, with Prolific third. Balto was trained by Maxime Bonaventure for the banker Andre Rueff, and was a first runner at Ascot for both of them.

Irish horses were in top form. Paddy Prendergast completed the three-year-old fillies' double on the Wednesday by winning the Coronation Stakes with Display and Ribblesdale Stakes with Tender Annie, both ridden by the Australian Garnet Bougoure. On the opening day, Prendergast had also won the Queen's Vase with Pavot, on whom Joe Sime put up 1 lb overweight at 7 st 9 lb. The other Irish winner at the meeting was the three-year-old filly Cassarate, ridden by Neville Sellwood for Vincent O'Brien's stable. Carrying the colours of Countess Margit Batthyany, she made all the running to beat La Tendresse by two lengths in the King's Stand Stakes.

The meeting had opened on a particularly cold day, such as is experienced at the Cheltenham Festival meeting in March rather than at Royal Ascot, and the 2000 Guineas winner Privy Councillor had

Scobie Breasley, benefited from the suspension of Lester Piggott to win the Hardwicke Stakes in 1962.

done nothing to brighten up proceedings by failing to justify favouritism in the Queen Anne Stakes. After being prominent early on, he dropped back rapidly, so that he was only fifth to Nereus, ridden for Ken Cundell's Berkshire stable by Peter Robinson – the other jockey involved in that affair at Lincoln in May which had such serious consequences for Lester Piggott.

The only owner to enjoy two successes at the meeting was Mr Jim Joel. As well as the St James's Palace Stakes with Court Sentence, who lacked a previous race in the season, he won the Rous Memorial Stakes with Henry the Seventh, trained by Bill Elsey at Malton. In August Henry the Seventh, a fine big chestnut with a large blaze and two long socks behind, was syndicated for £3500 a share, but after he had disappointed badly by being beaten by

Vienna at Sandown Park on his final appearance Mr Joel, with typical generosity, reduced the price to £2500 a share.

Two-year-olds that are beaten at the opening fixture of the season rarely make amends by way of success at Royal Ascot. Major H. R. Broughton's little filly Summer Day, trained by Jack Waugh, proved one of the exceptions. Starting at 2/1 on, she won her sixth race off the reel by making all the running to beat Queen's Hussar, the sire of Brigadier Gerard, by two lengths in the Windsor Castle Stakes.

Fillies dominated the Chesham Stakes that year. Another to lead all the way was Major L. B. Holliday's Narrow Escape, who beat Visualise by three lengths, with Ampney Princess the same distance away third.

The Royal Hunt Cup was won by Smartie, trained by his owner Ron Mason, who ran a small stable at Guilsborough in Northamptonshire together with a haulage business. This man of many parts, who had once been a speedway rider, gave up training in 1981 to run a stud that he had bought in Queensland, Australia.

Noel Murless accomplished what was probably his finest feat of training when winning the Gold Cup with the inexperienced Twilight Alley in 1963. Lady Sassoon's Twilight Alley was a massive chestnut colt by Alycidon out of the Mieuxce mare Crepuscule, and therefore three parts brother to the Derby winner Crepello. Like Crepello he always wore "Newmarket Cloths", shaped pieces of box cloth, between knees and fetlocks, to support the tendons. Inevitably he was much too backward to run as a two-year-old, and on his only appearance as a three-year-old won the Cranbourn Chase Stakes at Ascot in July. Reappearing at Sandown Park in early June 1963 he was second to Gaul over two miles, then in what was no more than his third race this immature giant won the Gold Cup, for which the French horse Taine was favourite at 6/4. The previous month Taine had beaten Misti IV by three parts of a length in the Prix du Cadran. Lester Piggott rode a beautifully judged race on Twilight Alley, whom he took to the front straight away to set a moderate pace to the other six runners. Going round the Paddock bend the big chestnut gave evidence of his immaturity by checking fractionally,

but Piggott soon had him into his stride again. A mile from home Piggott increased the pace and on the turn into the straight Taine was racing in ominous proximity. Soon afterwards Taine came under heavy pressure, as Twilight Alley strode away to beat Misti IV by a length without being anything like extended, with Taine three lengths away third.

As Trelawny was by Black Tarquin and Twilight Alley by Alycidon, sons of the two horses who had been the protagonists in the Gold Cup of 1949 had almost made a clean sweep of the long-distance races at the Royal Meeting of 1963. On his only subsequent appearance Twilight Alley broke down in the King George VI and Queen Elizabeth Stakes, for which he was favourite. He retired to the Beech House Stud, Newmarket, at a fee of 400 guineas, but was not a success as a stallion, though he got a number of useful horses, the best of which was the Jockey Club Stakes winner Queen of Twilight. This fine stayer had to be put down owing to emphysema at the age of 17 in September 1976.

The other winners saddled by Noel Murless at Royal Ascot in 1963 were The Creditor, also owned by Lady Sassoon, in the Jersey Stakes, and Mr St George's El Gallo in the Cork and Orrery Stakes. In contrast to Twilight Alley, The Creditor had been so small as a two-year-old that she had not been broken until August.

Just as the 1899 Coventry Stakes winner Democrat became the charger of Field Marshal Kitchener in India, so Marcher, who won the Wokingham Stakes for David Hanley's stable in 1963, also went abroad to be the mount of a celebrity. He was acquired by Audie Murphy, the most decorated American soldier in the Second World War and later a film star, who rode the Royal Ascot winner around his ranch for a number of years.

Following his enforced absence the previous year, Lester Piggott was once again the leading jockey of the meeting in 1963, having ridden six winners. As well as those three races for Noel Murless, he had won the Royal Hunt Cup on Spaniards Mount for the stable of Fred Winter senior, the Bessborough Stakes on Raccolto, one more useful handicapper trained by Sam Hall, and finally the King's Stand Stakes on Majority Rule trained by Paddy O'Gorman.

As Piggott unsaddled Majority Rule, the old Royal Enclosure was emptying for the last time.

MODERN MAGNIFICENCE

AS THE royal procession drove up the course on the opening day of the meeting of 1964, the Queen and her party could see that the stands had changed out of all recognition since the outset of the reign. Not only had the splendid Queen Elizabeth II Stand replaced the old Tattersalls structure, but now the modern Royal Enclosure stood proudly beside it. After the 1963 July meeting the course had been closed, and the September fixture transferred to Newbury, then the October one to Kempton Park, while the old stand was demolished, and its successor, designed by Eric V. Collins A.R.I.B.A., was erected by Wimpey. The work of the builders and other contractors involved in this outsized undertaking was badly hampered by the severe weather of early 1964. March was so cold that when the turfs for the lawns arrived they were frozen solid, and fires had to be lit so that they could thaw out before being laid. Even while the spring meeting was held at Newbury in early May there was still no turf on the course, but Hugh Mounsey the Bailiff, or Head Groundsman, remained quite confident that he and his staff would have everything shipshape in time for the opening of the world's most fashionable race meeting. His expectations were completely fulfilled, and the course, together with the paddock and lawns, was looking quite immaculate when the Queen arrived on 16th June. It was impossible to believe the whole area had looked like a bomb-site just three months earlier. The new stand, which cost £1,750,000, provided viewing facilities for 8000 people, more than twice as many as had been accommodated in the old one, and had escalators running to all levels, as well as lifts at either end.

The splendid new stand could hardly have come into use in more inauspicious circumstances, unless the entire meeting had had to be cancelled. As it was, half the fixture was lost. For the first time since its inaugural running in 1807, an event other than world war occasioned the cancellation of the Gold Cup. Rain fell on the course on the first day, though only enough to have minimal effect on the going, which was on the soft side of good. The same ground prevailed on the following day, but soon after the completion of Wednesday's card, the deluge began and by midday on Thursday 0.65 inches of rain had fallen. By lunchtime the sun was shining as picnics were taken in the car parks while the crowds made their way into the various enclosures, and the inevitably heavy going seemed to be the only legacy of more than 12 hours of downpour. Then it all started again. The dark clouds rolled across the sky, and still more torrential rain was all that could be seen from the beautifully appointed new stands. The Stewards announced that racing had been postponed for a quarter of an hour, though only the most optimistic or most ignorant members of the crowd experiencing the damp that seeped under every available bit of shelter really thought there was any prospect of horses running that day. Course, paddock, lawns and car parks were all awash so as to form one great quagmire, and at 3.15 came the now inevitable news of abandonment. The likelihood of the course drying out fast enough to permit racing on Friday was too remote to be given serious consideration, especially as still more rain was forecast, and after an inspection in the morning, that card, too, was abandoned. The Duke of Norfolk and his colleagues on the Ascot Authority now found themselves in the distinctly uncomfortable position of having the finest stands in the country and a course on which racing could not be guaranteed because of the

In 1964 the rains came causing the cancellation
of the Gold Cup.

indifferent drainage of the Bagshot Sands on which
it lies.

The only trainer to saddle more than one winner
at that truncated meeting in 1964 was Ian Balding,
who had just taken official charge of the horses of
the Queen, Lord Sefton, Mr Paul Mellon and the
other patrons of the historic Kingsclere stable,
following the death of Captain Peter Hastings-Bass
at the tragically early age of 43 less than a fortnight
earlier. As well as the Coventry Stakes with Mr
Mellon's Silly Season, Ian Balding won the Bessborough Stakes with Linnet Lane, owned by Mrs
Priscilla Hastings, widow of Captain Hastings-Bass,
who had not been obliged to assume the additional
surname of Bass to conform to a will of an uncle of
her husband. Both Silly Season and Linnet Lane
were ridden by Geoff Lewis.

Like Captain Hastings-Bass, who had played rugger at Oxford and in the army, Ian Balding is a natural athlete as well as a highly successful trainer of
racehorses. After playing cricket for Marlborough,
he both boxed and played rugger for Cambridge,
and later played rugger at county level. In addition
he was an accomplished amateur steeplechase rider,
winning the National Hunt chase on Time at Cheltenham's Festival Meeting in 1962 and the Rhymney
Breweries chase on Caduval at Chepstow the following year. He is the son of Gerald Balding, who

had the Weyhill stable in Hampshire, and brother of
the present Weyhill trainer Toby Balding. Before
taking charge of the Kingsclere stable during the
final illness of Captain Hastings-Bass, Ian Balding
had been assistant to the Royal Ascot specialist
Herbert Blagrave at Beckhampton. In 1969 he
married Captain Hastings-Bass's daughter Emma.

Much the most important of the other ten
winners at Royal Ascot in 1964 was Windmill Girl,
who had been second to Homeward Bound in the
Oaks before beating Fusil by a length and a half in
the Ribblesdale Stakes. Windmill Girl, a bay filly by
Hornbeam out of the Chanteur II mare Chorus
Beauty, was trained at Whatcombe by her breeder
Arthur Budgett, who had leased her to Lieutenant-
Colonel Sir Jeffrey Darrel for her racing career. On
retiring to Arthur Budgett's Kirtlington Stud in
Oxfordshire, Windmill Girl achieved the distinction
of becoming the dam of two Derby winners –
Blakeney (by Hethersett) and Morston (by Ragusa).

John Oxley, who had won the Oaks with Homeward Bound, landed the Coronation Stakes for the
second year running when Mr R. D. Hollingsworth's Ocean beat Words and Music by a neck
with the 1000 Guineas winner Pourparler three
lengths away third. Twelve months earlier John
Oxley had been responsible for the success of Lady
Halifax's Fiji in the race.

Steps to reduce the likelihood of the Royal Meeting ever again being washed out were taken immediately. A great deal of work was undertaken by
a Dutch firm, with long experience of coping with
flooding in Holland, and by the time an extensive
operation had been completed there were no less
than 28 miles of drains beneath the Ascot course.

The Royal Meeting 1965 all but belonged to
Lester Piggott. On the Thursday in particular he
was very nearly unbeatable, as he won on four of
his five mounts, and was beaten by a neck on the
other. In all, his 19 rides over the four days yielded
eight winners, two seconds and three thirds. Perhaps it was on Colonel John Hornung's Casabianca,
whom he rode for Noel Murless in the Royal Hunt
Cup, that he was seen at his brilliant best. Three
furlongs from home Casabianca was nearer last
than first of the 26 runners. Having begun to make
progress from that point, Piggott shot Casabianca
through a gap in the final furlong, and was at his

Trainer Ian Balding and his wife Emma, daughter of Captain Hastings-Bass.

most powerful as he very nearly knelt on the horse's withers in order to squeeze the last scrap of energy out of him, with the result that Casabianca got up almost on the post to beat Weeper's Boy by a head.

For the first time in recent history the Gold Cup was not the most valuable race at the meeting. Like the Hardwicke it carried £10,000 added money, but as the Hardwicke attracted a larger entry it was worth £11,936 to the winner as opposed to the £10,801 that was the first prize for the Gold Cup. To win the Hardwicke Geoff Lewis produced a strong run out of Soderini in the final furlong to beat Earldom, owned and trained by Herbert Blagrave, by a neck, with Gladness's son Bally Joy five lengths away third. Soderini was trained by Staff Ingham for his breeder Mr "Laudy" Lawrence, and had been third in the St Leger of the previous season. Whether his ability was of suffi-

ciently high order to warrant his winning the most valuable race of the Royal Meeting was very much open to doubt.

In the Gold Cup Lester Piggott rode Fighting Charlie, and for the second time in five years won the race on a promoted handicapper for Freddie Maxwell's Lambourn stable. Taking the lead a furlong and a half out, Fighting Charlie ran on in fine style to beat the French challenger Waldmeister by two and a half lengths. On Fighting Charlie, who had won a £2000 handicap over two miles at Kempton Park on his previous appearance, Lester Piggott wore the all-rose jacket of Lady Mairi Bury, that had belonged to her grandfather Harry Chaplin, Lord Hasting's rival in racing and love.

Mr T. Marshall's Harvest Gold won the Ascot Stakes. As he began to tire in the final furlong Harvest Gold, the mount of Frankie Durr, hung right away from the far rail and wandered towards the middle of the course. All the same, he held the strong challenge of Philemon by a head, with Tropical Song just another head away third. Convinced that his mount had been hampered as Harvest Gold came across the course, Paul Cook, the rider of Philemon, lodged an objection. Unfortunately the camera patrol had broken down at one of the times when it was most needed, not uncharacteristically of such contrivances, and after hearing the evidence of Frankie Durr and Paul Cook, the Stewards allowed the result to stand.

Trained by Tommy Robson in Cumberland, Harvest Gold was bred by Queen Elizabeth, the Queen Mother, for whom he won a small race at Brighton as a three-year-old in 1962. At the end of that season he was bought out of Captain Boyd-Rochfort's stable by Tommy Robson for 1900 guineas. A remarkably versatile man, Tommy Robson is a qualified veterinary surgeon, and enjoyed considerable success as an amateur rider, winning the 1953 Scottish Grand National on Queen's Taste and Kempton's Heathorn Handicap Hurdle on Straight Cup, whom he owned and trained under a permit. In 1961 he turned professional, and won the Scottish Grand National again on Sham Fight in 1962.

The Windsor Castle Stakes of 1965 was won by a remarkably tough and consistent two-year-old in Sky Gipsy, trained by Gordon Smyth at Arundel. Sky Gipsy, who raced in a hood for all that he could not have been more genuine, had already won seven races, and went on to further successes in the July Stakes at Newmarket and the Richmond Stakes at Goodwood. A bay colt by Skymaster out of Tudor Gipsy, he was bred at the Ballymorris Stud in Ireland and bought by the Anglo-Irish Agency for 2000 guineas on behalf of the Duke of Norfolk's daughter Lady Sarah FitzAlan-Howard as a yearling. Just before the Royal Meeting he was acquired by the Texas oilman Mr R. E. Hibbert.

Sir Gordon Richards had another winner at Royal Ascot as a trainer when Mr R. F. Watson's home-bred filly Greengage was successful in the Coronation Stakes. Ridden by Scobie Breasley she got up in the last stride to win by a short head from Major Holliday's 1000 Guineas winner Night Off.

Two questions, of very different kinds, exercised the minds of the racing community at the outset of the Royal Ascot Meeting of 1966. How many, or rather how few, winners would Lester Piggott ride without the backing of a powerful retaining stable? How many people would win the jackpot, the new form of pool betting to be introduced by the Tote?

The previous month Lester Piggott had dropped a bombshell by severing his formal association with Newmarket's Warren Place Stable, as he wanted to ride Valoris in the Oaks for Vincent O'Brien, rather than Varinia for Noel Murless, and would therefore become a free-lance. Piggott's judgement was duly justified, as he won the Oaks on Valoris, with Varinia third. Very many people, unaware that he had declined to accept a retaining fee for 1966, were quick to accuse him of the grossest disloyalty, and eagerly prophesied that he had ruined his career, and thrown away the jockeys' championship, for the sake of an Oaks winner.

By the end of the meeting those who foretold the doom of Lester Piggott felt themselves more than justified. As well as the New Stakes on Falcon, he had landed the King George V Stakes on Marcus Brutus, owned by his close friend Mr Charles St George, and the Windsor Castle Stakes riding On Your Mark for his father-in-law Sam Armstrong; thus he had ridden just three winners as opposed to the eight 12 months earlier. To make things worse he had decided not to renew his partnership with the previous year's winner Fighting Charlie in the Gold Cup. Instead he rode Aegean Blue, on whom he had won the Chester Cup very easily, and had to be content with fourth place behind Fighting Charlie, ridden by Greville Starkey.

To win the jackpot, which seemed to offer untold wealth, backers had to name all six winners, by the use of combinations at five shillings (25p) a line on coupons issued by the Tote. If it was not won, the pool was carried forward to the next day of the meeting, but it had to be won on the final day. If nobody nominated all the winners on the last day, the pool was shared among those who found most consecutive winners starting from the first race. In the case of Ascot, the fixture was deemed to include Saturday's card, even though it was not part of the Royal Meeting.

This new form of wagering proved immensely popular with both racegoers and clients of the Tote credit service. The pool was not won on the first

Fighting Charlie won the Gold Cup in 1965 (above, partnered by Lester Piggott) and 1966, ridden by Greville Starkey.

Greville Starkey skilfully balanced stricken Fighting Charlie to win the 1966 Gold Cup for the second successive year.

day, nor on the second, and so things went on in the same vein until it had to be carried over to the Saturday, when there was just one winner, a widow from Ipswich. She scooped a pot of £63,114 by finding the first five winners.

That nobody should have been able to pick all six winners on any of the four days of the Royal Meeting was hardly surprising, as Ascot was never better described as "The Graveyard of Good Things" than it was in 1966. Former speedway rider Ron Mason nailed two huge nails into backers' coffins by completing a double with Track Spare at 100/9 in the St James's Palace Stakes and the 33/1 chance Petite Path in the Queen Mary Stakes. The Irish horse Continuation won the Royal Hunt Cup at 25/1 and on the fourth day the apprentice George Cadwaladr brought off a double on 20/1 chances by winning the Wokingham Stakes on My Audrey for his master Eric Cousins, and the King's Stand Stakes on

Roughlyn for the Cheshire stable of Doug Francis, brother of former champion jockey and successful novelist Dick Francis.

The Queen Mary Stakes was generally reckoned the roughest race seen at the meeting since the King Edward VII stakes that had cost Lester Piggott his licence 12 years earlier. Under the strong driving of Jimmy Lindley, Petite Path held a renewed challenge from Broadway Melody, with Floosie two and a half lengths away third. Recrimination came swiftly. Geoff Lewis, rider of Broadway Melody, objected to Petite Path for crowding him, and Taffy Thomas, who had ridden Floosie, objected to both the winner and runner-up for interference. Probably thinking that once they started apportioning blame there would be no end to the process, the Stewards decided to take no action, and the result stood.

As Great Nephew had been beaten by a short head in the 2000 Guineas he was generally expected to win the Queen Anne Stakes, for which he was a well-backed favourite. Two furlongs from home he threw down his challenge, which proved totally ineffective, so that he dropped back to finish fourth to the Irish-trained Ballyciptic, who won from Tesco Boy. The Stewards immediately instituted an enquiry, and after seeing the film, relegated Ballyciptic to last place, and awarded the race to Tesco Boy, trained by Staff Ingham for Mr J. E. Cohen, and ridden by Ron Hutchinson.

The 1000 Guineas winner Glad Rags, ridden by Lester Piggott, was hot favourite for the Coronation Stakes. Soft Angels, who had delayed the start of the 1000 Guineas by her mulishness, was again on her worst behaviour, and when the race started nine minutes later, recoiled from the tapes momentarily, Glad Rags also being slowly away. After recovering enough ground to be in touch with the leaders by halfway, Glad Rags could find nothing extra in the final furlong, and was only third to Haymaking, ridden by Joe Mercer in the colours of Lincolnshire landowner Clifford Nicholson for Fulke Johnson Houghton's stable. Haymaking became the dam of Hayloft, whose son Wassl won the Irish 2000 Guineas in 1983, while Glad Rags was the mother of Gorytus, impressive winner of the Acomb Stakes at York and of Doncaster's Champagne Stakes before his inexplicable failure in the Dewhurst Stakes in 1982.

Fulke Johnson Houghton is the son of Major Gordon Johnson Houghton, who was assistant to Jack Colling before beginning to train in his native Cheshire in 1935. Following service in the war, the Major resumed training at Blewbury in Berkshire until tragically killed in a road accident while hunting with the Old Berkshire in 1952. His widow Helen, twin sister of Fulke Walwyn, then ran the stable until Fulke Johnson Houghton could take it over on coming of age in 1961. He achieved immediate success by winning the Greenham Stakes, the Sussex Stakes and the Queen Elizabeth II Stakes with Romulus in 1962, and then trained the full brothers Ribero and Ribocco to bring off the double in the Irish Derby and St Leger in 1967 and 1968 respectively.

Because of the outbreak of swamp fever in France, the government had banned the import of horses from that country in 1966. That eased the task of Fighting Charlie in the Gold Cup, though it was a near miracle that he won a second time. Turning into the straight he went so wide that the commentator mistakenly announced that he had run out. The stands rails prevented him drifting any further to the left, but he was clearly in distress, and seemed to have broken down. With a characteristically consummate feat of horsemanship, Greville Starkey had him balanced again, and, displaying immense courage, Fighting Charlie went in pursuit of the leaders. Taking the lead again with two furlongs to go, he strode away to come home eight lengths clear of Biomydrin. After Fighting Charlie had received an ovation worthy of a royal winner, Freddie Maxwell revealed that both the horse's fore legs had been so badly inflamed four days earlier, that it was 100/1 against his running. The apparently disastrous situation had been saved by Lambourn veterinary surgeon Frank Mahon.

With no challenge from France the Hardwicke Stakes seemed at the mercy of Colonel Hornung's four-year-old filly Aunt Edith, ridden by Scobie Breasley for Noel Murless. As she came under pressure two furlongs from home it was clear that the odds-on chance was not going to reproduce the running that had won her the Yorkshire Cup so easily the previous month. Dropping back rapidly, Aunt Edith finished a remote fifth of six to Mr Jim Mullion's Prominer, trained by Paddy Prendergast.

Aunt Edith was quite obviously not right, and there was the obvious possibility of her having been nobbled, but tests revealed no evidence of her having been doped. All the same, many people were of the opinion that the verdict was not proven, rather than negative. Happily for her connections, she left the form right behind her when returning to Ascot to win the King George VI and the Queen Elizabeth Stakes in July.

The stars of the Royal Meeting of 1967 were the Duke of Devonshire's filly Park Top, trained by Bernard van Cutsem in the Stanley House stable at Newmarket, and Be Friendly, a colt trained at Epsom by Cyril Mitchell for Peter O'Sullevan, the greatly respected racing journalist and outstanding television commentator. Park Top was one of those bargains to come good at Ascot. A robust bay by Alycidon's son Kalydon, bred by Mrs Leonard Scott at the Buttermilk Stud in Oxfordshire, she had been bought by her trainer for just 500 guineas as a yearling. Like so many horses that are too backward to run as two-year-olds she repaid the patience of her connections many times over. After being successful at Windsor and Newbury on the first two appearances of her second season, she stepped into the top league by beating St Pauli Girl, runner-up in the Oaks and 1000 Guineas, by half a length in the Ribblesdale Stakes. That was not to be her only tenancy of the winner's enclosure at Royal Ascot.

Although he cost a bit more than Park Top, Be Friendly was by no means expensive, as Peter O'Sullevan had been able to secure him with a bid of 2800 guineas at Tattersalls September Sales. A handsome chestnut colt of 16½ hands bred by Mr W. J. Madden in Ireland, he was by Skymaster, who had obtained a Royal Ascot success in the Windsor Castle Stakes, out of Lady Sliptic, by Preciptic. By the end of his two-year-old days he had done much more than recover his purchase price as he had won the first running of the Vernons Sprint Cup, worth £5337, and three other races. Scobie Breasley rode this high-class sprinter in the King's Stand Stakes, and going to the front with a perfectly timed challenge a furlong and a half out he beat the French colt Yours by half a length.

Watering overnight did not have the desired effect of taking the sting completely out of the

Australian jockey George Moore and Noel Murless with owner Lady Sassoon in 1967.

ground, and the surface beneath the turf was still quite firm by the third day of the meeting. The principal sufferer from man's failure to control nature was Danseur, who was odds on for the Gold Cup on the strength of his having won the Prix du Cadran for François Mathet's stable. Stan Mellor, who had been three times champion steeplechase jockey, made the running on the blinkered Bally Russe for a mile, after which Danseur took over. As he came under pressure with a furlong to run, Danseur faltered and Parbury went into the lead. One hundred yards from home Mehari struck the front, but Parbury, powerfully, rhythmically ridden by Joe Mercer got up to win by a short head. The

winner carried the colours of Major H. P. Holt, and was trained by Major Derrick Candy in the Kingstone Warren stable, which the Major handed over to his son Henry on his retirement at the end of 1973. A kind and approachable man, who earned and received the complete loyalty of his owners, Major Candy died in 1983.

The season of 1967 was notable for the riding of the Australian George Moore, whom Noel Murless had brought to England to be the first jockey to the Warren Place stable. From only 233 mounts, as opposed to the 552 of Lester Piggott, he rode 72 winners, a 30.9 percentage of success. Three of those winners were at Royal Ascot, where he brought off a double for Noel Murless on Mrs Murless's St Chad in the Jersey Stakes and Mr R. C. Boucher's Fleet in the Coronation Stakes on the Wednesday. The following day Moore won the Cork and Orrery Stakes on Mr Con Pollock's Siliconn, trained by former steeplechase jockey Atty Corbett, who was killed in a road accident while walking with his string at Newmarket in November 1976.

Fleet provided 43-year-old George Moore with the 2000th winner of his career. His first had been on the other Ascot racecourse, that at Brisbane, on Eagle Farm on New Year's Day 1940. Moore's stay in England was marred by threats of physical violence from less scrupulous members of the gambling fraternity, whom he had declined to oblige, and he did not return in 1968.

Mr Michael Sobell's Reform, the most important horse to be trained by Sir Gordon Richards, won the St James's Palace Stakes. Ridden by Scobie Breasley with characteristic tenderness, he beat Chinwag by a head, which would have been a far wider margin under the guidance of a less self-confident jockey. At stud Reform proved a considerable success by getting the Prix du Jockey Club winner Roi Lear, the Oaks winner Polygamy and other horses of undoubted class. A number of his daughters made their marks as brood mares, notably Lady Tavistock's Mrs Moss, dam of the Hardwicke Stakes winner Jupiter Island (by St Paddy), Precocious (by Mummy's Pet), successful in the Gimcrack Stakes, and Pushy (by Sharpen Up), winner of the Queen Mary Stakes.

Starting stalls were used at Royal Ascot for the first time in 1967. They supplanted the old-fashioned barrier, and were widely welcomed by reason of their reducing the likelihood of a horse being left. This went a long way to ensure that every backer had a run for his or her money. As the betting public had been making a substantial financial contribution to the support of racing through the levy since the passing of the Betting Levy Act of 1961, it was no more than right that its interests should be protected to the uttermost. On the other hand, the introduction of stalls did have the deleterious effect of levelling down the talents of jockeys. Hitherto one of the most prized skills of a rider was his ability to get a "flier" from the gate. To many people it seemed an act of gross injustice

to deprive the rider who had made a fine art of getting away from the barrier the opportunities to profit from it, and to remove the premium it put upon his services. The first winner from the stalls at Royal Ascot was Mr G. Dudley's Good Match. Ridden by little David East at 7 st 3 lb for Jeremy Tree's Beckhampton stable, the three-year-old made all the running to hold the challenge of Arenaria by a neck in the Queen Anne Stakes.

Doug Smith, who had ridden Alycidon to his momentous revenge over Black Tarquin in the Gold Cup of 1949, appeared in a new role at the Royal Ascot meeting of 1968. At the end of the previous season he had retired from the saddle to train some 40 horses in the newly constructed Loder Stable on Hamilton Road, Newmarket. No man could have made a better start to his second profession. With his first runner, Mr A. G. Samuel's Owen Anthony, he won the first race of his first season, then he won with his first runner at Royal Ascot when Mr J. F. Lewis's Virginia Gentleman beat Lady Halifax's Lincoln winner Frankincense by a length and a half in the Queen Anne Stakes.

The following day Doug Smith performed a notable feat by saddling both the winner and the runner-up for the Royal Hunt Cup, in which Gold Mean, the mount of Frankie Durr, beat Owen Anthony, ridden by Ray Still, by half a length. Not only were those two horses stablemates, but they were also half-brothers out of the Arctic Star mare Oweninny.

With George Moore declining to return to England, Noel Murless appointed Sandy Barclay, the 20-year-old Scot who had been champion apprentice in 1966, as his stable jockey for 1968. Barclay had never ridden a winner at Royal Ascot, but was leading rider of the meeting that year with five successes. For Noel Murless he brought off a treble on Mr Jim Joel's Royal Palace, winner of the Derby the previous year, in the Prince of Wales' Stakes, on Connaught, also owned by Mr Joel, in the King Edward VII Stakes, and on the Queen's Hopeful Venture in the Hardwicke Stakes. Barclay also won on Virginia Gentleman, and rode Mr H. H. Renshaw's Hopiana to win the Windsor Castle Stakes for Arthur Budgett's stable.

Although the meeting was, as usual, dominated by the most powerful stables in England and

Ireland, with the occasional French runner intensifying the competition, Ted Goddard, who had just 25 horses in his West Horsley yard between Guildford and Leatherhead, brought off a double, a prodigious feat of giant-slaying. With Mr S. A. Thorne's Q.C. he landed the Bessborough Stakes and with Tubalcain the Queen Alexandra Stakes; both were ridden by Geoff Lewis. While indentured to Colledge Leader at Newmarket, Ted Goddard showed talent in the boxing ring, and won several trophies at the National Sporting Club. After having had a number of mounts as an apprentice he rode quite a few winners over hurdles in the season preceding the outbreak of the Second World War. For 21 years he was attached to the West Horsley stable while Bertie Holland trained in it, and on Holland's surrendering his licence, Ted Goddard took over that little establishment in 1950, his son Peter being his head lad for many years. On retiring at the age of 67 in 1975, Ted Goddard lost none of his enthusiasm for racing, and regularly attended meetings in the London area.

French horses completely dominated the Gold Cup in 1968, although the previous year's winner Parbury took the field again. There was a massive public gamble on Countess Margit Batthyany's Samos, ridden by Lester Piggott for Albert Klimscha's stable.

A furlong and a half from home Pardallo II, on whom the Australian Bill Pyers wore the colours of Mme Suzy Volterra, struck the front, then after another 10 yards Lester Piggott suddenly produced the favourite. Samos challenged ferociously throughout the final furlong, but he never got on terms with Pardallo II, who beat him by a length. Another French horse, Petrone, was third, Parbury having been out of contention throughout the race.

Pardallo II was trained by Charles Bartholomew. The five-year-old's previous target in England had been the Champion Hurdle. That particular project had, however, to be abandoned after he had fallen in the Grande Course de Haies de Quatre Ans at Auteuil.

For the first time lounge suits, as opposed to the hitherto mandatory morning coats, were acceptable attire in the Royal Enclosure in 1968. Very few availed themselves of this sartorial concession to the Age of the Common Man, with the result that the

Trainer Doug Smith (left), seen at the yearling sales in 1968 with the Hon. David Montagu.

experiment was soon discontinued.

Names that had seemed indelibly written on Royal Ascot were missing from the racecard in 1969. Captain Sir Cecil Boyd-Rochfort had handed over the Freemason Lodge string to his stepson Henry Cecil at the end of the previous season, and Sir Jack Jarvis, who had laid the foundation of his reputation by winning the Wokingham Stakes with Golden Orb almost half a century earlier in 1920, died suddenly on 18th December 1968 while preparing for his annual holiday in South Africa. Sir Jack had never retired. Sir Cecil had received his knighthood in the New Year's Honours in 1968, and Sir Jack his in the Birthday Honours of 1967. Both had been born in 1887. Sir Cecil spent his retirement in his native Ireland, and had reached the great age of 95 when he died in March 1983. Walter Nightingall, who had trained so many Royal Ascot winners in the historic South Hatch stable at Epsom, also died in 1968, while Geoffrey Brooke, past master at the handling of precocious two-year-olds, had retired at the end of 1967. In some respects Royal Ascot was coming to the end of an era as well as a decade.

Following the death of Sir Jack Jarvis, Lord Rosebery turned Park Lodge into a private stable and had his horses, and those that his friend Lord Sefton had in the yard, trained by Doug Smith, who simultaneously ran the Loder Stable as a public establishment. Having made a flying start to his career at Loder, Doug Smith commenced his association with Park Lodge in similar style. On the second day of the Royal Ascot meeting of 1969 Doug Smith brought off a double for Lord Rosebery by winning the Jersey Stakes with Crooner and the Ribblesdale Stakes with the grey Sleeping Partner, who had won the Oaks on her previous appearance. Both were ridden by the 23-year-old South African jockey John Gorton, who had been apprenticed to Fred Rickaby, elder brother of Bill Rickaby. For good measure, on the day that Crooner and Sleeping Partner won, Doug Smith completed a hat-trick as he sent out Mr Danny van Clief's Farfalla from the Loder Stable to be ridden by Tony Murray to win the Queen Mary Stakes.

A little piece of history was made when Mrs Rosemary Lomax became the first woman to be the official trainer of a winner at Royal Ascot, as she was responsible for the success of Mr R. J. McAlpine's grey colt Precipice Wood in the King George V Stakes. The Jockey Club had only been granting women licences to train since losing the case brought against them by Mrs Florence Nagle in the Court of Appeal in July 1966. Previously the licences of women trainers had been held by assistants or head lads, as that of Mrs Helen Johnson Houghton had been by her cousin Peter Walwyn when she won with New Move at Royal Ascot in 1960.

Peter Walwyn, formerly assistant to Major Geoffrey Brooke, had opened his own stable at Lambourn in 1961. At that Royal Ascot meeting of 1969 he brought off a double with Mr Evelyn de Rothschild's Town Crier in the Queen Anne Stakes

and Mr Louis Freedman's high-class filly Lucyrowe in the Coronation Stakes, Duncan Keith being the successful rider in each instance.

On the second day Kamundu was ridden by Lester Piggott to land a huge gamble in the Royal Hunt Cup for flamboyant Scottish bookmaker John Banks, who operates on the rails. After being backed to win thousands of pounds, Kamundu, trained by Frank Carr at Malton, held the challenge of Lorenzaccio by half a length.

The future champion jockey Pat Eddery, then just 17 years of age, obtained his first success at Royal Ascot when claiming the 7 lb apprentices' allowance on Sky Rocket in the Wokingham Stakes. Sky Rocket was trained by Major Michael Pope. Only two months beforehand Eddery had ridden his first winner on Alvaro, also trained by Major Pope, at Epsom. Eddery has been the most successful of several good riders who served their apprenticeships with "Frenchie" Nicholson at Cheltenham. He is the son of Jimmy Eddery, who won the St James's Palace Stakes on Chevastrid in 1957 as well as many other races for the McGrath stable.

When the Duchess of Devonshire persuaded her husband to keep Park Top in training as a five-year-old, the Duke was left with no cause to regret having acquiesced. Following her success in the Coronation Cup that wonderful mare made a second appearance at Royal Ascot, and, ridden by Geoff Lewis, beat Chicago by an extremely comfortable length and a half in the Hardwicke Stakes.

In October 1969 Major-General Sir David Dawnay, who had been Clerk of the Course since 1957, retired and was succeeded by his former assistant, Captain the Hon. Nicholas Beaumont. After 13 years' service in the Life Guards, Captain Beaumont had become the Assistant Clerk of the Course at Ascot in May 1964. The post was created when jumping was to be staged on the course for the first time the following year. As General Dawnay lived in Ireland, there had arisen the necessity for somebody in authority to live on the spot so as to advise the Stewards of the necessity for inspections of the course during the winter. A man of great charm and tact, Captain Beaumont has worked hard to maintain, and in many cases improve on, the standards of his predecessors. Under his supervision the amenities in all enclosures have been enhanced, while the quality of the racing has never been higher.

The first Royal Meeting at which Captain Beaumont officiated as Clerk of the Course was disrupted by the General Election of 1970. In accordance with a long-established custom, since discontinued, there was no racing on polling day, and Thursday's card was transferred to Saturday, while that scheduled for Saturday was abandoned. Having been the first woman to be the official trainer of a winner at the meeting the previous year, Rosemary Lomax proceeded to become the first to saddle the winner of what is now classified a Group race when Precipice Wood took a step up in class successfully in the Gold Cup. Going into the lead two furlongs from home, Precipice Wood was ridden out by Jimmy Lindley to beat Blakeney, winner of the 1969 Derby, by three parts of a length.

The first two days were all but dominated by Noel Murless and Sandy Barclay, who began the meeting by bringing off a double for Mr Jim Joel, Welsh Pageant winning the Queen Anne Stakes and Connaught the Prince of Wales Stakes for the second year running. They also shared the success of Mr Stanhope Joel's Saintly Song in the St James's Palace Stakes, while the following day they won the Bessborough Stakes with Mr Jim Joel's Prince Consort and the Ribblesdale Stakes with Lord Howard de Walden's Parmelia.

Prince Consort was a big bay, half-brother to the Derby winner Royal Palace by Right Royal V, and Connaught was an even bigger colt of the same colour with a long blaze and socks on his hind pasterns. How little Sandy Barclay managed to keep such huge animals balanced was a mystery to most people. On his first appearance in public as a two-year-old Connaught, doubtless conscious of his size and afraid of claustrophobia, had flatly refused to enter his stall at York and had to be withdrawn.

By giving an encore of his 1969 success in the Prince of Wales Stakes, Connaught joined the select band of horses that have won at Royal Ascot three years running, as he had lost his maiden status in the King Edward VII Stakes in 1968. Connaught was by St Paddy out of the Goyama mare Nagaika, whom Mr Joel bought – through the good offices of Lavinia, Duchess of Norfolk – by reason of her being entirely free of Nearco blood. At stud Connaught

has got a number of offspring of genuine class, including the champion German miler Lirung, winner of the Prix Jacques le Marois, the Yorkshire Oaks winner Connaught Bridge, and Remainder Man, runner-up in the 2000 Guineas and third in the Derby.

At a time when colts with aspirations to winning the Derby were ever less frequently seen in the first half of their first season, Mr Paul Mellon's Mill Reef proved an exception to the rule, as he was to so many others. On the strength of his having made all the running at Salisbury in the middle of May, he started at 11/4 on for the Coventry Stakes, and justified confidence by beating Cromwell by eight lengths. He was the third winner of the race to be ridden by Geoff Lewis for Ian Balding, following Silly Season, as already mentioned, and Murrayfield in 1969. Ian Balding and Geoff Lewis also won the Ascot Stakes for the Queen with Magna Carta in 1970.

One of the best horses ever to win the Coventry Stakes, Mill Reef was a bay colt by the Nasrullah horse Never Bend out of Milan Mill. Of enormous quality, he gave the impression of being smaller than he actually was because of his perfect proportions. As a three-year-old he completed the great treble in the Derby, the King George VI and Queen Elizabeth Stakes, and the Prix de l'Arc de Triomphe. At stud he sired the Derby winners Shirley Heights and Reference Point, together with a plethora of other high-class horses.

An intense anglophile and a member of a famous American banking family, Mill Reef's owner Mr Paul Mellon was born in Pittsburgh, Pennsylvannia in 1907. While reading history at Cambridge, he developed a passion for foxhunting, and subsequently took to steeplechasing. After his first racehorse, the Irish-bred Drinmore Lad, had won several races for him in the United States, Mr Mellon was persuaded to bring that chaser back to England by his compatriot Ambrose Clark, whose wife had won the Grand National of two years earlier with Kellsboro Jack, a stablemate of Brown Jack in the Wroughton yard, which was being run by Ivor Anthony in association with the widow of Aubrey Hastings. Drinmore Lad duly joined the horses of his owner's friend Ambrose Clark at Wroughton. Mr Mellon thus came to know Mrs Hastings, with

Connaught, ridden by Sandy Barclay, gains the first of his two successes in the Prince of Wales' Stakes in 1969.

Henry Cecil and owner Charles St George.

whose family his friendship has endured for more than 50 years.

Soon after the end of the war, Mr Mellon renewed his interest in English racing by sending two horses for the flat to Aubrey Hastings' son Peter Hastings-Bass who moved the stable from Wroughton to Kingsclere.

The former champion jockey Scobie Breasley, who had retired from riding two years earlier, brought off a training double at Royal Ascot in 1970 with Yellow River in the Queen's Vase, and Great Wall, who had been fourth in the Derby, in the King Edward VII Stakes. Both were owned by Mr David Sung, whose red colours with gold fringed hoop and armlets were said to make a jockey look more like a lampshade than a race rider. Breasley's old rival in the saddle, Doug Smith, produced his sixth Royal Ascot winner in six years in Mr Benny Schmidt-Bodner's Virginia Boy, who beat Koala by a neck in the Wokingham Stakes.

Sir Reginald Macdonald-Buchanan's Parthenon became the first of many Royal Ascot winners to be trained by Henry Cecil by beating Hickleton by a comfortable three lengths in the Queen Alexandra Stakes in 1970. Henry Cecil and his twin brother

David were born in January 1943, the posthumous sons of Captain the Hon. Henry Cecil, who had been killed in action a fortnight earlier, and Rohays, daughter of Major-General Sir James Burnett, 13th Baronet of Leys. Captain Cecil, a younger brother of Lord Amherst of Hackney, had had horses with George Lambton.

In July 1944 Rohays Cecil married Captain Cecil Boyd-Rochfort. Henry Cecil and his three brothers were brought up amongst racehorses in the Freemason Lodge stable at Newmarket, and in 1945 the family was increased by the birth of Arthur Boyd-Rochfort. After being educated at Canford, Dorset, Henry Cecil worked on studs in France and the United States, completed a year's course at Cirencester Agricultural College, and further enlarged his experience by studying the anatomy of the horse at the Equine Research Station at Newmarket. In November 1964 he became assistant trainer to Captain Boyd-Rochfort, and two years later married Julie, daughter of Sir Noel Murless.

On the retirement of Captain Boyd-Rochfort at the end of the season of 1968, Henry Cecil took over the string, moving from Freemason Lodge to the newly constructed Marriott Stables on the other side of Newmarket in 1970. There has never been anything spectacular about Henry Cecil's methods. Rather than depend on plenty of strong gallops, like Reg Day, Jack Jarvis and other trainers of the old school, to bring his string to peak fitness, he economises on the expenditure of a horse's energy on the working grounds to the utmost, bringing his charges to form with good, healthy exercise. Moreover, he never stages the formal trials, racing paced gallops, which the old-fashioned trainers used to ascertain the relative merits of their horses. Instead he relies on his own evaluation of the way horses move in sensibly paced work. The formula for success of the order enjoyed by Henry Cecil necessarily defies analysis, but there is no doubt that his instinctive ability to interpret the evidence of his own eyes, and the accumulation of an extraordinary amount of it, both by watching work on the Heath and going around stables morning and evening, makes a vital contribution to his achievements.

Henry Cecil obtained his first classic success with Cloonagh, owned and bred by his half-brother Arthur Boyd-Rochfort, in the Irish 1000 Guineas in

1973, and won his first English classic with Bolkonski in 1975. The following year he finished champion trainer on the first of eight occasions to date, and following the retirement of Sir Noel Murless at the end of 1976 took over the Warren Place stable. Since then he has won the Derby with Slip Anchor in 1985 and Reference Point in 1987. In the latter year he won 180 races, a seasonal record for a trainer.

Like Henry Cecil, George Duffield enjoyed success at Royal Ascot for the first time in 1970. The 23-year-old Newmarket jockey won the Jersey Stakes on Mr R. D. Hollingsworth's Fluke for John Oxley's Newmarket stable, and just over an hour later completed a double by riding Mr C. W. Engelhard's Calpurnius to win the Royal Hunt Cup. Calpurnius was trained at Newmarket by Bill Watts, great-grandson of Persimmon's jockey Jack Watts. At the end of that season Bill Watts went north to take over the Hurgill Lodge stable at Richmond in Yorkshire.

Forty-five years after obtaining his first success at Royal Ascot on Lord Glanely's Sunderland, Sir Gordon Richards enjoyed his last when Edward Hide rode Marcia, Lady Beaverbrook's Richboy to win the Britannia Stakes of 1970. At the end of that season Sir Gordon disbanded his string, as his lease on the Whitsbury stable had expired and he was unable to find another suitable establishment. In retirement he managed the horses of Lady Beaverbrook and Sir Michael Sobell. He died at the age of 82 in November 1986.

The Rock Roi saga opened at the Royal Meeting of 1971. Then a four-year-old, trained by Peter Walwyn for Colonel Roger Hue-Williams, Rock Roi was ridden by Duncan Keith to finish four lengths clear of Random Shot in the Gold Cup. Rock Roi was then subjected to a routine dope test which revealed traces of oxyphenbutazone. The Stewards held a five-hour enquiry on 27th August, at which the colt's trainer Peter Walwyn explained that on veterinary advice he had given Rock Roi a course of Equipalazone, of which oxyphenbutazone is a constituent, as a cure for the stiffness with which he walked out in the morning. The manufacturers recommended that treatment should be discontinued 72 hours before running. In this case it had ceased 118 hours prior to running, the last dose having

been administered with Rock Roi's morning feed on the Saturday prior to the race. The Stewards totally exonerated Peter Walwyn and his head lad; but as a non-normal nutrient that could have affected performance had been found in his urine, the Stewards were obliged to disqualify Rock Roi and award the race to Random Shot, whom Arthur Budgett trained for Mrs G. S. Benskin.

It was a great pity that the oxyphenbutazone should have remained in Rock Roi's system for so much longer than the manufacturers, or anybody else, anticipated, as he was clearly the outstanding stayer of the season. On his only subsequent appearances of 1971 that chestnut colt by Mourne out of the Court Martial mare Secret Session won the Goodwood Cup, in which Random Shot finished a respectful eight lengths behind him in third place, and beat Russian Bank by a length in the Doncaster Cup.

While the rain teemed down throughout the opening day of the 1971 meeting, and the ground eased perceptibly all the time, misgivings about the unbeaten Brigadier Gerard being able to show his brilliance on soft going in the St James's Palace Stakes were voiced. Each of the five races that Mrs John Hislop's colt had won up to that time had been run on good or fast ground, and in the most recent of them he had turned in a fine performance by beating Mill Reef by three lengths in the 2000 Guineas. The question as to whether the Brigadier would like the underfoot conditions was quickly determined. He loathed them. But Brigadier Gerard had other qualities besides class of an outstandingly high order. One of them was courage. And it was the combination of class and courage that decided the issue on that damp and depressing afternoon at Royal Ascot. A furlong from home he was already under heavy pressure from Joe Mercer, but giving every last ounce of energy that he had in response to the desperate calls that were being made upon him, he got up in the last few strides to beat Sparkler, ridden by Lester Piggott, by a head.

Brigadier Gerard was a fine, big bay colt of great quality, with no white except a small star, bred by Mrs Hislop in partnership with her husband John, the former top amateur steeplechase jockey who was third in the Grand National on Kami in 1947. As well as having been a successful rider, and having won the Military Cross while serving with the Special Air Services, John Hislop is a writer of great talent. The titles of his two volumes of autobiography – *Anything But a Soldier* and *Far From a Gentleman* – reflect his somewhat sardonic sense of humour. In addition he has written *The Brigadier*, an account of the racing career of the great horse he bred, while his *The Theory and Practice of Flat Race Riding* is regarded as a classic of its kind. He was well qualified to write it, as he was champion amateur on the flat for the 10 years from 1946 to 1955.

Brigadier Gerard was trained by Major Dick Hern at West Ilsley. Earlier on that wet opening day of the Royal Meeting of 1971 Major Hern had initiated a double by winning the Coventry Stakes with Mr Michael Sobell's 20/1 chance Sun Prince.

By the second day the going was predictably heavy and Greville Starkey rode Mr R. R. Ohrstrom's Fleet Wahine to win the Ribblesdale Stakes for Tom Jones's stable. Eight years earlier the jockey had won the Coronation Stakes on Fiji, the dam of Fleet Wahine. That success by Fleet Wahine renewed another old association, as Greville Starkey had begun his career as an apprentice with Tom Jones. Unlike so many flat race jockeys, Greville Starkey is a horseman, as he showed in his handling of Fighting Charlie in the Gold Cup of 1966, as well as a race rider whose skill in riding a hard puller in the hunting field has commanded as much admiration as his ability to produce a colt to snatch the verdict in a photo finish to the Derby. The twin peaks of a long and successful career were the winning of the Derby on Shirley Heights in 1978 and the Prix de l'Arc de Triomphe on Star Appeal in 1975. He retired at the end of 1989.

While in his first season in Richmond's Hurgill Lodge stable in 1971, Bill Watts returned to Royal Ascot to win the Queen Mary Stakes with Mrs Richard Stanley's Waterloo. That filly was another of the comparatively few recent two-year-old winners at the meeting to graduate to classic honours, as she was to be successful in the 1000 Guineas of 1972.

For the second consecutive year the combination of owner Benny Schmidt-Bodner, trainer Doug Smith and jockey Dennis McKay shared success in the Wokingham Stakes with Whistling Fool getting up close to home to beat Golden Tack by a head. The going brought about a diametrical reversal of form in the Queen Alexandra Stakes. Whereas Parthenon had beaten Hickleton by three lengths on a sound surface 12 months earlier, Hickleton now ploughed through the heavy ground to beat Parthenon by five lengths.

Because of the state of the going the form shown at the meeting was highly suspect. Sparkler, for instance, was a great deal further behind Brigadier Gerard at level weights than the head by which he had been beaten in the St James's Palace Stakes. When they met on firm going in the Queen Elizabeth II over the same course and distance in the September of the following year the Brigadier gave Sparkler 7 lb and a beating of six lengths. Though so many questions had been left unanswered by the end of the Royal Meeting of 1971, the efficiency of the new drainage system had certainly been proved.

Along with the pageantry and splendour attendant upon the presence of the sovereign on a formal occasion, the cream of European thoroughbreds, and fashion, elements of theatre have always been inseparable from Royal Ascot. Two episodes of high drama were the features of the meeting in 1972, one that had a most unsatisfactory outcome, so far as most parties were concerned, and the other that had a happy ending. On the one hand, almost incredibly, Rock Roi was disqualified in the Gold Cup for a second time; on the other, Brigadier Gerard and Joe Mercer were successful again – but this time it was the courage of the rider, not his mount, that richly deserved the ovation of the huge crowd.

Rock Roi started at 11/4 on to obtain compensation for his misfortunes of 12 months earlier in the Gold Cup. Six furlongs out Duncan Keith sent him to the forefront, and he led into the straight from Russian Bond and the grey Erimo Hawk. With more than a furlong still to run Rock Roi was already being hard ridden, and at the distance marker was headed by Erimo Hawk, racing on his outside, under heavy pressure from Pat Eddery. Rock Roi, on the rails, rallied well for Duncan Keith, and a battle royal ensued over the final furlong. Duncan Keith had his whip in his right hand, and as Rock Roi hung away from it towards his left, inevitably hampered Erimo Hawk. Although

Brigadier Gerard and Joe Mercer, the only jockey ever to partner him in public.

unbalanced, Rock Roi continued to fight back tenaciously and securing a narrow advantage in the last few strides, passed the post a head to the good. The inevitable Stewards' Enquiry followed, and as the head-on camera made it clear that Erimo Hawk would have won had he not suffered interference, the grey was awarded the race with Rock Roi relegated to second berth.

That then was the end of the tragedy of Rock Roi. Later that year he was exported to France, where he had been able to show his true excellence by beating Parnell by a length on soft ground in the Prix du Cadran four weeks before he was disqualified at Royal Ascot for a second time. He was, without doubt, one of the finest stayers to have contested the Gold Cup without having his name on the roll of winners painted on the panelling in the office of the Clerk of the Course.

Erimo Hawk was owned by the Japanese businessman Mr S. Yamamoto, and trained at Newmarket by Geoffrey Barling, whose father Frank Barling had won those seven races at Royal Ascot for Lord Glanely in 1919. Geoffrey Barling was a tall, dark man, of great charm and totally unassuming. He loved training stayers, though he could well do justice to a sprinter as he showed in the case of Tower Walk. In 1973 he was obliged to retire when the council demolished his Primrose Cottage stable in the process of redeveloping the centre of Newmarket. He died at the age of 83 in October 1984.

Two days before the Royal Meeting of 1972 was to open, Joe Mercer had been booked for a number of mounts in Belgium, and was to fly to Brussels from Newbury racecourse in company with the Whitsbury trainer Bill Marshall, and two others. As soon as the plane took off it struck an overhead cable and was sent crashing to the ground. The pilot was killed instantly, but Joe Mercer was thrown clear. With total disregard for his own safety Mercer rushed back to the wreckage to pull the badly injured Bill Marshall and another passenger clear.

The ordeal left the jockey badly shaken and suffering from shock, so that there was inevitably doubt as to whether he would be able to ride Brigadier Gerard in the Prince of Wales' Stakes and fulfil his other commitments at the Royal Meeting. John Hislop maintained that the rider should be the sole judge of whether he would be able to take the mount on The Brigadier, whom no other jockey had partnered in public. Mercer finally decided he could do justice to the colt, who required none of the forceful assistance from the saddle he had done on the soft ground 12 months earlier, and won by a comfortable five lengths from the three-year-old Steel Pulse. Well aware that he had risked his life to save those of others 48 hours earlier, the crowd gave Joe Mercer a wonderful reception as he brought Brigadier Gerard back to the winner's enclosure; but by that time he was close to collapse, and rightly decided to forego the remainder of the rides at the meeting.

Joe Mercer was always one of the most popular riders. His principal loyalty was to the West Ilsley stable over the many years he was retained as first jockey there, and he never rang owners and trainers begging for mounts, or tried to supplant younger or less successful riders. Only once did he break that self-imposed rule. Knowing that Henry Candy's jockey Billy Newnes had been injured on the gallops, and nobody else had been booked for Time Charter in the King George VI and Queen Elizabeth Diamond Stakes in 1983, he rang the Kingstone Warren trainer, was engaged instantly and won the race. When his contract to ride for West Ilsley came to an end in 1976, he spent four years as stable jockey to Henry Cecil, and was champion in 1979. Subsequently he rode for Peter Walwyn, and retired in 1985. Joe Mercer rode 2810 winners under Jockey Club rules, a total surpassed only by Sir Gordon Richards, Lester Piggott and Doug Smith.

On the same afternoon that Brigadier Gerard was successful in the Prince of Wales' Stakes, the West Ilsley stable also won the St James's Palace Stakes with Sun Prince, ridden by Jimmy Lindley. Thus Dick Hern achieved the remarkable feat of bringing off a double on the first day of the Royal Meeting with the same horses two years running.

By the end of the third day, the betting on who would be top jockey of the meeting was wide open. Jimmy Lindley and Willie Carson had ridden three winners, Lester Piggott, Pat Eddery and Tony Murray two, and six other jockeys one apiece. There was no change in the position when the final day opened, with Dick Marshall landing the Windsor Castle Stakes on Adam's Pet, and Brian Taylor the Queen

Rock Roi (left), ridden by Duncan Keith, was disqualified for the second consecutive year after finishing first in the Gold Cup.

Alexandra Stakes on Celtic Cone. The rest of the afternoon belonged to Geoff Lewis, who suddenly transformed the situation by winning each of the last four races of the fixture. As well as landing a double for Noel Murless on Selhurst in the Hardwicke Stakes and Redundant in the Britannia Stakes, he also won the Wokingham Stakes for the Epsom stable of John Sutcliffe junior on Le Johnstan, and finally the King's Stand Stakes on Sweet Revenge, trained by Atty Corbett. As he had also won the Bessborough Stakes on Collector's Slip on the second day, Geoff Lewis became top jockey with five successes.

During the course of 1972 the Duke of Norfolk relinquished his responsibilities as Her Majesty's Representative at Ascot, and was succeeded by the Marquess of Abergavenny. The extent of Ascot's debt to the Duke of Norfolk is impossible to estimate. With remarkably clear foresight he appreciated that if the stands were not replaced in the early 1960s Ascot would never be able to afford the amenities to match the quality of the racing at the Royal Meeting, and would thus become the poor relation of Longchamps and the other great courses of Europe. The cost of building the Queen Elizabeth II Stand and the new Royal Enclosure Stand had been £2,250,000, much of which necessarily had to be borrowed. Had the work been undertaken 10 years later, more than three times the amount would have been required to meet the cost, and the raising of such a sum would have been quite out of the question. As the Queen wished to pay the Duke the compliment of naming a race after him, the New Stakes became the Norfolk Stakes.

TOWARDS THE END OF
A THIRD CENTURY

NEVER has Royal Ascot opened on quite such a sensational note as it did in 1974. Not only was the winner of the Queen Anne Stakes disqualified, but so were the runner-up and the third horse too. The favourite Royal Prerogative hit the front with well over a furlong to go, as Pat Eddery on Gloss, desperately squeezed for room, tried to challenge, and Confusion, the mount of Greville Starkey, also entered into contention. Inside the final furlong the aptly named Confusion secured a slight advantage though hanging left all the time, and at the post held Gloss, who had been denied a clear run, by a head. Royal Prerogative, who also hung left towards the stands rails, could not go through with his effort, and was three parts of a length away third.

At the subsequent Stewards' Enquiry each of the first three was found to have transgressed the rules, and the race was awarded to Brook, a rather wiry grey colt ridden by Brian Taylor who had finished six lengths adrift of Royal Prerogative. My Friend was promoted second, and Coup de Feu third. Brook was trained in Italy for the Milanese industrialist Dr Carlo Vittadini, whose chestnut colt Grundy was to be the outstanding two-year-old of the season and winner of the 1975 Derby. Brook's rider Brian Taylor reached the high point of his career when winning the Derby on Snow Knight the previous month. Ten years later the racing world was shocked when he was killed at the age of 45 after taking a heavy fall on the Sha Tin course in Hong Kong.

The following day Old Lucky brought off a substantial gamble in the Royal Hunt Cup. Having been backed from 12/1 to 8/1 he was pushed out by Willie Carson to beat Fabled Diplomat by two lengths. His tall, dignified trainer Bernard van Cutsem, who loved a tilt at the ring for all his ardent advocacy of a Tote monopoly, was as impassive as ever in the winner's enclosure, with just a flicker of a smile on his lips. Asked by Dai Davies, chief reporter of the Press Association, what the plan for Old Lucky was, he replied crushingly: "That was the plan."

In the December of the following year Bernard van Cutsem lost his amazingly brave fight against cancer. Not infrequently he had quit a hospital bed in the early morning to supervise his horses working on Newmarket Heath, just as, in happier times, he had left the gaming tables in a dinner jacket for the same purpose. For all that he had a natural niche in high society, Bernard van Cutsem was greatly esteemed for his professionalism, and a very popular member of the Subscription Rooms, where people of all ages found him the most companionable of men.

No trainer of modern times has experienced such extremes of luck at Royal Ascot as Peter Walwyn. On the one hand he has endured the misfortunes of Rock Roi, and on the other has enjoyed meetings like that of 1974, at which he had three winners for the second year in succession. After Aura had won the Queen's Vase for him on the Wednesday, he brought off a double on the third day with Mrs Vera Hue-Williams' English Prince in the King Edward VII Stakes and Mrs June McCalmont's Red Cross in the Chesham Stakes, all three horses being ridden by his then stable jockey Pat Eddery.

English Prince, a robust brown colt of excellent bone, followed up his success in the King Edward VII Stakes by winning the Irish Derby, but recurrent trouble in his off-fore prevented him from contesting the St Leger, and he retired to stud. When sent to Japan in 1980 he left behind a bay filly foal out

**The Duke of Norfolk retired in 1972, after 27 years as
the Sovereign's Representative at Ascot.**

of Sunny Valley. Given the name of Sun Princess, she won the Oaks and St Leger in 1983.

The son of Colonel Taffy Walwyn, of the Royal Horse Artillery, who won the Grand Military Gold Cup on White Surrey in 1920, and first cousin of the champion jumping trainer Fulke Walwyn and his twin sister Mrs Helen Johnson Houghton, Peter Walwyn was educated at Charterhouse. After National Service as a corporal in the Intelligence Corps, he was assistant to Geoffrey Brooke at Newmarket from 1953 until 1955. After holding the licence while associated with the Blewbury stable of Mrs Johnson Houghton, he commenced training on his own account at the Windsor House yard at Lambourn in 1961, moving to the historic Seven Barrows stable in the same quarter four years later. He was leading trainer in 1974 and again after winning the Derby with Grundy the following year, having obtained his first successes at Royal Ascot with Mr Evelyn de Rothschild's Town Crier in the Queen Anne Stakes and Mr Louis Freedman's Lucy-rowe in the Coronation Stakes in 1969. An immensely hard-working and well-read man, with a wide circle of friends, Peter Walwyn has done a great deal to promote Lambourn as a training centre.

The Duke of Norfolk, then 66 years old, crowned his long association with Royal Ascot by winning the most famous race of the meeting, the Gold Cup, with his home-bred brown colt Ragstone, trained by John Dunlop at Arundel. Ridden by Ron Hutchinson, Ragstone took the lead inside the final furlong, and staying on strongly won by three parts of a length from Proverb, with the French-trained favourite Lasalle, winner of the race 12 months earlier, a neck away third. Ragstone was a four-year-old bay colt by the Ribot horse Ragusa out of Fotheringay, who was by Hyperion's grandson Right Royal V, a mating devised by bloodstock expert Peter Willett by reason of his belief in the mixing of the blood of the great Italian horse Ribot with that of Hyperion.

Henry Candy reached his first milestone after taking over the Kingston Warren stable, near Wantage, from his father at the end of the previous season by winning the Ascot Stakes with Kambalda, ridden by Joe Mercer. Kambalda, favourite at 8/1, held the late challenge of Cadogan Lane by a short head.

The renewal of the partnership of Vincent O'Brien and Lester Piggott proved fruitful, as they shared the successes of Mr John Mulcahy's Lisadell in the Coronation Stakes and Mr Charles St George's American-bred Saritamer in the Cork and Orrery Stakes. The grey Saritamer became a successful stallion, and, rather surprisingly for a sprinter, sired an Oaks winner in Time Charter. He was exported to Saudi Arabia in 1982. Lester Piggott also won the Hardwicke Stakes on Relay Race and the Wokingham Stakes on Ginnie's Pet to become leading jockey of the meeting.

To no small extent the results at the Royal Meeting of 1974 mirrored those of 1973. In the latter year Pat Eddery also rode three winners for Peter Walwyn – Mr Louis Freedman's Loyal Guard in the Bessborough Stakes, Dr Vittadini's Habat in the Norfolk Stakes and Mrs McCalmont's Tudor Rhythm in the Britannia Stakes. Meanwhile Lester Piggott brought off a double for Vincent O'Brien by winning the St James's Palace Stakes on Mr Mulcahy's Thatch and the King's Stand Stakes on Mr St George's Abergwaun. Although the St James' Palace Stakes was reduced to a match there was a lively market, with Owen Dudley, trained by Noel Murless, fractional favourite at 11/10 on, and Thatch evens.

The race was by no means as close as the betting, as Thatch made all the running to win by 15 lengths.

There were some red faces in the winner's enclosure after the odds-on Daring Boy had proved himself one of the best of his age by winning the Windsor Castle Stakes. Trained by Arthur Budgett for Mrs G. Trimmer-Thompson he had been gelded as a yearling as a result of being mistaken for another horse.

When successful in the Ribblesdale Stakes, Miss Petard became a first Royal Ascot success for Ryan Jarvis, who had the historic Phantom House stable in which Tom Jennings trained Gladiateur at Newmarket. He is the son of royal trainer Willie Jarvis, and grandson of Cyllene's trainer Bill Jarvis. Miss Petard was by the St James's Palace Stakes winner Petingo out of Miss Upward by Alcide, and became the dam of Kiss (by Habitat) whose daughter Casey (by Caerleon) was another high-class middle-distance filly as she showed by winning the Park Hill Stakes at Doncaster in 1988.

After partnering Brigadier Gerard in the landing of a double for Major Hern's stable in each of the two preceding years, Sir Michael Sobell's Sun Prince achieved more success by gaining a third victory at the meeting in 1973. Driven right out by Joe Mercer, he beat Sparkler by a length in the Queen Anne Stakes.

The best horse to win at Royal Ascot in 1973 was Mr Henry Zeisel's Rheingold, ridden by the French champion Yves Saint-Martin. Starting at 5/1 on, he beat the filly Attica Meli by six lengths in the Hardwicke Stakes. Rheingold had been beaten by a short head by Roberto in the Derby the previous season, and in the autumn of 1973 won the Prix de l'Arc de Triomphe. Rheingold was by Faberge II out of Athene, a mare that fetched just 300 guineas when she came up at the Ascot Sales conducted by Messrs J. P. Botterill at the outset of her three-year-old days in 1963. A bay horse of considerable quality, Rheingold sired a number of good-class performers, including the dual Gold Cup winner Gildoran, before being sent to Japan as a 10-year-old in 1979.

Rheingold was the first good horse to be trained by Barry Hills, then 36 years old and fast establishing himself in the ranks of the leading trainers. The son of William Hills, who was head lad to Tom

Rimell at Kinnersley after riding over fences, and then trained successfully under Pony Turf Club Rules, Barry Hills was apprenticed to George Colling. While claiming the allowance he won a number of races on Lord Derby's Peter Pan and other horses, and later was head lad for John Oxley, who took over Newmarket's Hurworth House stable on the death of George Colling, for 10 years. Having made a considerable amount of money over the success of Frankincense in the Lincoln of 1968, Barry Hills was able to begin training on his own account in the South Bank stable, where Lester Piggott had served his apprenticeship, at Lambourn the following year. In only his third season he obtained his first success at Royal Ascot when Hickleton beat Parthenon in the Queen Alexandra Stakes. A trim, easily recognisable figure, usually to be seen with a large cigar, Barry Hills is an enthusiastic rider to hounds.

Another champion in the classic mould made his first appearance at Ascot in 1975. This was the four-year-old Sagaro, trained for his breeder Mr Gerald Oldham by François Boutin at Lamorlaye. Arguably the outstanding stayer to race in England since Alycidon just after the war, he was a chestnut of unusual depth in front, by Espresso (a son of Alycidon's brother Acropolis) out of Zambara, by Mossborough. He was to make history by becoming the only horse to win the Gold Cup three times. Before his debut at Ascot, this imposing individual had already demonstrated class versatility. Unlike so many high-class stayers, he was sufficiently precocious to win as a two-year-old. The following season he beat the subsequent St Leger winner Bustino in the Grand Prix de Paris, over a mile and seven furlongs.

In each of his three Gold Cups Sagaro was ridden by Lester Piggott. To win the first of them in 1975, he turned into the straight in fifth place behind Kambalda, began his run a furlong and a half out, took the lead at the furlong marker, and strode away to beat Mistigri by an extremely easy four lengths. Mistigri hung badly right in the final furlong and was relegated to last place, so that Le Bavard was promoted second and Kambalda third.

Twelve months later Lester Piggott rode Sagaro with even greater confidence. Taking the lead a furlong from the post again, Sagaro beat Crash Course

Sun Prince and Joe Mercer win the Queen Anne Stakes in 1973 from Sparkler, ridden by Lester Piggott.

by a length, with a great deal in hand. When completing the hat-trick in 1977, Sagaro was second into the straight behind Buckskin, took up the running rather earlier than he had in the two previous years, and went clear to win by a fluent five lengths.

As Sagaro had won every season from two to six years of age, he had consistency as well as conformation and class to recommend him as a stallion, and he was acquired by the Levy Board to stand at the National Stud at Newmarket for £175,000. Forty-four shares in him were advertised at £700, with another £700 to pay on the birth of a live foal. Despite the prejudice against Gold Cup winners all the nominations in him had been sold by the end of January 1978. Unfortunately, and rather surprisingly, Sagaro was not a success as a sire. Although he got a number of useful horses, such as the Cambridgeshire winner Sagamore, he never sired a horse approaching the same calibre as himself. Eventually,

in August 1985, he was transferred to the Emral Stud, Clwyd, as a National Hunt Stallion, to stand at £400, no foal no fee. There he died of a heart attack in March 1986.

Not for the first time, the riding of Lester Piggott was the feature of Royal Ascot in 1975. From 22 mounts he rode eight winners, finished second five times, and third four. On the first day he had a double, on the second a treble, on the third another double, and one more winner on the fourth.

Mr Robert Sangster's Boone's Cabin, on whom he won the Wokingham Stakes for O'Brien, carried 10 st, a record for the race and 4 lb more than Trappist had on his back in 1878. With his habitual imperturbability, Piggott lay some way off the leaders in the early stages, not asking his mount for an effort until two furlongs out. After little more than another 100 yards, Boone's Cabin burst to the front, and ran on resolutely to hold the late chal-

Vincent O'Brien, trained six winners four of which were ridden by Lester Piggott at the 1975 meeting.

Stakes with Dr Carlo d'Alessio's high-class miler Bolkonski, running for the first time since his success in the 2000 Guineas, and the Bessborough Stakes with Lord Howard de Walden's Fool's Mate in 1975.

Gavin Pritchard-Gordon, who had taken over Harvey Leader's Newmarket stable three years earlier, obtained two of the most notable of his earlier successes at the meeting. With Record Run he won the Prince of Wales' Stakes and with Ardoon the Royal Hunt Cup.

Of those eight races that Lester Piggott won at Ascot in 1975, four were on horses trained by Vincent O'Brien. Before landing the Wokingham Stakes on Boone's Cabin, he had won the Ribblesdale Stakes on Gallina, the Jersey Stakes on Gay Fandango and the Queen's Vase on Blood Royal. In all, O'Brien won six races during the course of the four days as he was also responsible for the success of Imperial March in the Queen Anne Stakes, as well as that of Swingtime in the Cork and Orrery Stakes.

A milestone in the story of Royal Ascot was reached in 1976, when Noel Murless had his final runners at the meeting prior to retiring at the end of the season. The last of the 56 winners that he saddled at it was Mr George Pope's Jumping Hill, appropriately ridden by Lester Piggott, with whom he had long been reconciled, in the Royal Hunt Cup.

The races that Noel Murless won most frequently at Royal Ascot, the races that he rarely won, and even those he never won at all, faithfully reflected his overriding aim of developing excellence over distances from a mile to a mile and a half, while willingly keeping older horses in training. He won both the King Edward VII Stakes and the Hardwicke Stakes six times, and the Rous Memorial Stakes, which used to be a mile event for three-year-olds and upwards, no fewer than eight times, with the likes of Petite Etoile and Landau. When the mile-and-a-quarter Prince of Wales' Stakes was revived to replace the Rous Memorial Stakes in 1968 he won it with Royal Palace, and he won it again in each of the following two years with the massive Connaught.

Given his limitless patience, and refusal to ask anything of a horse before it was ready to begin to

lenge of Tolspring, ridden by Pat Eddery, by three parts of a length.

Memories of Royal Ascot in pre-war days were evoked when Piggott wore the green and yellow halved colours made famous by Brown Jack to win the Coronation Stakes on Roussalka, owned by Mr Nicholas Phillips, the grandson of Sir Harold Wernher. A filly of very considerable ability, Roussalka had a disposition that was hardly calculated to endear her widely. Out with Henry Cecil's string at Newmarket, she would lash out at anything that came too near her, and in the box her teeth were as dangerous as her heels. A half-sister to Oh So Sharp, winner of the 1000 Guineas, Oaks and St Leger, she is a bay by Habitat out of Graustark mare Oh So Fair, and had made her mark as a brood mare by transmitting her own ability as well as her courage. Her daughter Gayane (by Nureyev) won both her races as a two-year-old in 1986, then as a three-year-old was successful in listed races at Goodwood and Haydock Park, and ran Ajdal to a head in the July Cup. As well as the Coronation Stakes, Henry Cecil won the St James's Palace

Lester Piggott, winner of eight races at the Royal Meeting in 1975.

The crowded enclosure in 1976.

do justice to itself, it is not surprising that he won the five two-year-old races at the Royal Meeting just once apiece – the Coventry Stakes with Royal Forest in 1948, the Queen Mary Stakes with Abelia in 1957, the New Stakes with Philip of Spain on the day that his granddaughter Katie Cecil was born in 1971, the Chesham Stakes with Abernant in 1948 and the Windsor Castle Stakes with Carnoustie in 1958. The only two races that Noel Murless never won at Royal Ascot were the Ascot Stakes and the Queen Alexandra Stakes, as he did not persevere with stayers unless they were absolutely top-class, like his Gold Cup winner Twilight Alley.

The great service that Noel Murless had done racing was recognised by the knighthood he received in the Silver Jubilee Honours list of June 1977. The following month he was elected to the Jockey Club.

A tall man with a weatherbeaten face and grey hair brushed back from the forehead, he had no liking at all for the limelight that his achievements brought upon him, and was far happier in the quiet of the stableyard than amidst the bustle of the racecourse. Beneath what was only a superficial reserve, Sir Noel had an extremely warm personality, was a delightful host, and was never short of a good story. He did not bet, and helped many a young man make his way in racing. In retirement Sir Noel managed the Woodditton Stud, where he made his home, at Newmarket, and the Cliff Stud, which he owned in partnership with Lady Murless, near Helmsley in Yorkshire. He was 77 when he died in May 1987.

The only success for the North in 1976 came when the King's Stand Stakes was won by Mr

Charles Spence's four-year-old Lochnager, trained by Mick Easterby and ridden by Edward Hide. A brown colt by Dumbarnie, Lochnager beat the French colt Realty by three parts of a length. After having been no more than a handicapper as a three-year-old, Lochnager had trained on to be one of the outstanding sprinters of the day. On his only two appearances subsequent to the King's Stand Stakes, he won the July Cup at Newmarket and the William Sprint Championship at York. He fulfilled hopes that he would get fast horses by siring Reesh, winner of the Palace House Stakes, Imperial Jade and other useful sprinters.

Considering he had commenced training with 14 horses at Racecourse Farm, Bescaby, near Melton Mowbray, only the previous season, 44-year-old Neil Adam did well to bring off a double at Royal Ascot in 1976. Cawston's Clown won the Coventry Stakes for him, and then Gentilhombre the Cork and Orrery Stakes. Neil Adam, a veterinary surgeon, relinquished his licence in June 1980. During recent years he has managed the Collin Stud at Stetchworth, near Newmarket.

In the course of the Derby meeting of 1976 came the totally unexpected announcement that Joe Mercer's retainer from the West Ilsley stable would not be renewed for the following season, after his having been first jockey there since the days of his apprenticeship almost 25 years earlier. The owners of the yard, Sir Michael Sobell and his son-in-law Lord Weinstock, had decided they needed a younger jockey and secured the services of Willie Carson. Having received a number of offers, Joe Mercer accepted that of Henry Cecil. The first Royal Ascot winner that he rode for Cecil was Mr Charles St George's Lucky Wednesday, on whom he made all the running in the Prince of Wales' Stakes on the opening day of the 1977 meeting.

Lester Piggott enjoyed another particularly successful meeting, riding seven winners. After Sagaro, the most notable was the sprinter Godswalk, who had been acquired by Mr Robert Sangster since winning the Norfolk Stakes for Christie Grassick's stable 12 months earlier, and transferred to Vincent O'Brien. Although stumbling as he came out of the stalls in the King's Stand Stakes, Godswalk was able to begin to make progress two furlongs from home, and, driven out by Piggott, got up inside the dis-

tance to beat the French filly Girl Friend by three parts of a length.

That enthusiastic cricketer Michael Stoute opened his score at Royal Ascot when Etienne Gerard, from the first crop of Brigadier Gerard, won the Jersey Stakes. Three days later Stoute was back in the winner's enclosure after Mr Raymond Clifford-Turner's Finite was awarded the Britannia Stakes, Petronisi having been disqualified as a result of wandering badly in the straight.

Then 31 years of age, Michael Stoute had been born at Gun Hill in Barbados, where his father was Commissioner of Police. The family home adjoined the island's racecourse at Garrison Savannah. In early boyhood he became fascinated by watching the horses trained by Freddie Thirkell, who had served his apprenticeship with Mat Peacock at Middleham, being worked on the course. Soon he began to ride out with Thirkell, whom he came to know well, and resolved to make a career in British racing. His only, somewhat tenuous, contact was through Sir Eric Hallinan, the Chief Justice of the West Indies, who had been a neighbour of the mother of Pat Rohan in Ireland. Through Sir Eric he obtained an introduction to Rohan, and in 1965 arrived in England to commence work in his stable. Soon afterwards he nearly abandoned the idea of training when he was short-listed for a job as racing correspondent with the BBC, but the post went to Julian Wilson, who has become so familiar to viewers when conducting interviews from the first-floor balcony above the winner's enclosure at Ascot.

After three years with Rohan, Michael Stoute went to Newmarket to be assistant to Doug Smith. He was made responsible for the Park Lodge yard, where he had charge of Sleeping Partner, winner of the Oaks and Ribblesdale Stakes. Subsequently he spent a year-and-a-half with Tom Jones, being associated with another classic horse, the 1971 St Leger winner Athens Wood, and in 1972 began training with just 15 horses at Newmarket. Rapidly advancing in his profession, he was champion trainer by 1981.

During the latter part of his career, the formidable, and often controversial, Captain Ryan Price was much in evidence at Royal Ascot. In 1978 he landed his third double there after having gained his first success at the meeting less than 10 years earlier with Lexicon in the Ascot Stakes of 1969. The jaunty angle at which he wore his trilby spoke volumes for Captain Price. Never short of confidence in his own talents, he went through life totally indifferent to what anyone thought of him. He held few of his fellow men in high regard, and certainly not those in authority. Captain Price held strong views about many aspects of racing, and expressed them with a vehemence that made verbatim reporting of him impossible in a family newspaper.

Born at Hindhead, Surrey, where his father bred show hacks, Captain Price had many point-to-point winners, before serving with distinction in Normandy and elsewhere during the war. Following the end of the war, Captain Price made his name as a trainer of jumpers, and his Findon stable, situated on the Sussex Downs, some five miles inland from Worthing, became one of the most successful in the country. He won the Champion Hurdle with Clair Soleil in 1955 and on two subsequent occasions, and the Grand National with Kilmore in 1962. After he had won the Schweppes Gold Trophy with Rosyth in 1963, the Stewards of the National Hunt Committee expressed themselves dissatisfied with the previous running of the horse, and he was warned off for a short time. Captain Price was again the centre of violent controversy when the heavily backed Hill House won the Schweppes by 12 lengths after being a moderate fourth at Sandown Park on his previous appearance. A dope test revealed a large quantity of cortisone in Hill House's urine, and an enquiry that lasted 171 days ensued. After exhaustive tests the Stewards finally concluded that Hill House manufactured his own cortisone.

With those triumphs and vicissitudes as a jumping trainer behind him, Captain Price devoted himself to flat racing from 1970, and was not long in augmenting his initial success at Royal Ascot with Lexicon. In 1972 he won both the Ribblesdale Stakes with Star Ship and the Queen Mary Stakes with Truly Thankful; the Queen Alexandra Stakes with Peacock in 1973 and King Levanstell the following year; both the Prince of Wales Stakes with Anne's Pretender and the King Edward VII Stakes with Marquis de Sade in 1976; then after winning the Queen Anne Stakes with Jellaby in 1977, he

After three doubles at the Royal Meeting Captain Ryan Price in partnership with Brian Taylor, brought off a treble in 1979.

completed that third double with Lake City in the Coventry Stakes and M-Lolshan in the King George V Stakes in 1978.

Twelve months later Captain Price reached the highwater mark of his success at Royal Ascot by bringing off a treble with Varingo in the Coventry Stakes, Romeo Romani in the Norfolk Stakes and Obratsovy in the Hardwicke Stakes. All three were ridden by Brian Taylor. The last winner to be saddled by Captain Price at Royal Ascot was Spin of a Coin, whom Brian Rouse rode to beat Cannon King by three parts of a length in the Bessborough Stakes in 1982. At the end of that season Price retired. One of the greatest characters seen on the racecourse during the four decades that followed the end of the Second World War, Ryan Price died on his 74th birthday, 16th August 1986.

Greenland Park became the first company-owned horse to be successful at Royal Ascot when she won the Queen Mary Stakes of 1978 for the stable of Willie Hastings-Bass, grandson of Brown Jack's first English trainer Aubrey Hastings, and son of Captain Peter Hastings-Bass. The filly belonged to Greenland Park Ltd, a firm of contractors, builders and electrical engineers based at Berkhamsted in Hertfordshire.

As had been the case 10 years earlier, when Connaught was successful in the King Edward VII Stakes, that race was won by a maiden. This time the winner was Ile de Bourbon, ridden by John Reid and trained by Fulke Johnson Houghton. A rather tall brown colt by Nijinsky, Ile de Bourbon carried the colours of Sir Cecil Boyd-Rochfort's nephew Major David McCall, who had managed the Triple Crown winner Nijinsky and the many other good horses that the American industrialist Charles Engelhard raced in England and Ireland for some years prior to his death in 1971. Like Mr Anthony Holland, owner of the 1972 Coventry Stakes winner Perdu, Major McCall who runs his own Blood-stock Agency, with great success, lives close to Ascot in the village of Windlesham. Ile de Bourbon fulfilled the promise of his performance at the Royal Meeting by training on to be top-class. In July he returned to Ascot to win the King George VI and Queen Elizabeth Diamond Stakes, and as a four-year-old made all the running to win the Coronation Cup by seven lengths. Before being exported to Japan in 1986, Ile de Bourbon had sired the Derby winner Kahyasi, while the German Derby winner Lagunas came from his first crop.

Bill Watts enhanced his family's record at the Royal Meeting by bringing that useful stayer Mountain Cross to Ascot in 1978. Ridden by John Lowe, Mountain Cross joined Trelawny in that select group to have completed the double in the Ascot Stakes and the Queen Alexandra Stakes in the same year.

With 10 weeks at the end of the long and dismal "Winter of Discontent" so bedevilled by strikes that even the dead could not be buried, the Royal Meeting of 1979 opened amidst feelings that the country was embarking on a new era. In the General Election on the first Thursday in May, the Labour Government, which had been in power since 1974, was defeated, and the Conservatives under Mrs Margaret Thatcher were returned. Mrs Thatcher soon made it plain that she had a refreshingly new approach to age-old problems, and was determined to ensure that the expansion of industry was no longer hampered by deplorable industrial relations, by repealing or revising the relevant legislation. In commercial and financial circles, spirits were buoyant.

The tip of the shadows of other things to come touched Royal Ascot in 1979, when Abeer, the mount of Willie Carson, won the Queen Mary Stakes. Carson was wearing the green jacket with pink sash and white sleeves of Mr Khalid Abdullah, a 37-year-old Saudi prince who was running horses for the first time that season. A close relation of King Fahd of Saudi Arabia, Mr Abdullah has extensive banking interests in his own country and Chicago. He was at the head of the phalanx of Arab owners who were to revolutionise the pattern of ownership in England, by their huge investment in bloodstock, and the acquisition of studs and training establishments, over the next decade. Before long Mr Abdullah would be racing against the Maktoum brothers, sons of the ruler of Dubai, namely Sheikh Maktoum Al Maktoum, the Crown Prince; Sheikh Hamdan Al Maktoum; Sheikh Mohammed Al Maktoum, the Cambridge-educated Minister of Defence of Dubai; and Sheikh Ahmed Al Maktoum, together with their cousin Sheikh Marwan Al Maktoum. These owners from the Middle East, on whose behalf millions of pounds would be spent at the sales, as well as in private transactions on both sides of the Atlantic, during the next few years, were quickly able to acquire a dominant position in British racing, with enormous strings spread amongst the most successful stables in the country. In 1989, for instance, Sheikh Mohammed, who had been leading owner in each of the previous four seasons, had 46 horses with Michael Stoute, 42 with Henry Cecil, 23 with Luca Cumani, 11 with Ian Balding, 8 with Clive Brittain, 5 with Paul Cole, 12 with Barry Hills, 11 with Major Dick Hern, 10 with John Dunlop, 7 with Bill Watts, 14 with Guy Harwood, and another 62 with John Gosden in his private stable, Stanley House, which he bought from Gavin Pritchard-Gordon, at Newmarket.

Inevitably ownership on that massive scale brought success at Royal Ascot. Although national dress is acceptable in the Royal Enclosure, the Sheikhs and other Arab princes are always to been seen immaculately attired in morning coats and top hats. Many of them have purchased or built large houses in the vicinity of Ascot, where they take up residence during the Royal Meeting.

Henry Cecil saddled the first and second in the Gold Cup in 1979, when Le Moss, ridden by Lester Piggott, won by seven lengths from Buckskin, the mount of Joe Mercer, still stable jockey at Warren Place. Yet Cecil described it as the saddest moment of his career. He had desperately wanted to win the race with the six-year-old Buckskin, a horse that he really loved. Buckskin combined character, class and courage to a remarkably high degree, with the result that he was a great favourite with the racing public of the late seventies. On the course this big, rangy bay enjoyed his racing to the full, winning by as far as he could, and at home his presence was all-pervasive in the yard, of which he had free range. Visitors to Warren Place would often be startled by a lot of cackling. Looking round, they would see Buckskin chasing a chicken.

Owned and bred by M. Daniel Wildenstein, the Paris art dealer, Buckskin had beaten the triple Gold Cup winner Sagaro by three parts of a length in the Prix du Cadran while still being trained in France as a four-year-old in 1977. After joining Henry Cecil's stable in the middle of 1978, Buckskin put up a splendid performance by beating Billion by eight lengths, with that season's Gold Cup winner Shangamuzo third, and Sea Pigeon fourth in the Doncaster Cup. He then beat Shangamuzo by eight lengths without even being challenged, when they met again in the Jockey Club Cup. He remained in training with the Gold Cup of 1979 as his solitary objective.

Buckskin had dropped soles to his feet, so that he had to have built-up shoes. To add to his trainer's problems, he had a very suspect ligament on his off-fore joint, so that he had to spend many hours each day having a hosepipe played on it. In consequence of these defects, there was always the very real risk of his breaking down, and the amount of work he did had to be severely restricted. Henry Cecil has expressed the opinion that Buckskin could have been a high-class middle-distance horse, had he been able to do the necessary sharp work. As it was, he had to be confined to the long, steady work horses do preparatory to long-distance races.

On the strength of his having turned in another highly impressive performance by beating the York-shire Cup winner Pragmatic by 15 lengths in the Henry II Stakes at Sandown Park first time out in 1979, Buckskin started slightly odds-on for the Gold Cup. As he cruised to the front just before making the turn into the straight, the mission seemed accomplished. But it was one more race than the leg could stand. Poor Buckskin was as desperately keen to win as ever he had been, and fought on gallantly, as everybody who knew him would expect him to do. Had his leg stood him in as good stead as his heart he would have won again. As it was he had nothing with which to answer the relentless progress being made by his stablemate Le Moss, and defeat, albeit as honourable a one as there has ever been, became inevitable.

As against the disappointment occasioned by the defeat of Buckskin, the Royal Meeting of 1979 had more than one highlight for Joe Mercer. In addition to the St James's Palace Stakes on Lord Howard de Walden's brilliant miler Kris, he won the Coronation Stakes on One In a Million, though only on the disqualification of Buz Kashi, and the Britannia Stakes on Mr Jim Joel's Welsh Chanter for Henry Cecil's stable. That season he finished champion jockey for the only time, at the age of 45, having ridden 164 winners, as opposed to the 142 of the runner-up Willie Carson, who had brought off a double for the Queen and Major Hern at Royal Ascot by winning the Ribblesdale Stakes on Expensive and the Queen's Vase on Buttress.

Henry Cecil was again leading trainer at Royal Ascot in 1980, though he saddled only three winners, whereas Major Hern enjoyed four successes. Le Moss gave an encore in the Gold Cup, still the most valuable race of the meeting, and his trainer also won the Queen Mary Stakes with Lord Tavistock's Pushy, and the King Edward VII Stakes with Mr Jim Joel's Light Cavalry, who was to go on to win in the St Leger. Like so many of Mr Joel's other Royal Ascot winners, Light Cavalry came from the Absurdity family. He was a bay colt by Brigadier Gerard out of Glass Slipper, a half-sister to the Derby winner Royal Palace, their sixth dam being Absurdity.

Among those four races won by Major Hern in 1980 was the Prince of Wales' Stakes with Ela-Mana-Mou, who had gone to West Ilsley since landing the King Edward VII Stakes 12 months earlier. At that time Ela-Mana-Mou had been trained by Guy Harwood, who had bought him for

Le Moss and Buckskin, both trained by Henry Cecil at Warren Place came home first and second in the Gold Cup in 1979.

4500 guineas as a yearling. In the winter of 1979/80 he changed hands for £500,000, some 100 times his original price, on being acquired by the Weinstock family in partnership with Tim Rogers of the Airlie Stud. The investment proved a sound one. After his second success at Royal Ascot, Ela-Mana-Mou won the Coral Eclipse Stakes and the King George VI and Queen Elizabeth. In three races he had recovered very nearly half his purchase price. On retiring to Airlie, Ela-Mana-Mou rapidly acquired a reputation for siring high-class middle-distance horses like himself. He has got Almaarad, winner of the Hardwicke Stakes for Sheikh Hamdan Al Maktoum in 1988, the William Hill Futurity winner Emmson, and the Nassau Stakes winner Ela Romara among others.

Walter Swinburn senior and his son and name-sake brought off a family double on the third day of the Royal Meeting in 1981. After the son had won the Cork and Orrery Stakes on The Quiet Bidder, trained by Reg Hollinshead at Hednesford in Staffordshire, the father landed the Norfolk Stakes on Day Is Done for Dermot Weld's Irish stable. The elder Swinburn was born in Liverpool in 1937, and apprenticed to Sam Armstrong from 1951 to 1958, coming to prominence when he rode By Thunder! at 6 st 12 lb to win the Ebor Handicap by a dozen lengths in 1954. On completing his apprenticeship he went to Ireland to ride for Paddy Prendergast, for whom he won the Coventry Stakes on Martial in 1959. He was twice champion jockey of Ireland, and in 1977 became the first flat race jockey to ride

The superb Kris and Joe Mercer.

As well as the Cork and Orrery Stakes for Reg Hollinshead, Walter Swinburn the younger won the Prince of Wales' Stakes on Hard Fought, owned by Mr L. B. Holliday, son of the Major, and the King's Stand Stakes on Mr Edmund Loder's filly Marwell in 1981. Both were trained by Michael Stoute. Marwell, one of the outstanding sprinters of her era, was yet another high-class horse tracing back to Pretty Polly in tail female line to be bred by a member of the Loder family at the Eyrefield Lodge Stud. She was a bay by Habitat out of Lady Seymour, by Tudor Melody out of My Game, whose dam, Flirting, was half-sister to The Cobbler, winner of the Wokingham Stakes in 1949.

Rasa Penang became the first winner at the Royal Meeting to be trained by Robert Armstrong, whose brother-in-law Lester Piggott rode him to beat Star Pastures by three lengths in the Jersey Stakes of 1981. Another family tradition was thereby maintained, as Robert Armstrong is the grandson of Bob Armstrong, who won the Ascot Stakes with Dan Dancer almost 100 years earlier, and the son of Walter Swinburn's mentor Sam Armstrong. Robert Armstrong had taken over the St Gatien Stable at Newmarket at the end of 1972, following the retirement of his father, who died at the age of 78 in 1983.

All down the years from Georgian times, winners at Royal Ascot have continued to come from widely divergent backgrounds. One remembers that the mighty Ormonde, successful in the Hardwicke Stakes in 1886 and 1887, was bred on the rolling acres of his owner, the Duke of Westminster. Victor Wild, winner of the Royal Hunt Cup a few years later, had been bought out of a selling race at a minor meeting, and belonged to a London publican. The two-year-olds Horage and Widaad, winners of the Coventry Stakes and Queen Mary Stakes respectively in 1982, could hardly have had more disparate antecedents either. Horage cost 8000 guineas and came from the 15-horse string trained by Matt McCormack, Peter Walwyn's former work rider, at Wantage, while Widaad, the first Ascot winner for a member of the Maktoum family, had been purchased for $220,000, then worth £92,502, and was one of the 120 horses in Michael Stoute's fashionable Newmarket stable.

Owned by Mr Abed Rachid, a Lebanese bus-

more than 100 winners in a season in that country. On retiring from riding in 1982 he spent a year as assistant to Day Is Done's trainer Dermot Weld, and in 1984 purchased the Genesis Green Stud from Harry Carr.

Whereas his father had spent the formative part of his career with Sam Armstrong, the outstanding tutor of young riders in the 1950s, Walter Swinburn junior, born in Oxford in August 1961, served his apprenticeship with the former top steeplechase jockey "Frenchie" Nicholson, who had assumed the mantle of Armstrong, at Cheltenham. Walter Swinburn the younger rode his first winner on Paddy's Luck at Kempton Park at the age of 17 in 1978, and his first at Royal Ascot on Mon's Beau in the Ascot Stakes the following year. Rapidly reaching the top of his profession, he was appointed first jockey to Michael Stoute's stable in 1981, and that season won the Derby on Shergar, trained by Stoute. He later won another Derby for Stoute's stable on Shahrastani, in 1986.

inessman, Horage was ridden by Pat Eddery when making all the running to beat Kafu by a length and a half in the Coventry Stakes. In all, the colt won nine of his ten races in his first season, thereby earning £105,916. As a three-year-old he consolidated his reputation on returning to Ascot to win the St James's Palace Stakes. Leading from start to finish again, Horage held the challenge of Tolomeo, who had been runner-up in the 2000 Guineas by a head.

Horage was bought by his trainer at the Doncaster Sales, which were revived by Hardwicke trainer Ken Oliver and the late Willie Stephenson in 1962. All the yearlings that go through the ring there are selected by the directors, who specialise in the sale of precocious stock, so that Harry Beeby and his colleagues have gained a reputation, to which Horage made a substantial contribution, for selling horses likely to show their owners an early return by winning as two-year-olds. At the end of his second season, Horage retired to the Ballygoran Stud, Maynooth, Co. Kildare. Amongst his first crop was that useful middle-distance horse Dust Devil, who amassed more than £30,000 by winning at Ascot and Doncaster for John Dunlop's stable at the back-end of 1988.

Widaad carried the colours of Sheikh Maktoum Al Maktoum. To win the Queen Mary Stakes she took the lead well over a furlong from home, and ran on well to beat Crime of Passion by a length and a half.

Rather surprisingly it was not until 1982 that former American champion jockey Steve Cauthen rode his first winner at Royal Ascot when successful on Mr Tony Shead's Kind of Hush in the Prince of Wales' Stakes. The following day he won the Jersey Stakes on Merlin's Charm, and on the fourth the Windsor Castle Stakes on Prince Reymo for Robert Armstrong's stable. Steve Cauthen had come to England to ride for Barry Hills and Mr Robert Sangster at the beginning of 1979. Born at Covington, Kentucky, on 1st May 1960, Steve Cauthen was brought up with horses, being the son of Tex Cauthen, a former trainer who became a farrier, and his wife Myra, who had trained winners on her own account. At the age of five he was already riding fast work and within a week of having his first mount in public, he rode his first winner on

Red Pipe, trained by his uncle, Tommy Bischoff, at River Downs on 17th May 1976.

Rapidly acquiring recognition as a completely natural jockey, Steve Cauthen became the youngest rider to win America's Triple Crown, the Kentucky Derby, Preakness Stakes and Belmont Stakes, when riding Affirmed in 1977. He also won the Washington International on John D at Laurel Park, and rode six winners in one day at New York's Aqueduct track that season, at the end of which he was champion jockey with 487 winners.

Extremely intelligent and modest, Steve Cauthen is a likeable man who would have had no difficulty in earning a good living in another walk of life. One of his greatest assets as a race rider is his almost uncanny judgement of pace, having been brought up to ride against the clock, like all other American and Australian jockeys. Consequently he excels when making his own running, as he knows to a nicety exactly how fast he is going at every stage of a race. The saying on the racecourse is that he has a clock in his head.

After winning the Gold Cup with Le Moss in 1979 and 1980 as well as with Mr Charles St George's Ardross in 1981, Henry Cecil won that stayers' championship for the fourth year in succession when Ardross gave an encore, and at the same time provided Lester Piggott with his 11th success in the race in 1982. The wheel had turned full circle when Lester Piggott became first jockey to Cecil in 1981 and returned to Warren Place, the stable that he had left for that ride on Valoris in the Oaks of 1966, back in Sir Noel Murless's day. For the fourth year in succession Henry Cecil was leading trainer at Royal Ascot in 1982.

After 10 years in office as Her Majesty's Representative, the Marquess of Abergavenny resigned in 1982. Much had been achieved during the decade that he had directed the destinies of the course, by way of raising the level of racing through the constant increase in prize money to attract the strongest possible field. In addition, amenities for racegoers in all enclosures and the paddock had been further improved, and, equally importantly, the accommodation for the runners and those in charge of them was brought up to a standard that would have been unimaginable in the days when Dan Dancer spent the night before the Ascot Stakes of 1888 in a cow byre with an extra rug. In 1974 the Ascot Authority decided to abandon the yard on the Windsor Stud, in which runners had stood since the demolition of the Royal Ascot Hotel; and built stabling with 140 boxes and tack rooms together with administrative offices, all within a wire perimeter fence for reasons of security, on land lying behind the car parks on the other side from the course of the Virginia Water to Bracknell Road.

Alongside the new stables, the Ascot Authority built a new hostel, to ensure stable staff were afforded the maximum comfort during their stay at the course. With accommodation for 120 travelling head lads, lads and girls, and no more than three to a room, the hostel has a spacious lounge with colour television, large dining room, bar, table tennis room and a room in which tack can be dried. The third structure to appear in the course of this development was the ring, in which Messrs J. P. Botterill, the Yorkshire-based auctioneers, conduct their sales approximately once a month. The late Jack Botterill, whose father trained at Malton, founded these sales at the Royal Ascot Hotel in 1946.

Lord Abergavenney's successor as Her Majesty's Representative at Ascot was Colonel Sir Piers Bengough, who had joined the Ascot Authority in 1972. A member of a well-known Herefordshire family, he had been a professional soldier until his retirement in 1973, having risen to command his regiment, the Royal Hussars, of which he is now Honorary Colonel. While having jumpers in training with Alec Kilpatrick, he proved a highly competent amateur steeplechase jockey, winning the Grand Military Gold Cup at Sandown Park four times, on Joan's Rival in 1960 and Charles Dickens in 1971, 1972 and 1973, while he also had four mounts in the Grand National. He now runs a farm in tandem with a small stud at Canon Pyon in Herefordshire.

The heroine of Royal Ascot in 1983, the first full year that Sir Piers Bengough was Her Majesty's Representative, was the Irish mare Stanerra, one of the gamest and toughest horses of either sex to be seen on the racecourse in those days. On the first day she beat the heavily backed Sabre Dance by four lengths in the mile-and-a-quarter Prince of Wales' Stakes, and on the fourth she came home a

length and a half clear of Electric at the end of the mile and a half of the Hardwicke Stakes, setting a record time for the track. A rather rangy chestnut by Guillaume Tell out of an Aureole mare, Stanerra was ridden in both races by 43-year-old Brian Rouse for her owner-trainer Frank Dunne. A Londoner born in Fulham, Brian Rouse had worked very hard indeed to receive the recognition that he deserved as one of the most competent and dependable jockeys in the country. Apprenticed in Ted Smyth's Epsom stable, he rode his first winner on Gay Bird at Alexandra Park in July 1957. On coming out of his time without another winner, he spent a spell away from racing before returning to work in the stables of Brian Swift and John Sutcliffe until eventually renewing his licence on the suggestion of the latter in 1972, obtaining a belated second success on New Tack, trained by Sutcliffe, at Chepstow in the May of that year. Thereafter he was increasingly frequently employed by the Epsom trainers, as well as those in other areas. In both 1977 and 1978 he won the Northumberland Plate on Tug of War for Dermot Whelan, and in both 1978 and 1980 the Cambridgeshire on Baronet, for John Benstead, another Epsom trainer. In 1978 his score rose to 60 winners in the season, and in 1980 he obtained a classic success when winning the 1000 Guineas on Quick as Lightning for John Dunlop.

The other notable performer at Royal Ascot with whom Brian Rouse has been associated is Blue Refrain, a horse that always came to his best in early summer while trained by John Benstead. Brian Rouse won on Blue Refrain at the meeting in three consecutive years, landing the Windsor Castle Stakes in 1978, the Jersey Stakes in 1979 and the Queen Anne Stakes in 1980. Besides those two races on Stanerra, Brian Rouse also won the Cork and Orrery Stakes on Sylvan Barbarosa, trained by former top amateur rider Philip Mitchell, in 1983.

Horses owned by members of the Maktoum family were in evidence more forcibly than ever before in 1983. Sheikh Mohammed won the Ribblesdale Stakes with High Hawk as well as the Windsor Castle Stakes with Defecting Dancer, and Sheikh Maktoum Al Maktoum the King Edward VII Stakes with Shareef Dancer, who had cost $3,300,300 (£1,380,753) as a yearling.

High Hawk, acquired for a relatively modest 31,000 guineas, is rated by John Dunlop among the best fillies that he has ever trained. During the last 20 years Dunlop has made the Arundel stable one of the most consistently successful in the country. As well as the Derby with Lord Halifax's Shirley Heights, the St Leger with Lavinia, Duchess of Norfolk's Moon Madness and the Oaks with Sir Robin McAlpine's Circus Plume, he has won most of the other big races in the Calendar, and was responsible for the late Duke of Norfolk reaching the summit of his career as an owner by winning the Gold Cup with Ragstone. John Dunlop was born at Tetbury in Gloucestershire in July 1939, the son of a country doctor of Ulster descent. From early childhood he went racing regularly, as his father was a founder member of Chepstow and also a member of Cheltenham. After completing his National Service in the Royal Ulster Rifles, he decided to make a career in racing. Accordingly he placed an advertisement in the *Sporting Life* offering enthusiastic but untutored services, which were eventually accepted by Neville Dent. After two years with Dent, who had a string of some 20 horses in the New Forest, Dunlop became assistant to Gordon Smyth at the Duke of Norfolk's establishment at Arundel. When Gordon Smyth left to train at Lewes, John Dunlop took over the stable.

An immensely energetic man, with sometimes close on 200 horses in a stable where there were only 60 when he first trained there, he travels to the continent to saddle runners most Sundays during the season. Despite his heavy commitments to his profession, Dunlop devotes a great deal of time to working for charity. As one of the three organising secretaries, he played a big part in staging the equestrian day in Ascot's Silver Ring, where racing personalities were sponsored to participate in show jumping and other events, as part of the racing industry's contribution to raising funds for the Stoke Mandeville Hospital in July 1981.

Former jockey Ron Sheather, who had commenced training at Newmarket in 1978, stepped into the limelight when winning the Coventry Stakes with Mr J. C. Smith's Chief Singer in 1983. A tall brown colt with the substance to match his height, Chief Singer was running for the first time, and,

The 1983 Gold Cup winner Little Wolf, with Willie Carson.

ridden by Ray Cochrane, beat Hegemony by four lengths. Twelve months later he emulated Horage by returning to win the St James's Palace Stakes. He retired to Newmarket's Side Hill Stud, owned by the Marquess of Hartington, a member of the Ascot Authority as well as Senior Steward of the Jockey Club at the time of writing.

The Queen's Racing Manager Lord Carnarvon, then Lord Porchester, won the Gold Cup of 1983 with Little Wolf, ridden by Willie Carson for Major Hern's stable. Second on the turn into the straight, Little Wolf took the lead two furlongs out and drew away to beat Khairpour by five lengths.

The following year, Major Hern was leading trainer at Royal Ascot as a result of his having won the King Edward VII Stakes with Sheikh Mohammed's Head for Heights and the Prince of Wales' Stakes with Lord Rotherwick's Morcon. Sheikh Mohammed had purchased Head for Heights from Mr John

Horgan, following his success in the Chesham Stakes the previous season.

The leading owner at the meeting in 1984 was Mr Robert Sangster, who won the Gold Cup with Gildoran, the Cork and Orrery Stakes with Committed and the Bessborough Stakes with Sikorsky. The colours of Mr Sangster, whose father Vernon Sangster was the founder of Vernon's Pools of Liverpool, were the best known on British race-courses, after those of the Queen, until the full impact of the Arabs began to be felt. He was leading owner in 1977 and 1978, again in 1982 and 1983, and for a fifth time in 1984. Domiciled in the Isle of Man, Mr Sangster came into racing as a patron of the Cheshire-based trainer Eric Cousins, who won the Ayr Gold Cup for him with Brief Star in 1969. Soon afterwards he increased his interests in bloodstock considerably, spreading his horses among the stables of his longstanding friend Barry Hills, Captain Ryan Price, Bill Watts, Michael Stoute, Henry Cecil, Jeremy Hindley and other trainers, while in Ireland he was a patron of the stables of Vincent O'Brien and Dermot Weld. In association with O'Brien, or in partnerships and syndicates with other owners in his stable, Mr Sangster demonstrated the commercial profitability of importing American-bred horses, and syndicating them on this side of the Atlantic after they had proved themselves at the highest level on the race-course. The considerable success that Mr Sangster and his partners achieved by the implementation of that policy introduced new dimensions to the international bloodstock market. By way of contrast to what was the case 20 years ago, almost all the leading British trainers attend the major yearling sales in the United States. Among the most important American-bred horses to have carried Mr Sangster's emerald green jacket with royal blue sleeves are the Derby winners The Minstrel and Golden Fleece, together with Lomond and El Gran Senor, each of whom was successful in the 2000 Guineas, and the Eclipse Stakes winners Solford and Sadler's Wells. As can be gathered from gossip columnists, Mr Sangster entertains lavishly in his home, and is also a generous host on the race-course.

Bill Shoemaker, the most successful jockey the world has known, added a success at Royal Ascot to the broad spectrum of his achievements by winning the Bessborough Stakes of 1984 on Sikorsky. Born near Fabens in Texas in August 1931, Shoemaker, who is no more than 4 ft 11 inches tall, has ridden more than 8800 winners as he nears the end of his career, as opposed to the British record of 4870 set by Sir Gordon Richards. Shoemaker rode his first winner at Los Angeles in April 1949, and in 1953 set a then world record for the number of races won during a year, with 485 successes. Famous horses with whom he has been associated include Swaps, Round Table, Sword Dancer, John Henry and Spectacular Bid.

Of the other two horses that won for Mr Sangster at the Meeting in 1984, Gildoran was ridden by Steve Cauthen, and Committed by the 26-year-old New Zealand-born Brent Thomson, who had recently arrived in England to ride for Mr Sangster. Thomson returned the following year, and was stable jockey to Barry Hills during the season of 1986. He rode Gildoran when the horse won the Gold Cup for a second time in 1985. Twice champion apprentice in his own country after riding his first winner in 1973, Brent Thomson made his name in Australia.

Another outstandingly fast filly was seen at Ascot in 1984, when Mr M. Mutawa's Habibti was ridden by Willie Carson to win the King's Stand Stakes for John Dunlop's stable. All but flying in the last furlong, she got up in the last strides to beat Anita's Prince, the mount of Lester Piggott, by a short head.

A third of a century after riding his first winner at Royal Ascot on Malka's Boy in the Wokingham Stakes of 1952, Lester Piggott brought an era to an end by gaining the last of his 113 successes there by winning the King's Stand Stakes on Mr E. D. Kessly's Never So Bold for the stable of his brother-in-law Robert Armstrong in 1985. The Royal Enclosure and stands were packed with young people – as well as others not so young – who were not born when the Boy Wonder rode Malka's Boy. For older racegoers, memories stretched back down the years to the drama of his ride on Never Say Die in the King Edward VII Stakes and its dire consequences for him in 1954, which was to be followed by so many splendid feats of riding: the wonderful judgement of pace he displayed when making all the running on Twilight Alley in the

Happy hatters in 1983.

Gold Cup; the almost unbelievable strength he employed to force Casabianca home in the Royal Hunt Cup; the coolness with which he brought the top-weight Boone's Cabin through from the back of a large field to win the Wokingham Stakes, and so many more. Like Chifney the younger, Fordham, Archer, his own great-grandfather Tom Cannon, Steve Donoghue and Gordon Richards, Lester Piggott had brought a touch of magic to the Royal Meeting.

During that last season of his long career in the saddle, Lester Piggott rode as a freelance, Steve Cauthen having succeeded him as first jockey to Warren Place. At the first Royal Ascot of their association Henry Cecil and his American stable

jockey reaped a rich harvest, sharing the successes of Mr Stavros Niarchos's Gwydion in the Queen Mary Stakes, Mr Charles St George's Lanfranco in the King Edward VII Stakes, M. Daniel Wildenstein's Grand Pavois in the King George V Stakes, and Mr Jim Joel's Protection in the Britannia Stakes.

Once again horses carrying the colours of the Arab owners were frequently seen in the winner's enclosure in 1985. On the first day Sheikh Mohammed brought off a double when Bairn, the mount of Lester Piggott, won the St James's Palace Stakes for Luca Cumani's stable, and Sure Blade, ridden by Brent Thomson for Barry Hills, the Coventry Stakes. The following afternoon Newmarket-based Tom Jones brought off a double with Sheikh Hamdan Al

Sure Blade, after winning the Coventry Stakes in 1985, ridden by Brent Thomson for Barry Hills.

Maktoum's Al Bahathri in the Coronation Stakes and Sheikh Ahmed Al Maktoum's Wassl Merbayeh in the Queen's Vase. In addition Mr Khalid Abdullah won the Queen Anne Stakes with Rousillon and the Chesham Stakes with Bakharoff, both horses being ridden by Greville Starkey and trained by Guy Harwood.

As well as being a trainer of meticulous professionalism, Tom Jones has long been regarded as one of the most amusing men at Newmarket, where his poems, not all of which give expression to delicate compliments, are widely read by the racing fraternity. As might be expected of a man who won the Headmaster's French Prize at Eton, Tom Jones is gifted with an intelligence that matches his wit, and frequently propounds cogent arguments in favour of reform of various aspects of the administration of racing. Following service with the Royals, Tom

Jones spent two years as assistant to Brud Fetherstonhaugh in Ireland, and then another four in the same capacity with Sam Armstrong, before commencing to train at Newmarket at the age of 26 in 1951. At first he was better known as a trainer of jumpers, but gradually built up his team for the flat until he had no hurdlers or chasers in the yard in 1981. The following year he was responsible for Sheikh Maktoum Al Maktoum's Touching Wood finishing second in the Derby and being successful in the St Leger, the classic that he had already won with Athens Wood in 1971. Several other good riders besides Greville Starkey have served their apprenticeship with Tom Jones, including his present stable jockey Richard Hills.

Richard Hills and his brother Michael, also a successful jockey, are the twin sons of Barry Hills. Their elder brother John trains at Lambourn. When riding Wassl Merbayeh in the Queen's Vase, Richard Hills gained his first success at Royal Ascot. He has since won the Norfolk Stakes on Sizzling Melody in 1986 and Petillante in 1989, as well as the Prince of Wales' Stakes on Mtoto in 1987.

Despite the immensely strong competition from the Arabs, and other overseas owners such as the Aga Khan and the Greek shipping magnate Mr Stavros Niarchos, English owner-breeders had their share of success at Royal Ascot in 1985. Mr Bob Cowell, formerly a successful point-to-point rider, won the Ribblesdale Stakes with his home-bred filly Sally Brown trained by Michael Stoute. As well as managing his Bottisham Heath Stud, Mr Cowell farms in the Newmarket area. Sally Brown is by Posse out of the Above Suspicion mare Unsuspected. While trained by Ryan Jarvis for Mr Cowell's father, the late Mr Cecil Cowell, who also farmed near Newmarket, Unsuspected won eight races.

The tragedy of the Royal Meeting of 1985 occurred when Michael Seth-Smith collapsed while giving the commentary on the Prince of Wales' Stakes on the first day. He was immediately operated on for a tumour on the brain, and underwent intensive treatment in a Guildford hospital, but sadly, he died at the age of 57 in May 1986. A completely straightforward man of great charm and energy, Michael Seth-Smith derived as much pleasure from golf and bridge as he did from his work. As well as being a broadcaster, he was a distinguished editor of *The European Racehorse*, and the author of several books, among which his biographies of Sir Gordon Richards and Steve Donoghue are standard works.

Resplendent in light grey morning coat and top hat, instead of racing silks, Lester Piggott returned to the Royal Meeting as a trainer in 1986, and won with his first runner. That was Mr Mahmoud Foustok's Cutting Blade, whom the American Cash Asmussen rode to beat Polemos by a short head in the Coventry Stakes.

Twenty-four-year-old Asmussen, who had come to Europe to ride for the French trainer François Boutin in 1982, also won the King George V Stakes on Mood Madness for Lavinia, Duchess of Norfolk, whose husband had been the Queen's first Representative at Ascot. One of those horses who make

constant improvement, Moon Madness won the King George V Stakes by five lengths, and in the autumn was ready to take a big step up in class by beating Celestial Storm in the St Leger. He was a bay colt by Vitiges out of Castle Moon, a half-sister to the late Duke of Norfolk's Gold Cup winner Ragstone.

John Dunlop also won the Ribblesdale Stakes with Lord Halifax's Gull Nook, while for the Royal Hunt Cup he saddled both the second favourite Siyah Kalem, ridden by Willie Carson, and the 20/1 chance Patriach, the mount of Richard Quinn. Taking the lead two furlongs out, Patriach held the challenge of his stablemate by three parts of a length. Coincidentally both Willie Carson and Richard Quinn are natives of the Scottish city of Stirling. As a result of his having brought off that treble with Moon Madness, Gull Nook and Patriach, John Dunlop finished the meeting as leading trainer.

Having become the first Arab to be leading owner at Royal Ascot in 1985, Sheikh Mohammed was again leading owner, and set another record by becoming the first to amass a six-figure sum in the course of the four days in 1986, having £111,696 to his credit by Friday evening. As well as the St James's Palace Stakes with Sure Blade and the King Edward VII Stakes with Bonhomie, he won the Coronation Stakes with Sonic Lady, one of the outstanding milers of either sex of her generation. All three had been expensive purchases as yearlings. Sure Blade had cost 270,000 guineas at Tattersalls Highflyer Sale, Bonhomie $350,000 (£241,379) at Keeneland, and Sonic Lady, who came from the same family as the Gold Cup winner Quashed, $500,000 (£344,827) at the Fasig Tipton Kentucky Sale.

Henry Cecil's stable was in all but invincible form throughout the Royal Meeting of 1987, at the end of which the Warren Place horses had won seven races. For Lord Howard de Walden, Cecil won both the Gold Cup with Paean, who avenged the defeat of his tail-female ancestress Pretty Polly by Bachelor's Button in that event back in 1906, and the Queen's Vase with Arden.

Lord Howard de Walden's father, the eighth holder of a title created by Queen Elizabeth I for a younger son of the 4th Duke of Norfolk, had won the Gold Cup with Zinfandel 82 years earlier in 1905. The story that he was sitting under a tree in the paddock, musing over the score of an opera while Zinfandel was winning, is probably apocryphal, but could well have been true, for he was a highly cultured man, a classical playwright, and the composer of three operas, *Bronwen, Dylan* and *The Children of Don*. He chose his all-apricot colours on the advice of Augustus John, who told him apricot would show up better against the green of the racecourse than anything else. The owner of a great deal of property in the Harley Street area of London, which has been inherited by his son, Lord Howard had had horses with Dawson Waugh at Newmarket for nearly 20 years when he retired from racing in 1936. He sold the Snailwell Stud at Newmarket the following year, and was only 66 when he died in 1946.

Like many another owner, the present Lord Howard de Walden developed his taste for racing as an undergraduate at Cambridge, just 13 miles from Newmarket. He subsequently studied German in Munich, where he met his first wife, and ran over an aspiring politician called Adolf Hitler while driving up the high street. Always punctiliously polite, he sought an interview with the future Fürhrer to apologise. Some 15 years later, in 1948, Lord Howard embarked upon ownership by acquiring the colt Jailbird and the filly Sanlinea, whom he sent to Jack Waugh, nephew of his father's trainer Dawson Waugh. Jailbird gave him his first success, at Chepstow in 1949, while Sanlinea, who was third in the St Leger, became the dam of the Coventry Stakes winner Amerigo, and one of the foundation mares of his stud. Two years before bringing off the double in the long-distance races at Ascot, Lord Howard reached the summit of his success as an owner-breeder by winning the Derby of 1985 with Slip Anchor.

Henry Cecil's first success of the 1987 meeting came when Prince A. A. Faisal's Midyan beat Linda's Magic in the Jersey Stakes. Cecil also won the Bessborough Stakes with Mr Stavros Niarchos's Primitive Rising, the Ribblesdale Stakes with Mr Louis Freedman's Queen Midas, the Windsor Castle Stakes with Mrs Maria Niarchos's Space Cruiser, and the Hardwicke Stakes with Orban, another of Prince A. A. Faisal's horses.

Another piece of history was made at Royal Ascot in 1987 when 23-year-old Gay Kelleway became the first woman to ride a winner at the meeting. Partnering Sprowston Boy, she brought him home eight lengths clear of the Irish-trained Naevog, the mount of Willie Carson, at the end of the marathon Queen Alexandra Stakes. Sprowston Boy was trained by her father Paul Kelleway, the former top jumping jockey, who won the Cheltenham Gold Cup on What A Myth in 1969, and the Champion Hurdle on Bula in 1971 and 1972. He had begun training at Newmarket, where he was apprenticed to Harry Wragg, in 1977. Gay Kelleway rode her first winner on Aberfield as an amateur at Ripon in June 1981. After seven more successes she turned professional, to be apprenticed to her father.

The heavens opened just before racing began on the Wednesday of the 1987 meeting, and the rain continued almost incessantly for three days, so that by the Friday the going was decidedly heavy. Such conditions were ideal for Mr Fahd Salman's Bel Byou, who became the third winner of the Wokingham Stakes to be trained by Paul Cole. He beat Dorking Lad by two and a half lengths. Cole had won that race for the first time with Calibina, owned and bred by Mr Alec Badger, an Oxfordshire farmer, 10 years earlier in 1977, and again with Mrs L. d'Ambrumenil's Queen's Pride. He had also won the Prince of Wales' Stakes with Mr Hubert Spearing's Crimson Beau in 1979, and the Queen Alexandra Stakes with Mr Salman's Otbari in 1986.

The son of Major Harold Cole, Paul Cole belongs to a hunting and farming family from the West Country, so that he has been accustomed to handling livestock since early boyhood. After spells in the stables of Trelawny's trainer George Todd and Les Kennard, he became assistant to Richmond Sturdy, who had the Shrewton stable, in which Bob Sievier had Sceptre, on Salisbury Plain, then commenced training with 11 horses in the Hill House stable, Lambourn, at the age of 26 in 1968. In the May of that year he obtained his initial success with Optimistic Pirate at Beverley, and really came to the fore when winning three races with Florintina on the July course at Newmarket in 1971. John de Coombe became his first Group One winner by landing the Prix de la Salamandre at

Bluebird, winner of the King's Stand Stakes in 1987, and jockey Cash Asmussen, being led in by Mrs Robert Sangster.

Longchamps in 1977. At the end of 1985 he left Lambourn to take over the historic Whatcombe stable, in which Dick Dawson had trained the flying Mumtaz Mahal to win the Queen Mary Stakes in such sensational style in 1923, and in 1986 he was 10th in the list of winning trainers. A tall, athletic man with a thatch of black hair streaked with grey, who takes his relaxation on the tennis court, Paul Cole runs an internationally orientated stable, and was leading overseas trainer, with stake money to the value of £614,625, in 1987.

Richard Quinn, who won the Wokingham Stakes on Bel Byou, is one of three champion apprentices to be indentured to Paul Cole, having held the title in 1984. The others have been Robert Edmondson and David Dineley, who were at the head of the list in 1972 and 1976 respectively.

As members of the Jarvis family have had stables at Newmarket since long before trainers were officially identified, it is impossible to say how long

they have been sending winners to Ascot, but Willie Jarvis belongs to at least the fourth consecutive generation to have enjoyed success at the Royal Meeting. He had his first winner there when Mrs F. G. Allen's Colmore Row, ridden by Bruce Raymond, beat Classic Ruler by half a length in the Chesham Stakes in 1987. Willie Jarvis's great-grandfather William Jarvis had been responsible for the success of Northern Dancer's forebear Cyllene in the Gold Cup in 1899; his grandfather and namesake won the Queen Mary Stakes with Aloysia, and other races, for King George V; while his father, Ryan Jarvis, won the Ribblesdale Stakes with Miss Petard in 1973. Moreover, Willie Jarvis also has strong family connections with Ascot through his paternal grandmother, who was a sister of Frank Butters. Willie Jarvis spent five valuable years as assistant to Henry Cecil at Warren Place between 1979 and 1984, and also went well beyond the confines of his native Newmarket to learn the rudiments of his profession. In Australia he was attached to the stable of T. J. Smith in Sydney, and G. Hanlon in Melbourne. His second success at Royal Ascot was obtained with Lord Howard de Walden's Weld in the Queen's Vase in 1989.

So great had the attendance at Royal Ascot become that the stands were packed as never before in 1987, and with some 12,000 people in the Royal Enclosure alone on Gold Cup Day, still the most popular of the four, the crowd was widely felt to be becoming too large for even the capacious new Ascot stands to accommodate comfortably. To enter the Royal Enclosure it is necessary to apply for a voucher from the Ascot office in St James's Palace, London, by the end of April. Vouchers can then be exchanged for badges for the Royal Enclosure at a cost, by 1989, of £28 a day, or £69 for one covering the four days. People applying for vouchers for the first time were asked to fill in a form giving a few personal details, countersigned by a sponsor who had been admitted to the Royal Enclosure at least eight times. As it was obvious that Ascot was rapidly becoming in danger of being the victim of its own popularity, Her Majesty's Representative, Colonel Sir Piers Bengough, and the Ascot Authority decided that the list of people admitted to the Royal Enclosure would have to be closed, so that no vouchers would be issued to new applicants for the time being, while admission to the Grandstand on the Wednesday and the Thursday would only be obtained by the purchase of tickets in advance.

Not for the first time the Gold Cup gave rise to drama, albeit of a thoroughly unsatisfactory nature, in 1988. In a field of 13, the largest since Supertello won in 1950, Guy Harwood saddled Sheikh Mohammed's Sadeem, ridden by Greville Starkey, and pacemaker El Conquistador, the mount of Tony Clark. With Sadeem favourite, the other fancied runners were Primitive Rising, from Cecil's stable, the French-trained Royal Gait, with Cash Asmussen up, and Sergeyevich, who had won the Goodwood Cup and the Italian St Leger for John Dunlop's stable the previous season. El Conquistador went off into an immediate lead, and was still in front turning into the straight. Half a furlong later, El Conquistador, on the rails, began to weaken, while Royal Gait, on his outside, was moving into a challenging position, and, still wider, Sadeem was im-

proving. Soon, El Conquistador, Royal Gait and Sadeem were racing so closely together that Asmussen on Royal Gait, in the middle, was badly squeezed for room, with El Conquistador in a still more parlous situation, hopelessly unbalanced to the extent that Tony Clark was unseated. With El Conquistador finally out of contention, Royal Gait was able to forge ahead, and drawing right away, finished five lengths clear of Sadeem, with Sergeyevich third, and Chauve Souris, ridden by Paul Eddery for Geoff Wragg, in fourth place.

At the subsequent Stewards' Enquiry, Royal Gait was found to have caused the unseating of Tony Clark. In consequence he was relegated to last place, and Cash Asmussen was suspended for seven days. Sadeem, therefore, was awarded the race, with Sergeyevich promoted to second place, and Chauve Souris to third. As Royal Gait, who broke the course record by three seconds, was clearly the best horse in the race, his disqualification predictably produced a renewal of demands for an amendment of the rules so that owners, trainers and backers of a horse obviously best on merit should not be penalised for the transgressions of its rider.

Trainer John Fellows and Asmussen lodged an appeal against the disqualification of Royal Gait, but after hearing legal arguments for two and a half hours, the Jockey Club Disciplinary Committee, Lord Vestey, John Sumner and Bruce Hobbs, rejected it. Their statement confirming the verdict read: "Having considered the evidence, the committee found that approaching the two-furlong marker Royal Gait had bumped Sadeem (USA) and had then interfered with El Conquistador due to there being insufficient room to pass between El Conquistador and Sadeem (USA). The interference was the cause of the jockey of El Conquistador being unseated. Furthermore the committee was satisfied that El Conquistador did not come off a straight line until the interference had taken place."

Within two hours of being adjudged the winner of the Gold Cup on the second-best horse in the race, 48-year-old Greville Starkey, the senior British jockey, was involved in a second drama while riding Ile de Chypre, also trained by Guy Harwood. He set off to make all the running in the King George V Handicap, and was still well clear of the field inside

Royal Gait was first past the post in the 1988 Gold Cup, but relegated to last place after a Stewards' Enquiry.

the final furlong when the colt swerved violently left towards the stands, unseating his rider. The colours were ripped away from Starkey's right arm, and he was obviously badly shaken. However, he was not seriously hurt, and after missing his only mount on Friday, staged a successful return to the course on Mazzacano on Saturday. Guy Harwood was totally unable to explain the behaviour of Ile de Chypre. Far from having shown any signs of waywardness on the gallops, the horse had often led work. Following the sudden defection of Ile de Chypre, the King George V Handicap was won by Mr Stephen Roots' grey colt Thethingaboutitis, ridden by apprentice Tony Culhane for the Epsom stable of former top jockey Geoff Lewis.

Prince Yazid Saud's Persian Heights acquired the distinction of winning the first race at Royal Ascot with a first prize of more than £100,000 when Pat Eddery rode him to beat Raykour by a length and a half in the St James's Palace Stakes in 1988. That success on the part of Persian Heights came about as a result of a fine feat of training on the part of

Newmarket-based Geoff Huffer, once a minor member in a pop group, who had bought the colt for 25,000 guineas at Tattersalls Highflyer Sales. Persian Heights had split his near pastern in the Middle Park Stakes the previous autumn, and was confined to his box for six months until the pin could be removed in February. This left his trainer with a race against time in order to bring him to peak fitness for the Royal Meeting, where more than one of his immediate relatives had also been seen to advantage. A chestnut horse by Persian Bold, Persian Heights comes from a female family developed by Major Holliday, as his dam Ready and Willing is by Reliance II out of No Saint, second in the Ribblesdale, and half-sister to Noble Chieftain, who won the Coventry Stakes for the Major in 1954.

When High Estate won the Coventry Stakes of 1988 the colt became the 24th winner at the Royal Meeting for 93-year-old Mr Jim Joel, long the doyen of British owners, and enabled him to match the record of his father, Jack Joel, for whom Tag

End had become the last of 24 winners with his success in the King's Stand Stakes 59 years earlier in 1929. High Estate, ridden by Steve Cauthen for Henry Cecil's stable, was also the last home-bred winner at the meeting for his owner. Two years earlier, Mr Joel had sold off his brood mares, as his failing eyesight prevented him from reading pedigrees, and robbed him of much of the pleasure of planning matings, so long one of the most fascinating aspects of breeding for him. At 5200 guineas, the American-bred Regal Beauty, dam of High Estate, was cheapest of the 20 mares and fillies sold by Mr Joel.

Once again horses owned by the Maktoum brothers were well to the fore in 1988. Besides the Gold Cup with Sadeem, Sheikh Mohammed won the Ascot Stakes with Zero Watt; Sheikh Hamdan Al Maktoum brought off a double with Waajib in the Queen Anne Stakes and Almaarad in the Hardwicke Stakes; and Sheikh Maktoum Al Maktoum won the Britannia Stakes with Foreign Survivor, while Sheikh Ahmed Al Maktoum's Mtoto won the Prince of Wales' Stakes for Alec Stewart's stable for the second year running, making six successes for the family from Dubai.

At a time when so much of the best stock is concentrated to an increasingly great extent in the large studs of these and other overseas owners, Mr John Moore achieved a quite remarkable feat by breeding two winners at the Royal Meeting. As well as Mtoto, Powder Blue, successful in the Wokingham Stakes for Peter Makin's stable, was bred by Mr Moore, a solicitor and Lloyd's underwriter, at the Biddestone Stud, Wiltshire, where he had just ten mares. Powder Blue is by He Loves Me out of Ridalia, whose dam Wharfedale became the first mare to be acquired by Mr Moore when he bought her for 1750 guineas from Lady Macdonald-Buchanan at the December Sales of 1964. Mtoto is by Busted out of the Mincio mare Amazer, whom Mr Moore bought for 5800 guineas when Sir Robin McAlpine submitted her to the December Sales of 1976. Mr Moore is a great believer in buying from established breeders like Lady Macdonald-Buchanan and Sir Robin McAlpine, by reason of their mares invariably belonging to the best families. In these instances, Wharfedale comes from the same female line as the Derby winner Nimbus, and

Amazer has the 1000 Guineas winner Zabara for her grandam.

By riding eight winners at Royal Ascot in 1989, Pat Eddery emulated the achievements of Lester Piggott, who had reached that tally in both 1965 and 1975. As contract rider for Mr Khalid Abdullah, Eddery won five races for that owner, namely the Queen Anne Stakes on Warning, the Prince of Wales' Stakes on Two Timing, the Royal Hunt Cup on True Panache, the King George V Stakes on Carlingford, and the Hardwicke Stakes on Assatis. As Eddery could not do the weight for Mr Abdullah's Danehill in the Cork and Orrery Stakes, Willie Carson took the mount, and Danehill, who had been third in the 2000 Guineas, won in a record time for Ascot's six furlongs.

Eddery sent True Panache to the front after three furlongs in the Royal Hunt Cup, only to lose the advantage to Sleepline Fantasy a furlong and a half out, but Eddery, at the top of his form, forced True Panache back into the lead a furlong out, and eventually brought him home a length clear of the fast-finishing Wood Dancer. Like the dual Gold Cup winner Gildoran, True Panache is out of that high-class mare Durtal, who in 1977, when she was favourite for the Oaks, unseated Lester Piggott, crashed into the rails, and had to be withdrawn.

The successes of Panache, Two Timing and Danehill were extremely popular as they constituted a treble for Jeremy Tree, who, the previous week, had announced that he would retire at the end of the season. For 36 years he had run the Beckhampton stable in an exemplarily straightforward manner, winning his first race at Royal Ascot with Persian Road in 1966.

Greville Starkey, who had wound up the meeting on such a disastrous note on account of the erratic behaviour of Ile de Chypre in 1988, could not ride at all in 1989. While in Spain the previous Sunday he had caught his foot against some of the photo-finish equipment sticking out on to the course, and torn ligaments so badly that he returned to London on crutches.

In consequence Willie Carson deputised for him on Sadeem when Sheikh Mohammed's chestnut six-year-old earned his place on the roll of Gold Cup winners, rather than have the race awarded to him as had been the case the previous year. Taking the

Persian Heights, ridden by Pat Eddery, won the first prize of more than £100,000 in the St James's Palace Stakes in 1988.

lead three furlongs out, Sadeem forged clear to win by eight lengths from his stablemate Mazzacano. But for that accident in Spain, the luckless Starkey would also have won the King Edward VII Stakes on the Derby third Cacoethes, whom Pat Eddery brought home three parts of a length clear of Zayyani.

As well as the Gold Cup with Sadeem, Sheikh Mohammed won three other races at Royal Ascot in 1989. His filly Golden Opinion, trained by André, Fabre in France, was successful in the Coronation Stakes, while Alydaress won the Ribblesdale Stakes for Henry Cecil's stable, and Shaadi, trained by Michael Stoute, the St James's Palace Stakes.

No stable lacking the support of the Maktoum family, or another of the Arab owners, has flourished to a greater extent than that of Richard Hannon in recent years, and in 1989 he was responsible for Mr A. F. Budge's Rock City winning the Coventry Stakes. Richard Hannon is the son of Harry Hannon, who came to England from Ulster to ride as a steeplechase jockey, subsequently training at Lewes, Lambourn and finally East Eversleigh near Marl-

borough in Wiltshire. On the retirement of his father at the end of the season of 1969, Richard Hannon took over the East Eversleigh yard. Quickly making a name for himself, he won both the Princess Elizabeth Stakes at Epsom and the Nassau Stakes at Goodwood with a very smart filly in Crespinall in 1972, then the following year he did still better by landing his first classic, the 2000 Guineas, with Mon Fils. In 1987 he won the 2000 Guineas with Don't Forget Me, who went on to complete the double in the Irish 2000 Guineas.

In these days when running a stable profitably is a major commercial undertaking, Hannon, a thick-set, genial man, is a good deal more relaxed than many of his colleagues, and rarely without a good story with which to amuse his friends in the bar after racing. To a large extent the East Eversleigh stable is supported by small owners, whose interests he has served well by buying them useful horses at modest prices. Fly Baby, who gave him his first Royal Ascot success in the Queen Mary Stakes in 1981, had cost only 2000 Irish guineas at Goffs' Kill Sale.

Henry Cecil's stable once again enjoyed multiple success in 1989. As well as the Chesham Stakes with Mr Peter Burrell's home-bred Be My Chief, Cecil won the Britannia Stakes with Polar Boy, bred and partly owned by Mr Burrell, a former director of the National Stud.

The last Royal Ascot winner of the 1980s was Captain F. Samdan's grey five-year-old Ala Hounak, trained by Liverpool-born Frank Durr, the former top jockey, and ridden by his fellow Liverpudlian Billy Newnes. Zero Watt, winner of the two-and-a-half-mile Ascot Stakes in 1988, was long odds on, but was under pressure five furlongs from home; and so after taking the leader early in the straight, Ala Hounak, a 20/1 chance, stayed on in great style to come home three lengths clear of Sergeyevich.

One of the longest established of all English institutions, Royal Ascot is fast coming to the end of the first 300 years of its existence. All down the years the shape of the meeting has continually evolved, while still owing its ethos to the heirs of the sovereign, who founded it. Queen Anne originated it in order to race hunters, more remarkable for their stamina than their speed, on a hastily cleared piece of heathland in the forest. During the reigns of the early Hanoverian kings, who were totally indifferent to the charms of the turf, Royal Ascot reached the nadir of oblivion so that there was no meeting at all some years. King George IV, with his love of pageantry and panoply as well as sport, brought high fashion to Royal Ascot; he built the first Royal Box, and established the Royal Procession. Although Queen Victoria had little interest in racing, did not attend more than two days, and never attended again after widowhood in 1861, Royal Ascot continued to become more important and a better organised meeting during her reign, until her eldest son the Prince of Wales, later King Edward VII, made it the pivotal event in the social calendar. King George V and King George VI assiduously maintained the traditions of Royal Ascot, and during the reign of Queen Elizabeth II, most knowledgeable of racing enthusiasts, the meeting has become one of the highlights of the year for tens of thousands of her subjects, and enjoys a popularity undreamed of by Queen Anne.

Always adaptable, Royal Ascot has accepted the demands made by the development of racing. Back in the days of the Regency, towards the end of the eighteenth century, the Oatlands Stakes was the most coveted event of the meeting, but it gradually declined in prestige until it was translated into a handicap, the Ascot Stakes. For more than a century the Gold Cup was by far the most important race in the country for older horses. Derby winners were kept in training as four-year-olds, even five-year-olds, with the winning of it as their principal objective, and success put the seal on the careers of the likes of West Australian, Gladiateur, Doncaster, Isinglass and Persimmon.

In the course of the last 25 years or so, there has been ever more demand for ability at middle distances and a mile, reflecting American priorities. The Gold Cup, last contested by a Derby winner (Blakeney) in 1970, has become almost the exclusive preserve of the specialist stayers, and has ceased to be the most valuable event of the four days – during which classic winners are tested over distances from a mile to a mile and a half. To meet the needs of the age, the Prince of Wales' Stakes was reintroduced over a mile and a quarter in 1968, and consistently attracts horses of the very highest class, along with the St James's Palace Stakes, the Hardwicke Stakes and the King Edward VII Stakes. In 1989 the St James's Palace Stakes was the most valuable race of the meeting with a first prize of £113,994 as opposed to the £79,740 of the Gold Cup.

In the course of close on 300 years Ascot has been transformed from rough and ready heathland into an immaculate racecourse, with magnificent stands and a host of ancillary facilities, while the development of the international bloodstock industry has occasioned the laying out of great racecourses, almost the world over. France has Longchamp and Chantilly; Ireland has The Curragh and Leopardstown; Germany has Baden-Baden and Cologne; the United States has Belmont and Churchill Downs; Australia has Flemington and Randwick; Hong Kong has Sha Tin, and Japan Fuchu. Elaborate splendour, often allied with elegance, and even sheer beauty, is the hallmark of them all, but none has the indefinable quality that the presence of the sovereign, pageantry, fashion and racing of the highest quality combine to give to Royal Ascot.

In the Winner's Enclosure – Two Timing, winner of the Prince of Wales' Stakes in 1989.

THE ROYAL FAMILY AND ASCOT

*(Members associated with Ascot appear in bold capital letters: **ANNE**.)*

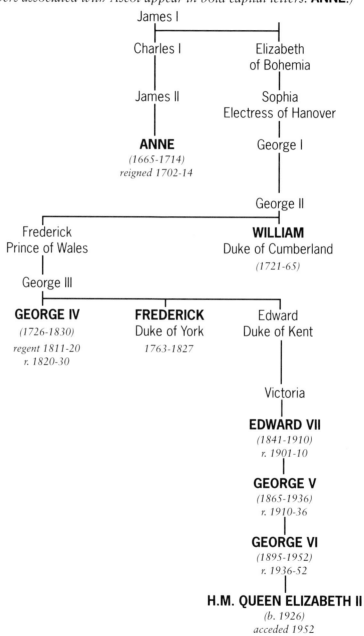

James I

Charles I   Elizabeth
of Bohemia

James II   Sophia
Electress of Hanover

ANNE   George I
(1665-1714)
reigned 1702-14

George II

Frederick   **WILLIAM**
Prince of Wales   Duke of Cumberland
(1721-65)

George III

GEORGE IV   **FREDERICK**   Edward
(1726-1830)   Duke of York   Duke of Kent
regent 1811-20   *1763-1827*
r. 1820-30

Victoria

EDWARD VII
(1841-1910)
r. 1901-10

GEORGE V
(1865-1936)
r. 1910-36

GEORGE VI
(1895-1952)
r. 1936-52

H.M. QUEEN ELIZABETH II
(b. 1926)
acceded 1952

SIMPLIFIED TREE OF THE JARVIS, BUTTERS, LEADER AND HALL FAMILIES

(Names of members who trained, or have trained, winners at Royal Ascot are in bold capitals.)

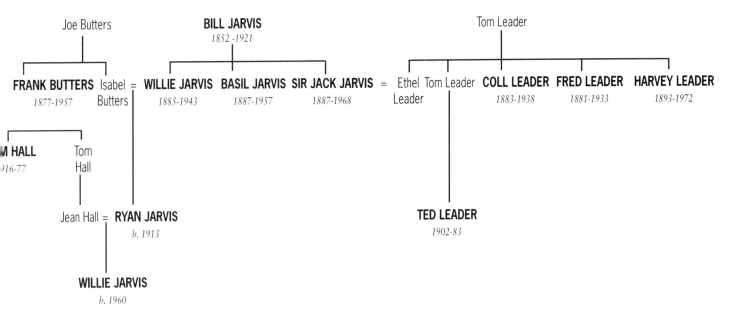

THE DAY, CANNON, PIGGOTT, RICKABY AND ARMSTRONG FAMILIES

(Names of members who trained or rode winners at Royal Ascot are in bold capitals.)

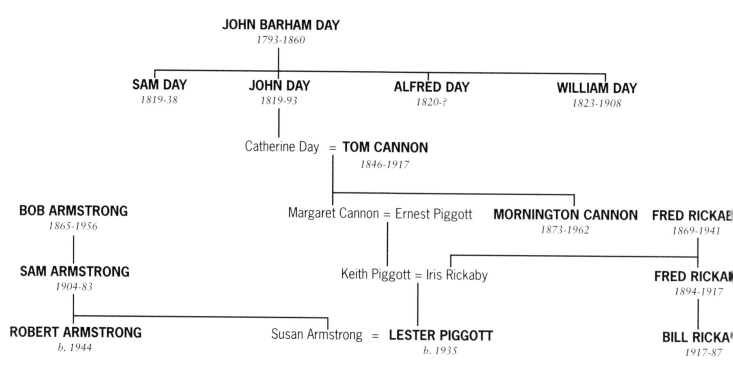

ROYAL ASCOT WINNERS IN THE TAIL MALE LINE FROM STOCKWELL

(The line runs from Stockwell, dubbed the 'Emperor of Stallions', and beaten a head in the Gold Cup of 1853, to Northern Dancer, most successful stallion in the world, during recent times.)

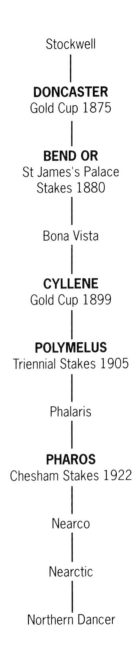

Stockwell

DONCASTER
Gold Cup 1875

BEND OR
St James's Palace
Stakes 1880

Bona Vista

CYLLENE
Gold Cup 1899

POLYMELUS
Triennial Stakes 1905

Phalaris

PHAROS
Chesham Stakes 1922

Nearco

Nearctic

Northern Dancer

BIBLIOGRAPHY

AGA KHAN. *Memoirs of Aga Khan* (Cassell, 1954)

ALLISON, William. *Memories of Men and Horses* (Grant Richards, 1922)

AXHELM, Pete. *The Kid* (Paddington Press, 1979)

BIRD, T. H. *Admiral Rous and the English Turf* (Putnam, 1939)

BLACK, Robert. *The Jockey Club and Its Founders* (Smith, Elder, 1891)

BLYTH, Henry. *The Pocket Venus* (Wiedenfeld & Nicholson, 1966)

— *Old Q* (Wiedenfeld & Nicholson, 1967)

BRITT, Edgar. *Post Haste* (Frederick Muller, 1967)

BUTLER, Ewan. *The Cecils* (Frederick Muller, 1964)

CARR, Harry. *Queen's Jockey* (Stanley Paul, 1966)

CAWTHORNE, G. J. and HEROD, R. *Royal Ascot* (Treherne, 1902)

CECIL, Henry. *On the Level* (Harrap, 1983)

CHETWYND, Sir George. *Racing Reminiscence* (Longman, Green, 1891)

COWLES, Virginia. *Edward VII and his Circle* (Hamish Hamilton, 1956)

— *The Rothschilds* (Wiedenfeld & Nicholson, 1979)

CURLING, Bill. *The Captain* (Barrie & Jenkins, 1970)

— *Derby Double* (William Luscombe, 1977)

DARLING, Sam. *Sam Darling's Reminiscences* (Mills & Boon, 1914)

DAY, William. *Reminiscences of the Turf* (Richard Bentley, 1891)

DIXON, Sydenham. *From Gladiateur to Persimmon* (Grant Richards, 1901)

"THE DRUID". *Post and Paddock* (Vinton, 1895. 1st pub. 1856)

— *Silk and Scarlet* (Vinton, 1895. 1st pub. 1859)

— *Scott and Sebright* (Vinton, 1895. 1st pub. 1862)

FAIRFAX-BLAKEBOROUGH, J. F. *Malton Memories and l'Anson Triumphs* (Truslove & Bray, 1925)

— *Paddock Personalities* (Hutchinson, n.d.)

— *The Turf Who's Who, 1932* (The May Fair Press, 1932)

— *York and Doncaster Races* (J. A. Allen, n.d.)

FALK, Bernard. *The Royal Fitzroys* (Hutchinson, 1950)

FELSTEAD, S. Theodore. *Racing Romance* (Werner Laurie, 1949)

FITZGEORGE-PARKER, Tim. *The Guv'nor* (Collins, 1980)

FRANCIS, Dick. *Lester* (Michael Joseph, 1986)

FULFORD, Roger. *George the Fourth* (Duckworth, 1935)

GALTREY, Sidney. *Memoirs of a Racing Journalist* (Hutchinson, 1934)

GILBEY, Quintin. *Queen of the Turf* (Arthur Barker, 1973)

GOOD, Meyrick. *Good Days* (Hutchinson, n.d.)

— *The Lure of the Turf* (Odhams Press, 1957)

GUEDALA, Philip. *Palmerston* (Ernest Benn, 1926)

HERBERT, Ivor, and O'BRIEN, Jacqueline. *Vincent O'Brien's Greatest Horses* (Pelham Books, 1984)

HISLOP, John. *Far from a Gentleman* (Michael Joseph, 1960)

— *The Brigadier* (Secker & Warburg, 1973)

HODGMAN, George. *Sixty Years on the Turf* (Grant Richards, 1901)

HUMPHREYS, A. L. *Crockfords* (Hutchinson, 1953)

HUMPHRIS, Edith M. *The Life of Mathew Dawson* (Witherby, 1928)

JARVIS, Sir Jack. *They're Off!* (Michael Jarvis, 1969)

JOEL, Stanhope. *Ace of Diamonds* (Frederick Muller, 1958)

KENT, John. *The Racing Life of Lord George Cavendish Bentinck, M.P.* (Blackwood, 1892)

LAIRD, Dorothy. *Royal Ascot* (Hodder & Stoughton, 1976)

LAMBTON, the Hon. George. *Men and Horses I Have Known* (Thornton Butterworth, 1924)

LEACH, Jack. *Sods I Have Cut on the Turf* (Victor Gollancz, 1961)

LECHMERE, Jocelyne. *Pretty Polly* (The Bodley Head, 1907)

LONDONDERRY, the Marchioness of. *Henry Chaplin* (Macmillan, 1926)

LYLE, R. C. *Brown Jack* (Putnam, 1934)

— *The Aga Khan's Horses* (Putnam, 1938)

MARSH, Marcus. *Racing with the Gods* (Pelham, 1968)

MARSH, Richard. *A Trainer to Two Kings* (Cassell, 1925)

MENZIES, Mrs Stuart. *Lord William Beresford, V.C.* (Herbert Jenkins, 1917)

MORRIS, Tony and RANDALL, John. *Horse Racing Records* (Guinness Publishing, 1988)

MORTIMER, Roger. *The Jockey Club* (Cassell, 1958)

— *The History of the Derby Stakes* (Michael Joseph, 1973)

— *The Flat* (Allen & Unwin, 1979)

MORTIMER, Roger, ONSLOW, Richard and WILLETT, Peter. *Biographical Encyclopaedia of the British Turf* (Macdonald Jane, 1978)

MORTON, Charles. *My Sixty Years on the Turf* (Hutchinson, n.d.)

"NIMROD". *The Chase, the Road and the Turf* (Bodley Head, 1927 edn.)

OAKSEY, John. *The Story of Mill Reef* (Michael Joseph, 1974)

ONSLOW, Richard. *Headquarters* (Great Ouse Press, 1983)

OSBOURNE, John. *The Horsebreeders' Handbook* (Edmund Seale, 1898)

PLUMBTRE, George. *The Fast Set* (André Deutsch, 1985)

PORTER, John. *John Porter of Kingsclere.* (Grant Richards, 1919)

RADCLIFFE, John. *Ashgill. The Life and Times of John Osborne* (Sands, 1900)

RICKMAN, John. *Eight Flat-Racing Stables* (Heinemann, 1979)

RODRIGO, Robert. *The Racing Game* (Phoenix Sports Books, 1958)

ROSSMORE, Lord. *Things I Can Tell* (Eveleigh Nash, 1912)

ST AUBYN, Giles. *Edward VII – Prince and King* (Collins, 1979)

SARL, Arthur. *Horses, Jockeys and Crooks* (Hutchinson, 1935)
— *Gamblers of the Turf* (Hutchinson, 1938)

SCOTT, Alexander. *Turf Memories of Sixty Years* (Hutchinson, 1925)

SETH-SMITH, Michael. *Bred for the Purple* (Leslie Frewin, 1969)
— *Lord Paramount of the Turf* (Faber and Faber, 1971)
— *Steve* (Faber and Faber, 1974)
— *Knight of the Turf* (Hodder and Stoughton, 1980)
— *A Classic Connection* (Secker and Warburg, 1983)

SILTZER, Frank. *Newmarket* (Cassell, 1923)

SLOAN, Tod. *Tod Sloan* (Grant Richards, 1915)

SMIRKE, Charlie. *Finishing Post* (Oldbourne, 1960)

SMITH, Doug. *Five Times Champion* (Pelham, 1968)

SMITH, Eph. *Riding to Win* (Stanley Paul, 1968)

SUTHERLAND, Douglas. *The Yellow Earl* (Cassell, 1965)

"THORMANBY" *Famous Racing Men* (James Hogg, 1882)

VOIGHT, C. A. *Gentlemen Riders at Home and Abroad* (Hutchinson, n.d.)

WELCOME, John. *Fred Archer* (Faber and Faber, 1967)
— *Neck or Nothing* (Faber and Faber, 1970)

WESTON, Tommy. *My Racing Life* (Hutchinson, 1952)

WHYTE, James Christie. *A History of the British Turf* (Henry, Colburn, 1840)

WILLETT, Peter. *An Introduction to the Thoroughbred* (Stanley Paul, 2nd edn. 1975)
—*The Classic Racehorse* (Stanley Paul, 1981)
— *The Story of Tattersalls* (Stanley Paul, 1987)

WILSON, Julian. *Lester Piggott* (Queen Anne Press, 1985)

WRIGHT, Howard. *The Encyclopaedia of Flat Racing* (Robert Hale, 1986)

The General Stud Book
The Racing Calendar
The Sporting Life
Ruff's Guide to the Turf
Racehorses of 19-
Raceform
Horses in Training
The European Racehorse
The Directory of the Turf
Tote Investors' Who's Who in Racing
Cope's Racegoers Encyclopaedia
Racing Illustrated

GENERAL INDEX

INDEX OF HORSE NAMES

ACKNOWLEDGEMENTS

The Author and Publishers are grateful to the
following for permission to reproduce photographs:

The Mansell Collection:
9, 11, 12, 16, 23, 29, 32, 37, 41, 47, 51, 57.
Mary Evans Picture Library:
15, 21, 27, 35.
Illustrated London News:
25, 39, 43, 44, 61, 68, 70, 73, 75, 89,
91, 95, 97, 98, 111, 121, 122.
Racing Illustrated:
33, 40, 52, 53, 59, 62, 66, 69, 78, 82, 85.
Sport and General:
87, 96, 133, 137, 147, 174, 192, 195, 205.
The Hulton Picture Company:
101, 102, 105, 106, 109, 110, 112, 114, 117, 118, 126, 130, 134,
141, 143, 145, 148, 153, 155, 156, 159, 162,
163, 165, 166, 168, 170, 173, 177, 179, 181, 183, 186, 188, 191.
Gerry and Mark Cranham:
184, 185, 197, 198, 201, 203, 207.

COLOUR PLATES:
(Between pages 72 and 73)
Mary Evans Picture Library:
1, 2, 3, 5 (bottom), 8 (bottom), 10, 12, 15.

The Mansell Collection:
4, 5 (top left), 5 (top right), 9, 11.

Illustrated London News:
12 (top), 14, 15 (bottom), 16.
ET Archive:
6.
The Jockey Club:
8 (top, both pictures).
Gerry Cranham:
16 (inset).

(Between pages 152 and 153)
Illustrated London News:
1, 2, 6.
Sport and General:
7.
The Hulton Picture Company:
3, 4 (inset), 5.
Gerry and Mark Cranham:
8, 9 (both pictures), 10 (both pictures), 11, 12, 13, 14, 15 (both pictures), 16.

Jacket Pictures:
Front, Gerry Cranham (main picture) and Mary Evans Picture Library.
Back and flap, Mary Evans Picture Library and The Hulton Picture Company.